THE REVEAL

THE NEXT STAGE OF HUMAN AWARENESS

ickonic
publishing

First published in September 2024.

ickonic
publishing

New Enterprise House
St Helens Street
Derby
DE1 3GY
UK

email: gareth.icke@davidicke.com

Cover Illustration & Book Design: Neil Hague

British Library Cataloguing-in
Publication Data
A catalogue record for this book is
available from the British Library

ISBN 978-1-8384153-5-8

Printed and bound by
CPI (UK) Ltd, Croydon CR0 4YY

THE REVEAL

THE NEXT STAGE OF HUMAN AWARENESS

DAVID ICKE

Dedication:

To my amazing daughter Kerry who has left us at the age of 48. Now she is free and ageless, but so missed by all who knew her.

The Reveal is the third book in the 'Reality Trilogy' along with *The Trap* and *The Dream*. The book is written to be read either by itself or in conjunction with the other two. Each book in the series is both self-contained and part of an interconnected sequence.

THE DREAM

THE EXTRAORDINARY REVELATION OF WHO WE ARE AND WHERE WE ARE

DAVID ICKE

Other books and DVDs by David Icke

The Dream

The Trap

Perceptions of a Renegade Mind

The Answer

The Trigger

Everything You Need To Know But Have Never Been Told

Phantom Self

The Perception Deception

Remember Who You Are

Human Race Get Off Your *Knees* - The Lion Sleeps No More

The David Icke Guide to the Global Conspiracy (and how to end it)

Infinite Love is the Only Truth, *Everything* Else is Illusion

Tales from the Time Loop

Alice in Wonderland and the World Trade Center Disaster

Children Of The Matrix

The Biggest Secret

I Am Me • I Am Free

… And The Truth Shall Set You Free – 21st century edition

Lifting The Veil

The Robots' Rebellion

Heal the World

Truth Vibrations

DVDs

Worldwide Wake-Up Tour Live

David Icke Live at Wembley Arena

The Lion Sleeps No More

Beyond the Cutting Edge – Exposing the Dreamworld We Believe to be Real

Freedom or Fascism: the Time to Choose

Secrets of the Matrix

From Prison to Paradise

Turning Of The Tide

The Freedom Road

Revelations Of A Mother Goddess

Speaking Out

The Reptilian Agenda

Details at the back of this book
and through the website **www.davidicke.com**

Those who are able to see beyond the shadows and lies of their culture will never be understood, let alone believed, by the masses.

Plato

Today's mighty oak is just yesterday's nut that held its ground.

David Icke, 1991

(Icke is spelt 'Eik' in Dutch and means 'oak')

Is not this world an illusion? And yet it fools everybody.

Angela Carter

This is your last chance. After this, there is no turning back.
You take the blue pill – the story ends and you wake up in
your bed and believe whatever you want to believe.
You take the red pill and you stay in Wonderland and I show
you how deep the rabbit hole goes.

Morpheus, *The Matrix*

Contents

CHAPTER ONE

Mind Prison

*We are captives of our own identities living in prisons
of our own creation*
Theodore 'T-Bag' Bagwell in *Prison Break*

What do we know for sure? I mean REALLY know? Not *think* we know. *KNOW* we know? Well, next to nothing. We live in a 'world' in which we are fed a constant stream of illusion and our illusion-infested thoughts and emotions then manifest the illusory *experience* that we falsely believe to be real. We call this illusion 'human life'.

I mean 'falsely believe to be real' in the sense that we think we are experiencing reality as we perceive it to be when we're not. What can we know for sure in such circumstances? Precious little. We can scan the illusion for patterns, as I have done for 35 years, and establish that it *is* an illusion. We can add to that, step-by-step as more patterns emerge, and begin to piece together *why* it's an illusion; what creates the illusion; and what is behind the illusion. We can be aware as we explore the illusion that it *is* an illusion and realise that even what we think we know can be illusory. British wartime Prime Minister Winston Churchill described Russia as 'a riddle wrapped in a mystery inside an enigma'. The sentence would be far longer if he had been talking about reality. Maybe 'an illusory riddle wrapped in an illusory mystery inside an illusory enigma, which is perplexing, inexplicable, baffling, confusing, befuddling, bizarre, weird, odd, strange, peculiar and bewildering'. I could go on. But there is one thing that we do know that cannot be credibly questioned or denied: Whatever we *think* we know there is always, always, *more* to know – an *infinity* of more to know in our case. To understand the world and reality we must be constantly aware of what we don't know. That means almost *everything*. Ancient Greek philosopher Socrates is famous for seeing this most basic truth. Among quotes attributed to him are: 'To know is to know you know nothing. That is the meaning of true knowledge.'; 'The only true wisdom is in knowing you know nothing'; '… in knowing that you know nothing that makes you the smartest of all' (Fig 1 overleaf).

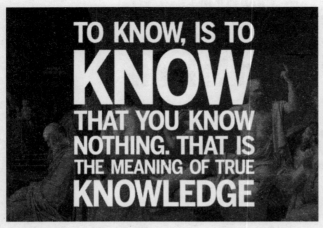

Figure 1: Any researcher that doesn't heed these words is destined for self-censorship and here-and-no-further.

These words are most obviously correct and this awareness has driven me and everything that I have done in the last three-and-a-half decades since my extraordinary awakening which I describe in *The Trap*. Humility is the foundation of this. The humility of saying: 'I don't know – so *what* don't I know?' This propels and inspires you to seek out what you don't know. There is never a point where you say: 'I've got it'. You realise that this is the biggest illusion of all and one that entraps vast swathes of humanity in the perceptual prison cell of 'I know'. Exploration is over once you believe that. Why should I explore what I don't know when I *do* know? American historian Daniel J. Boorstin said: 'The greatest obstacle to discovery is not ignorance – it is the illusion of knowledge.' Unwavering belief that cannot be questioned and the human need for certainty amid blatant uncertainty are the very keystones of religion, including the religion that we call 'science'. They both seek certainty in an infinite reality of infinite possibility, infinite potential, infinite *un*certainty. How is certainty even possible if perception dictates behaviour and experience? The only certainty must be *un*certainty – must be *choice* in its deepest sense. Uncertainty is the gift that brings new experience and with that new knowledge, awareness, and the potential for wisdom. We must make peace with it. Curiosity drives us to embrace uncertainty, to seek

Figure 2: Without wonder and curiosity there can be no wisdom. Wonder embraces and celebrates uncertainty.

out the cutting edge and go beyond it. Cliff Morgan, the Welsh rugby legend, said to me when he was an executive at the BBC: 'David – never lose your sense of wonder.' I never have. Lose your sense of wonder and you lose your sense of life (Fig 2).

Dictating perception

I have been exposing since 1990 (to great hilarity and dismissal until relatively recently) that humanity is controlled by a non-human demonic force that works through a global network of secret societies to hijack the perception of the population. I call this network the Global Cult. We will see throughout this book how control of perception is the foundation of *all* control. Secret societies fiercely impose their own compartmentalisation of knowledge to ensure that only the inner circle knows how the pieces fit – and even then not all of them. These are the secret society compartments known as 'degrees'. The most elite secret societies are *so* secret that almost all of their members have no idea of the *real* reason for their existence. Only the inner core or circle knows that. You can accurately symbolise this covert structure as a spider's web of secret societies and semi-secret groups with a 'spider' at the centre directing events and dictating its agenda for humanity (Fig 3). The web

Figure 3: The Global Cult structure. The dystopian agenda is projected from the spider and passes through the secret society web into the world of the seen to be implemented by governments and corporations via secret groupings, non-governmental organisations (NGOs), and 'think tanks'. The web is strictly compartmentalised on the 'need to know' principle. Only the inner core and its closest gofers know the real picture. The rest only know enough to contribute to an outcome they either have no idea about or only partially understand. (Image by Neil Hague.)

has been manipulating humanity towards a dystopian society founded on a world government dictatorship (Fig 4). I warned about this from the wilderness for a long time as the agenda unfolded covertly. Since the advent of the 'Covid' hoax the direction we are being taken has become ever more obvious. The web structure can also be portrayed as a pyramidal hierarchy. The controlling core is at the top and each succeeding level below them knows less and less until you reach the mass of humanity at the bottom. They are manipulated to know next to nothing. Each level obeys orders from the one above and imposes them on the one below. Down the hierarchy this goes

Figure 4: This is where the plan is heading – a global unelected technocratic dictatorship that I have warned about all these years and it's being constructed all around us day by day. (Image by Gareth Icke.)

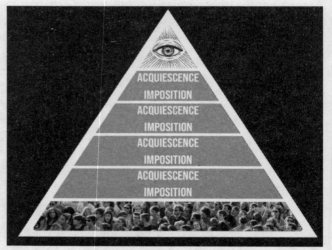

Figure 5: How the inner core of the Cult imposes its will on the world population through a sequence of imposition and acquiescence. Each level of the global and national hierarchy acquiesces to the commands from above and imposes them on the level below. If the population unquestioningly obeys government and human authority at its level of the pyramid a circuit is completed through which the agenda of the Cult inner core dictates the direction of human society. (Image by Gareth Icke.)

until you reach the masses. At this point the will of the tiny few at the top is 'imposed' on the entire population and all it has taken is a sequence of imposition and acquiescence (Fig 5). Cult demands are not so much imposed as *obeyed* into being.

We have two 'worlds' within human society divided by their very different access to *knowledge*. Advanced knowledge is passed through the generations in the inner core of the Cult about the hidden nature of reality and the Cult plan for a global dystopia controlled by artificial intelligence (AI). The rest of the web is aware only of what they need to know to make their specific contribution. 'Occult' means 'hidden'. Perception-transforming knowledge must be hidden from the people you seek to enslave. These non-Cult billions in the other 'world' are subjected to lifetimes of knowledge *suppression* through the Cult-created-

and-owned 'education' system and media (Fig 6). I have described the Cult in enormous detail in previous books going back to the early 1990s and, since the second half of that decade, how a non-human demonic force in another dimension of reality is ultimately dictating the direction of human life. We are talking about a very few controlling the very many. Add the

Figure 6: The two worlds divided by access to knowledge. The secret society web has need-to-know information passed on through the levels of 'degree' about the plan for humanity and the true nature of reality. The population has its knowledge suppressed by the Cult-created 'education' system and Cult-owned media..

demonic entities beyond human sight to those few secret society members that fully understand what they are doing and the maths becomes laughable. The controllers are dramatically outnumbered by the controlled. The demonic few must control the *perception* of the population if they are to prevail. They do this by hijacking the individual and collective consciousness of their targets. We have a human reality in which control of perception is constantly pursued through control of information from which those perceptions are formed. This is the reason for today's mass censorship which is planned to dramatically increase from 2024 onwards and especially through the implementation of AI. From perception, comes behaviour, and from collective behaviour comes human 'life'. Control perception and you control human experience.

The story goes deep into other dimensions of reality – far deeper than even 95 percent of the alternative media understands let alone the mainstream. We are going deeper than I think any book has gone in presenting the totality of the human plight (with always more to know) and build on the revelations in *The Trap* and *The Dream*. I want to start in the human realm of the illusory 'physical', and what is termed 'everyday life', to show how perceptions at this level are manipulated. This will include the exposure of 'alternative' information and 'big names' that are helping, some knowingly, most unknowingly, to divert people away from the core knowledge they need to have and into irrelevant byways of politics and little picture obsession. We will then delve deeper into those other realms from where the plan is all ultimately orchestrated. A key to perceptual control is manipulating the human targets into a sense of certainty that is solid-gold *wrong*. If you can also get them to worship what they think is their 'God' while they are actually worshipping *you* – the demonic – so much the better. This is happening as I will explore.

The need to be 'certain'

Humanity is systematically manipulated into such states of insecurity (uncertainty) by constantly challenging events and experience which trigger a need for certainty – the need to think you *know*. Phew! In a world of such uncertainty at least I *know* this. There is a certainty that I can cling to. I have just described why religious belief dominates human life. Belief in a religion is to have the *certainty* of believing that 'I know'. We are told there are eight billion humans and of that number an estimated 2.382 billion follow Christianity; 1.907 billion are Muslim; and 1.161 billion are Hindu. These three beliefs alone account for 5.45 billion of the eight billion. Then add Buddhism, Sikhism, Judaism, Baha'i, Jainism, Shintoism, Caodaism, Rastafarianism, Chinese religions, African religions, the list goes on and on. Only some 1.193 billion are said to be secular, non-religious, agnostic, or atheist. Break these down and they, too, are belief systems held largely in perpetuity. Secular refers to 'not overtly or specifically religious'; an atheist is 'a person who does not believe in the existence of a god or any gods'; and only the agnostic is aware that 'any ultimate reality (such as God) is unknown and probably unknowable'. Well, at least unknowable

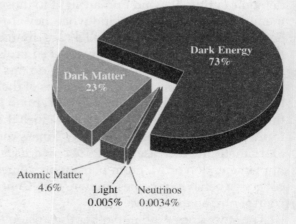

Figure 7: Mainstream science says the electromagnetic spectrum – basically human experienced reality – is only 0.005 percent of what exists in the Universe. In truth, it is far less even than that.

to consciousness trapped in the severe, almost laughable, limitations of human form. How laughable? This laughable:

Mainstream science says that the electromagnetic spectrum or 'light' (which is basically human experienced reality) is only 0.005 per cent of what exists in the Universe as energy in all its forms (Fig 7). Some go as high as 0.5 percent, but the point remains. It is infinitesimal. More than that, we can 'see' only a tiny fraction of that 0.005 percent known as visible light (Fig 8). Take on board that the 'Universe' itself is only a

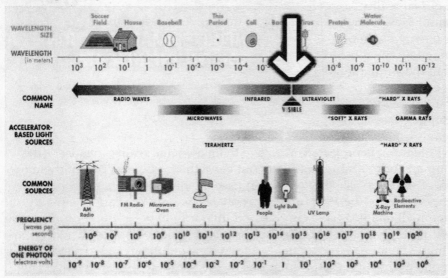

Figure 8: We can 'see' a mere fraction of the 0.005 percent within a frequency band known as 'visible light'. Humans are blind to the infinity of what exists in the 'space' they occupy and call the 'human world'.

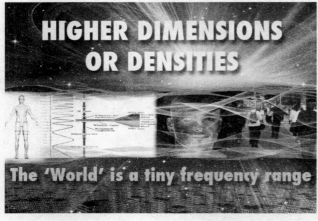

Figure 9: The 'human world' is a tiny band of frequency sharing the same 'space' as infinite reality. (Image by Neil Hague.)

smear of Infinite Reality and to say that humans are pretty much blind is the understatement of eternity (Fig 9 and Fig 10 overleaf). One question that immediately comes from this is 'why?' – *why* can we see so little? The last thing you want if you are seeking to control humanity from a hidden realm or dimension is for your targets to have a frequency range of visual perception that allows you to be seen. Our human reality is a *virtual* reality simulation if you do the research, and to maintain the illusion that the simulation or movie is real you can't allow your stooges to see those levels from where the

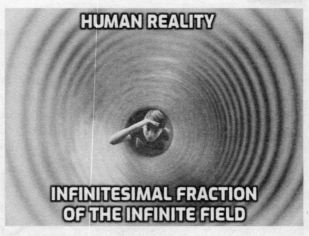

Figure 10: This fact should be taught to every child the moment they are old enough to understand with its potential to transform perception of self and reality.

whole thing is projected. You give them a virtual reality 'headset' (the human body/brain) that filters out everything you don't want them to see. I am often asked why we can't see the hidden rulers that I have exposed since the 1990s and my reply is always: 'You can see next to damn all, mate.' I have emphasised this early in book after book because without this understanding there can *be* no understanding. Children should be taught the frequency limitations of human sight from the first moment they can digest what this means for their sense of reality. This doesn't happen when such knowledge has to be kept from us to control perception and deliver a sense of isolation and limitation – illusion. Another reason, connected to the first, is that most adults teaching children don't *themselves* realise the astonishing scale of their visual confinement. 'The blind leading the blind' was never more appropriate.

Our reality is holographic rather than solid, and holograms have an extraordinary feature in that every part of a hologram is a smaller version of the whole. This results from the way that holographic information is encoded. Information of the whole is encoded in every part. Cut a

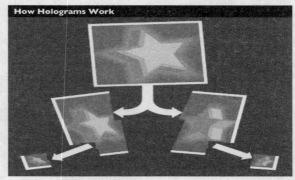

Figure 11: Holograms have an extraordinary characteristic in that every part of a hologram is encoded with the information of the whole hologram – as above, so below. This explains so many things that appear to be 'mysteries'.

holographic print into four pieces and you won't get a quarter of the picture in each piece. You will get a quarter-sized version of the *whole* picture (Fig 11). The body, like everything else in the human realm of fake 'physical', is a hologram and this is why acupuncture, reflexology, and other forms of healing can find points all over the body that relate to the information of the *entire* body. There are points in the ears, hands, and feet, which are smaller versions of body organs that follow the holographic principle of 'as above, so below'. These can be used to affect those organs through the body's interconnected nature. Skilled palm readers can see the whole body reflected in the hand for the same reason (Fig 12). I will expand on all this as we go along.

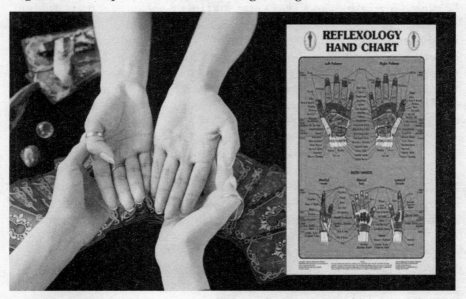

Figure 12: A skilled palm reader can see the whole body in the hand because the body is a hologram.

You must *believe* (what I do)

The great majority of the human race believes they *know* what they need to know thanks to religious and 'scientific' (religious) belief and seek to indoctrinate subsequent generations with the same delusion. The Global Cult achieves this through repetition programming from the earliest moments of human life and through childhood intimidation, guilt and fear: 'This will happen to you if you don't believe what I tell you.' To me this is child abuse. Some simple facts reveal this truth. Those born to Christian families in the southern states of America will invariably become Christians. Kids in Muslim families become Muslims, Hindus become Hindus, and Jewish children follow Judaism. This is clearly not because all of them have decided through free-thought that this is how they choose to perceive reality. Indoctrination, often intimidatory indoctrination, is how this is done. Each generation should be given access to all information and possibility available and then respected in how they choose to respond. I hear people demanding freedom in the so-called 'alternative' media who would never define freedom that way. You mean I can't tell my children to believe what I do? You mean my children have the freedom *not* to believe in Christianity, Islam, Judaism, Hinduism? *'Never!'* they say. They then return to their demand for 'freedom' from tyranny without seeing that they are part of the tyranny.

Religions are prisons of the mind that build impenetrable walls around limited belief and block the exploration of infinity beyond them. I contend in *The Trap* and *The Dream*, and other books, that reincarnation of consciousness is the trap that recycles 'souls' in and out of this insane reality for reasons I will explore later. Judeo-Christianity and Islam don't believe in reincarnation at all (except for Christian 'Jesus') while Eastern religions like Hinduism say that reincarnation is necessary to 'learn lessons' to reach a state of 'enlightenment' to be free of the cycle on the Buddhist 'Wheel of Samsara'. Either way, a non-belief in reincarnation, or a belief that it is 'God's plan', means that any suggestion that reincarnation is a calculated trap is dismissed by reflex action. Such is the role of belief in preventing exploration of Infinite Possibility. How can we know more by refusing to go further than we think we already know – but don't? There is the essential component whenever the few control the many of divide and rule. We have religious wars and ongoing conflicts along the fault-lines of ongoing beliefs. Divide and rule is a doddle once you have rigid beliefs to play off against each other.

The fine detail of perceptual imprisonment is extraordinary. Practicing Buddhists cut their hair short while Sikhs don't cut their hair

Figure 13: Buddhist: Cut your hair short. Sikh: Don't cut your hair at all. Is 'God' confused?

at all which is why they wear a turban (Fig 13). What is this fixation that 'God' has with hair? There's a similar obsession with uniforms. Buddhists wear robes because Buddha did; Sikhs wear robes because long ago gurus did; Muslims wear beards because Muhammad did; and Southern Baptists wear jackets, shirts, and ties because Jesus did. Well,

no, er ... they must wear them because that's their Sunday best. You can see a New Ager from 100 yards by what they are wearing. Group-think needs a group uniform, I suppose. The Shafi'i school of 'Islamic jurisprudence' within Sunni Islam is named after the founder and 'father of Muslim jurisprudence' who lived more than a thousand years ago. He and others apparently decreed that a full beard is recommended, not obligatory, and it is 'neither unlawful to shave it nor to shorten it, even when this is done without an excuse'. Gillette breathes

Figure 14: Muslims wear beards because someone a thousand plus years ago decreed it.

a sigh of relief there, then. However, it is 'disliked to shorten or shave the beard because it contravenes the prophetic command to grow a full beard' (Fig 14). People must believe whatever they want, but WTF? I read that an initiated Sikh is required to keep the following on their body at all times, day and night, regardless of circumstances: Loose undergarment; wooden comb; iron bangle; unshorn hair; ceremonial short sword. These are five articles of faith known as 'kakar'. You can recognise an initiated Sikh by their loose underpants. I must be a Sikh then. I show my faith by sleeping with a short sword. Thank goodness it only has to be short.

'Move over, dear, your bum's on me sword.'

'Oh, sorry, my love, I thought you were just pleased to see me.'

You have got to laugh or you would cry for the human race.

Each religion has its own funeral rituals which 'God' demands even though they are all different. Hindus are cremated, ideally on a pyre near a river before the next sunrise or sunset, with the eldest son lighting the fire. Muslims bury their dead within 24 hours with the head positioned to face Mecca. This is where the Prophet Muhammad, founder of Islam, lived some 1,500 years ago and that is considered enough to dictate which way Muslims must face when they are dead or how they must pray on their knees five times a day. Everyone to their own, I guess, but *is* it 'their own', or what they are *told* has to be 'their own'? It's the latter, obviously. How easy must it be to control human perception if you can program people to this extent through what is claimed to have happened 1,500 years ago, or even thousands of years before that? My mind is free so long as I conform to God's clearly schizophrenic 'will' as interpreted by the bloke standing at the front with the book in his hand. Muslims are divided into Sunni and Shia and these factions can hate each other with a vengeance over their disagreement over the rightful successor to Muhammad after the year 632. It's a head-shaker. Saudi Arabia is the centre of the Sunni faction while Iran is the premier Shia nation and you understand something of why they don't get on. We see the same with Catholic and Protestant Christianity. Create a religion and then sub-divide it into hostile factions. Divide and rule and then divide some more and rule some more.

Blueprint religions

What appear to be 'different' religions are really the same blueprint in different disguises. At the top you have the perception of 'God', or gods, called Almighty God, Yahweh, Allah, Krishna, whatever. At the bottom there is the congregation and followers who worship the 'God'. In between are the middlemen (a few middlewomen now) who tell the followers what 'God' wants them to do and the consequences for not obeying 'His' word. These are called popes, priests, bishops, imams, rabbis, among endless others in the religious hierarchies. In their befrocked uniforms and fancy dress they interpret what 'God wants' in 'His' sacred places called cathedrals, churches, mosques, synagogues, and temples. Observe almost any religion and you will see the same deal at work. This is the blueprint for religious perceptual control and it is not only confined to what my father described as 'bricks and mortar religion'; the same structure is everywhere and can be seen in everything from politics to mainstream science; academia; human-caused climate change fanaticism; and the software program known as 'Woke'. They all have a belief (their 'God'), their leaders (priests), and the unquestioning repetition of that belief (followers). The 'God' – or Goddess – can be anything from Allah to Mother Earth, or 'Gaia', to the 'equity' of Woke that appears to mean 'equality' but really means the opposite. Religion is defined as 'the belief in and worship of a god or gods, or any such system of belief and worship'. We are awash with religions with such wide interpretation. Religions are nothing more than unquestionable belief with a different name-tag. The financial system that pervades human society and dictates choice (freedom) has its God (money), its priests (bankers, hedge fund managers, stockbrokers), and its congregation (those for whom money is the meaning of life and a focus of worship). Show me, for example, a Christian, Muslim, Jewish, or Hindu money-obsessive and I'll show you someone lost in illusion, contradiction, and cognitive dissonance worshipping two gods for the (negotiable, let's do a deal) price of one. Make that three if they believe in the manipulated hoax of human-caused 'climate change'. We have a perceptual prison within a prison within a prison.

Religions emerge from this human need for certainty. Most humans are ill-at-ease with states of flux in which the outcome is unknown because reality is unknown. This is the major reason that the nature of reality has to be denied us by the Global Cult and its demonic masters through control of 'education' and 'science' (not least with funding). We could enjoy uncertainty and see each experience for what it is while being aware that experience always changes. We could be happy with the true diversity this brings as we explore Infinite Possibility infinitely. Such people are awake to their infinite nature of consciousness forever experiencing forever. A world of billions expressing their infinity and respecting the right of others to express a different infinity would be impossible for the few to control as they currently do. We have to be disconnected from that Infinite Self and our perceptions must be parked in the bodily illusion of names, titles, and labels, which are mere brief experiences that we are constantly pressured, manipulated, and encouraged to believe is the 'I'. From this comes division, bewilderment, confusion, and fear. Who are we? Where are we? How did we get 'here'? We cover the anxiety of what we *don't know* with a manufactured construction of beliefs through which we deceive ourselves that we *do know*. This is what religion really is and *why* it is.

The neurological prison

I have said since the 1990s with ever more detail that the human body is akin to a biological computer that has been created to limit our range of sight and perception. I will develop this theme as we proceed. The human brain is the computer's 'central processing unit', or CPU, which is known as the brain of a computer. The body's genetic communication system is the motherboard and so on. I describe in *The Trap* and *The Dream* how the body connects us to our simulated reality. Think computer and computer game. One decodes the other. The body decodes the simulation into what we experience as the 'physical world' as a computer decodes Wi-Fi into a very different form that we see on the screen. Reality may be multidimensional, but we perceive only this one in the normal course of human life. I will concentrate first on how our perception is manipulated in what we *believe* to be the physical world and then we will go deeper and deeper into the Great Beyond. The human brain is specifically designed to limit our sense of reality and especially the left hemisphere. The 'why?' will become clear if you haven't read the first two books in this trilogy.

The brain has right and left sides with a bridge connecting them known as the corpus callosum (Fig 15). All information is encoded throughout the body in accordance with its holographic structure and both brain hemispheres are involved in all aspects of perception. The *big* difference is the way they process that information. The brain has two realities or centres of awareness; two types of *attention*. The left hemisphere sees the detail and processes reality as a

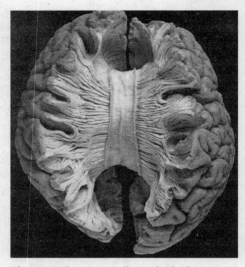

Figure 15: The corpus callosum bridge between the two hemispheres of the brain.

series of parts. Its world is black and white without nuance or dot-connected meaning, and a bit like looking at the world through a magnifying glass. The right hemisphere sees relationships and connections between everything. It sees the tapestry, not the strands (Fig 16). The right is where we find meaning and *context* which the left cannot process. The left can tell you *what*; the right tells you *why*. Human society is dominated by the left side which, in the way it processes information, demands that word again … *certainty*. I quote in *The Dream* the open-minded psychiatrist Dr Iain McGilchrist, author of *The Master and His Emissary, The Divided Brain and the Making of the Western World.* The book

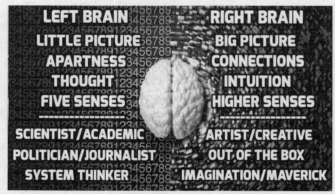

Figure 16: The left and right hemispheres process reality in very different ways.

describes how the left-brain seeks certainty. To achieve this it must collapse *un*certainty into a sense, however illusory and misguided, of certainty.

McGilchrist says of the left-brain: 'It's black and white thinking,

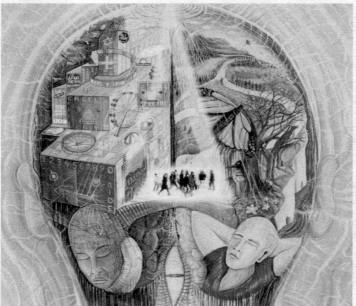

Figure 17: Human society is structured by the Cult to emphasise left-brain reality at the expense of the right and prevent people becoming whole-brained. Academia, science, medicine, media, politics, and much religion are guards at the gate to block right-brain influence on left-brain reality. (Image by Neil Hague.)

dogma, cut and dried thinking, unnuanced thinking, the craving for certainty …' A picture that could either be seen as a duck or a rabbit depending on the angle of observation would throw the left-brain into bewildered confusion with the absence of certainty. It would say: 'Either this is a duck or a rabbit, what do you mean?' Mainstream science, academia, medicine, politics, media, and corporations are all locked away in the left side of the brain and so is religion which satisfies the need for certainty. 'If I believe in Jesus, I'll be saved'; 'If I obey Allah, I'll be saved'. There is no evidence or logic to this. No matter. The certainty that it's true is all the left-brain requires. From this comes 'faith' – a faith in the certainty in the absence of supporting evidence. At least there is one certainty that gives me comfort amid the uncertainty of daily life: 'God' will save me through Jesus, Muhammed, Yahweh, or Shiva. Mainstream science, academia, medicine, politics and media are all religions in that sense and fulfil the criteria for what a religion must be. They follow a dogma that shall not be questioned and those who refuse are the equivalent of blasphemers who must be fired, cancelled, dismissed, demonised, and ridiculed. 'Education' indoctrinates the dogma of false certainty into each new generation as it is designed to do by its creators. 'Education' as we know it was established by the Global Cult which also controls mainstream science, academia, medicine, politics, media, and religion (Fig 17 and overleaf Figs 18 and 19).

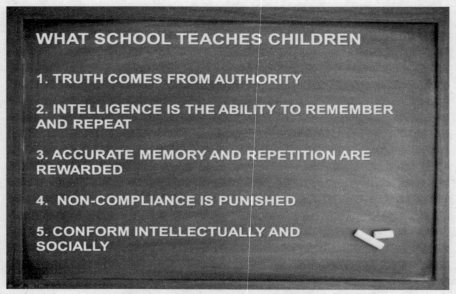

Figure 18: 'Education' is systematic perception programming.

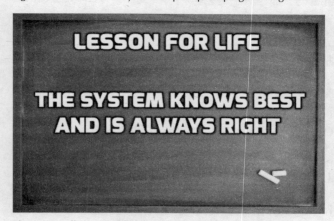

Figure 19: 'All you need to know children – *follow the rules.*'

'Seeing' is deceiving

Left-brain certainty is expressed in the way that it perceives (decodes) reality itself. McGilchrist says the left-brain has a 'very narrow beam, perhaps 3 degrees out of 360 targeted on the detail'. The left-brain produced 'a world of tiny fragments, a bit here, a bit there … static, fixed, known, familiar, bits and pieces'. The left-brain presents us with the world of the five senses with everything appearing separate from everything else. This entraps perception in the illusory world of 'physical' in which the sight-sense sees only 'matter' within what appears to be 'empty space', but isn't. Our eyes can only perceive energy within the minuscule frequency band of visible light which means they can only see the frequency of what is called 'matter'. Energy at frequencies beyond 'matter' is invisible to us. The perceptual result of left-brain limitation was perfectly described by German philosopher Arthur Schopenhauer (1788-1860) with this quote: 'Every man takes the limits of his own field of vision for the limits of the world.' We have the illusion (only one aspect of the total illusion) that we are living in a reality of 'material things' and 'empty space'. Famed scientist Albert Einstein (1879-1955) put it this way:

> Concerning matter, we have been all wrong. What we have called matter is really energy, whose vibration has been lowered as to be perceptible to the senses. There is no matter. There is only light and sound.

'Energy whose vibration has been lowered' to within the frequency of visible light, which is all our eyes can see without expanded psychic sight. The hidden manipulators of humanity (and their now not so hidden Cult gofers on the public stage) seek to imprison perception in the left-brain where reality is wired through the five senses to see only detail and separateness. These include mainstream scientists, academics, doctors, politicians, 'journalists', and system-thinkers dominated by the brain decoding process that we know as 'thought'. If you want to control the masses you must control who they look to for information. They must be 'head' people whose awareness resonates in the frequency realm of the left-brain:

> I am the left brain. I am a scientist. A mathematician. I love the familiar. I categorise. I am accurate. Linear. Analytical. Strategic. I am practical. Always in control. A master of words and language. Realistic. I calculate equations and play with numbers. I am order. I am logic. I know exactly who I am.

The right hemisphere processes more expanded frequencies of perception to present a different sense of human reality. Right-brain-driven people are artists, creatives, and those that think outside of the left-brain 'box':

> I am the right brain. I am creativity. A free spirit. I am passion. Yearning. Sensuality. I am the sound of roaring laughter. I am taste. The feeling of sand beneath bare feet. I am movement. Vivid colours. I am the urge to paint on an empty canvas. I am boundless imagination. Art. Poetry. I sense. I feel. I am everything I wanted to be.

Right-brainers are often mavericks with a more expanded awareness and active imagination. They have the potential to see beyond apparently random dots to how those dots connect. It doesn't mean that they *do*. This depends on how much the right-brain is activated. Some can be creative people (right-brain) yet still perceive reality in general through official narratives (left-brain). Many who are creative in their field donned a mask, stayed at home and took the jab during 'Covid'. Extreme right-brain people can be 'off with the fairies' and find it difficult to function in a left-brain society. It is about balance and to be *in* this world (left-brain) but not *of* it (right brain). The corpus callosum 'bridge', a thick bundle of nerve fibres connecting the hemispheres, is supposed to provide that balance by sharing information and perception between them.The two distinct 'personalities' of the hemispheres are confirmed by the fact that when the corpus callosum is deactivated the person operates in two realities or personalities that perceive independently of each other. There are more limitations when communication between them is severed (often to stop severe epileptic seizures) and the hemispheres go their own way. This can cause literally a split personality ('split-brain syndrome') like neural schizophrenia. One side can do something or perceive something without the other being aware of it. Studies have revealed that people with a disconnected or non-functioning corpus callosum can be shown the same image with each eye, but the second one has no memory of already seeing it with the other. The right-brain controls the left side of the body and vice versa. A woman having a stroke in her corpus callosum said that her left hand had 'a will of its own'. The hand would close doors that the right had opened, close books that the right had opened, or 'snatch money back that the right had paid'. They were making decisions independently of each other.

The corpus callosum does not have to be severed to impact communication between the two sides. This can happen through malfunction whether 'natural' or systematic via chemical/electrical/electromagnetic interference. The brain communicates and processes information electrically and electromagnetically and on one level has a chemical structure. Frequencies are decoded into thought and perception. Put that lot together and you have incredible potential to manipulate brain function and corpus callosum *mal*function through electrical, electromagnetic and chemical influence. What must be the impact on the brain of technologically-generated electromagnetism – the 'Cloud' – as it moves through 4G, 5G and on to 6G and 7G as its reach is expanded across the world thanks to the burgeoning low-orbit 'Starlink' satellite system of Elon Musk's SpaceX and other companies, including Amazon? The effect on the corpus callosum could, for instance, induce a state of cognitive dissonance which is to believe two contradictory things at the same time while thinking both are true. Human society is drowning in this. Humanity is dominated by the left-side of the brain through lack of activation or communication from the right. Corpus callosum blockages will be a major cause of this although not the only one.

Left-right? No – left-left-left

Another reason is the life-long bombardment of information and perception that stimulates the left-brain at the expense of the right. The Cult system seeks to influence this by emphasising the left, putting the right to sleep, and suppressing activity in the corpus callosum 'bridge' between them. This can be overridden if your mind is powerful and independent enough, but it can be a challenge given that brain programming starts at the earliest age. Calculated 'education' (programming) focuses on left-brain, five-sense, subjects such as numbers, language, memorising 'facts' for examinations, and presenting the world as a place of apartness and division. At the same time right-brain stimulation is marginalised or deleted in the fields of art, music, drama, poetry, creative sports, and imagination through spontaneous, ad-lib play and improvisation. When do kids of school age have time to *play* anymore and set their imagination free? The format of Western 'education' (left-brain indoctrination) has been established across the world thanks to first colonialism and then funding from charities and non-governmental organisations (NGOs). Life is lived through information, specialisation, and 'reductionism' – 'the analysis and description of a complex phenomenon in terms of its simple or fundamental constituents' and 'an explanation of complex life-science processes and phenomena in terms of the laws of physics and chemistry'. Reductionism sees parts, not wholes. The result of all this in 'education' can be seen in a major study by Kyung Hee Kim, professor of education at the College of William and Mary in Virginia, of large numbers of school-age children between kindergarten and 12th grade. She found the following:

A massive decline of creativity [right brain] as children have become less emotionally expressive [right brain], less energetic, less talkative and verbally expressive, less humorous [right brain], less imaginative [right brain], less unconventional [right brain], less lively and passionate [right brain], less perceptive [right brain], less apt to connect seemingly irrelevant things [right brain], less synthesizing [right brain], and less likely to see things from a different angle [right brain].

The control system wants us locked away in the left side of the brain. *End of.* This means locked away in a perceptual myopia which can be defined as 'unable to understand a situation or the way actions will affect it in the future' and 'unable to see clearly things that are far away'. That's 'far away' literally and in the sense of realities beyond the range of the left-brain and five senses. Global Cult fake 'education' is designed to slam the door and the Cult mainstream media (plus major tracts of the 'alternative') and societal institutions work to keep you there for the entirety of a human experience. This system is administered by those who are themselves left-brain prisoners called politicians, journalists, scientists, doctors, academics, and most of the rest of the human race. Left-brainers perpetuate leftbrainism which means that those in full knowledge of what they are doing, and why, can be very few compared with the target population. And they are. Human society is structured as an overall hierarchy (the Global Cult) overseeing smaller hierarchies known as governments, corporations, science, medicine, finance, media, 'education', and many more. Operating through this is a system of carrot and stick in which conforming to left-brain reality is rewarded, or at least not condemned, while being right-brain and whole-brain driven is to be ridiculed, rejected, or demonised for the crime of being 'different'. This cumulatively batters so many of the would-be 'different' into left-brain conformity. Emerging from this, or refusing to succumb in the first place, is called 'awakening'.

Whole-brain balance

The Cult and its demon masters fear whole-brain people the most. They can function 'down here' and 'out there'. I use these only as symbolic terms because all realities and dimensions are sharing the same 'space' (like radio and television frequencies of the analogue system made possible by different bands of frequency or wavelength). There is only 'interference' – awareness of their existence – if the frequencies are very close on the dial. Otherwise we are not aware of other realities even though they share the same 'space' as ours. Whole-brain people can function in the human world (left-brain overwhelmingly) and are influenced by expanded levels of consciousness in higher dimensions (frequency-bands). They can take concepts perceived by the right brain and communicate them to the left to be described in the language of the left and through symbolism and analogies when dealing with a sense of reality which no words can adequately describe. Ancients and their shamans worked this way by using symbols and analogies familiar to their societies and eras. Modern historians and anthropologists come along and take the symbolism literally to declare that their beliefs were 'primitive'. Not necessarily so, but then historians and anthropologists are left-brain professions and process reality that way.

Iain McGilchrist said in a Netflix documentary that his official training in psychiatry had all been focussed on the left-brain and what happened in the right was not considered important. He quoted Michael S. Gazzaniga, a professor of psychology at the University of California, as saying that the right hemisphere has about as much intelligence as a chimpanzee. 'Science' and academia think they understand the brain and much more besides when they don't have a clue about the connections and panorama that their left-brain prison-eyes cannot see. A reviewer of McGilchrist's book said that he 'debunks the old 1960s notion that the left side of the brain was the reliable, dependable, rational one, and that the right side was creative and spiritual and filled with mumbo-jumbo'.

McGilchrist rightly observes that the left-brain is 'colonising the world with potentially disastrous results' and had taken over humanity. He says that 'people behave as if the right hemisphere is damaged' and it has been, or at least closed off to suppress its influence. McGilchrist contends that this has cost left-brainers 'the means to understand the world' and my goodness how that explains so much about human behaviour.

Reflecting the demonic

There is an even bigger panorama to all this. I have studied over the decades the mentality of Cult operatives and their demonic realm masters and it long ago became clear that the traits of the left-brain are the traits of the cultists and demons. They have turned humanity into *them* with the need to control and their terror at states of flux with the outcome uncertain or unknown. The left-brain is fixed while the right wants to ride with the flow. The demonic must be in control of the outcome (it must have *certainty*) or it runs home crying to its mum. Cultists seek to control all sides for this reason as they are now seeking to control the alternative media. The demonic mind is expressed through the left-brain and human society reflects that demonic mind. McGilchrist speaks of the left-brain needing rules, regulation, and order. We had 'recreated outside ourselves a world which very much looked like the interior world of the left-hemisphere – rigid lines of things that are rolled out mechanically and were non-unique'. Bureaucracy was in its element with this and depended on the left-brain for its 'organised ability, anonymity, standardisation, uniformity'. Authority was always measuring, quantifying, categorising. The obsession today with data, data, data, is the left-brain at work and what is the Woke obsession with race if not categorisation?

The financial system is left-brain which is one reason why its operatives in the markets don't see or care about the consequences for others of their number crunching. They ignore the connection, or don't see it. Cities are left-brain phenomena with their categorised 'order' of rigid lines, grids and blocks. Buildings of the ancients with their right-brain/whole-brain creativity have given way to the straight lines and right angles of high-rise towers. Show me by comparison the straight line or right angles in what we call 'nature'. McGilchrist points out that the civilisations of ancient Greece, early Rome and the Renaissance (a cultural movement of the 15th and 16th centuries) came from a much more balanced brain 'but eventually moved towards the left and collapsed'. The Industrial Revolution is a left-brain phenomenon and has become ever more extreme in its impact as we enter an era of total control through dependency on seriously left-brain AI and technology. Why has the world become incessantly more standardised and uniform wherever you go? Now you know.

The left-brain can *appear* to be intelligent through memorising information (see exams) which defines what intelligence is for many. This is only *taught* 'intelligence' and the use of memory. Such 'intelligence' can be the village idiot without input from the right to see connections and context. That is innate intelligence, Infinite Intelligence. McGilchrist says there's 'a lot of evidence that the really critical [side] from the point of view of intelligence is the right hemisphere' which has knowledge that the left-brain's perception of 'logic' cannot understand. The left-brain may memorise words. The right-brain provides the gestures and tone that delivers them. Show me a boring speaker and I'll show you a left-brainer. The left hemisphere has 'enormous capacity for denial', to ignore things, and 'keep them shut out', says McGilchrist. Current human perception is founded on denial and the same is true with most 'alternative' thought (which is why I have had as much ridicule from that direction as the mainstream over the years for saying that a non-human force, working through a simulated reality, is behind human affairs). The left-brain has laughed at what I have said, but the right-brain can see it. Humanity has been locked into the left hemisphere with cold calculation. Political correctness is left-brain rigidity with its fine detail of rules, dos and don'ts, and limitation. Humour is a right brain speciality and comedy is being destroyed by Wokery with its demands that 'you can't say this' and 'you can't laugh at that'. Go to a Woke 'comedy' show and watch fake 'comedians' trying to make people laugh while upsetting and offending no one. Not a pretty sight.

Culture and environment affect the way the brain is wired and now the left-brain Western mentality has been imposed upon the world. The throttle goes both ways in that the left-brain changes the culture and the culture can make people more left-brained as minds adapt to the world around them. Ideally we merge the two types of attention into a balanced whole. Pushing against that is the calculated manipulation of perception designed to create hemisphere imbalance that leads to societal imbalance and breakdown. Then there is the phenomena of brain 'plasticity' in which information that the brain processes changes (or solidifies) the way the neural networks connect and fire. Scientists believed until quite recently that once the brain was formed this is how it stayed throughout a human life. They now know differently. The *type* of information (frequency) the brain decodes dictates how the neural networks interact. These networks solidify if they constantly process the same information (hence a 'closed mind'). A constant stream of left-brain information from a left-brain society will hold the population in a left-brain perception through plasticity solidification. In contrast when the right-brain is stimulated and activated through the input of other information/perception the networks rewire to reflect that ('open mind'). The brain is not static unless we choose to make it that way by not being open to other possibilities and ideas. Iain McGilchrist says that the problems of society are caused by an imbalance in the human brain and at that level this is true. I will suggest later that the brain is only responding to *consciousness* and that our state of consciousness *outside* the brain decides how the brain processes reality – left, right, or whole.

Before I address that I want to explore how the left-brain dominates the 'alternative media' which I say is being hijacked by the Global Cult to ensure that it doesn't expose those levels of the dystopian control conspiracy that would truly set us free from The Trap. You will see as we explore the deeper levels of reality how these early chapters about the here-and-now, and people like Elon Musk, fit perfectly with what is happening on the macro scale of human control.

'As above, so below', was never more apt.

CHAPTER TWO

Barricade Brigade

*You get diminishing returns when you are
restricted to your comfort zone*

Sunday Adelaja

There was no alternative or independent media when I had my explosive awakening in 1990 (see *The Trap*). A small number of largely disparate individuals worldwide were exposing the 'conspiracy' in those days. I would talk to minute audiences and rows of empty chairs and only dogged determination drove me on.

I watched the 'alternative media' appear and grow and I have observed with a shaking head as it has been hijacked since 'Covid' by many main chancers, superstar wannabees, repeaters of other peoples' research, and a few key agents of the Cult. Demonic conspirators seeking to impose global dystopia would rather everyone just believed their lies and official narrative that society must become authoritarian because of 'Covid', the human-caused climate change hoax, and all the other manipulated 'crises'. They know since the emergence of the alternative media, now massive by comparison with decades ago, that increasing numbers of their target population won't buy those narratives. A fall-back position is necessary. This requires the infiltration and hijacking of the 'New Media' to hold the line of here-and-no-further, to misdirect, and give them 'conspiracies' to chew on while ensuring they are the *wrong* conspiracies. Locking away the 'alternative' in the left side of the brain would be another bonus. Meanwhile, those who won't compromise on the truth or limit where their research will take them are marginalised while 'safe' people are algorithmically and financially promoted. The mainstream media ridiculed me as a 'nutter' for a long time after 1990 and this turned to abuse and demonisation as my research expanded and I refused to disappear. The approach changed again after early 2020 when I accurately exposed the 'Covid' hoax and since then I have been largely ignored and banned. I am currently banned from 29 European countries of the Schengen border system and Australia. I would find that I am banned from many others if I tried to enter. There is one law for the 'safe' and another for the 'dangerous'.

The truth went *that* way, no, *this* way, no, *that* way.

An example of calculated misdirection of the now-hijacked centre of the
New Media is that the 'Covid virus' was released by design by the
Chinese government from a bio-lab in Wuhan where the 'virus'
supposedly first appeared. Conspiracy researchers jumped on the
release-by-design 'bio-weapon' story and fantastic numbers of hours,
days, weeks, years, have been wasted following this fabricated false trail
to the point where even many politicians, including presidential
candidate Robert Kennedy Jr, have picked up the theme. This has
diverted attention from the fact that there is no 'Covid virus' and so no
'variants' or need for the global campaign of mass vaccination with a
'vaccine' which does not fulfil previous definitions of a vaccine.
Kennedy has done great work exposing the fake vaccine, but in other
ways he promotes the Cult agenda. He named 'American entrepreneur'
Nicole Shanahan as his vice-presidential running mate in 2024.
Shanahan was married to Google founder Sergey Brin until 2022 when
the marriage ended after she reportedly had an affair with Elon Musk.
She donated $4 million of the $7 million cost of a 30-second commercial
for Kennedy played during the Super Bowl. It's small world at the 'top'.
The fake 'Covid pandemic' is a wonderful example of how the Cult's
perceptual manipulation works and why being seriously informed and
streetwise to the techniques is essential to be a proper 'alternative
journalist' which, by that criteria, there are relatively few. How do you
get billions of people and most of the alternative media to believe that a
'virus' exists, when, well, it doesn't? Here's how:

1) Repetition. You repeat through a compliant and unquestioning media
that there is a 'virus' which is potentially deadly. You induce the belief
that it must exist because everyone else believes that it does. Why?
Everyone falls for the same repetition. As the Nazis said:
'Repeat a lie often enough and it becomes the truth.' These lies are
underpinned by images of people with the 'virus' collapsing in the street
in China (but not subsequently anywhere else) and hospitals 'overrun'
with 'virus' patients when they were really *empty*. Yes, empty. They were
cleared of other patients to cope with the victims of the 'virus' of which
there were few and in truth none. How could there be when there is no
'virus'? Britain's ITV produced a docudrama series in 2024 grotesquely
misrepresenting what happened. *Breathtaking* was perception-
manipulating gaslighting in the extreme, portraying 'overrun' hospitals
that were, in fact, virtually devoid of patients (Fig 20 overleaf). The
series will have been made for calculated reasons of misdirection in
readiness for the next 'pandemic'. Even the few patients that *were* in

hospital with 'Covid' were misdiagnosed on the basis of symptoms of the 'virus' claimed by medical authorities taking direction from the Cult-owned World Health

Figure 20: Fantastic amounts of money were spent creating unused 'temporary hospitals' to cope with the 'Covid pandemic' when regular hospitals were all but empty. They were designed to fuel the hype and panic rather than for necessity.

Organization. The WHO was created by the Cult Rockefeller family in 1948 and is run on their behalf by major funder and Rockefeller gofer, Bill Gates. The left-brain is ensnared by the need for the virus to exist to explain all the illness. The right-brain and whole brain says, 'but *why* are they ill? Is there more to know?'

2) Symptoms were described as 'flu-like' and immediately flu was re-diagnosed 'Covid' (along with pneumonia and any other respiratory disease). More symptoms were constantly added to draw in other conditions that could be redesignated 'Covid'. This is why cases of flu *disappeared worldwide* once the 'Covid' hoax began. You don't need a 'virus' to generate illness when you can redesignate illness from other causes as your fake 'virus'. The right-brain and especially whole brain can see this. The left-brain cannot. It sees parts, not connections.

3) The illusion of 'cases' came from testing 'positive' for 'Covid' with the PCR test that was *not testing for the virus*. PCR test creator, the Nobel Prize-winning American biochemist, Kary Mullis, had long confirmed this. Mullis conveniently died just before the 'Covid' hoax was played. He would otherwise have been screaming from the rooftops what he had said about his PCR test when it was used to 'diagnose' the equally never-proven-to-exist 'HIV virus'. He said: 'The PCR test cannot tell if you are sick.'

4) The concept of 'asymptomatic' or no-symptom transmission was lied into being to justify lockdowns, increase the fear, and explain why everyone with no symptoms had to be constantly mass-tested with a PCR test not testing for the 'virus'. Billions of perfectly healthy people were decreed to be a 'Covid case' when there was *nothing* wrong with them. The PCR protocol tests for fragments of genetic material and the

more you amplify the test the more fine detail of genetic material is accessed to ping the result as a 'positive'. Amplification levels used around the world were purposely so high that samples from a goat, paw-paw fruit, even cola, came back 'positive' for 'Covid'.

5) Fictitious 'Covid' deaths were secured by the outrageous policy of putting 'Covid' on the death certificates of anyone who died from *any other cause* within 28 days (and sometimes more) of a 'positive' test not testing for the 'virus'. People were recorded as 'Covid' deaths or 'Covid-related' when they died in road accidents, fell down the stairs, or were killed by gunshots. They were even testing *dead people* after they died of other causes to increase the delusion of 'Covid fatalities'. The left-brain is limited by the perception of 'they would never do that'. The right-brain and whole brain has the perceptual expansion to see that they would and they were.

6) Other magician-level techniques included the tens of thousands of old people who died in UK 'care homes', and in other countries, after being literally murdered using a combination of the drugs Midazolam and morphine. Midazolam is an end-of-life drug used to usher people into the next world and is employed by some American states in the execution process. Record quantities of Midazolam were ordered by the UK government under 'Health' Secretary Matt Hancock in the spring of 2020 and used in record quantities to produce the mass deaths they called 'the first wave of Covid'. One of the consequences of Midazolam in the doses used? *Respiratory failure*. Oh, look – it's 'Covid'.

7) US government 'Covid' overseer Anthony Fauci, a mass-murderer on an industrial scale, decreed that the drug Remdesivir be used on people who tested positive for 'Covid' with a test not testing for it. He well knew the consequences of Remdesivir from studies he had seen in relation to Ebola for which it was soundly rejected as a treatment. Fauci knew that Remdesivir would cause multiple-organ failure. Remdesivir blocks kidney function and the abdominal cavity fills with fluid. This enters the lungs to cause *respiratory failure* which is recorded as 'Covid'.

8) Financial incentives were given to hospitals and medical facilities to diagnose other conditions as 'Covid'. The US government paid them $4,600 dollars for a patient diagnosed with regular pneumonia; $13,000 for each diagnosis of '*Covid-19*' pneumonia; and $39,000 for every 'Covid' diagnosed patient put on a ventilator that would almost certainly kill them.

These were just some of the ways they made billions believe in a 'virus pandemic' without any need for the 'virus' to exist. Key players such as Bill Gates, World Health Organization 'chief', Tedros, Anthony Fauci, and their like were well aware there was no 'Covid virus' when they used the lie of its existence to fake vaccinate billions for reasons I will be explaining. These jabs have killed or destroyed the health for life of staggering numbers of people. See my book *The Answer* for a detailed and absolutely devastating demolition of the 'Covid' hoax. The almost unimaginable level of deceit that I have described is only a glimpse of what we are dealing with. The Cult is expert at manipulating perception in extremely subtle (as well as obvious) ways. To see through it requires the streetwiseness that comes from detailed research and long experience picking through the calculated cul-de-sacs and diversions. It most certainly requires a mind free from preconceived beliefs of any kind and one that has no limits on where it is prepared to go – a mind that is free of concern about what others think of what is presented. The fear of what others think, the fear of damaging your 'image', is the death knell to accurately researching the world.

Left-brain domination of the mainstream 'alternative' arena meant that its perceptual limitations resisted the idea that the conspiracy was so deep that there was no virus. 'People are ill, I saw it on the news, so there *must* be a virus.' To left-brain 'logic' it must have come out of the Wuhan laboratory where 'viruses' are researched in the city where 'Covid broke out'. They didn't research the shockingly ludicrous techniques through which all 'viruses' are claimed to exist (see *The Answer*) and that made them pawns in a game that they largely didn't understand. The right-brain/whole brain can see that the literal existence of a 'Covid virus' was not necessary; only the *perception* of its existence. If they scammed the cases through an illusory test; scammed the illness by diagnosing other conditions as 'Covid-19'; scammed the fatalities with fraudulent death certificates; and murdered people with Midazolam, morphine and Remdesivir while calling it 'Covid' – *where was the sodding 'virus'* then? Where's the 'bio-weapon' when you need to set up all these manipulations to produce your alleged 'cases' and 'deaths'?

The right-brain/whole brain can see that if you want to lead alternative researchers into a diversionary dead end you give them crumbs to follow to the Wuhan lab. You know that *how* and *why* they believe the 'virus' was real is irrelevant as long as they *do* believe in it. Once that is achieved they must further believe there is a tangible threat of some kind to deal with. The Wuhan lab 'bioweapon' theory was born from a belief in the 'bioweapon virus' when the bioweapon was always going to be the fake vaccine. Seeing there was no 'virus' meant there was nothing to deal with. 'Covid' wasn't just partly a scam – it was *all* a scam, every last syllable. This is the difference between what I call the

Mainstream Alternative Media (MAM) and pursuing the unfiltered truth without regard for how people will react. Some MAMs call me a 'purist' and if that means that I want the truth for the truth's sake no matter what people think of me then I am fine with that.

How independent is 'independent'?

The alternative media has exploded since I started out and especially since 'Covid'. That's great, but it doesn't mean the 'alternative' must never be questioned. We must question *everything*, including ourselves. How much of this 'alternative' is truly 'independent' and always in search of greater understanding? If we mean financially independent, well, no, it's not. Many are far *less* dependent than the mainstream which exists only because of advertisers, sponsors, and often billionaire owners, all of which have self-interest as their driving force. The mainstream media needs to keep those people happy and that means not publishing material at odds with their personal or collective agendas. Mainstream media reflects the 'norms' that don't upset the advertisers, sponsors, and billionaire owners, and don't expose the Global Cult's plans for humanity. The Cult *owns* the mainstream media through its gofers and assets. This, by definition, ensures mainstream 'journalism' is firmly trapped in the left-side of the brain and 'here-and-no-further'. It reports the world of 'physical' illusion and tells us lies by reflex action either directly or through suppression of the truth. The alternative, too, depends on advertising, product sales, subscriptions, and 'clicks'. The difference has been that such support has come from far more open-minded sources that want to see beyond the lies. There has been until more recently far more independence and leeway before potential supporters and funders say that is far enough and this has allowed more expression of the right-brain/whole brain. The question is – how much? To what extent is that leeway in the 'independent' sector now being curtailed by a combination of funder resistance and self-censorship? The answer dictates what the 'independent' will report and how far it will go.

Some will say that I am going too far in my criticism and questioning of the mainstream of the alternative media. I trust that before the book is complete you will see why I am so unrelenting and concerned about the way things are shaping up. 'Covid' changed the game in that many more people saw that the world is not as they believed it to be. Rapid alternative media expansion reflected that. Are we really so naïve that we believe the Global Cult would leave it alone and not seek to infiltrate and misdirect? It can't close the stable door, but it can make sure the horse ends up in another field of limitation. This is happening as I will detail. The alternative media that I knew has been hijacked by newbies who have arrived since 'Covid', many of whom bought the 'Covid' hoax, and now present themselves as stars of the New Media while marginalising those who have been researching for decades and exposed 'Covid' from the start. The newbie stars are being massively promoted to vast audiences thanks to algorithmic boosting while the real alternative is artificially suppressed, or 'shadowbanned', by the same algorithms, or banned altogether. This is very dangerous in that genuine truth-seekers are being eclipsed in reach by basically no-littles who hold the line of here-and-no-further as the Cult presses on with its agenda of total human control. The Titanic is sinking while so much of the Mainstream Alternative Media (MAM) focuses its efforts and its audience's attention on rearranging the deckchairs.

Religious limitation

Great swathes of the 'alternative' media, especially in North America, are founded on the Christian belief system which represents a crucial block on free and open research. Possibilities and provable facts are dismissed if they would demolish or even challenge Christian belief. You cannot uncover the expanded truth of what is happening if you have any built-in 'no-go' areas and much of the 'alternative' operates this way. I have been told by Christians that they like some of what I am saying, but they can't support me if I don't believe in Jesus. Others have called me satanic for not accepting the literal existence of Jesus as 'our saviour'. Many times I have been asked if I believe in Jesus as my saviour as a test for the credibility of what I say and write. When is humanity going to grow up to the extent that teeming masses of them don't think they require a 'saviour'? 'Please *save me*!' No problem. We have a long list of saviours on our payroll. We have political saviours, religious saviours. Take your pick. Famed (infamous) American Freemason and Cult operative Albert Pike (1809-1891) said: 'Whenever the people need a hero we shall provide him.' Stop looking for a hero and *be* one. The existence of the Christian version of Jesus is confined almost entirely to a Bible written by who knows who, who knows when, in who knows what circumstances, and then re-written by the 'Church'. Religious belief is their certainty and their left-brain must have that for comfort and solace. To have those claiming to be exposing deceit and lies blindly following a religion founded on deceit, lies, and symbolism taken literally, is quite a contradiction.

Biblical history and especially Old Testament Jewish history is easy to debunk. You have the meticulous documentation left us by ancient Egyptians not even mentioning what should have been the major event of Moses and the Israelites fleeing the pharaoh across a parting Red Sea. Where is any evidence of the '40 years of desert exile' that followed? Shlomo Sand, Professor of History at Tel Aviv University, set out to prove the biblical Israel story was true and soon found there was no evidence for it. This led to his 2008 book *The Invention of the Jewish People*. Christians in the 'truth movement' ignore this and crack on regardless in their belief that the Bible is the word of God. I have met some who do see the lack of Old Testament evidence and still go on believing that the book is God's word – just not that bit. The biggest conspiracy that must be exposed in my view is the reincarnation trap that manipulates 'souls' to keep returning to this simulated shit-hole while believing they are 'learning lessons' to 'evolve and grow'. Where do you start with Christians and Jews that don't even accept the possibility of reincarnation not mentioned in the Bible? Or with Muslims who also reject reincarnation? Or Hindus who believe the reincarnation cycle is 'God's plan' so we can 'evolve and grow'? That's 5.4 of the eight billion humans spoken for straight away.

Padlocked mind

I was invited to do a live interview in front of a large audience in Manchester, England, by James Delingpole, a Christian believer who now claims to be an alternative journalist. He is definitely MAM material. Delingpole had a career in the mainstream with major UK newspapers including the *Daily Mail* and *Telegraph*. His awakening and intelligent sister had been reading my books since the 1990s much to the amusement of Delingpole. Then 'Covid' arrived in 2020 and he changed his mind. Well, sort of. The audience in Manchester was a mix of people who came to hear me and others that came for Delingpole. He introduced the subject of religion and reality. I gave my views on this, including the non-human manipulation and simulated nature of the human world, and he became very discourteous and belligerent. I was questioning his certainty. The next day he posted on Twitter that we had disagreed, but it was all good debate, while posting on Telegram to his followers an aggressive condemnation of me and my views. It was fascinating to see at close range how a believer reacts to someone with a different opinion. He posted: 'My take home from this is that I am authentic. Icke is not.' This was the guy who had laughed at the idea of a conspiracy until 2020 now condemning someone as inauthentic who had been calling it out since 1990. He followed this with further abuse and said I was leading people into 'the New Age'. I have seen this so many times with biblical ignorance. Talk about metaphysics and frequencies and you must be 'New Age' even though I have exposed the New Age movement as a diversion. Delingpole derided my mention of frequencies. I guess it's not in the Bible. His Christian supporters were cheering him on. One posting tagged 'Ben Bootneck' said of me:

Finally the truth. The man is a fraud, a charlatan, a bullshitting con artist and a 33 degree Freemason/Jesuit agent. Thank god you've seen through this

charade Dellers and exposed him as such. He's under the control of Satan and
as such should now be chided, derided and mocked as such. Odious
despicable Luciferians as are his cunt sons.

How very Christian. Apparently my 35 years of work and taking untold
abuse and ridicule was only 'to provide an adequate release valve for
public dissatisfaction and frustration at the system' and 'to provide very
precise glimpses of the enslavement plan' while providing 'no solutions
apart from waking people up' (which is one hell of a solution!). These
Brains of Britain decided this was not good enough. From those
comments alone such people have no idea what I am saying and can't be
bothered to find out. They are unbelievably superficial while claiming to
be some intellectual giant. I asked Delingpole while he was condemning
me on stage how many books of mine he had read and he replied 'none'.
Great swathes of the 'alternative' are full of shit and taking people
nowhere except dystopian oblivion. This is only one small example of
how Christian belief and religious belief in general is a reinforced
concrete wall blocking the way to where we need to go to understand
the scale of this conspiracy and how to overcome it.

The Christian-dominated 'truth movement' has a foundation of here-
and-no-further on that basis alone and there are other incentives for self-
censorship in the 'independent' sector. Audiences for much alternative
content, again especially in North America, are dominated by Christian
believers and this makes hosts and channels often very reluctant to
upset or lose those people by saying anything that would outrage them.
Here we have another research and communication blocker. If you (a)
have a rigid belief system or (b) give a damn about what anyone thinks
of you then you will always go so far and stop. That's not very far,
either, in many cases. Only by working on the premise of knowing how
little we know (constantly fluid perception), and refusing to censor
ourselves in fear of what others think, can we cast aside all limitation of
where we will go and let information and evidence be our only criteria
for what we do and say. The truth will always elude us without the dot-
connecting right-brain that sees the panorama and connections. The
right-brain connects the dots while the left sees *only* dots and apartness.
How much the right-brain is involved, and how unblocked or restricted
is the corpus callosum communication channel, will dictate how far and
deep we will go.

Much of the mainstream alternative is dominated by the left-brain
with some input from the right although often not that much. The prime
theme of this level of the alternative is seeing the manipulations of the
five-sense, left-brain realm of politics and finance. This involves the
World Economic Forum of Cult-gofer Klaus Schwab, blatant Cult
operative Bill Gates, and other 'globalists' behind the centralisation of

global power via Cult-fronts such as the Rockefeller-Gates-controlled World Health Organization, International Monetary Fund (IMF), G-20, NATO, European Union, and the Bank for International Settlements in Basle, Switzerland, which is the *private* (Cult) organisation that covertly coordinates global financial policy between 'national' central banks. Only a little right-brain is required to chart the connections between that lot once you start. I am not saying that exposing this level of the conspiracy is not important. I have been doing that myself for 35 years and long before today's alternative media even existed. I do it every day on Davidicke.com. I am saying that while these matters have to be exposed they are only symptoms of an infinitely greater conspiracy for human enslavement that is far more essential to know. Those that attract the biggest alternative audiences are largely ignoring this and focusing only on the five-sense here and now. I don't think that this is a coincidence. I cringe a little bit when I hear people talk about the 'globalists'. I have observed how this is often code for a here-and-no-further mind. The 'globalists' are a fraction of what is going on.

The MAM

I refer to the central core of the 'New Media' as the Mainstream Alternative Media, or MAM, and its advocates and 'stars' now stride the centre stage of 'alternative' attention. They include people like Joe Rogan, Andrew Tate, Jordan Peterson, Tucker Carlson, Russell Brand, and Bret Weinstein. They have since been joined by Alex Jones and others. MAMs are invariably supporters and followers of the new MAM God, the now everywhere-you-look, Elon Musk. I have been tracking Musk for a very long time and if I have ever seen a fraud, a wolf in sheep's clothing, it is him. I saw this way before the Cult sold him Twitter, now X. I knew when this happened that it was a scam with a longer-term motive and that 'free speech' was only a cover. Most of the MAMs – with the exception of people like Alex Jones – are very or relatively recent additions to the 'alternative' and they have taken it over in terms of public and mainstream attention. I am not saying for a second that they are knowingly working for 'them'. Some MAMs will be plants, including Musk in my opinion. Most will not. Mass promoting those with a limited knowledge of the Big Picture that suits your here-and-no-further ambitions is all that you need.

Media personality, comedian and briefly Hollywood actor Russell Brand did not appear on this scene until after 'Covid' broke and indeed took the piss and used me as a prop for his jokes when I was on some of his shows long before he 'saw the light'. Brand has reinvented himself many times and now he is a 'campaigner for truth'. Joe Rogan was paid a reported $200 million by the very mainstream Spotify for his Internet podcast and in February 2024 Spotify announced a new deal estimated by the *Wall Street Journal* to be worth $250 million which would also make his show available on other platforms including Apple, Amazon, and YouTube. You don't get that phenomenal sum for a podcast and that mainstream Internet exposure if you are a threat to the system. Reading some of the comments on the story from people supposedly 'awake' was perhaps even more shocking:

> 'Those efforts by the Left to cancel him really paid off, huh?'; 'Sounds like the perfect time for Joe Rogan to interview Tucker Carlson'; 'He deserves every penny of it. Joe has the constitution to stand up for everyday Americans. The most rare quality among his peers'; 'Wow, the most influential podcast is going to get louder'; 'Joe Rogan continues to push the envelope in terms of what a podcast can accomplish'; 'This is wonderful news!'; 'Big win for free speech'; 'Arguably the most influential person on Planet Earth right now is about to have even more reach. This is massive considering how important the election this year is.'

These were literally only among the first few and it went on and on like that. I didn't see any at the time asking why someone they believe is a 'threat to the system' would be paid $250 million *by* the system to broadcast on mainstream Internet platforms owned by the system. You ask this question and what comes back is: 'You're just jealous.' These people are not 'awake'. They are in a coma. The most prominent MAMs, Joe Rogan, Tucker Carlson, Ben Shapiro, Alex Jones, Andrew Tate, Russell Brand, and Jordan Peterson mostly promote, defend, and interview each other. There is friction between a few, but mostly that's how it works. Carlson interviews Brand. Brand interviews Carlson. Carlson interviews Tate. Rogan interviews Peterson. Brand interviews Peterson. Carlson interviews Peterson. Rogan interviews Carlson. Peterson interviews Shapiro. Shapiro interviews Peterson. Brand interviews Shapiro. Rogan interviews Shapiro. Jones interviews Tate. Rogan interviews Jones. Jones interviews Rogan. Rogan interviews Brand. Rogan interviews Musk. Jones interviews Musk. Carlson interviews Jones. People like Tate, Peterson and Shapiro also enjoy many mainstream interviews for apparently 'alternative' people. Among mainstream hosts who invite them is Piers Morgan once of the Murdoch station, Talk TV, and now on YouTube. Russell Brand was 15 when I began my journey of exposure in 1990 and Joe Rogan was a 22-year-old hoping to be a comedian while I was facing decades of ridicule and abuse for exposing what these people now attract multiple millions for basically repeating in a much milder version. Tucker Carlson was a 21-year-old and still a year from graduation. Jordan Peterson was 28 and working for his PhD in clinical psychology in Canada. Andrew Tate was *four.* I have been on this road a very long time, but they are here now and they are promoted to worldwide public attention.

So what's the problem?

None of this explains why I am so vehement in my exposure of Elon Musk and those who are building a limitation barricade around the alternative media. The reason is that they are hijacking the focus of the alternative arena and reacting – *reacting* – to only five-sense events. These are the symptoms of the conspiracy, not the *cause*. Without getting to the cause there can be no deletion of the cause, or as a result, a deletion of the problem. Andrew Tate, the Muslim-converted son of a CIA operative (he says), is supposed to be persona non grata and yet has been given a stream of high-profile mainstream media interviews to promote himself as a champion of men. His one trick is to correctly point out that there is a war on the male (ignoring the gathering war on the female). Both sexes are being targeted because the Cult is in the process of eliminating both to create a new far more synthetic technologically-procreated androgynous human (Human 2.0) as I have highlighted in my books for many years and is now becoming blatantly obvious. We have the mass fake vaccination of self-replicating synthetic material in the 'Covid' jab and the emergence of synthetic biology, or 'SynBio', as a fast-growing discipline of mainstream science with its obsession with replacing the perceived 'natural' with synthetic copies. This includes body parts and, in the end, whole bodies. Rapidly falling sperm counts around the world is the calculated elimination of male-female procreating Human 1.0.

All of this is lost on Tate who meets the challenge of male suppression by telling young men to assert themselves with women and equate power and success with having lots of money and an expensive fancy car. You want to be a *man*? Get yourself a Bugatti like me. It's not barely-one-dimensional or anything. Andrew Tate is not a threat to the 'New World Order', but his promotion as a threat gives him credibility with his audience. As I write, he is not allowed to leave Romania over sexual abuse allegations which he vehemently denies. He was a kickboxer who came to the fore in 2016 on the UK TV show *Big Brother* created by Dutch media tycoon, John de Mol Jr, who was named as one of the 500 richest men in the world. Joe Rogan is a former small-time kickboxer who got his first TV break on a US game show called *Fear Factor* produced by John de Mol Jr. Andrew Tate has made endless claims and boasts about his life that researchers say are not supportable by the evidence. He claims to be 'the smartest person on this planet' when you only have to listen to his self-obsessed bullshit for 60 seconds to know that this is seriously not the case.

Another MAM Barricade Brigadier is Canadian psychologist and academic Jordan Peterson who came to prominence in 2016 for his refusal to bow to the tyranny of the enforced use of 'preferred pronouns' and political correctness in general. Good on him, too. If someone with a male body wants to call himself 'Miss' or 'They/Them' that's up to 'They/Them'. It's none of my business what they call themselves. Just don't tell me to refer to someone as a female when they are obviously a bloke. I won't do it. I have self-respect and I'll decide how I see reality, not some Woke extremist. I am with Peterson on this. The problem with the Barricade Brigade is that they come into the arena via one 'dot' or subject and then think they know what is going on across the spectrum when they are babes in arms to the real panorama. This makes them easy to manipulate through their lack of knowledge. Peterson, for example, has made dismissive comments about people 'believing that reptiles run the world' when he has no idea if that is true or not. The severe limitations imposed by his left-brain tell him that it can't be true when it breaches his perception of 'normal'. There is no need for an open mind or further research. His left-brain has spoken and decreed the limits of his reality. He is a classic left-brainer along with the great majority of the MAM. He has a few interesting things to say about psychology here and there from a left-brain perspective. Mostly he only states the obvious. His allegedly profound statements when broken down are often meaningless and he reminds me of the Peter Sellers character in the movie, *Being There*, released in 1979. Sellers plays the gardener of a wealthy resident of Washington DC and he never left the property. His benefactor dies and events lead to him becoming celebrated as a genius intellectual who is introduced to the US President. He is talking about gardening which they mistake for incredible insights on the world and economy. Sellers says:

> As long as the roots are not severed, all is well. And all will be well in the garden ... in the garden, growth has its seasons. First comes the spring and summer, but then we have fall and winter. And then we get spring and summer again.

This is taken as a statement about the economy (there will be growth in the spring) when he is a gardener talking about his garden. I see this theme in many of Peterson's perceived profound statements that are actually not. He nevertheless built an enormous following and began to comment on matters that he knew nothing about. This is a major defect of the MAM. It has become top-heavy since 'Covid' with people who are clueless about the totality of the conspiracy and how that impacts on world events. Peterson was hired on a stupendous salary by *The Daily Wire* in the United States, headed by the ultra-Zionist, Israel first, second and last, Ben Shapiro, who, like Peterson, had the 'Covid' jab and then complained that the government had lied to him about it. You would think that as a self-proclaimed alternative journalist this would have been a gimme. Not so. The idea is to expose lies, not fall for them. Peterson said during 'Covid':

> Why did I get the vaccine? Balance of risk, I suppose. I don't need Covid. I've had enough health trouble and I had Covid. So I had Covid and I got the vaccine because some of my blood markers indicated that my immunity might not be what it should be. Was it the right thing to do? How the hell do I know? I don't bloody well know.

> I don't think that vaccine makers are conspiratorial fundamentally or any more than any other organisation … I wanted to stop worrying about Covid. It seemed to me that case rates plummeted after the vaccine was strong … I am sick and tired of the lockdowns and assume that if in Canada we reach a certain threshold of vaccinated people that it would be done with and I'm ready for that and willing to take some risk for it.

If I needed a single quote to justify my contention that know-nothings have hijacked the 'alternative' media then that is it. To think this bloke is even considered alternative when he fell for every lie and perceptual trap of the 'Covid' hoax says everything about the MAM. The guy who spoke those words was even being praised in March 2024 for attacking a Big Pharma and 'Covid' supporting chap in an interview. This is a theme of the 'New Media' MAM – those who bought the hoax now being promoted as activists against something they bought in its entirety at the time. More than that, they are considered experts on a global conspiracy about which they know *nothing*. The idea of 'alternative' journalism is not to be wise *after* the event when you have bought the hoax and the gathering consequences make it more acceptable to challenge. It is being researched, streetwise, and courageous enough to call it out *when it is happening*.

Defend Israel At All Costs (DIAAC)

Shapiro took Peterson on the Israel propaganda tour to meet the many times Prime Minister Benjamin 'Bibby' Netanyahu. What followed was Shapiro interviewing Netanyahu like a little boy in awe of his dad. Another recording had Netanyahu talking with Peterson who let the mass-murdering tyrant get away unchallenged with outrageous claims. Netanyahu even boasted that he turned the Israeli people into a 'Pfizer lab' for their fake vaccine during 'Covid'. Peterson drooled over his 'Bibby' and when the latest mass bombing by Israel of Gaza was about to begin in October 2023 he posted on Twitter/X: 'Give 'em hell @netanyahu. Enough is enough.' Netanyahu's Israeli Defense Forces (IDF) went on to bomb Gaza into oblivion at the cost of more than 30,000 lives in an open-air prison camp where 43.5 percent of the population was aged 14 or under. The comment came from pure ignorance of Israel-Gaza history and the dynamic between the two cultures. There was no mention of the most obvious fact that Israeli military and intelligence (the IDF, Mossad, and Shin Bet) are among the most technologically advanced and sophisticated in the world and they clearly *allowed* Hamas terrorist operatives to breach the Gaza border fence in multiple places. The Israeli government *created* and funded Hamas as opposition to the Palestinian Liberation Organization of leader Yasser Arafat. This is well known.

I have written in great detail in books like *The Trigger* about the cutting-edge nature of Israeli intelligence and surveillance technology (in which it is a world leader). Former members of the Israeli Defense Forces (IDF) stated publicly after the Hamas October 7th attacks that the fence sensors are so sophisticated that if a cockroach or bird went near them the IDF would immediately know. They said it was not possible for Hamas to breach the fence in multiple locations without the knowledge and response of the IDF, but that is what happened. The Israel government subjected its own population to what followed to provide the excuse for the Gaza genocidal mass bombing. There was no mention of this by the MAMs Peterson or Shapiro or that Hamas was a creation of the Israeli government. Did the cerebral genius not know? Even if Peterson *had* known, and made these points, Shapiro would have been furious at such insubordination. The academic faced a fierce and immediate public backlash for the Netanyahu tweet and many re-evaluated their view of him. A chunk of his followers walked away. Large numbers didn't. This is what happens when you promote MAM people to 'alternative' prominence that have no idea what they are talking about and would not say it if they did. For sure, this is no accident.

The attacks that Egypt warned Israel were imminent were allowed to happen because it gave Israel the excuse to take control of Gaza and continue the ethnic cleansing of Arabs from what the Israeli government claims for its own. It is the technique that I dubbed in the 1990s Problem-Reaction-Solution – create the problem, trigger a public reaction of 'do something', and then offer the solutions to the problem you have yourself created. There's a version that I call NO-Problem-Reaction-Solution which we see with 'human-caused climate change' and 'Covid'. You don't always need a real problem, only the public *perception* of one. The Cult-owned government of Israel bombed Gaza into oblivion (again) thanks to the actions of its gofers leading Hamas who would have well known what the consequences would be for the people of Gaza when it has happened so many times before. Hamas leaders, meanwhile, were making video statements from … *Qatar*. If Netanyahu and his fellow psychopaths had been genuine, rather than in on the whole scam, they would have taken action against Qatar for hosting Hamas leaders. They didn't.

Candace Owens, a presenter with Shapiro's *Daily Wire*, did challenge Israel's genocidal mass murder in Gaza and when the Cult-owned Anti-Defamation League (ADL) began to target her the outcome was inevitable. She was fired by *Daily Wire* boss man and Netanyahu stooge Shapiro. He made his name attacking the Woke cancel culture, but, of course, that aversion to censorship has never included criticism of Israel and ongoing mass murder of Palestinian civilians. This was still more evidence of the Israel-centric hijack of the Mainstream 'Alternative' Media (MAM) which transformed into the DIAAC – Defend Israel At All Costs (Fig 21). MAM God Musk jumps to attention when Israel barks its orders and they are invariably unquestioning advocates of Israel

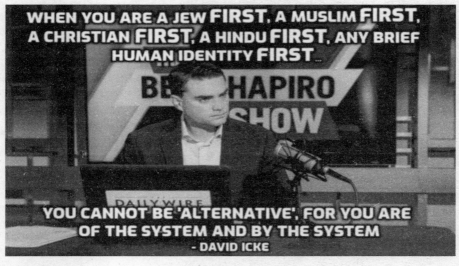

Figure 21: Ben Shapiro at work. We are all expressions of Infinite Awareness and to identify with human labels is to identify with limitation and illusion. It also makes divide and rule a cinch.

which can do no wrong, or terrified of criticising HE who must be obeyed. Some of us have rather more integrity and a backbone made of steel, not jelly. My congratulations go to Candace Owens for having both on this issue. She suited the Shapiro agenda as a black woman brilliantly calling out the Black Lives Matter scam, but crossed the line with Israel which would potentially enter the Cult's inner sanctum and she was gone – from *The Daily Wire* anyway. Owens revealed her own cognitive dissonance by converting to Roman Catholicism a few weeks later, of which more in a moment.

Some in the MAM did begin to break ranks on Israel when the Gaza slaughter showed no sign of ending and charity food aid workers were killed in an Israeli attack in Gaza that clearly targeted them. I have been exposing the Israel connection since the mid-1990s and been mass-censored ever since as a result. I hope that as the Israel link to the Global Cult becomes ever more obvious that those MAMs who are not agents of Israel will be speaking out more on this subject by the time you read this. To ignore the Israel-connection is to show you are not informed and/or you have no spine when it matters. No one needs to see the Israeli government for what it is more than Jewish people who are being mercilessly manipulated by their Cult-owned 'leaders'.

Boarding the ARC

Jordan Peterson is fronting up the most obvious controlled opposition organisation known as 'ARC', the Alliance For Responsible Citizenship, with its highly-symbolic catch-phrase 'Welcome aboard the ARC' (Fig 22). I watched a very informative investigation of the ARC and its

Figure 22: Old Testament symbolism for the Old Testament 'ARC'.

backers in an Internet video by a researcher posting under the pseudonym Polly St George on her Rumble channel 'Amazing Polly'. We would certainly disagree on many things, not least religion, but on the theme of the MAM hijack we see many of the same patterns. She noted that Jordan Peterson announced the creation of ARC in an interview with Joe Rogan – another MAM-MAM interview – in January 2023. ARC's first conference was in London the following autumn attended by some of the most non-alternative people you could imagine. These included former Australian Prime Ministers Tony Abbott and long-time Cult gofer John Howard, the second longest serving Aussie PM, who has appeared in my books many times over the years. There was former Australian Deputy Prime Minister John Anderson and US Representative Dan Crenshaw who serves on the House Energy and

Commerce Committee and the House Permanent Select Committee on Intelligence. All are on ARC's Advisory Board. Crenshaw was a Lieutenant Commander in the US military SEAL Teams and was named a Young Global Leader of the World Economic Forum of Klaus Schwab which ARC claims to oppose. Crenshaw says he was named without his knowledge.

Another speaker at the London ARC conference was UK government minister Michael Gove, an ultra-Establishment figure who could not spell the word 'alternative'. Let's give him a clue – it starts with an 'a', mate. Gove has filled a number of Cabinet positions under Conservative Prime Ministers David Cameron, Theresa May, Boris Johnson, and Rishi Sunak. He is a member of the far-right-dominated Henry Jackson Society that locks into the Neoconservative or 'Neocon' network in the United States that was behind the invasions of Afghanistan and Iraq in 2001 and 2003. Gove contended that the UK did not need UN approval to invade Iraq because the UK is a democracy while non-democratic countries on the UN Security Council had a veto over military action. He is vehemently pro-Israel, as with all Neocons, and argues that Israel's seizure of Arab land was legitimate. No wonder he and Peterson get on. The ARC mix involves those supporting the carbon net zero policy that employs fraudulent 'climate change' to justify dystopia and those building 'digital cities' that allow total control through AI.

Who is really behind ARC?

Polly St George gets to the core of ARC when she delves into the backers, funders and creators of the organisation. Peterson claims in his ARC videos that he had the idea for the organisation after meeting people organically around the Western world from North America to Europe and Australia/New Zealand who supported his idea for what became ARC. He had a vision for 'another story' for the world. Letting individuals decide their own story was not enough, it seems. They need others to tell them what that story should be. Peterson said that he began to formulate ARC with people he knew in the UK. The cornerstone of ARC is the Legatum Institute, the 'philanthropic' arm of a massive global investment fund, Dubai-based Legatum Capital. Baroness Philippa Stroud, a co-founder of ARC, is the Legatum Institute CEO and a member of the House of Lords who founded the Centre for Social Justice in 2003. Two ARC notables are Kevin Tebbit, former director of the British Intelligence GCHQ 'listening centre' and a permanent secretary at the Ministry of Defence; and Paul Marshall, co-founder and chairman of Marshall Wace, one of Europe's largest hedge fund groups which was launched in 1997 with a $25 million investment from major Cult operative, George Soros. The company was worth £630 million by 2020. Marshall is one of the driving forces behind ARC and his friend Baroness Stroud became CEO of ARC in November, 2023. Her occupation is described as 'think tanker' and among her policy priorities are more 'refugee' children coming to the UK and government becoming more involved in 'family relationships'. Both are Cult agendas that I have been exposing for a long time. These connections are a glaring example of what constitutes the 'alternative' since 'Covid'.

Legatum was founded in 2007 by Christopher Chandler. His brother Richard founded the Chandler Foundation and has connections to the Bill and Melinda Gates Foundation, the Rockefeller Foundation, World Bank, and US Intelligence front, USAID. Alan McCormick is another partner of Legatum and a former vice-president of marketing with JP Morgan. Cult-owned MasterCard is a funder of at least one Legatum 'philanthropic' venture while MasterCard also partners with George Soros. If you wanted a group of the least alternative people then here they are and 'Peterson's' ARC is their baby. The pseudo 'alternative' UK television station GB News was founded in 2020 by Legatum and Legatum-connected Paul Marshall. There are few more obvious here-and-no-further operations than GB News who happily fire anyone who crosses the line into real journalism and exposure of the Cult agenda. Needless to say that, as with Joe Rogan and Tucker Carlson, GB News refuses to interview me, including MAM presenter Neil Oliver. An interview was arranged with my sons, Gareth and Jaymie, but cancelled once it was publicised and GB News lied to them about the reason. GB News is there only to *appear* to be alternative by questioning Woke and climate policy (a common theme with 'New Media' activists and billionaires). Cross the line into anything close to Cult connections and you are out the door.

How can you claim to be 'alternative' when GB News employs Conservative Party politicians to present their shows, including 'Covid' Prime Minister Boris Johnson? It's crazy, crazy. GB News and ARC are masks on the same face controlled by the same people. Paul Marshall backs another UK alternative operation called UnHerd which says that its mission is 'to push back against the herd mentality with new and bold thinking'. Okay, *how* 'bold'? Prosperity UK was another Marshall company and when Polly St George checked out ARC on the UK Companies House website she found that its *previous name* was *Prosperity UK*. Peterson claims ARC emerged from support for his idea on his travels and it should not have had any previous name. Oh, but it *did* – the organisation created by hedge funder Paul Marshall. She also found two directors listed for ARC -- Marshall and Legatum partner Alan McCormick. ARC is a front for billionaires and the only-so-far agenda of the Cult-infiltrated Mainstream Alternative Media (MAM). Is Peterson aware that his 'organic' story is not true or is he just not bright enough to see how he is being used? Only he knows although I concluded a long time ago that people like Peterson are not even nearly as intelligent as many believe. Word-salad narrators may sound intelligent and 'intellectual'. This does not mean that they are.

ARC and WEF: What's the difference?

ARC claims to be challenging the Cult-owned World Economic Forum of Klaus Schwab. I don't agree. I say that ultimately ARC is another version of the WEF designed to pull in the naive. ARC 'opposes' the WEF hard sell agenda and instead goes for the soft sell of basically the same agenda. Pushbackers on Cult plans reject the hard sell and the idea is to convince them to buy the soft sell to the same end. Schwab, who announced a change of role at the WEF from 2025, was 'mentored' (psychologically cloned) by the infamous Cult operative, Henry Kissinger. The WEF coordinates the Cult's dystopian agenda between world leaders and the intellectual elite and has its infamous Young Global Leaders training scheme in which targeted young people are promoted and prepared to become world leaders of the future and, in the words of Schwab, 'penetrate the cabinets'. These have included British Prime Minister and Cult-clone Tony Blair; Angela Merkel, long-time Chancellor of Germany, Nicolas Sarkozy, President of France; Emmanuel Macron, President of France, a former Rothschild employee; Jacinda Ardern, the Blair-aide Prime Minister of New Zealand and 'Covid' extremist; Justin Trudeau, Prime Minister of Canada and 'Covid' extremist; Chrystia Freeland, Deputy Canadian Prime Minister, Minister of Finance, 'Covid' extremist, and WEF operative; and Gavin Newsom, Governor of California and 'Covid' extremist. Schwab has claimed that Russia's Vladimir Putin is a WEF Young Global Leader 'graduate'. Others include Bill Gates; Jeff Bezos, Amazon founder and owner of the *Washington Post*; Larry Page, an official founder of Google; Mark Zuckerberg, official founder of Facebook; Niklas Zennström, founder of Skype; Jimmy Wale, founder of Cult-narrative-promotor Wikipedia; Jack Ma, founder of Chinese Internet tech giant Alibaba; Leonardo Di Caprio, actor and UN 'climate ambassador'; Bono (rock singer and Bill Gates arse-licker); David de Rothschild, the 'Green' activist; and Ricken Patel, founder of climate change promoting Avaaz along with other Cult agendas. Control politicians and sources of communication and you control laws and perception. Don't worry – a few people can't control the world, right?

Peterson's ARC has its version of WEF Young Global Leaders and among them is Dutch activist Eva Vlaardingerbroek. Once again, as with other MAMs, she has some relevant things to say about particular dots. Most prominently in her case is the seizing of farming land in the Netherlands and Europe, mass migration, and the WEF. She is clearly unaware of the scale of the human and spiritual panorama and there lies the problem. This makes her a cul-de-sac, not a freeway. I wish her well with what she does. My point is that we should not fall for the idea that this is the limit of the conspiracy. It goes *way* deeper. Vlaardingerbroek's conversion to the Roman Catholic Church in 2023 at the age of 26, attended by colleagues from GB News, is an example of how a little knowledge has its dangers (Fig 23). Few organisations in human history have been a bigger block on freedom of thought and belief than the

Figure 23: Dutch MAM activist Eva Vlaardingerbroek very publicly converted to Roman Catholicism.

Roman Church which is the relocated Church of Babylon. I have exposed the Vatican-based networks in detail over the years for their central role in mind manipulating followers through fear, guilt, intimidation and mass-murder of 'heretics', plus its infamous history of child abuse. Popes have been some of the most bloodthirsty satanic tyrants ever to walk the Earth and we have had a stream of modern popes serving the Cult with the likes of Pope Francis, Pope Benedict, and Pope John Paul II. The latter's predecessor, Pope John Paul I, Albino Luciani, somehow eluded the white smoke mafia to become Pope in 1978 only to be murdered after the Freemasonically-significant 33 days in office while preparing his plans to rid the Vatican of Freemason control. His murder coincided with the exposure of the Rome-based Propaganda Due, or P-2, Freemasonry lodge of Mussolini fascist Licio Gelli which was manipulating all major aspects of Italian society through its members in government, media, intelligence, military, and business. See David Yallop's 1984 book, *In God's Name: An Investigation into the Murder of Pope John Paul I,* and my own books for the background to P-2. A 'truth activist' claiming to know about the global conspiracy while converting to a central pillar of the conspiracy betrays the level of ignorance that pervades the MAM. Vlaardingerbroek said she did so because we are involved in a 'spiritual war'. Well, unfortunately, Eva, you chose the wrong ally, mate, and that should have been obvious to you. She posted at Christmas 2023:

Over 2000 years ago a child was born that came to die for all of our sins. He is the Christ, the living God, the Saviour of the world. Love Him with all your heart, because He loves you. Have a blessed Christmas everyone.

What someone believes is nothing to do with me. That's not the issue. It is the monumental contradictions between a 'researcher of truth' and those statements which cannot be supported by evidence outside of the Bible and the Christian narrative – a Bible whose content was decided and dictated by the *Roman Church*. If Jesus died to forgive all human sin that must include Vlaardingerbroek's targets Schwab, Gates, and Dutch Prime Minister Mark Rutte. If Jesus is the 'Saviour of the world', born 2,000 years ago, when is he going to start with the saviour bit? Humanity's need for left-brain certainty (which depends on corpus callosum suppression) instigates the cognitive dissonance necessary for such contradictions to prevail. I read this in a Christian Internet article:

> Jesus' death brings forgiveness because it serves as a substitutionary sacrifice. His perfect life, without sin, made Him the only suitable candidate to pay the price for humanity's sins. By willingly giving up His life, Jesus offered Himself as a perfect sacrifice that satisfied the demands of justice, allowing God to extend His forgiveness to humanity.

> The death of Jesus reveals the immense love of God for humanity. It demonstrates that God was willing to give up His own Son, the ultimate sacrifice, to reconcile humanity back to Himself. It is a vivid display of God's unconditional love and desire for restoration with His creation.

If any of that is true, we have a 'God' that is both masochistic and stupendously stupid. The idea that 'God' would want 'his son' sacrificed for the sins of psychopaths and Satanists has got to be a very definition of ridiculous and it kicks shapeshifting reptilians way out of the park when it comes to being 'weird'. How can the same brain that believes this to be true also believe that it's researching the conspiracy based on pursuing facts? Only by the right brain not talking to the left, I guess.

MAMs 'find religion' and stardom

Eva Vlaardingerbroek has posted pictures of herself walking around an airport wearing an ash cross on her forehead. I think it's fair to say that she is a fanatical Catholic and good for her. I just don't see how this fits with the uninhibited pursuit of what is going on. I can't comment on any of her Twitter/X posts since she blocked me in 2023. She gets serious promotion from Tucker Carlson, Jordan Peterson, and the MAM which is dominated by the Christian belief system. The MAM clique has become full of itself with its stars believing their own publicity and hype. I saw Vlaardingerbroek portray herself as a Joan of Arc figure on horseback brandishing the hammer of pagan god, Thor. This was not very Roman Catholic and when the story becomes you *covering* the story, and not the story itself, the true meaning and reason for the alternative media evaporates. Her religious conversion would seem to have been prompted by hearing a speech in 2017 by Dr Peter Kreeft, a Catholic philosopher and convert, called '7 Reasons Why Everyone Should Be Catholic'. Among them was that the Catholic faith is true; it's good; it's beautiful; it's veracity is proved by the facts of history; it produces saints; it gets people to heaven; and it's where people actually meet Jesus Christ. None of this is supported by any evidence whatsoever except that the Roman Church does declare 'saints' – many of which have been some of the most violent mass-killers of non-believers that history has recorded. It's very 'alternative'. Eva Vlaardingerbroek posted a clip of Kreeft on Twitter/X with the line: Beware of the 'I'm spiritual, but not religious' types. I must be a blasphemer then. The clip had Kreeft saying:

> The Devil is very spiritual, he hates matter, and religion means relationship – relationship with God. If you know who God is that relationship starts with humility. But spirituality lacks humility. 'Oh, I'm very spiritual.' That's what the Pharisees said, too. I think that's ridiculous and dangerous. I'm not spiritual. I'm religious.

'Humility' is to kill vast numbers of people who see reality differently and to exploit fear and guilt to ensnare the minds of children for life? I am staggered that someone so barely-one-dimensional could have convinced Vlaardingerbroek to buy this crap. We can't expand into the enormity of what is happening while its advocates sit on the barricade with guards at every exit. They are promoted to attract the biggest audiences which then believe that what they are seeing is 'it' when what they are being told is only a fraction of 'it'. The theme of religion is very relevant in the MAM hijack. The alternative media has always been dominated by Christian belief and this is being ramped up today. I have noticed, and I am not alone, that many MAM personalities are converting to a religion, voicing their religion more loudly than they did before, or changing their anti-religion stance. I doubt this is a coincidence.

American activist Candace Owens converted to Roman Catholicism in the spring of 2024 while Russell Brand posted a video of himself doing the Catholic Rosary and saying Christian prayers. He was later baptised and said that Jesus is real. Brand's wife is Roman Catholic and Jordan Peterson's wife has converted to Roman Catholicism with support from Vlaardingerbroek after she was 'cured of cancer' by praying with rosaries blessed by the Pope and another owned by her great grandmother. This would have nothing to do with Roman Catholicism and rather the power of the mind and belief on the body. What you believe, you perceive and what you perceive you experience. We'll see how this works later. Even

Figure 24: Humanity on its knees to a bloke raised above them on a throne. The human condition revealed in a single image.

people like Candace Owens, who I respect for her unrelenting stance on many issues, has her reality founded on 'Christ is King'. I have no idea what this is supposed to mean. He's king of what? I would just say think it through and apply open-minded research and logic to what is constantly repeated by reflex action. I watched an outpouring of 'Christ is King' on Twitter/X after it was apparently suggested that the phrase is 'anti-Semitic' (but then what isn't?). One post included this highly symbolic picture of the human plight (Fig 24). The post said: 'Christians – ignore the campaign to mark "Christ is King" as antisemitic. Ignore it with all your might. Christ is King, and every knee will bow and confess that He is Lord.' The same people talk about the need to be free. What – on your *knees*? My reply did not go down well with many, but it was heartfelt:

> When humanity stops bending the knee to ANYONE we might just have a shot at this freedom we talk about. Human race get off your KNEES! You'll never be free while you're on them – whatever the reason.

How people can't see the obvious contradiction of demanding freedom while telling people to bend the knee to Jesus as their Lord is truly beyond me. Alex Jones and the vast majority of the MAM inner core go along with 'Jesus is Lord' or 'Jesus is King'. Russell Brand says he's now a born-again Christian, wears a cross, and follows Jesus. He said he is 'reading the Bible a lot more'. YouTube 'influencer' and anti-Woke comedian JP Sears announced that he was converting to Christianity:

> I was excluding some amazing traditional Christian values, beliefs of God and ways of connecting with God that I now really value but, out of what I would call spiritual arrogance, I was excluding them, just judging them. I didn't believe in the immense power of prayer.

Why do you have to convert to Christianity for any of this? Prayer is the

interaction of intent with the simulation field, or consciousness beyond
the simulation, which can manifest in matter what you pray for. Joe
Rogan had not been a religious advocate before, but he has been
covering Christianity more frequently and said this on his podcast:

> I think that as time rolls on, people are going to understand the need to have
> some sort of Divine structure to things. Some sort of belief in the sanctity of
> love and of truth. And a lot of that comes from religion. A lot of people's
> moral compass and the guidelines that they've used to follow to live a just and
> righteous life, this has come from religion.
>
> And, unfortunately, a lot of very intelligent people , they dismiss all the
> positive aspects of religion because they think that the stories are mere
> superstitious fairy tales, that they have no place in this modern world, and
> we're inherently good, and your ethics are based on your own moral
> compass, and we all have one. And that's not necessarily true.
>
> We need Jesus. I think for real. If he came back now it'd be great. Like Jesus, if
> you're thinking about coming back, now's a good time.

There is surely more to know about this MAM religion deal and we'll
see where it goes from here, I guess. Focusing on a religious hero to
come and save us is certainly a benefit for the Cult. Jesus will come and
sort it out. Have faith. The Psyop that was 'QAnon' during the first
Trump presidency was a version of this. We were told by an anonymous
source known as 'Q' that there was a plan to replace the 'bad guys' with
the 'good guys'. Arrests were going to be made. My goodness how
many times I have seen this card played under different guises since I
set out in 1990. A mythical 'good guy' group of insiders had everything
in hand. 'Trust the plan' was the mantra when it was a Cult Deep State
Psyop. There was never any plan except to mislead and stitch-up
Trump-supporting pushbackers. The whole fiasco was only buying time
for the Cult agenda to further advance unmolested.

'The plan' led to the breach of the Capitol Building in Washington DC
on January 6th 2021 after which a long list of decent, if misguided,
people were arrested and jailed for high crimes that were simply a case
of communal trespass. They were clearly allowed into the building (as
was Hamas into Israel). I wrote from the day it happened that the
Capitol breach had been manipulated to allow the trespass to be labelled
an 'insurrection' with all the police state and political potential that
offered. January 6th was a Deep State (Cult) Psyop sting and tens of
millions in the United States and others around the world bought the
QAnon lie because it told them what they *wanted to hear*. What a mind
control technique this is. Tell people what they want to be true and the

door of acceptance is already swinging open. Tell them what they don't want to hear, as I have done for 35 years and the door is padlocked. A cascade of abuse awaits anyone with the backbone to go there.

'Donald will save us' is just another case of telling people what they want to hear. A belief that Jesus is 'coming back' is a global version of the QAnon sting. Trust the plan. God has a plan. 'Oh, thank you Jesus for sending your John the Baptist, the blessed Donald, to prepare for your return.' I wish that was happening. I really do. How much easier it would be for someone else to come and make everything right. Jesus isn't coming and 'The Donald' is a Psyop to buy still more breathing space for the Cult agenda to reach its goal.

WE have to do it. Bad news, I know. True all the same.

CHAPTER THREE

'Dream Team'

Agreement in a dialogue can lead to a cul-de-sac

Christoph Grafe

I have watched American talk show host Tucker Carlson evolve over the years from a classic mainstreamer to someone questioning world events from a far more expanded perspective.

He crossed the mainstream collective party line to the point where he was fired by Rupert Murdoch's Fox News despite having by far the biggest audience on US cable channels. Well, maybe that was the reason. Who knows for sure? I would watch his show every morning on the Internet year after year. He was only scratching the surface of the real conspiracy, but he was scratching a lot more than anyone else in mainstream 'journalism'. Carlson's father, Dick Carlson, is a 'diplomat and lobbyist' and was director of the Voice of America in the last six years of the Cold War with the Soviet Union. Voice of America is a US propaganda operation owned and funded by the government which broadcasts TV and radio in nearly 50 languages. Dick Carlson was also director of the former US Information Agency, another government operation, and the Documentary Film Service. The agency had a stated mission 'to understand, inform and influence foreign publics in promotion of the national interest, and to broaden the dialogue between Americans and US institutions, and their counterparts abroad'. Translated from the Orwellian this means communicating US propaganda and covert manipulation through its connections to the Intelligence network. Dick Carlson ran the American government-funded Radio Marti which was broadcasting US propaganda into Cuba in an attempt to hasten the fall of Cuban leader, Fidel Castro. That's some career in American government agencies, state-funded media, and propaganda. His son, Tucker Carlson, once applied to join the CIA.

Tucker Carlson moved to Elon Musk's Twitter/X after his Fox departure and his audience skyrocketed from a few million to often stupendous numbers due to heavy promotion, mega-supportive algorithms, and the kudos of his Murdoch sacking. In doing so he entered the MAM clique of Musk, Rogan, Peterson, Tate, Brand, and company, all of which, apart from Rogan, he has interviewed in the MAM round-robins that underpin the barricade. He later announced the launch of a subscription service, the 'Tucker Carlson Network' (TCN). He has quickly become a pivotal figure in the MAM with a familiar CV with many new stars of the New Media. Carlson was at Fox in 2020 while I was exposing 'Covid' as a scam to justify mass vaccination and he said he felt a 'moral obligation' to meet with President Trump to warn him personally about the seriousness of the coronavirus pandemic. Carlson told *Vanity Fair* that he met with Trump at his Mar-a-Lago resort in Florida on March 7th and two nights later issued a warning to viewers to prepare for the coming 'Covid virus' storm: 'People you know will get sick. Some may die. This is real. That's the point of this script – to tell you that.' How many new MAM stars and stalwarts who bought and promoted the 'Covid' hoax are now portrayed as 'Covid' dissident heroes? A lot. Carlson has continued to interview many of the same people that he did on Fox News to a much bigger audience and with a wider perspective. This is welcome, but far from the scale of knowledge that humanity needs to know about. You will see the real level of the conspiracy a few chapters hence. The Cult and its demonic masters are terrified that this will be revealed to the imprisoned masses on a global scale. Carlson's every X interview is ferociously promoted and his main guest list has become known as the 'Dream Team', and also Musk's term, 'Team Humanity', often repeated by Alex Jones.

The masked crusader

The more I have seen of Carlson since his switch to X the more questions that I have. He interviewed Bret Weinstein, a podcaster and former professor of evolutionary biology, about 'Covid' in January 2024. Weinstein became an instant 'Covid' hero for many by citing someone else's research, without acknowledgement, that 17 million people had been killed by the jab. Aware people with a memory began posting clips of Weinstein from 2020, 2021, and 2022 in which he called for more intense lockdowns and told Joe Rogan (naturally) that he was 'very concerned' about the 'Covid virus' because it was 'brand new evolutionarily'. He was a professor of evolutionary biology and I left school at 15 without taking a major exam. He bought the 'virus' hoax. I didn't. Such is the 'Dream Team'. Weinstein deleted old tweets that recorded his earlier views on 'Covid'. A video that survived had him explaining during the fake pandemic that he wore a bandana scarf around his neck at home that could be pulled over his face whenever he answered the door. He said he bought 25 of them from Amazon. Weinstein said he would pull up the scarf whenever he left his car and put on 'safety glasses'. He told an interviewer:

> Any droplet I encounter, if I walk through a cloud that someone has coughed
> out, could it get in my eye? Sure. Is it likely to? No … it has a complex path to
> get past my glasses.

Weinstein said he also wore cloth gloves. He had 'multiple sets' and got them 'very cheap' from a hardware store. He said that anything he touched went on the glove and not his hands. The intellect of an 'evolutionary biologist' is extraordinary. Weinstein said that he could take the gloves *off* which compounds my previous statement to still new levels of extraordinary. He would also immediately take off his clothes after any trip outside and put them in the laundry room (Fig 25). This is Carlson's and Rogan's MAM 'go-to' on 'Covid'?? Suddenly all these people appeared on the scene criticising 'Covid' *after* the fact when it was acceptable to do so and bought it when it mattered. Weinstein's appearance with Carlson coincided with an obviously coordinated campaign to label those few that called 'Covid' from the start to be guilty of 'infighting' by

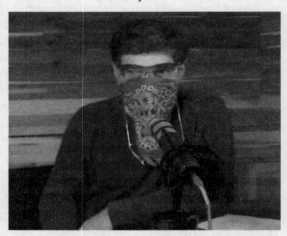

Figure 25: The MAM's new go-to 'Covid expert' Bret Weinstein as he was during the 'Covid' fake 'pandemic'. It's another laugh-or-you'll-cry scenario. 'Pathetic' has no meaning.

exposing those who were trying to re-write their history to become perceived 'anti-Covid heroes' of the alternative media. Weinstein took this same line:

> We have an epidemic of friendly fire within the dissident community. The
> people involved need to level up or get off the battlefield. That should be
> obvious.

The arrogance of that statement beggars belief. Those who have been on the road long before him – I mean *long* – and called 'Covid' when *he didn't* should disappear from the scene if they chose to criticise him and his sudden and unwarranted elevation? Would saying that the WEF is bad for humanity be considered 'disunity'? No, and neither is highlighting the Dream Team for their takeover and here-and-no-further limitation. This Weinstein post captures his theme:

> … the petty infighting among dissidents is a distraction at best and a circular firing squad at worst … Individuals and new dissident institutions argue about who gets to take credit for victories. Purists criticize latecomers for not getting things right initially. But how do you expect to expand a movement if you don't allow for converts, and are not grateful when people change their minds and come over to your side?

> Many dissidents do not understand media and communications, and think that shouting the truth, even when nobody is listening, will move the ball down the field … when the team wins we all win and it does not matter who gets credit for the game winning shot.

This may sound reasonable on first hearing without the context that those who were silent or even promoted the conspiracy should now form the 'Dream Team'; and the context of taking over the public face of the alternative media to push a narrative that will not ultimately dismantle the tyranny. This has happened. Weinstein's intellectual and seriously left-brain arrogance in saying many 'dissidents' do not understand the media (like Weinstein is the implication) is shocking. I have worked in the media at all levels, mainstream and alternative, for more than *50 years* straight. He delivers his spiel with a charisma bypass and says again and again that he doesn't know what's behind what he claims to expose. *He doesn't know?* Then why is he being interviewed by such high profile people like Carlson and Rogan? Is it not time for him to get off the battlefield and allow in those who *do* know after decades of research? I have faced untold abuse for pointing out the MAM hijack when I was saying things long ago that the Dream Teamers ridiculed. They then claimed after 'Covid' that they knew all along. It's a scam people and it is bizarre how many of the alleged 'awake' have fallen for it.

Bret Weinstein was back on Carlson's mega-audience X broadcast within days of his 'Covid' interview talking about the open southern border which was a Musk theme in the same period. Of all the people Carlson could have credibly talked to about the border situation and its real agenda Weinstein would have been a long way down the list as he was with 'Covid'. Weinstein was suddenly *everywhere* among the MAM clique. I highlighted in an interview with American talk show host Alex Jones how ridiculous it was for Carlson to have promoted Weinstein as a 'Covid' expert while he ignored those who exposed the hoax and fake vaccine at the time. I also pointed out that the MAM was giving Elon Musk a free pass when he was fronting up companies that were obviously advancing the Cult and WEF agenda. Jones introduced a caller during the interview in audio only who sounded remarkably like Elon Musk and turned out to be a sound-like called Adrian Dittmann who pushed the line that AI is inevitable and that reality enhancement by AI can be beneficial. *Inevitable* when calculated and coordinated decisions have *made* AI 'inevitable'? Other decisions could have been made had it not been for the Cult agenda. Days later Jones had Weinstein on his show and they both gave propaganda eulogies for Elon Musk. Immediately after that Weinstein was on Joe Rogan's podcast in which they both agreed that Elon Musk is 'one of us' and fighting for freedom. I take it as a compliment that my interview with Jones about Musk and Weinstein was so well received by viewers that it was felt they had to go to these lengths in damage control. Adrian Dittmann was another Jones guest soon after my interview and again in audio only.

Welcome in, Alex

Tucker Carlson was instrumental in inducting Alex Jones into the Dream Team MAM clique. I had observed Alex moving closer and closer to the MAM clique for quite a while and I warned him in an email about the emerging takeover. He was fully absorbed by the Dream Team crowd in the latter months of 2023. I have agreed with many things that Alex Jones has said over the years and disagreed with many, too. I have, however, had great respect for how he has worked tirelessly to expose the political levels of the conspiracy over a long period and it was sad to see him disappear into the black hole of awareness which is the MAM. I don't say that he knows what he's doing. I do say he's been pulled in at the time of writing and maybe that will change. You can always hope. Jones, like Rogan, became ever more obviously a Musk groupie after the acquisition of Twitter, now X, despite Musk's apparently clear statement that Jones would never be allowed back on his platform over what he said about Sandy Hook. Events began to move very fast in December 2023 and led to Jones being restored. First Carlson interviewed him on Twitter/X to great fanfare and I said to my son Jaymie that Musk would have Jones back on the platform very soon. It took only days before a laughable Musk-designated Twitter/X public 'poll' voted for his return. Musk said he would abide by the decision 'of the people'. You have got to laugh. It was sickening to see personalities in the MAM pleading for the Cult-owned Musk to reinstate Alex Jones and Jones himself posting a video urging people to vote for his return. Talk about human race get off your knees. I posted at the time that it was already a done-deal and what was happening was an intelligence-insulting mind-game:

Is it just me? This is an embarrassing farce, a pathetic ritual of power dynamics in which the master in control rubs his chin and ponders while people who should know better (but don't) plead with the master to view them with favour. Alex calling Musk a hero will surely help the case, sir.

Just reinstate him Mr Musk – you know you are going to but people have to plead a bit, right? Makes you feel powerful? Shows the little people where the power really is? As for those doing the pleading – get a bloody grip.

You are pleading to someone who is fronting up major aspects of the Cult agenda. 'Please Cult that we claim to be opposing, please reinstate our man. Please sir, thank you, sir.' Pathetic. Just do it Mr Musk and cut the power ritual crap. I never cease to be amazed at the unresearched naivety of many who claim to be awake and aware.

So it was. On the day that his return was announced Jones appeared on a live Twitter/X 'Spaces' event *with Musk*. They were joined by Andrew Tate, then US presidential candidate Vivek Ramaswamy (more later) and other MAMs for his official initiation into the clique. That is some renaissance to go in days from exclusion by Musk to a Twitter/X interview with Carlson, to his Musk ban being lifted, to going live with Musk. None of this was by chance or 'organic', of course. Alex Jones completed his initiation on Spaces with the obligatory eulogy to Musk:

Elon Musk [is] the biggest maverick in the last 500 years. I'm not kissing ass here [you *are* mate, you *are*, and big-time]. Elon, you've got big ones man on every front. You are literally overturning the entire power structure … I just want to say this while you are here. I mean, you are literally changing the entire paradigm and you have definitely got the system scared. So everyone needs to support X, everyone needs to support the sponsors on X. I am personally doing all my Christmas shopping this year on X …

I found it so tragic to see a bloke who has done a tremendous amount to awaken people to the five-sense, political, financial, level of the conspiracy hand over his self-respect in totality to this most obvious fraud and take so many of his followers with him. Musk is 'the biggest maverick in the last 500 years'? He's not the biggest maverick in the last 500 minutes. Suddenly the 'outcast' Alex Jones was everywhere which on one level was good, but the whole thing was just too organised. Someone had pressed a button and pre-planned events followed wham, bang, bang. Alex Jones' style and approach is very different to mine with his nightly 'bombshell emergency broadcasts' on his Infowars show. That's no problem. People are different and they should be. The greater good, however, is far more important than any individual's sensitivities and the time had arrived to call a spade a shovel. My own view is that Alex was invited into the fold to give the MAM Psyop the credibility of someone who had been on the case long before the 'New Media' fake heroes moved in after 'Covid'. I emphasise again that I am not saying that Alex Jones knows this. He still does good work within the barricade. I am saying that the 'New Media' suits the Cult agenda of holding the line at politics and repackaging what is already known so the expansion of knowledge is thwarted.

I have been highlighting the Cult-serving activities of Elon Musk for years, but to do so after 'he' bought Twitter and turned it into X was to face the mass abusive wrath of MAM believers. I was exposing their 'saviour' for what he is and it was like condemning Jesus in Alabama. I have continued anyway. The truth is what matters, not the reaction to it. You may see Musk rather differently to Alex Jones and company when I get to him and his real agenda shortly and ask questions that MAMs refuse to ask. When you have a need for a saviour, as Jones appears to do with Musk and Trump, balance is the first casualty. Cognitive dissonance kicks in and the corpus callosum displays no-entry signs. I was already seeing the chess pieces moved to hijack the alternative arena when I wrote *The Dream* and I made these very points. This has since been kicked into overdrive with the likes of Musk, Carlson, Tate, Rogan, Peterson, Brand, and Jones and the hundreds of millions of people they take with them.

One rule for one ...

Tucker Carlson called Alex Jones 'the world's most censored man' while remaining silent as I have been banned from entering 29 European countries, Australia, and endless others if I tried to get in. I have been banned from YouTube, Facebook, Spotify, on and on, since I exposed 'Covid' as a hoax in April 2020. This is the same Spotify that pays Joe Rogan hundreds of millions to host his podcast. I am in effect banned from the UK broadcast media by decree of the government censor, sorry 'regulator', Ofcom, in the wake of my 'Covid' exposure. What have the MAM 'stars' had to say about any of this? *Nothing*. Carlson described Russell Brand in his introduction to an interview as akin to one of the greatest voices for freedom 'in the English speaking world'. Carlson said of his second interview with Brand: 'It's one of the most brilliant explanations of the modern world you'll ever hear.' Both statements were as outrageous as they were absurd. Carlson said that 'Governments colluded to shut down and destroy Russell Brand.' Meanwhile I sat at home banned from nearly 30 European countries and Australia. Brand was demonetised by YouTube in 2023 after several women made sexual allegations against him which he strongly denied. Jones, Carlson, Tate, Musk, and Peterson immediately supported Brand along with Peterson's *Daily Wire* ATM, Ben Shapiro. None of them knew if the allegations were true or not true and yet they decreed that it was only to 'silence Russell'. But it didn't silence him. He was only *demonetised* by YouTube and could go on posting his videos. He wasn't banned from anywhere on the Internet. I was demonetised by YouTube in 2018 and banned in early 2020. The UK's Toby Young of the Free Speech Union condemned the taking down of *one* Russell Brand YouTube video in 2022. What was Young's response to my ban from all those countries and when my entire YouTube channel was deleted in April 2020? *Silence.* Young and his Daily Sceptic website again have relevant information to share and do some good work while being full-blown expressions of the MAM. Joe Rogan and Tucker Carlson are quite happy to interview between them Brand, Jones, Tate, Peterson, Shapiro, and their like, but as I write they refuse to even consider interviewing me. Alex Jones gets a live Twitter/X Spaces event with Elon Musk. Why won't Musk come on with me so I can ask him some *real* questions? Who knows what will happen from hereon and by the time you read these words, but Rogan has had the chance to interview me since his first podcast and vehemently refuses while interviewing people who know next to nothing. Why?

I knew all along – honest!

Another aspect of the MAM is to ignore what non-MAMs have been saying since the 1990s and claim they were the ones that knew all along. Alex Jones's Infowars ran the following headline: 'BREAKING VIDEO: Tucker Carlson Warns of Hostile Interdimensional/Spiritual Forces Influencing the Human "Ant Farm".' Carlson was saying this from his Christian perspective while ignoring the fact that I had been exposing the interdimensional manipulation of human affairs and with far, far, more detail in a stream of books, talks, and videos since 1996. Carlson talked about concluding his views from *his* research. What followed in the article was Alex Jones saying how he had long been saying the same. Again there was not a mention of the man who has faced constant ridicule and dismissal out there alone exposing for 30 years that a non-human force was manipulating human society via the Global Cult. I had introduced the non-human interdimensional aspect of human control many times on Jones's Infowars show much to the ridicule of a large section of his audience. Now *he* knew about it all along if you read the article.

This was the same Alex Jones who likened me and my work in a TV documentary in 2001 to 'a turd in a punchbowl' for saying that non-human entities in the hidden realms were ultimately behind human control. The 'turd' was me saying this which he claimed discredited the *real* conspiracy that was confined to the world of political and financial manipulation. The documentary, *The Secret Rulers of the World* on the UK's Channel 4, reported that the then emerging alternative media was 'scandalised' by what I was saying about the non-human foundation of the global conspiracy. They featured Alex Jones condemning me for this and saying that my claims about a blood-drinking elite were 'asinine'. He went on: 'He's either a smart-ass opportunist conman or he's completely insane or he's working for them directly.' Okay, he apologised for saying that many years later, but now here he was, 23 years after those statements, presenting himself as the fountain of knowledge on the subject of non-human manipulation with no acknowledgement of the guy who has taken decades of shit for exposing this. 'These major conclusions reached by Carlson have been communicated at length by Alex Jones', said the article on his website. Jones was then quoted as saying the following. Every word is straight from my interviews with him and the content of my books over decades:

Jones then referenced the electromagnetic spectrum and visible light to illustrate how humans can only see very little of what's going on around them.

'Remember, your sight is a TINY band of visible light – and light itself is just a tiny band of all the other energies,' said Jones. 'There's so much energy it's hard to quantify. Let's just say we see 1% of what's going on … Your eyeballs are only set to pick up a VERY small amount of stuff that's going on.'

Similarly, back in 2019, Jones talked about how the human body is functionally an electrochemical antenna that connects to higher and lower dimensions. Jones said that cultures throughout the ages chronicled how good and evil entities of these dimensions were capable of interfacing with humans.

Readers of my books will know that this is virtually word for word what I have been saying since the 1990s and now the 'turd in the punchbowl' guy was claiming this as his own. It reminded me of Andrew Tate when he said in 2023 that he predicted things and they happened because he had been 'talking about the Matrix for two years'. *Two years*?? He doesn't even begin to know what the Matrix is, anyway. Meanwhile, there are other really great and genuine people in the conspiracy research arena. The genuine ones don't get a fraction of the promotion of the MAMs and there lies the intent. Polly St George began to post perceptive comments about the 'Dream Team' and what she called the 'cross-promotional network' (MAM-MAM interviews). 'This group ignores knowledgeable voices in order to "keep it in the family" and control info', she wrote. 'None of these guys do any digging either. They just repeat narratives, interview each other and let "experts" talk.' Exactly right. I stress again that I am not saying they are all knowingly manipulators and diversions. Many simply have a different opinion from their level of knowledge which they are entitled to have. I also think that Christian believers have to be careful in their interpretations and labels of 'New Age'. I have been branded 'New Age' myself when I have a big problem with that mindset. Talking about metaphysics does not have to mean 'New Age'.

We should not forget that Musk and Twitter/X control the algorithms and which posts are boosted and suppressed. Those he and his controllers want promoted are widely algorithmically boosted while those that don't toe the desired line are shadowbanned and lost in cyberspace. Musk posts are the most boosted of all with millions, even tens of millions, of views for the most inane comment. Anything reposted by Musk and divinely blessed with a 'well done', 'good', or 'wow' from the MAM God rides the wave of his algorithm while others, like me, are blatantly shadowbanned. An example are Musk retweets of pretty run of the mill posts by two MAM members, the big picture clueless Tim Pool in America, and the English Israel fanatic, Douglas Murray. Pool posted: 'Google is rigging the 2024 election.' Murray said: 'Google's push to lecture us on diversity goes beyond AI.' Such comments are two-a-penny. Musk's retweets gave them 14 million and 10 million views. An Eva Vlaardingerbroek speech about immigration retweeted by Musk ensured her tens of millions of views for a subject I had been warning about for decades before. This is how the 'chosen' are promoted. Tim Pool said in April 2020 that the psychopathic liar and mass murderer Anthony Fauci was a 'good dude'. His fellow host Luke Rudkowski said something similar. I knew Rudkowski way back and he did some good work in those days. Then during 'Covid' he promoted masks and social distancing throughout 2020 and accused those who saw through the hoax of killing people by going outside without a mask. Years later he was criticising Trump for not acknowledging he was wrong on 'Covid' and the fake vaccine. Breathtaking stuff and a short memory is essential for MAMs.

Right is right. Er, that's it

I am glad on one level that the MAMs are talking about the five-sense manipulation, however mildly, and I would not be challenging them if they widely allowed into their largely closed circle those who describe a much more expanded conspiracy in which reality *itself* is the conspiracy. My pokes in their chest may lead to that, who knows? That's the idea anyway. For now at least they sell us their political heroes of 'the right' in the form of Donald Trump, Argentina's President Javier Milei, and Eva Vlaardingerbroek's Dutch political champion, Geert Wilders. All are Israel fanatics with Milei and Wilders embarrassingly so. All you have to do is criticise 'communism' and take a few aims of the World Economic Forum and you are immediately a MAM hero even though, when you cut through the bullshit, they are promotors of that same agenda. Milei says he is selling state assets and the MAM cheers him for a blow against communism. He is selling them to global corporations and the Cult owns both the state *and* the corporations. Vlaardingerbroek and Wilders were both silent while the Dutch government and media were vilifying me to prepare the way for my ban from eventually 29 European countries. Where were they when freedom was being deleted in their own country? Their concern for freedom is unbelievably selective. The MAM is basically right-wing politics.

Donald Trump is the focus of 'hope' to 'stop the globalists' when he is owned by them and especially their ultra-Zionist inner core that I refer to as the Sabbatians which control the Israeli government and its worldwide manipulation web. Sabbatians have contempt for Jewish people and use them as a shield to hide behind. Anyone like me that uncovers their sinister activities is immediately branded an 'anti-Semite'. Jewish people in general and the Sabbatians are not the same and I have exposed this in great detail in *The Trigger*. Ironies just keep on coming. Wilbur Ross, a Rothschild employee of 24 years, bailed out Trump decades ago by orchestrating a group of 72 banks to save his backside when he admitted publicly that he personally owed a billion dollars – that's besides fantastic company debt. He made Wilbur Ross his Commerce Secretary when he won the presidency. Carl Icahn, an ultra-Zionist billionaire who was crucial to the bailout, was another given a role in 'the Donald's' administration. Trump was able to run for president thanks to the ultra-Zionists involved in that bailout alone. His major financial backer in his 2016 presidential campaign was Sabbatian ultra-Zionist and Las Vegas casino tycoon Sheldon Adelson who also funded Netanyahu. Trump's White House 'senior advisor' and ultra-Zionist son-in-law Jared Kushner is a life-long friend of Netanyahu. The Zionist connection goes on and on. Trump moved the US embassy from Tel Aviv to Jerusalem with its fundamental implications, symbolic and literal, for Palestinians. The few times he criticises Israel is just political expediency.

Trump continues to claim credit for Operation Warp Speed that delivered the deadly 'Covid' fake vaccine and goes on praising its affect even after the data emerged of its devastation to health and life. Trump is a Psyop as Musk is a Psyop as Jeffrey Epstein's paedophile ring ensnaring the influential with cameras and microphones was a Psyop. The MAM sees the obvious one with Epstein and misses the other two completely. Both Psyops are made possible by the MAM's worship of Trump and Musk as its saviours when they are systematically leading the alternative arena to glorious failure. Right wing political movements such as the Christianity-dominated Turning Point USA and its annual AmericaFest event are now considered 'alternative'. What a statement about how far from the frontline of knowledge the MAM has now pitched its tent. How ironic to hear Russell Brand say in a podcast: 'They're having to work so hard to keep you from awakening ... working so hard to keep you distracted.' Oh, I think the MAM is doing that well enough without any help, Russell. It is time to cast aside naivety and ask that simple question again. Enormous numbers began the awakening process after being shakened from their slumber during 'Covid' by the pre-MAM alternative media that existed then. Does anyone really think that in those circumstances the Cult is going to leave the alternative sources of information alone? Unknowing place people with the right mentality and limited knowledge are going to be promoted and Cult operatives sent in to infiltrate, limit, misdirect, and neuter. Anyone who can't see that needs a few sessions with Naivety Anonymous – more than a few.

The king of the castle, at the top of the MAM hierarchy, sits the exalted deity that is Elon Musk. He is a Cult gofer playing the role of opposing the Cult while serving it and how the MAMs have bought into this most obvious of Psyops.

Postscript: MAM hero Geert Wilders nominated 'former' spy chief Dick Schoof as Dutch Prime Minister in a technocratic government with many unelected members months after Wilders 'won' the Dutch election. *Unelected* Schoof is a civil service careerist, the senior official in the justice ministry, and led the AIVD domestic security service, counter-terrorism agency, and the immigration service, ALL of which were responsible for my ban from the Netherlands and nearly 30 European countries in the Schengen border group. He's also been connected to many cover-ups. Wilders is a blatant fraud backed by the naïve beyond belief Mainstream 'Alternative' Media (MAM) and 'freedom activists' like Eva Vlaardingerbroek.

CHAPTER FOUR

The Musk Myth

The best way to control the opposition is to lead it ourselves

Vladimir Lenin

We have reached such a point of insanity that a tidal wave of abuse follows whenever I point out Elon Musk's glaring contradictions. He really is the MAM God now – He who must never be questioned. You doubt 'The Lord', you *blasphemer*.

Those with genuinely open minds and eyes can see what Musk is being used for. They will invariably be the same people who seek the unfettered truth and comprise the real alternative that seeks out facts and not popularity. There are many of these, but they don't get the promotion, funding, and exposure. Elon Musk has a long history of deceit and deception in the way he rewrites history. He claims to be a co-founder of Tesla when he wasn't. He actually got rid of the founders when he moved in on the company. He claims to have been a co-founder of PayPal when he wasn't. Musk has a record of telling his company shareholders what isn't true. A group of Tesla shareholders accused Musk in a San Francisco court of lying in a tweet in 2018 about how he had secured funding to take Tesla private which drove up the share price. The tweet said: 'Am considering taking Tesla private at $420. Funding secured.' This didn't subsequently happen, the share price dropped, and shareholders claimed they lost considerable amounts of money. One newspaper reported: 'While the plaintiffs portrayed Musk as a reckless liar who caused "regular people" to lose millions, the defense team for the tech billionaire painted him as a well-intentioned visionary, who merely used the "wrong words" in describing the deal.' This was far from a one-off for the 'freedom champion' who would appear from my observations to have been born with a forked tongue and a Teflon-like quality that makes him untouchable.

The San Francisco jury cleared him of wrong doing after he said that he believed he had a handshake agreement in 2018 with Saudi Arabia's Public Investment Fund to take Tesla private. He said the Saudis reneged on the deal and that wasn't his fault. The fact that he made the tweet on 'a handshake' with no formal agreement seems to have eluded the jury. California District Court Judge Edward Chen had ruled that the tweets were false and reckless. He then told the jury not to include in their deliberations that Musk and Tesla had reached a $40 million settlement with the Securities and Exchange Commission (SEC) only a month after the tweets were posted. The money was later distributed to Tesla shareholders who lost money. The jury found Musk not guilty of doing what the SEC found to be true. A Delaware judge blocked Musk's record-breaking $56 *billion* Tesla pay package and described the sum granted by the Tesla board 'an unfathomable sum' that was unfair to shareholders. Just a little bit. Florida judge Reid Scott ruled there was 'reasonable evidence' that Tesla and CEO Musk were 'acutely aware' of defects in Autopilot systems in their vehicles and failed to fix them. Tesla continued to promote the system as 'safe'. I could go on and on about Musk's business practices. I want to focus on points relevant to my theme of Musk being a Cult agenda frontman. I can, however, recommend videos on YouTube headed *A Message to Elon Musk*, posted by the Anonymous Official channel, and *Elon Musk is a Dangerous Fraud – I'm Embarrassed That I Ever Believed Him.* See also the Common Sense Skeptic channel on YouTube for a long list of documentaries and videos exposing Musk for what he is even if the MAM chooses not to see the obvious. Musk's history suggests that no one should ever believe a word he says without checking every detail.

Musk is not some kind of maverick 'genius'. He's another Peter Sellers in *Being There* in my opinion. His persona is sold through myth and fawning interviews with his groupies like Joe Rogan who said he must be an 'alien' to do simultaneously all that he does (Fig 26). Well, Mr

Figure 26: Joe Rogan and his pot-smoking mate, Elon Musk.

Rogan, have you ever considered the possibility that he *doesn't* do all those things? Does anyone really think that Elon Musk runs SpaceX, Neuralink, Tesla, Twitter/X, xAI, plus others, while in his own words spending '80 percent of my time designing, engineering and manufacturing'? He somehow finds time to scattergun post on Twitter/X every day at all hours. Not all those posts in his name will be directly from him, but you get the point. The incredibly inarticulate 'genius' has promised so many things that never reach fruition including his Hyperloop transport system that we were told would propel pods full of passengers at speeds of up to 760 miles an hour. The company set up to make Musk's proposal reality closed in 2023, sacking workers and selling off assets. Richard Branson had invested in the project and said in 2017: 'After visiting Hyperloop One's test site in Nevada and meeting its leadership team this past summer, I am convinced this ground-breaking technology will change transportation as we know it and dramatically cut journey times.' I don't think so, mate, and why must everything go faster and faster anyway?

Keep it in the family

I have highlighted over the years the central involvement of Musk's grandfather in the Rockefeller-backed technocracy movement in Canada in the 1930s before moving to South Africa where Musk was born. Technocracy describes perfectly the world that is fast emerging today in which technology (now through AI) runs everything and controls the population in league with unelected appointed bureaucrats, technocrats, scientists, engineers, and medical 'experts'. Politicians requiring any form of public legitimacy would be confined to fading memory. Technocrats contend that traditional forms of government can't understand modern technological society and this has to be left to the 'experts'. They mean what happened with 'Covid'. That worked out well, didn't it? Technocracy dubbed itself the 'Science of Social Engineering'. Cult operatives tend to run in families with the CIA and Israeli Mossad for example seeking to recruit sons and daughters of their operatives. Some openly say that a parent was CIA to divert attention from the fact that they are, too. UK newspaper tycoon Robert Maxwell was a Mossad agent as confirmed by Mossad whistleblower, Victor Ostrovsky, who published two books, *By Way of Deception: The Making and Unmaking of a Mossad Officer* (1990), and *The Other Side of Deception* (1995). The second book said that Maxwell was a Mossad asset who was killed by them when his failing business and media empire crumbled and he became a problem. Israel's prime minister and president attended his funeral on the Mount of Olives in Jerusalem along with six heads of Israeli intelligence. The point of the story is that his daughter is *Ghislaine* Maxwell, the fixer for Mossad blackmail agent Jeffrey Epstein who ran a paedophile ring with hidden cameras and microphones on his island and in other properties to compromise influential people and decision-makers that Mossad sought to control. He was, like Robert Maxwell, deleted when he was in a Washington DC jail awaiting trial on paedophile charges that could have brought much to light.

Lawrence Preston Gise, grandfather of Amazon's Jeff Preston Bezos, was involved with the US military's Advanced Research Projects Agency (ARPA) that morphed into the infamous Defense Advanced Research Projects Agency (DARPA). This organisation is central to the Cult's technology and AI control agenda. DARPA is the Pentagon's agency for funding technology developments essential to the Cult dystopia and claims credit for making the Internet possible with military hardware. The agency was covertly involved in the emergence of key Internet corporations including Google (which owns YouTube) and Facebook (Meta) along with the CIA's technological development arm, In-Q-Tel (IQT). Bezos's grandfather was also Assistant Director of Military Applications at the US Atomic Energy Commission and has been connected by some researchers to the sequence of events through which Israel was able to develop nuclear weapons. Now we have Bezos and Musk, grandsons of Deep State and technocracy operatives, at the centre of the technocracy rollout through their companies Amazon, SpaceX, Tesla, Neuralink, Twitter/X, xAI, and more besides. A coincidence? Not a chance.

Satan's little helpers

Amazon is taking over global product purchase and distribution at the expense of independent businesses and has created a near-monopoly on book sales and distribution with the power to decide what people can and cannot buy in the wake of its demolition of independent publishers. This is exactly in line with the Cult agenda and Musk is doing the same Devil's work across a swathe of Cult operations. I have detailed in other books how the Cult is creating on behalf of its demonic masters a hive-mind control system based on artificial intelligence (AI). These are some of the elements involved and I will then relate them to Elon Musk:

1.) A technologically-generated electromagnetic field (the 'Cloud') of 4G/5G/6G/7G designed to connect the human brain to AI and the Internet. This is the so-called 'Internet of Everything' in which all devices, domestic appliances, energy systems, and the human brain/body would be connected by and to AI. The plan requires that the Cloud be projected to every inch of the planet to capture every human being. We are seeing 5G towers added incessantly to the 4G transmitters with 6G already in the pipeline and 7G to follow. Towers are fine to generate the Cloud in urban areas. To have the whole planet covered requires the electromagnetic field be projected from low-orbit satellites – tens of thousands of them and more. Already an expansion is being planned for a 'cyber-physical system spanning ground, air, and space' called the Internet of Space Things (IoST) which involves 'CubeSats'. These are mini-satellites little bigger than a Rubik's Cube.

2.) An AI connection to the human brain to control the population's collective perception from a central point via an in-brain connection to the Cloud. This is the hive mind that I have been warning was the plan over decades and there are other aspects to it that I will come to later. I have highlighted in book after book the words of Zionist Google executive Ray Kurzweil and Zionist World Economic Forum AI promotor Yuval Noah Harari as they describe how humanity is planned to be controlled by artificial intelligence. Kurzweil has even mentioned the year 2030 for this to be underway. The truth is that it's already happening. Kurzweil says that artificial intelligence will do more and more of human thinking once the connection is made until human thought as we know it will be 'negligible'. He means deleted.

3.) The AI/brain/body connection is being made via self-replicating nano-systems including those injected in the synthetic fake 'Covid' vaccines that are not vaccines by any previous criteria. They are genetic manipulation devices containing a substance called hydrogel specifically designed to trick the immune system, cells, and brain to accept the synthetic genetic material that it would otherwise immediately reject as a foreign entity. Hydrogels can be *programmed*, encrypted/decrypted, and provide a base material for a brain-computer interface through which humans can be fused with machines.

4.) Nanotechnology self-replicates in the body to build nano-systems to connect brain and body to the Cloud like a computer connecting with Wi-Fi. Now you see a key reason for all the lies and impositions to manipulate billions to have the 'Covid' jab multiple times. Other vaccines are being transferred to the synthetic system and they have developed the means to release these fake vaccines into the air so people *breathe them in* without even the choice of what goes into their bodies. Private stores are selling 'Covid' jabs over the counter with British chain Boots offering the Pfizer/BioNTech vaccine to healthy customers in England aged 12 and over at a cost of £98.95 a pop. I say *British* chain – it is owned by America's Walgreens Boots Alliance.

5.) We are in the midst of seeing Human 1.0 becoming Human 2.0 which would be much more synthetic and controllable by AI. The idea is to block access to expanded levels of consciousness outside the simulation as AI becomes the human mind.

6.) The prime excuse for an AI-controlled world is another hoax called 'human-caused climate change' in which carbon dioxide, a gas of life, is turned into a deadly pollutant purely through unremitting propaganda.

There would be no 'natural' world and no food supply without sufficient levels of CO2. No humans, no animals, no nothing. The ludicrous assertion that human-generated carbon dioxide is threatening our existence through 'climate change' provides the excuse to target the gas of life and what follows is simple. Society as we know it depends on the widespread use of CO2-producing fossil fuels and by setting the target for CO2 reduction known as 'net-zero' a chain of events is set in motion. You only need to set the target and get countries across the world to pursue that target to ensure human society must be transformed beyond measure; there is no way to meet the target with its dramatic reduction in fossil fuel use without changing the way humans live equally dramatically.

7.) The Cult plan seeks to imprison humans in what are termed '15-minute cities' which are really communities within cities, towns, and elsewhere in which the authorities (the Cult) say everything you need will be within a 15-minute/20-minute walk or cycle ride from your home. You will only be able to drive outside of your designated area so many times a month and numberplate cameras will police this fascism. Eventually you won't be able to drive out at all without specific permission. Numberplate cameras appearing everywhere to enforce policies like ultra-low-emission zones (ULEZ) are the very cameras that will be used to enforce 15-minute communities. 'Covid' isolation, social distancing and working from home were all part of the psychological preparation for this. The Cult is at war with movement whether long-distance through air travel or short by car. The modus operandi is to claim the need to reduce CO2 to save the world from a climate disaster (that isn't happening).

Essential to the plan of parting people from their vehicles is a mass belief that petrol and diesel engines must be banned and replaced by electric systems. Well, 'replaced' is what they say, but not what they mean. The idea is that the general population will no longer own a vehicle. Electric versions are far too expensive for all except a minority and there are simply not the resources available to make all the batteries necessary to replace petrol and diesel. The elite would have vehicles and the population would not. Some in the car industry have said the 'manic move' to electric vehicles would destroy car production and sales. *But that's the idea.* Travel would be only by public transport and by autonomous taxis run by computer. ULEZ policies penalise older vehicles and this has the added benefit of getting rid of those not connected to the Internet. New ones are step by step getting closer and closer to autonomous. Driverless vehicles have to be electric and that's the real reason they are being imposed along with deleting vehicle ownership for all except the few. You can drive a petrol or diesel vehicle anywhere you want pretty much with some exceptions; an autonomous car means the *computer* will decide where you can and cannot go. Fantastic tracts of the world will be denied to us when the 'computer says no'. It's all about control.

Some questions, Mr Musk

Okay, let's apply all this to Elon Musk, the people's friend and free-speech absolutist who has joined with Alex Jones to call for 'Team Humanity'. *Mmm* … Team Humanity? Elon Musk's SpaceX is at the forefront of creating the Cloud with low-orbit satellites plus the mini CubeSats in the pipeline. He brags on his Twitter/X how many satellites he is launching every month for his Starlink Wi-Fi system and he already has permission for thousands from the US government's (the Cult's) Federal Communications Commission (FCC). Musk's satellites are also making everyone trackable. This is quite a feat for such a 'defender of freedom'. SpaceX is the leader, but other companies are involved in surrounding the Earth with the electromagnetic Cloud, including the Kuiper system of Amazon's Jeff Bezos. I think they call it 'synchronicity'. Bezos and Musk, the grandsons of technocrats, are creating the Cloud essential to an AI-controlled technocracy. There were 5,500 Starlink satellites in orbit by March 2024 and that's more than half the active satellites orbiting the Earth. SpaceX secured FCC permission to deploy 12,000 first-generation Starlink craft with applications filed for another nearly *30,000* Starlink 2.0 satellites. Those permissions began to be instigated in late 2022. A 'mesh network' of lasers is also being created between the satellites as described by SpaceX engineer Travis Brashears. These already numbered nearly ten thousand lasers by the start of 2024 with obviously more to come as satellites constantly increase. Starlink satellites are on course to outnumber the nine thousand visible stars. Astronomers were complaining very early in this process that Starlink was obscuring the night sky. Research has confirmed that low-frequency radio waves used by Starlink are leaking into the sky and making it difficult to make astronomical observations. You've seen nothing yet. Or, rather, you *will* see nothing when these lunatics are finished.

SpaceX, like so much of the 'Musk Empire', is supported by phenomenal amounts of 'government' (taxpayer) money without which he could not survive. The official story says that Musk travelled to Russia with CIA executive Mike Griffin in 2002 to buy discounted intercontinental ballistic missiles and when the deal failed he decided to start SpaceX with the CIA's Griffin as a business partner. Musk offered him the job of SpaceX Chief Engineer. Griffin instead became president and chief operating officer of the CIA-funded major Cult operation, In-

Q-Tel, which scans for companies with new technologies to aid 'national security' (national control). Griffin was then appointed head of NASA (2005-2009) and awarded a $400 million contract to SpaceX at a time that it had yet to launch a single rocket and Musk had no experience of space flight. In 2008 came a $1.6 *billion* NASA contract for commercial cargo services. Griffin's NASA role included the oversight of a future spaceflight to Mars which has been much vaunted as one of Musk's major ambitions. Cult-serving Nazi rocket scientist and NASA founding stalwart Werner von Braun wrote a science fiction novel in 1949, *Project Mars: A Technical Tale,* in which he described a Martian government structure headed by a leader called 'the Elon'. He wrote: 'The Martian government was directed by ten men, the leader of whom was elected by universal suffrage for five years and entitled "Elon".'

Musk is 'independent'??

SpaceX is promoted as an independent Musk operation when it's not. The company is dependent on government/Pentagon/NASA funding and some very familiar names are among its prominent investors. There's the Founders Fund venture capital firm co-founded by Musk associate and PayPal founder Peter Thiel who has the intelligence community in his DNA. Thiel's Founders Fund handed Musk $280 million to launch his brain chipping company, Neuralink, later increased to $323 million. Thiel invested in Musk's The Boring Company and his name appears with significant regularity in Cult agenda companies. Fidelity Investments, a global trillion-dollar asset management firm, put $100 million into SpaceX besides investing in Jeff Bezos-founded space company, Blue Origin. Alphabet Inc., the parent company of Google and YouTube, invested massively in SpaceX. One report said that 'collaboration between these two tech giants has the potential to reshape the future of global communication and connectivity'. Yes, that's why they are doing it – to create the Cloud. SpaceX is clearly a NASA-CIA-Pentagon front operation with Musk as usual only the cover-story to hide the real background. Big parts of the US space program have been handed to SpaceX which is the only American company approved to transport NASA astronauts to the International Space Station. The Pentagon, through its Space Force operation, awarded SpaceX a contract in 2023 for its Starshield network which is a version of Musk's Starlink satellite Internet system for military and government. Reuters reported that SpaceX is building a 'network of hundreds of spy satellites' for the National Reconnaissance Office which is the arm of the US Defense Department charged with building and operating reconnaissance satellites in orbit. Musk tweeted that Starshield will be controlled by the Department of Defense's Space Force. He said that this was 'the right order of things'. *Musk is a danger to the Establishment??* He *is* the Establishment.

Musk's insider status would explain why the Federal Communications Commission (FCC) has awarded all those permissions for low-orbit satellites with more to come. Low-orbit space belongs to the United States, does it? How can the FCC give such permission as an agency of one country when it affects the whole world? It represents the Global Cult, that's how. Why doesn't Europe, China, Russia and the rest of the world challenge what is happening in low-orbit with even the astronomy of the night sky being rewritten? You would think they surely would, but they don't except for the odd statement here and there about potential military uses. They, too, are Cult owned and following the same agenda with their own satellite ambitions that would in truth combine with the Western system to create a Global Cult surveillance and weapons space network. Starlink 2.0 satellites can beam directly to cellphones. Never mind that there are big environmental costs with launching rockets and the effect on humans and wildlife of Cloud radiation especially around Musk's Starlink receiver dishes. One example is the animal deaths at a sanctuary in Guffey, Colorado, at 9,000 feet in the Rockies which followed installation of Starlink dishes by many residents. You can understand why this is so when you read the following article on the Activist Post website:

> Starlink is a 5G phased array technology from the sky. When a Starlink dish is online, that means a satellite is aiming a narrow beam at it. But by the time the beam reaches Earth from a few hundred miles up in space, the beam can be 8 miles in diameter or more. The dish also aims a beam of radiation directly at the satellite and scatters radiation around it. If there are a lot of dishes in a 10-mile radius, as there are in Guffey, radiation from Earth and space is scattered far and wide.

Add these sources together with the towers in towns and cities and you have the global Cloud. Musk said that AI could be the end of humanity and then launched a company called Neuralink with essential support from Peter Thiel to merge the human brain with AI and computers (Fig 27). Many dead and tortured monkeys are testament to this quest and Musk has since secured permission (yet another '*of course*') for human trials. Musk's cover story is that a chip would be surgically implanted in the brain to upload and download information and read brain activity. A Musk biographer described how a surgeon would remove a piece of skull and a robot would weave electrodes and super-thin wires into the brain. A unit would be located behind the ear with wires going into the brain. Musk may talk about a surgically-implanted chip with his Neuralink tech. This does not mean that's how it's really planned to be done and *is* being done. On face value

Figure 27: I made and published this meme long before Musk bought Twitter/X. One difference between me and the MAM is that I am still saying the same.

Neuralink implants have great limitations in how many people would sanction their skull being opened to insert a chip. An important point to know about Musk is that much of what he does surrounds selling a *concept* rather than actually making it happen in the way he originally describes. Implant chipping is nano in scale with no need to open the skull. Musk was asked in one interview about the problem of persuading people to have their skulls opened. His answer was very significant. He said that it would not necessarily have to be done this way: 'You could go through the veins and arteries.' Through the bloodstream in other words which is how 'Covid' fake vaccine nanotechnology is getting in the brain. Researchers who aren't fawning Muskovites have pointed out that the Star*link* system projecting the Cloud and Neura*link* with its brain implants both include the word 'link'. They are links to connect the human brain to the Cloud in the way I have said for 25 years was the plan.

Musk says 'his' SpaceX rockets will open the way to humanity's first inter-planetary travel. Anyone who has researched these subjects to any significant extent knows (as *he* does) that space technology in the secret projects and underground bases is lightyears ahead of SpaceX with interplanetary transport already happening with those craft. A wonderful way to hide his technology is to promote a fake public technological state-of-the-art. SpaceX is doing exactly this. Its rockets may be capable of delivering low-orbit satellites, but they are way behind what already exists far from the public gaze. See *The Trap* and the US Naval officer talking about US Space Command which he likens to apparently fictional sci-fi series such as Star Trek. You can also see the officer interviewed on the Ickonic series *Classified* with Richard Willett. Another bonus of not revealing this advanced technology is that it would give us all the warmth and power we need *without fossil fuel*. The human-caused climate change hoax would be dead in the water.

Poacher *and* gamekeeper

Musk's concern about AI and the end of humanity is a colossal contradiction when contrasted with his love of AI technology. Oh, but anyone who says that is not paying attention. He's the *good* billionaire, you see. He's just trying to mitigate the effect of AI. He's only connecting people to AI so that robots and machines don't take over through their superior intelligence. King Elon the Good is even warning about the dangers of AI (while being a vehicle to introduce ever more) and he's calling for regulation along with Bill Gates, Mark Zuckerberg, and other tech tycoons worth a total of more than $380 billion who convened for a behind-closed-doors hearing in the US Senate in 2023. Musk was interviewed by UK Prime Minister Rishi Sunak on what needs to be done to save us from AI. That's how serious he is. TV cameras were not allowed and the government released its own footage which was terrible by the way. Reporters were told they could not ask questions. I'm sure Sunak's concern about AI was genuine given that his father-in-law Nagavara Ramarao Narayana Murthy founded Indian multinational AI information technology company Infosys and Sunak's wife owns shares in the company reported to be worth £400 million. Musk told Sunak that AI offered 'a future of abundance where there is no scarcity' and described AI as a 'magic genie'. He said AI robots could become our friends. 'His' Tesla company is producing robots, be they, like Neuralink implants, rather less than state of the art. 'An AI with memory could know you better than you know yourself – you could actually have a great friend', the MAM God suggested. How AI sceptical of him.

Why would Musk promote himself as a defender of the people from AI while doing the opposite? Well, put it this way: If you want to traffic drugs without being suspected you do it through an anti-drug agency. If you want to traffic children you do it through a child protection agency. 'They would never do that – they are trying to *stop* drug/child trafficking.' I exposed in books in the 1990s how US drug agencies were running drugs for the Cult through the Bush and Clinton crime families not least through the Mena airstrip in Arkansas when Bill Clinton was state governor before becoming US president. Musk and American entrepreneur techy, Sam Altman, warn with others about AI dangers for the same reason. It takes attention from the fact that they are both fundamental players in making those dangers real and there is the need to be involved in AI regulation discussions so you can control it. Altman drones on about his AI concerns and at the same time the *Wall Street Journal* reveals his plans to raise between $5 trillion and $7 trillion to increase the capacity of global semiconductor production essential to AI expansion.

Musk and Altman co-founded OpenAI which launched in 2022 (after

Musk officially left) and has since given us the artificial intelligence 'chatbot' known as ChatGPT (see also GPT-4 and advancements that follow). ChatGPT is employed across the Internet by Cult fronts such as Bill Gates's Microsoft which has invested significantly in OpenAI. The public ask ChatGPT questions about anything they choose and it is being consulted as an oracle along with its competitors. This gives AI control of information and what many then believe to be true about people and events. 'News' stories written by AI are increasing at a fast pace in the mainstream for the same reason. The ChatGPT 'chatbot' phenomenon which has swept across the Internet also creates interaction – 'chat' – between humans and AI as if AI is human on the road to one absorbing the mind of the other. Children play with AI dolls and devices to put them under the same spell from the earliest age. New York start-up Hume AI secured $50 million in funding to launch a new 'emotionally intelligent' AI voice interface that imitates human responses with 'umms' and 'ahhs', laughs and sighs. An Activist Post article said: 'Many of us are already talking to our smart devices as if they are humans. In the future, smart devices may be able to talk back in a similar way.' Hume AI founder and former Google scientist Alan Cowen said:

By building AI that learns directly from proxies of human happiness, we're effectively teaching it to reconstruct human preferences from first principles and then update that knowledge with every new person it talks to and every new application it's embedded in.

Hume AI's 'Empathic Voice Interface' (EVI) is claimed to 'interpret emotional expressions and generate empathic responses'. The promotional blurb says: 'Meet the first AI with emotional intelligence.' Sam Altman and OpenAI launched Sora in early 2024 in which AI creates an entire scene based on a text prompt. Write into the system 'a cat walking through the woods' and you generate an AI video of a cat walking through the woods. The company said:

We're teaching AI to understand and simulate the physical world in motion, with the goal of training models that help people solve problems that require real-world interaction. Introducing Sora, our text-to-video model. Sora can generate videos up to a minute long while maintaining visual quality and adherence to the user's prompt.

The limit of a minute will soon be gone, and all this is coming from a company with Altman on the board who claims to be 'fearful' of where AI could go. What a joke. The OpenAI board as of March 2024 included: Sue Desmond-Hellmann, former CEO of the Bill and Melinda Gates

Foundation, former director of Proctor and Gamble, and on the board of 'Covid' fake vaccine maker, Pfizer; Nicole Seligman, an attorney and corporate director who represented Oliver North during the Iran-Contra hearings and President Bill Clinton during his impeachment trial; and ultra-Zionist Larry Summers, a long time financial manipulator within government and Cult to the tips of his toes. These are people you can trust not to use AI to control you! There's also the fake rivalry.

Cult 'competition'

Musk sued Altman for turning OpenAI into a profit-making company when it was supposed to be open source. Altman responded by releasing emails in which Musk indicates to Allman that OpenAI needs to raise money from investors. Don't be fooled by this 'open source' stuff either. 'Open to everyone' means you are circulating it everywhere and blurring, before destroying, the sense of what is real and fake. We are seeing reports of six-foot robot priests delivering sermons and conducting funerals. 'Religious' organisations, like the Turing Church, are founded on the premise that AI will give humans super intelligence. Robot priest Mindar has been reciting the Heart Sutra mantra to pilgrims since 2019 at a Buddhist temple in Kyoto, Japan. How enlightened. Musk launched a 'rival' to OpenAI in 2023 which he called xAI. He said in another MAM-MAM interview with fawning ask-no-real-questions Tucker Carlson that he would introduce a 'rival' to ChatGPT which he referred to as 'TruthGPT'. This would later be launched on Twitter/X as 'Grok'. He told Carlson that 'TruthGPT' (Grok) would be 'a maximum truth-seeking AI that tries to understand the nature of the universe'. He said he was worried that ChatGPT was 'politically correct'.

You see the scam. Musk advances AI control while presenting his intent in a way that keeps the MAMs on board. How he must be laughing at his sycophant 'truth seekers'. The apparent AI 'rivalry' between ChatGPT, Grok, Amazon's chatbot called 'Q', Google's Gemini, and Apple's Ferret, is only a front for Cult operatives to appear to be in competition while all are introducing the same control technology. Apple was apparently 'in talks' with Google over using its Woke-biased Gemini on its new iPhones. You have to look at the *outcome*, not the rhetoric. SpaceX has 'competitors' in positioning low-orbit satellites, including Amazon again. The *outcome* of this fake 'rivalry' is ever more low-orbit satellites. The MAM suffers from the same disease as most of the population which is naivety. A long-time AI development operation is Google's DeepMind and Musk recruited Igor Babuschkin from DeepMind to be Chief Engineer of xAI. He must have had to suspend posting on Twitter/X that day while he secured the deal. It's all mix-and-match to the same outcome. Musk is the best-known promotor of the electric autonomous vehicle agenda and while again Tesla has 'rivals' the outcome is the same in league with Cult-owned governments to enforce the deletion of petrol and diesel. A carbon tax is another long-time demand of the Cultists in which CO_2 use would be limited and people taxed beyond that. Musk has called for just such a tax for many years and continues to do so – 'It's high time there was a carbon tax' – and this is a Cult plan to transform human life right across global society. His justification is the classic Cult explanation of (non-existent) 'human-caused climate change' and he repeats the words of Bill Gates and Klaus Schwab. Musk is using his support from the MAM to stop legitimate exposure that he is 'Gates-lite' with both heading for the same outcome. Gates is hard sell, Musk is soft sell, and that's the only real difference.

We reached the point where the Alex Jones website Infowars was running stories about what Musk's AI system Grok was saying about conspiracies and MAM political targets. Headlines included: xAI 'Grok' Thinks Taylor Swift's Biden Support Is A Psy-Op; X's AI Chatbot Grok Roasts WEF Globalist Kingpin Klaus Schwab; Grok Exposes Globalist Plot To Destabilize America; Elon Musk's AI 'Grok' Gives Stunningly Accurate Description of Why Governments Destabilize Countries for Power. It's an *AI program* for goodness sake. Who cares what it says except as a critique of its dangers? It's programmable. The interaction with Grok, OpenAI's ChatGPT, Google's Gemini, Amazon's Alexa, and other systems and devices are to program people to get used to conversing with AI as if it is human. How many people now go on the Internet and have their questions answered by ChatGPT, Grok, or Gemini?

Agenda Man

Wherever you look the MAM God hero Elon Musk is serving endless central strands of the Cult agenda for human control. Musk further supports a universal basic income to control the population through dependency once manipulated economic collapse and AI have deleted jobs for humans. He supported the fake 'Covid' vaccines (just like MAM hero, Trump) and said: 'To be clear, I do support vaccines in general and Covid vaccines specifically. The science is unequivocal.' The 'science' is calculated garbage. Trump claims credit for the fake vaccine under Operation Warp Speed (really run by the military not the dumbo front man Trump) which has killed and maimed incredible numbers of Americans. The swamp-drainer continued to claim credit for the jabs and promote them for cancer into 2024. Who are the two biggest MAM heroes? Musk and Trump. Musk is friends with the Silicon Valley Mafiosi, including Google's Sergei Brin and Larry Page, and media notables like James Murdoch who is on the Tesla board. His father

Rupert Murdoch fired Tucker Carlson from Fox. Was there more to know about that given how much credibility it gave to Carlson with the alternative audience? Carlson would not even have to know any of this, but it was obvious what he would do after leaving Fox and how his alternative star would soar.

Ari Emanuel, one of Hollywood's most powerful agents, is another friend of Musk. He was the agent of Donald Trump and remains a close friend. Emanuel's father Benjamin was an operative with the Jewish terrorist group, Irgun, which bombed Israel into existence in 1948. He apparently specialised in bus bombing. I explained in *The Trigger* how many ultra-Zionists were relocated to the United States after Israel was established and Benjamin Emanuel was one of them. They wanted their children to be born as Americans. Emanuel duly obliged by spawning Ari Emanuel; Rahm Emanuel, Barack Obama's White House Chief of Staff (handler), mayor of Chicago and US Ambassador to Japan; and Ezekiel Emanuel who became Chief of the Department of Bioethics at the National Institutes of Health Clinical Center. He was a member of Joe Biden's COVID-19 Advisory Board. That's quite a range of influence for one family of first generational immigrants from Israel. Rahm Emanuel gofer Barack Obama has a background starting with his mother that is awash with CIA involvement and that means the influence of Israeli Mossad. Those with eyes to see will ask why the MAM are in awe of Musk and not calling him out in the light of all this. The answer is Twitter which Musk renamed 'X'.

The X spell

The Cult, through its Deep State operatives, had almost complete domination by 2022 of what was posted on major social media and video platforms of the mainstream Internet where most people sought their information. The Cult had created Google which went on to own YouTube, and the same with Facebook. To this was added Twitter and the list went on. I was banned from all of them in the spring of 2020 after revealing the 'Covid' hoax and the plan to use it for mass vaccination. These platforms were banning posts and posters who challenged almost any aspect of the Cult agenda. The bans applied to 'Covid', 'human-caused climate change', and the spectrum of Woke that included transgenderism and perceived racism against anyone except white people. Alternative views, even mild ones, were blocked. Russell Brand for whatever reason was allowed to continue on YouTube as was Joe Rogan with his Spotify contract worth $200 million, now $250 million. Most of the rest were either deleted or had to roll back what they said. What followed was therefore a real strange move by Cult-controlled Twitter if you were not aware of what the real game is. The Cult Deep State had exactly what it wanted with total control of what was posted and yet they suddenly sold it to Elon Musk who was proclaiming himself to be a free-speech absolutist. *What*? We are talking shareholders of Twitter at the time according to the list I saw that included mega Cult-connected global trillion dollar investment groups BlackRock, Vanguard, and State Street. Morgan Stanley was another. They were not going to sell to Musk unless the Cult *wanted* Twitter sold to Musk. End of story. Musk made a commitment to buy Twitter and they even threatened to take him to court to hold him to that deal when it seemed he may be seeking a way out.

'He' paid $44 billion, changed the name to X, a letter he is obsessed with, and appointed top NBCUniversal executive, Linda Yaccarino, as Twitter CEO. This was a bizarre pick for 'freedom-loving' Musk when Yaccarino was an Executive Chair of Klaus Schwab's World Economic Forum and headed the WEF's Taskforce on Future of Work. She began to describe Twitter/X policy as 'freedom of speech, not freedom of reach' which meant you could post information, but if it was considered the wrong information the ability of people to view it would be suppressed. This is known as 'shadowbanning' and they do it to me constantly. Yaccarino says that 'if it is lawful, but it is awful, it will be extraordinarily difficult for you to see it'. None of this seemed to matter to the MAM. Post-Musk Twitter/X was allowing previously banned people to return and that was proof enough that Musk was 'one of us'. He would tweet and state opinions increasingly supportive of MAM themes which further enhanced his 'one-of-us' reputation. He told Rogan that George Soros 'fundamentally hates humanity' and that he advances agendas that 'erode the fabric of civilization'. It was straight from the 'get them to trust me' script. Follow Musk's tweeting record and he repeats MAM talking points without ever adding anything new. He lets Yaccarino play the role of enforcer to allow him to maintain his 'free-speech' façade as the wrong opinions go on being shadowbanned, even deleted.

The longer this has continued the more Musk's glaring contradictions have been ignored by the MAMs and the more vehement has become the abuse when I've pointed them out. How can Musk become (officially) one of the world's richest men if he is really challenging the Cult that could destroy him financially in a day? The ridiculously inflated share price of Tesla alone, on which his (official) wealth status depends, would be an easy Cult target given the Cult-owned shareholder base of the company. Electric vehicle sales are falling anyway as I write this. There is the stupendous government financial support for his businesses that could be withdrawn if he was such a danger. Why would world leaders including Sunak, Macron, Modi, and Netanyahu flaunt their public meetings with him if his Twitter/X platform was such a threat to the prevailing order that they represent? Why can he be considered by the MAM to oppose the Cult agenda when he is fronting up SpaceX,

Neuralink, Tesla, x.AI, which are all supporting that same agenda?

Why sell it *him*, then?

Then there was the biggest question of all: Why would the Cult/Deep State that controlled what was posted on Twitter sell it to Musk if he was genuinely what he claimed to be? Musk even began to release what were termed the 'Twitter Files' through MAM members like Matt Taibbi and Rogan's mate Michael Shellenberger to reveal emails and documents proving what control the Deep State had over Twitter before him. Okay, so why would the Cult/Deep State that already dictated content on Twitter allow an alleged 'free speech absolutist' to take over unless *that suited them*?

Musk went back on the podcast of his groupie Joe Rogan to emphasise the same point about the Twitter Files proving what control the Deep State had of the platform. Nowhere to be seen or heard from

Figure 28: The Pied Piper.

Rogan (or Carlson) was the prime question: If the Deep State controlled Twitter and what was posted *why did they sell it to you??* By now Musk's eunuchs in the MAM were so spellbound that such obvious questions were off-limits (Fig 28). I experienced the outrage directed at me when I posed them. Musk-mesmerised MAMs were spitting outrage and fury. The answer to those questions is that Elon Musk is not genuine and a Pied Piper leading his entranced MAMs to the edge of the cliff. The scam works like this: Without the acquisition of Twitter, the MAM would have had to address all the ways that Musk is serving the agenda that they claim to be exposing. Once he became 'Chief Twit', everything changed. Cognitive dissonance seized control of the MAM which was overwhelmed by split-brain syndrome. Musk was serving the Cult in all those ways and yet he was still 'one of us' – 'Elon!, Elon!, Elon! Oh, thank you, sir!' This always happens when you are so desperate for something to be true, and someone to be genuine, that you block out everything that shows that it's not true and disingenuous. Musk and his masters appeared to have MAMs in some sort of trance in which all rational thought was suspended. Alex Jones in his 'New Year Message' at the dawn of 2024 said he wanted to see humanity as a 'space-faring nation, a space-faring world, and setting up humanity 2.0 which Elon Musk is talking about'. *Humanity 2.0?* WTF? Space-faring? Our reality is a holographic simulation, a perceptual trap. Should we be 'space-faring' the illusion or freeing our minds from it?

I came across a video of Eva Vlaardingerbroek from 2022 titled: 'Elon Musk is not your friend – he is a transhumanist.' She correctly highlighted how he and his companies like Neuralink were advancing the transhumanist agenda of human control through AI. Exactly right. *Now* she was suddenly praising Musk like a love-sick teenager. She spoke of 'Elon's inexhaustible commitment to free speech' and she reposted a tweet that said Musk is 'the most important voice for free speech in this country right now and the world'. What happened in her psyche for Musk to morph from a dangerous transhumanist into a saviour? What happened between that video and her eulogies a year later when she is beside herself when Musk posts his support for her to increase her reach by millions? 'Thank you, Elon!' Nothing had changed except that Musk had become the MAM God and MAMs were expected to show due reverence. I can't take people seriously who flip like that for no reason except expediency. Either he's a transhumanist danger or he isn't. You could see the theme emerging that 'we have to come together in unity' which is fine so long as the unity is based on truth and not diversion. Russell Brand in another hat-tip to Musk said: 'You may not like Elon Musk but you are going to have to start forming alliances with people standing up against the establishment ...' He completely missed the point of what is going on and added that he was in touch by phone with Musk. Funnily enough, Musk has never called me. Brand's words matched a recurring theme that we saw with Bret 'Covid Mask' Weinstein, Rogan, Jones, and others: Musk is on our side and we have to align with him. No thanks.

Who really owns Twitter/X?

We are told that Elon Musk controls Twitter/X, but does he? He merged Twitter in early 2023 into a new company, X Corp. The platform is not the property only of Musk. Prince Alwaleed bin Talal bin Abdulaziz of 'free speech' Saudi Arabia owns a major stake and other shareholders include billionaire Lawrence J. Ellison, Revocable Trust, Sequoia Capital, Vy Capital, Binance, A.H. Capital Management, Qatar Holdings, Alia Capital Partners, and Fidelity Management. Hardly a bunch of free speech absolutists. Ellison is listed as the world's eighth-wealthiest man with assets of $130 billion. He owns 98 percent of Lanai, the sixth biggest island in the Hawaiian group, and the Ellison Institute of Technology which involved war criminal former UK Prime Minister Tony Blair. He handed Blair tens of millions for his Blair Institute for Global Change which is Cult agenda to the quicks on its fingers. What interest would Ellison have in free speech which Blair seeks to destroy? Ellison is very focussed on life extension and biotechnology which is a major unifying force among the billionaire MAM crowd. Twitter/X owners, X Corp, is itself a subsidiary of X Holdings Corp. Twitter/X is therefore owned and controlled by X Holdings Corp which was registered only in March 2023 and some very interesting details emerged about this when a group of former Twitter employees fired by Musk filed a lawsuit to secure compensation. Judge Susan Illston ordered that Musk and his company must reveal all owners of X Holdings Corp which turned out to be 95 shareholders that he did not want to publicly name. Musk's lawyers responded by listing the 95 individuals, private families, trusts, and organisations that own Twitter via X Holdings Corp, but with *all the names redacted even including Elon Musk.* The lawyers argued that disclosing the names 'would result in injury'. Oh really – how? The lawyers then filed for the names to be kept secret and the *judge agreed.* She ruled that 'the Court grants the motion and orders that the unredacted statement shall be shared with petitioners' counsel subject to the condition that petitioners and their counsel shall maintain the confidentiality of the statement'. Musk was allowed to go on keeping secret the names of the 95 entities that own Twitter/X.

We do know that the state of Qatar invested in Musk's acquisition of Twitter through its Qatari sovereign wealth fund and in late 2022 Saudi Arabia's Prince Alwaleed bin Talal bin Abdulaziz said in a US Securities and Exchange Commission filing that he had invested $1.9 billion to become Twitter's second biggest shareholder after Musk. Qatar was awarded the 2022 World Cup purely for money and this was attended by Musk who was pictured with Donald Trump's ultra-Zionist son-in-

Figure 29: Jared Kushner with Elon Musk at the 2022 World Cup in Twitter/X investing Qatar.

law Jared Kushner who was 'senior adviser' to Trump during his years in the White House (Fig 29). Kushner was reportedly handed a $2 billion 'investment' at the end of the Trump presidency by the Saudi Public Investment Fund headed by Crown Prince Mohammed bin Salman. Remember the Saudi link that Musk claimed for the tweet about taking Tesla private? That involved the trillion dollar Public Investment Fund that invests on behalf of the Saudi Arabian government controlled by Mohammed bin Salman. There are some very dubious players and many of the usual suspects involved in Twitter/X and Musk companies in general. The website Techdirt.com said: 'We've already written a few times about Elon Musk's "Grok" AI from his company xAI, which may or may not be a part of ExTwitter, or possibly Tesla, but no one really knows because all of Elon's companies blend together in a mishmash of hell for anyone who believes in good, normal corporate governance.' He's a man you can trust alright.

Musk is summoned

The Qatar connection is interesting. Qatar is home to the real leaders of terrorist group Hamas who provided Israel with its latest excuse in October 2023 to mass murder in excess of 30,000 Palestinian Arabs in the open-air concentration camp that is the Gaza Strip. It is vital to understand that the Cult has no borders or nationality; its Jewish assets are as happy to target Jews as its Arab assets are to oversee mass-killing of Arabs. They are demons and have no national or cultural basis. Musk tried to exploit the outrage at the Israeli bombing by suggesting that his Starlink system could provide Internet access to Gaza which the Israelis had taken out. He never delivered and was never going to. It was still more Musk bullshit. He was summoned to Israel by his masters to be a propaganda stooge for psychopath Prime Minister Netanyahu whose propaganda he has retweeted. Musk told the world that Israel 'had no choice' but to kill those who insisted on murdering Israeli civilians. There was no mention of murder by Israel and the thousands of Palestinian civilians and children being killed as he spoke. Nor the crystal-clear fact that the Hamas attacks were allowed to happen by Israel and were met with no immediate response from one of the world's most advanced militaries. The Peter Sellers sound-alike said there needed to be education to stop the next generation becoming murderers. How did he think mass murder in Gaza would impact 'education' and affect the attitude of Palestinian children towards Israel? The man is not a 'genius'. He's an idiot reading his script like a good little boy. Musk also said:

> The rebuttal is often made that, well, Israel has killed civilians also in Gaza, but there is an important difference here, which is that Israel tries to avoid

killing civilians, doing everything it can to avoid killing civilians, and there's no sort of joy expressed.

The statement was as moronic as it was uninformed. Musk's suggestion that he could use Starlink to reconnect the Gaza Internet was always opportunist rhetoric. His masters would not allow it. This was a post during Musk's Israel visit from Shlomo Karhi, Israel's Minister for Communications:

> Elon Musk, I congratulate you for reaching a principle understanding with the Ministry of Communications under my leadership. As a result of this significant agreement, Starlink satellite units can only be operated in Israel with the approval of the Israeli Ministry of Communications, including the Gaza Strip.

Musk's vacuous bending of the knee to Netanyahu and Israel amid the Gaza slaughter did not go down well with many of his previous supporters and something had to be done to bring them back on board with the deceit. He immediately returned to America to appear on live TV at a conference to tell advertisers unhappy with his Twitter/X posting policy to 'Go fuck yourself'. The context was: 'If somebody is going to try to blackmail me with advertising, blackmail me with money, go fuck yourself. Go fuck yourself. Is that clear? I hope it is.' This was calculated and strategic, as always with Musk. The gang was back in line. Did you see what Elon said to them? *What a guy*! Andrew Tate was beside himself in a Twitter/X post:

> Look at Elon, Look at me, Look at Trump, We have FUCK-YOU money. And we WILL say 'Fuck you'. We are the epitome of free will, the indomitable human spirit … This is why you will always see the Mainstream Media bundle Me, Trump and Elon together … Trump was not supposed to win the 2016 US presidential election [Yes he WAS]. He was not meant to be the president of the USA [Yes he WAS]. Elon Musk was not supposed to champion free speech [He's NOT except as part of a wider strategy].

Wake up, Andrew. Blimey.

Shapiro's bagman

Musk upset many of his supporters again when he visited the Auschwitz concentration camp in January 2024 with his fellow MAM, Ben Shapiro, in another blatant propaganda trip (Fig 30). Musk knows that he must keep his owners in Israel happy or he's done. He and Shapiro said they were highlighting the mass murder of Jews by the Nazis in World War II while Shapiro was justifying the ongoing mass

Figure 30: Shapiro and Musk at Auschwitz.

murder of Palestinians in Gaza about which Musk had his lips sealed. Shapiro, a mate of Netanyahu and employer of Jordan 'give em hell, Netanyahu' Peterson, interviewed Musk on the trip in which the MAM God said:

I grew up around a lot of Jewish people, I went to Hebrew preschool – my name is pretty Jewish. I went to Israel when I was 13 – most of my friends are Jewish, sometimes I forget 'Am I Jewish?' I'm Jewish, aspirationally Jewish. Two-thirds of my friends are Jewish – I'm like Jewish by association, I'm aspirationally Jewish.

In other words you are Jewish, mate. Why not just admit it? Why so shy? The Jewish population of the United States has risen recently to more than seven million in a total US population (officially) of 335 million. That's only 2.2 percent and they have been massively overrepresented by ratio in key government positions over successive American administrations. Under Joe Biden they were appointed to positions of Secretary of State, deputy Secretary of State, Treasury Secretary, Attorney General, Homeland Security Secretary, and head of the Centers for Disease Control (CDC) during and after 'Covid', among many others. They are also overrepresented by ratio among funders and prominent 'influencers' within the post-'Covid' MAM. Some would respond by saying that they have particular abilities, but when you see the numbers and incompetence (for whatever reason) of those in the Biden line-up that really doesn't wash and it doesn't when it comes to knowledge within the conspiracy arena either.

I said when Musk 'bought' Twitter/X that EU and other government regulation would eventually allow him to block freedom of speech while remaining the hero of the MAM. 'He doesn't want to do it, but he has no choice.' Global government censorship is about to go stratospheric not least under the guise of 'hate speech'. The fascist European Union launched 'formal infringement proceedings' into X in late 2023 'for failing to counter illicit content and disinformation, a lack of transparency about advertising and "deceptive" design practices'. Reports suggested that the (Cult-owned, unelected) European Commission threatened to permanently delete the platform if it didn't comply. Margrethe Vestager, the EU's Danish executive vice president for digital policy, said the Commission would carefully investigate X's compliance with the Digital Services Act (DSA) 'to ensure European citizens are safeguarded online'. This means safeguarded from the truth and any other opinion that questions the Cult's narrative. EU law can fine non-compliant companies up to six percent of their annual global income or ban them from operating in the EU if it decrees a breach of its Hitleresque rules. Other countries and legislative blocs are going the same way and this would provide a long-planned means to both censor X content and maintain Musk's status as a MAM God. Alex Jones called on the public to defend Musk when there is absolutely another way to read the dynamics of the situation. AI technology is ready and waiting funded by governments and the Cult in general to override free speech and give Musk his getaway car. An article on the Technocracy News website said:

> What's happening is that a tool powerful enough to surveil everything that's said and done on the Internet (or large portions of it) is becoming available to the government to monitor all of us, all the time. And, based on that monitoring, the government – and any organization or company the government partners with – can then use the same tool to suppress, silence, and shut down whatever speech it doesn't like.

> But that's not all. Using the same tool, the government and its public-private, 'non-governmental' partners (think, for example: the World Health Organization, or Monsanto) can also shut down any activity that is linked to the Internet. Banking, buying, selling, teaching, learning, entertaining, connecting to each other – if the government-controlled AI does not like what you (or your kids!) say in a tweet or an email, it can shut down all of that for you.

Musk says he wants to turn 'X' into an 'everything app' that would combine banking, buying and selling, Internet, and social media posting. He said he wants X to handle everything in your life that deals with money and told X employees that he expected this to launch by the end of 2024 although many of his predictions for his businesses have not come to pass in his timescale. Musk said that an X email system – 'XMail' – was on the way. This is a centralised, cross-referencing wet dream for the Cult agenda which Musk so obviously serves.

But don't you worry. He's one of *us*.

CHAPTER FIVE

Selling Dystopia

Your eyes are wide open, but you see nothing

Kim Liggett

There is a Cult/Israeli link to Twitter/X data collection. The media reported in August 2023 that Twitter/X could harvest user biometric data and DNA. The Mail Online revealed: 'A new update quietly added to the platform's privacy policy says that X now has permission to harvest its users' fingerprints, retinal scans, voice and face recognition and keystroke patterns'. Keystroke patterns mean tracking how you tap your keyboard.

The update meant that unique biometric data could be catalogued by the company. No need to be concerned, though. Twitter/X said this was only happening 'for safety, security, and identification purposes,' and for 'educational background and job search activity'. Oh, that's okay, then. Musk's 'verification' partner for this is the Israel-based AU10TIX, a subsidiary of Netherlands-based ICTS International. ICTS was created by 'former' members of Israel's domestic intelligence agency, Shin Bet, which works closely with global spy agency Mossad. September 11th researchers will know that another subsidiary of ICTS is Huntleigh USA which was responsible for security on 9/11 at the Boston and Newark airports involving three of the four hijacked planes. Then there were the '7-7' London tube and bus bombings on July 7th, 2005. This is a quote from my 9/11 exposure book, *The Trigger*:

> ICTS subsidiary, ICTS UK, had its office in London's Tavistock Square and the bus bomb went off right in front of the building. Fortress GB, another Israeli company, had an office next to ICTS UK on the first floor of Tavistock House South and still another ultra-Zionist operation, Verint Systems, then a subsidiary of Israel's Comverse Technology, was given the contract the year before the 7/7 bombings to install a 'networked video system' across the underground.

There should have been a stream of CCTV images of the '7-7 bombers' walking through the tube system and getting on the trains. Where are they? This quote is from the exposure documentary *7/7 Ripple Effect*: 'Verint Systems is the security firm that is responsible for the CCTV surveillance cameras in the London Underground rail network ... why [has] no CCTV footage of the four Muslims boarding the tube-trains ... been released by Verint who claim that their cameras were not working?' How many times do we hear this when attacks happen that the authorities want to blame on the wrong people? Should we really be okay with Twitter/X using AU10TIX, a subsidiary of 'Shin Bet' ICTS and part of a wider Israeli network, to check and collect user data? The answer is obvious and again the MAM was silent. The potential for X to become a mass data collecting source and hub of centralised control is enormous. Musk said in October 2022 that buying Twitter was 'an accelerant to creating X, the everything app'. He said he was looking forward to working with WEF Twitter/X CEO Linda Yaccarino to transform the platform into the X everything app. Yaccarino said:

> X is the future state of unlimited interactivity – centred in audio, video, messaging, payments/banking – creating a global marketplace for ideas, goods, services, and opportunities. Powered by AI, X will connect us all in ways we're just beginning to imagine.

Oh, I think we can imagine a lot more than that. Consult the WEF plan promoted by Klaus Schwab and you will see. Musk has likened his 'everything app' to the Chinese platform, WeChat, through which people communicate with messaging, voice and video calls, social media posts, payment services, and much more. It is a one-stop shop that makes it easy for the Cult-owned Chinese fascist/communist government to track everyone. Musk said:

> If you're in China, you kind of live on WeChat. It does everything. It's sort of like Twitter plus PayPal plus a whole bunch of things all rolled into one, with a great interface. It's really an excellent app, and we don't have anything like that outside of China.

Many things come from this. I have been writing over the decades that China is the blueprint for the global system of mass control through AI and that's why the world has become ever more like China especially since 'Covid' which is *claimed* to have started there. It didn't, but the symbolism is appropriate. Musk has considerable contacts and business interests in China. His ambition to copy the Chinese WeChat is straight from the Cult script and the plan for an AI-controlled digital concentration camp that controls all financial transactions, decides what you can and cannot buy, and dictates what you can and cannot see through control of information. Musk promotes the concept of an X everything app as competition for China's WeChat when it is only the Western version of it. They are not competitors. They are on the same side. China controls its population through a Social Credit points system which decides through 24/7 surveillance if your compliant behaviour allows you to operate within mainstream society or your non-compliance means you are excluded to the margins. You have to incessantly centralise power and decision-making for the few to control the many and Musk's X everything app would be tailor-made to advance this agenda. You would think that anyone who really believed in freedom would be seeking diversity of power and decision-making away from the centre. Not Musk. He is a Cult-owned fraud selling the Cult agenda while claiming to oppose it. I saw a Musk Twitter/X post which had an X appearing over the Earth as if it was the Sun. Nothing 'he' posts is without an ulterior motive or reason. Another post said: 'X as humanity's collective consciousness.' You mean the AI Cloud you are creating, mate? A public reply to that post listed a predicted sequence that would follow:

> Elon buys Twitter; Everyone celebrates 'free speech' again; Earns trust of the people; Brings on Yaccarino; Changes name to X; X to become the 'everything app' for chat, purchases, and entertainment; Yaccarino now discussing a social credit score under the guise of 'brand safety' (see: 'lawful' vs 'awful'); 'Everything App' eventually ties to this Social Xredit Score; Everything App + Social Credit Score rolls into Neuralink; Neuralink mandated to use X/Everything App; Morons actually do it out of convenience; Voila! Microchipped and controlled population! Yayayay!!

The social credit score is a central pillar of control in China as I mentioned. Doing what the government demands earns you 'credits' and doing otherwise has them taken away. Once enough are removed for non-compliant behaviour and opinions you can no longer travel by train or plane or function within mainstream society. This is what is planned for the rest of the world. China is the blueprint after all. These plans put into wider perspective Elon Musk's stated goal to turn Twitter/X into his everything app that includes your finances. People being cancelled and losing their job for their views are stepping stones to full-blown social credit China.

What's with the 'X'?

Musk has long been obsessed with the esoteric/occult symbol of 'X'. He began at least in 1999 with X.com which was absorbed (without his input) into PayPal. Then followed SpaceX, Tesla Model X, X-Corp, X-

Holdings, Twitter renamed X, xAI, and he even named his son X Æ A-12, or 'X' for short. This was later changed to conform with California law to X Æ A-Xii. The name was apparently meant to indicate 'X Ash Archangel'. The X symbol denotes something mysterious or unknown. We have X-Files; X-Men (a group of mutants with superhuman abilities in the Marvel comics and movies); X chromosome (found in both men and women); Generation X (those born between 1965 and 1980); the skull and bones symbol of the X (a symbol of death) which is the logo of the sinister Skull and Bones Society in the United States (Fig 31). The Skull and Bones Society has produced significant political players in America including the two Bush presidents and the US Secretary of State and later 'Climate Czar', John Kerry. Artist and esoteric researcher Neil Hague explored the occult background to X in an article on Davidicke.com when Musk made the switch. Hague related X to

Figure 31: Skull and Bones Society crossbones X logo.

Figure 32: A mirrored X as in Twitter/X reveals a remarkable resemblance to the Freemasonic compass and the ancient Sigil of Saturn which is repeated in the logo of the British royal family residence of Balmoral Castle in Scotland. We will see later the significance of Saturn to the Global Cult.

'Hex' which is a negative spell. What is the effect of constantly seeing 'X' as you enter and surf Musk's platform as the symbol is being absorbed by your conscious and subconscious mind? A mirrored X from Musk's platform shows remarkable synchronicity with the Freemason compass, the occult Sigil of Saturn, and the logo of Balmoral Castle owned by the British royal family (Fig 32). Is this is a coincidence or a Hidden Hand behind world events founded on occult symbolism and hidden knowledge? An article at Spells8.com said the following under the heading 'What Does Being Hexed Mean?':

A hex is an energetic influence placed upon a person, place, or thing to create a negative experience. There are many ways to accomplish a hex, but the most common way is through spell-work. Hexes are a form of baneful magick and are more commonly used than commonly known.

A hex can change the overall energy field or add an energy attachment to the field with a specific intention. Someone who's been hexed may experience unfavorable events unfold in their lives. These experiences can be mental disturbances, physical ailments, emotional turmoil, or aspects of their lives becoming more negative.

Are regular visitors to Musk's X being hexed? I think 'yes' unless they are consciously aware of that intent which projects an energetic barrier. I believe many MAMs have been hexed which is why they can't see the obvious. Neil

Figure 33: X keys emblem of the Papacy.

Hague points out the widespread use of X on flags, logos and heraldry and how it was adopted by the Vatican (Fig 33). You see the cross or X used in ancient Egyptian symbolism and in the present day logo of Extinction Rebellion promoting the Cult climate change agenda (Figs 34 and 35). X relates to the number 10. In numerology the numbers are added together until there is a single digit. In this case the 10 is numerologically a 1, as in 'The One'. Hague says X

Figure 34: Egyptian god Osiris was said to have been buried with his arms crossed in an X and Pharaohs were buried with the same pose.

Figure 35: Extinction Rebellion X logo.

is symbolically linked to the constellation of Orion (Osiris) which appears in much Cult symbology, as does Saturn, and he suggests that the 'X spell' is being cast through symbols that speak to the subconscious mind. The X was used 'to draw our attention, to mesmerize us' and to keep many of us busy 'buying into the material world'. He says the X in corporate logos, products, and movies is there to cast a 'magic spell'.

When Musk rebranded to X he seized the @X Twitter handle account without warning or financial compensation and told the owner, Gene X Hwang, from the corporate photography and videography studio Orange Photography, that he would be offered a selection of X merchandise and a tour of the X headquarters as a 'reflection of our appreciation'. It is also a typical reflection of Musk arrogance and sense of entitlement. The *Wall Street Journal* reported concern in the first days of 2024 by Musk company shareholders, executives and board members about his drug use which was said to include LSD, cocaine, ecstasy, and ketamine. The article suggested these were often taken at exclusive parties around the world where guests have to sign non-disclosure agreements and hand over their phones. The *WSJ* said serious concerns over Musk's drug taking were raised in 2017 when he slurred his words and rambled incomprehensibly for fifteen minutes at a SpaceX meeting before someone else took over. There is so much more to know about this bloke.

The Gang (some of them)

I want to highlight some other players in the MAM takeover before we move into the deeper than deep areas that the Barricade Brigade is holding back from widespread public attention. Writer and film producer Jonathan Taplin penned an article in *Vanity Fair* describing how four very powerful billionaires, Elon Musk, Peter Thiel, Mark Zuckerberg, and Marc Andreessen are creating a world where 'nothing is true, and all is spectacle'. He called them technocrats and said they make up 'a kind of interlocking directorate of Silicon Valley, each investing in or sitting on the boards of the others' companies. That reminds me of the interlocking support, promotion, and interview network of the MAM 'stars'. Taplin said the vast digital domain of the 'Fab Four' controlled our personal information, affected how billions of people lived, worked, and loved, and sowed online chaos, inciting mob violence and sparking runs on stocks:

> These four men have long been regarded as technologically progressive heroes, but they are actually part of a broader antidemocratic, authoritarian turn within the tech world, deeply invested in preserving the status quo and in keeping their market-leadership positions or near-monopolies and their multi-

billion-dollar fortunes secure from higher taxes.

Taplin quotes Peter Thiel as saying 'competition is for suckers'. I have discussed Musk at length here, Zuckerberg is the Cult frontman for Meta/Facebook, and Andreessen is the American software engineer who co-founded Netscape, software company Opsware, and Silicon Valley venture capital firm Andreessen Horowitz. They are, with Thiel, all in their own way advancing the Cult agenda with their funding and actions. Peter Thiel requires especial mention because of his fundamental ties to the intelligence community and Pentagon (Fig 36). He was born in Frankfurt, Germany, and his father was Klaus Friedrich

Figure 36: Peter Thiel has fundamental ties to Intelligence and Pentagon networks.

Thiel, a chemical engineer who apparently helped to mine uranium in Namibia for South African, Israeli, French, and Chinese atomic bombs. Peter Thiel worked with serious insider companies as a securities lawyer at Sullivan & Cromwell and a derivatives trader at Credit Suisse. He was a speechwriter for Bill Bennett, the US Secretary of Education under Ronald Reagan, who was named by MKUltra mind-control survivor Cathy O'Brien as one of her mind manipulators and abusers. Thiel co-founded Palantir Technologies which is used for data and surveillance analysis by US Intelligence and the Department of Defense as well as state and local governments and corporations. Put another way, the Cult web. Palantir is very active in Israel and stated at the start of 2024 that 'We stand with Israel': 'The board of directors of Palantir will be gathering in Tel Aviv next week for its first meeting of the new year.' The name Palantir comes from J.R.R. Tolkien's *The Lord of the Rings* in which magical palantíri were 'indestructible balls of crystal used for communication and to see events in other parts of the world'. Palantir's first investor was the CIA's In-Q-Tel in line with Thiel's recurring CV. A head of In-Q-Tel, Mike Griffin, later head of NASA, was instrumental in the founding of 'Musk's' SpaceX in which Thiel is a shareholder through his Founders Fund. Palantir co-founder Joe Lonsdale has joined with a group including former *New York Times* opinion editor Bari Weiss, evolutionary biologist Heather Heying, and Harvard University professor Arthur Brooks, to create the University of Austin. This university is claimed to be dedicated to freedom of thought and discourse and is supported by a 'group of powerful venture capitalists' that include the said Marc Andreessen who joined Lonsdale as a lecturer in a programme called 'Forbidden Courses'. It's amazing how many billionaires and influencers suddenly want to position themselves in this 'freedom' arena.

Peter Thiel was a co-creator of PayPal and the Founders Fund, the first outside investor in Facebook, and supports research into 'friendly AI' – the usual story from these people. He invested in the Musk/Altman-founded OpenAI behind ChatGPT and so has the Rishi Sunak family's technology company Infosys. Thiel has massive investments in biotechnology which is 'the manipulation (as through genetic engineering) of living organisms or their components to produce useful usually commercial products such as pest resistant crops, new bacterial strains, or novel pharmaceuticals'. Put simply, this is genetic manipulation or engineering which a major, major, goal of the Cult. If Thiel is involved so somewhere is US Intelligence, Israeli Intelligence, and the military. He had a number of meetings with Mossad blackmail operative (among other things) Jeffrey Epstein and at one dinner at Epstein's New York mansion they were joined by film director Woody Allen. Another Thiel-Epstein meeting involved Bill Burns who at the time was Obama's deputy Secretary of State and is now head of the CIA. Burns was born at Fort Bragg, now Fort Liberty, in North Carolina, a centre of military psychological warfare operations (Psyops). Epstein was a vehicle to fund genetic engineering and biotechnology. Maryam Henein writing on the Activist Post website revealed claims that Epstein 'wanted to develop an improved super-race of humans using genetic engineering and artificial intelligence and impregnate women with his seed – 20 women at a time'. I have revealed many times how the Cult perpetuates its human-alien bloodlines through sperm banks (see *Everything You Need To Know But Have Never Been Told* and *The Perception Deception*). Thiel announced he is launching an alternative Olympics that allows athletes to take performance-enhancing drugs 'out in the open and honestly'. How long before 'performance-enhancing' will involve AI and robotics?

Thiel and the MAM

Thiel's path has crossed with Musk countless times going way back. An indication of Thiel's influence came in 2011 when he was granted citizenship of New Zealand after spending only twelve non-consecutive days in the country. He is a member of the Republican Party and describes himself as a conservative libertarian. He makes substantial donations to American right-wing figures and causes so beloved of the MAM. He donated to Trump's successful presidential campaign in 2016 and Thiel was a member of Trump's executive committee of the

President-elect's transition team. Trump, like the MAM, is supposed to be 'against the globalists' and yet Thiel is on the Steering Committee of the Cult's seriously-globalist Bilderberg Group that has been working for a world government since 1954. Thiel's connections are everywhere within the MAM. Vivek Ramaswamy was born to parents who emigrated to America from India and went on to become a prominent voice in the MAM. Ramaswamy, a former investment partner in a hedge fund, was given essential promotion and a public profile by Tucker Carlson, first on Fox News and then Twitter/X. He announced a run for US president for 2024. Ramaswamy founded the pharmaceutical company Roivant Sciences in 2014 and co-founded the investment firm Strive Asset Management in 2022. Peter Thiel is an investor in Strive along with Bill Ackman, an American Jewish billionaire hedge fund manager. Eric Weinstein, brother of Carlson-endorsed 'hero' Bret 'Covid mask' Weinstein, is an advisor to Thiel's venture capital company. Eric Weinstein has appeared many times on Joe Rogan's show.

The Cult is behind the Woke phenomenon. Thiel, Ackman, and the Weinsteins all claim to be 'anti-Woke'. If you want to make yourself a hero of the MAM you must be anti-Woke. It's the way into the fold and we have 'anti-Wokers' Thiel, Ackman, Ramaswamy, the Weinsteins, Trump, and Musk, but that's as far as they go. Here and no further. Bret Weinstein was a member of the 'intellectual dark web', a name coined by his brother Eric while working for Peter Thiel to describe academics and such like 'who oppose identity politics, political correctness, and cancel culture in higher education and the news media within Western countries'. Israel fanatic 'journalist' Barry Weiss promoted the 'intellectual dark web' while at *The New York Times*. Ramaswamy and Thiel's Strive Asset Management is not averse to Woke, it would appear. Strive lists some of its top holdings as Apple; Microsoft; Amazon; Alphabet (the parent company of Google/YouTube); Musk's Tesla; and 'Covid' vaccine-maker Johnson & Johnson. Ramaswamy went to law school on a scholarship partly funded by the late Paul Soros, brother of George Soros, who was often known as 'the invisible Soros'. *Newsweek* reported that Ramaswamy's Roivant implemented a classic Woke diversity, equity, and inclusion (DEI) initiative when he was CEO. Roivant Social Ventures aimed to foster 'DEI opportunities for future leaders in biopharma and biotech'. Roivant's biggest institutional investors included Morgan Stanley, Viking Global, and BlackRock which he criticises *by name*. *Newsweek* said: 'In a deeply ironic twist, Ramaswamy's anti-Woke campaign is being bankrolled by the profits reaped from the very policies he denounces.' Roivant under Ramaswamy bought a stake in Arbutus Biopharma Corporation which launched a joint 'RNA therapeutics' venture with Roivant called Genevant Sciences, This sought to develop lipid nanoparticles which are used to manipulate the immune system and deliver the contents of 'Covid' fake vaccines into the body. Arbutus and Genevant launched a lawsuit against Moderna for infringing patents related to this. Ramaswamy stepped down from Roivant's board as he made his brief bid to win the 2024 Republican nomination after which he pledged support for Trump. Some of his campaign speeches were remarkably similar, sometimes word-for-word, what Barack Obama had previously said. It is highly possible that he was Trump's surrogate in the televised Republican primary debates which Trump chose not to attend. Once they were over and the voting began Ramaswamy quickly left the stage to Trump.

Get ready to Rumble

Vivek Ramaswamy claims to be an 'outsider', the same as 'anti-Woke' MAM champion Trump. That is an insult to the intelligence in both cases. Ramaswamy is on 'Jordan Peterson's' ARC organising committee. Peterson is a friend of Carlson-endorsed Dave Rubin, a MAM podcaster and Israel-firster. Rubin said he became a friend of Peter Thiel through Thiel's friend and confidant (and venture capital advisor) Eric Weinstein, brother of masked crusader Bret. Dave Rubin promoted a Joe Rogan-Bret Weinstein interview on Twitter/X with the post: 'The Elites are on the march, but @elonmusk @BretWeinstein @joerogan and many others are putting up a fight.' What an example of the MAM cross-promotion network in all its glory. He said he was no longer a friend of

Figure 37: Dave Rubin – a classic MAM and don't criticise Israel if you want to be his friend. I think I can survive without that somehow.

Candace Owens after she criticised Israel for mass murder in Gaza (Fig 37). I personally wouldn't trust any of the people in this group. Rubin launched Locals Technology Inc., or Locals.com, in 2019, with his Israeli brother-in-law Assaf Lev. Locals attracted millions in funding from San Francisco venture capital firm Craft Ventures which was co-founded in 2017 by Musk's mate David Sacks, a Jewish chief operating officer and product leader with PayPal co-founded by their friend, Peter Thiel. Sacks has invested in SpaceX, Palantir, Facebook, Uber and Airbnb, and is a board member of Rumble. I have seen Musk repost comments by Sacks several times on Twitter/X ensuring them an audience of multiple millions. The MAM has become an almost unfathomable web of these billionaires.

Dave Rubin's Locals was bought by video-sharing site Rumble in 2021. Peter Thiel is a major shareholder in Rumble and this means that a member of the Bilderberg Group Steering Committee is a funder of this 'alternative' platform. J. D. Vance, US senator for Ohio, is another Rumble investor and was a principle at Peter Thiel's venture capital company Mithril Capital. 'Anti-globalist' Vance (don't laugh) co-founded Narya Capital with financial backing from Thiel, Marc Andreessen, the aforementioned tech billionaire, and Eric Schmidt, the former Google chief and Cult-globalism-operative-to-his-DNA. Vance is another investor in the Ramaswamy-Thiel operation, Strive, and yet *another* convert to Roman Catholicism. He said this deepened his commitment to Israel which has funded his political career via its American lobby group, AIPAC, along with … Peter Thiel. Thiel is everywhere in the MAM. Russell Brand's pivot to Christianity, the Rosary, and baptism came in the same period that he was promoting, presumably for a handsome fee, a Roman Catholic 'prayer app' called Hallow which is funded by … *Peter Thiel* who is not a Roman Catholic. Vance, who rails against Big Tech data collection, is also an investor in Hallow which gathers data from its subscribers that it reserves the right to exploit. This is a key to all of this tech business and includes personal information secured from Tesla drivers – data collection. The 'Christianity' and biblical explosion within the MAM is no organic coincidence. Jordan Peterson has connections to Thiel and Andreessen. The spokesman for the 2022 Canadian truckers protest, Benjamin Dichter, brought up in a Jewish family in Toronto, spoke with Thiel and Peterson at that year's Bitcoin conference in Miami Beach, Florida. The Trump Media and Technology Group announced an agreement in December 2021 for technology and cloud services with Rumble which included an association with Truth Social that Trump launched as a Twitter-like platform after being removed from mainstream platforms. Trump Media and Technology announced a merger in early 2014 with Digital World Acquisition Corp which could be worth to Trump a reported $3.5 to $4 billion. The idea that Trump is seeking to 'drain the swamp' is hilarious. He's a MAM Psyop, just like Musk and the rest of this mob.

Rumble was founded in 2013 by a Canadian technology entrepreneur Chris Pavlovski who publicly offered Joe Rogan $100 million over four years to move his podcast to his platform. Rumble's chief operating officer is Tyler Hughes, who was head of marketing for the AI software development arm of pharmaceutical and agribusiness giant Bayer Monsanto. Michael Ellis, Rumble's General Counsel and Corporate Secretary, held senior legal and policy roles in the Intelligence Community, White House, and Congress. Ellis has quite a CV. He was Senior Director for Intelligence Programs at the National Security

Council (NSC) under Trump; Senior Associate Counsel to the President; Deputy NSC Legal Advisor in the Office of the White House Counsel; and general counsel of the notorious National Security Agency (NSA). Before that he was General Counsel of the House Permanent Select Committee on Intelligence and an intelligence officer in the United States Navy Reserve. I think it's fair to say he has specialised in 'intelligence'. Rumble's 'partners and executives' connect into Microsoft, Yahoo, Bayer, and the US National Security Council. It's all very strange to have all these serious mainstream insiders funding and working for an 'alternative' platform supposedly challenging the system that they represent.

Rumble, needless to say, does nothing to promote my own work of now 35 years while heavily promoting MAMs. The policy appears to be in line with Musk at Twitter/X in that it suppresses search results for keywords which it claims are associated with 'hate speech' and 'extremists' while still allowing the material to be posted: 'Freedom of speech, not freedom of reach.' Rumble promotes Russell Brand; Steven Crowder and his Mug Club network that includes Alex Jones; Steve Bannon, the Trump political strategist; Charlie Kirk, Turning Point USA co-founder and Musk arse-kisser; Dan Bongino, Rumble investor, former Fox host, and Secret Service Agent; plus many more of a similar ilk. All are focussed on politics and the great majority are supporters of Trump. I don't say these people and others are knowingly manipulating their audience on the Cult's behalf. You once again only have to promote the mentality that suits your agenda and exclude those who don't.

'Dr' John

Big MAM names on Rumble interview MAM stars such as Vivek Ramaswamy, Robert Kennedy Jr, Jordan Peterson, Tulsi Gabbard, Dave Rubin, Ron DeSantis, Jimmy Dore, and 'Dr' John Campbell, a retired

'nurse educator', of whom it is worth saying more. He's another archetypal MAM of the 'New Media'. Campbell spent the 'Covid' years promoting the official story and the fake vaccines. He then became a MAM hero when he could no longer ignore the excess deaths from

Figure 38: 'Dr' John Campbell. In the top left of his backdrop we see 'follow the evidence'. If he had taken that advice a lot of people who watched his podcast during 'Covid' might not have had the fake vaccine. What has happened to some of them already?

the very fake vaccine he had promoted. Go figure again (Fig 38). Campbell calls himself 'Dr' which most people would take to be a medical doctor when he is discussing topics of health. The 'Dr', in fact, refers to Doctor of *Philosophy*, not medicine. He may say this here and there, but between those times his audience would think something else. If you did not want to mislead people you wouldn't use the term 'Dr' in these circumstances. In the context of what he does being a Doctor of Philosophy is irrelevant. It's the same with the mega-crook 'Dr' Tedros, the Gates-Rockefeller gofer who officially heads the World Health Organization. He is not a 'Dr' of medicine – he's another Doctor of Philosophy (the Cult's philosophy).

Campbell has more than three million subscribers on YouTube which drops you at the mere hint of challenging the official health narrative. He's no rebel, quite the opposite. Campbell pushed the official 'Covid' bullshit and the ludicrous 'asymptomatic spread'. When he reinvented himself as a 'Covid dissident' he told a different story to the same viewers that he had warned about the danger of 'asymptomatic spread', not least from children. Now suddenly, as Campbell rewrote history, the very idea was a 'myth'. He had the bare-faced cheek and nerve to ask where the myth of asymptomatic spread had come from and how it was perpetuated. Because of people like *you* – you fucker! What an extraordinary hypocrite. Now he's a 'Covid' hero interviewed by the Dream Team including Russell Brand. Another Johnnie-come-lately is British cardiologist Aseem Malhotra who promoted the 'Covid' fake vaccine and then turned against it when the consequences became clear. He supports all other vaccines. Sorry, the time to do your research as a doctor is *before* the fake vaccine is administered, not after you see the mayhem it has caused. Malhotra is not for me, that is for sure. Doctors who went early with their warnings about the jab have been struck off or are threatened with being so. People like British doctor Mohammad Iqbal Adil.

Keeping well

I know from my own experience that you are not popular when you challenge Weinstein, Campbell, and other MAMs and 'Covid'-promotors-come-'Covid'-dissidents. Polly St George experienced the same when she was on their case. The good news is that this led to her uncovering remarkable connections between many 'dissidents' and the 'alternative' health industry. She became aware of the widespread MAM funding network of The Wellness Company co-owned by Foster Coulson and Dave Lopez which sells health supplements and ways to detox the 'spike protein' in the fake 'Covid' vaccine when some credible alternative medical voices say the alleged 'spike protein' in the vials does not exist. The Wellness Company only began in 2022 in the wake of

the debunking of
'Covid' by the pre-
MAM alternative
media in 2020, 2021,
and 2022. It's public
front men with
Coulson are headed by
cardiologist Dr Peter
McCullough, and Dr
Paul Alexander, 'a
Canadian independent
scientist and

Figure 39: Foster Coulson after an interview with Tucker Carlson.

former Trump administration official during the 'Covid' hoax at the US
Department of Health and Human Services. The number of people who
bought the 'Covid' swindle and now tell us what is best for our health is
both shocking and embarrassing. Foster Coulson comes from a very
wealthy family (Fig 39). Among its companies is one that 'fights
wildfires' across the world with government contracts worth multiple
billions. The story goes that Coulson met his Wellness partner Dave
Lopez while visiting Bolivia on fire-fighting business. This seems very
convenient given the speed at which events moved from there.

Lopez is interesting in that he worked in Haiti for the 'anti-child
trafficking' operation Underground Railroad of Tim Ballard highlighted
in the movie, *Sound of Freedom*. Lopez began his own 'anti-child
trafficking' organisation, Mission Six Zero, with the tagline 'unleash your
inner soldier'. He's a former Navy SEAL who has been employed by US
Homeland Security. Lopez worked for Erik Prince, a CIA asset and
founder of the mercenary army operation Blackwater, one of the biggest
private security firms in the world used regularly over the years by the
CIA and Pentagon as an arms-length asset. Prince trained James O'Keefe
and staff at the hidden-camera exposure group, Project Veritas, and
O'Keefe now runs another MAM operation, the O'Keefe Media Group,
funded by the Wellness Company. Erik Prince relocated to the United
Arab Emirates where American investigative journalist Matthew Cole
says he built two 'secret armies' for the Emirates and in Somalia. Cole
said Prince returned to America in the Trump era and is not averse to
political 'dirty tricks'. Prince is now appearing on MAM shows with
people like former Trump aide Steve Bannon. Alex Jones once called
Prince a 'patriot' and Tucker Carlson described him in a Rogan interview
as 'a good friend of mine', a 'really a wonderful person', and 'one of my
favourite people, actually'.

The Wellness Company funds a whole raft of MAM stars, websites,
and video platforms and launched its own, the Vigilant News Network.
Wellness CEO Peter Gillooly has confirmed that those they financially

support are monitored for their content and the company would not tolerate 'fringe or hate speech'. 'Fringe' is code for outside the limits of the MAM. The Wellness Company is owned by Foster Coulson's Stardust Group and includes 1775 Coffee which has partnered with Rumble and has been promoted by Andrew Tate. The group says it is focussed on 'growing a truly parallel economy that champions freedom, liberty, and self-determination, and one that is free from the corrupting forces of big pharma, big tech, big media, and big government.' Wellness Company stalwarts, Foster Coulson, Dave Lopez, and Brandon Kuemper launched an American venture capital company, Integro Capital, in 2021. Investments include Nanobiosym, 'a physics, biomedicine, and nanotechnology' operation run by founder, chairman, and CEO, Dr Anita Goel. She is described as 'a world-renowned expert and pioneer in the emerging field of Nanobiophysics' which is 'a new science at the convergence of physics, nanotechnology, and biomedicine'. The recurring theme is clear as is the network all driving in the same direction. Goel is a serious insider with connections to the Clinton Global Initiative, Pentagon Big Tech arm DARPA, NASA, SpaceX, and AI-human fusion promotor, Peter Diamandis. She delivered a joint keynote speech with Cult operative and former UK Prime Minister Tony Blair on 'Tackling Global Challenges' at the Annual Novartis Forum. Novartis is one of the world's biggest pharmaceutical companies based in Basle, Switzerland. Nanobiosym is 'building innovative public-private partnerships with governments, NGOs, academic, industrial, and global thought leaders, to help bring emerging technologies to address some of the world's most pressing challenges'. It's the usual suspects with the usual script for AI takeover. I wonder after reading some of the background here if you think claims to be 'alternative' by The Wellness Company and its owners, operatives, and corporate connections have any credibility? So much of the MAM 'New Media' doesn't seem to be very 'alternative' at all.

Border Psyop

Musk was posting regularly by the start of 2024 about the open southern border of the United States. Post after post on Twitter/X saw him say how terrible it was and how it threatened the stability of the country. He would highlight how migrants were treated compared with the indigenous population. This was all correct and mirrored what I had been saying year after year about the plan to flood the West with migrants from other countries. Mass migration is a big theme of the MAM and the posts added to Musk's hero status. The question was why was he doing this? The MAM didn't think to ask. They were too busy cheering. The border situation had been building for decades and the numbers soared even further from the moment 'Biden' officially took office in 2021 as I predicted they would. Why now, Mr Musk? People need to understand that Musk's posts on Twitter/X are a Psyop. They are all calculated and I doubt that he even posts at least many of them. The mass movement of migrants into the West is happening for multiple reasons. Western culture is being diluted (a long-time Cult goal) and young adult men of military age pour into a country who have no allegiance to their new location or its people. Look at almost any image of the migrant hordes in Europe and North America and you will see that very few of them depict families and children. They are young adult men.

A major study into fertility and human population decline appeared in the science journal *The Lancet* in 2024 funded by the Bill & Melinda Gates Foundation and this is most relevant to mass migration. The funding source means that the content both suited the Cult agenda and was meant to be widely circulated – as it was. The study said the global population would fall within decades because of dramatically reduced fertility rates and may never recover. By 2050 the great majority of countries were on course to have birthrates that would not replace the dying population. Co-author Dr Natalia Bhattacharjee said declining fertility rates 'will completely reconfigure the global economy and the international balance of power and will necessitate reorganising societies'. This would represent the biggest population decline since the bubonic plague or 'Black Death' killed up to 50 million in the mid-1300s. Mass migration would be necessary to replenish the workforce and aging populations from those areas of the world where populations were projected to increase. These countries with a 'baby boom' were focused in sub-Saharan Africa. The United Nations has said something similar about the need for mass migration from other cultures to 'save the West'. A study author, Professor Stein Emil Vollset, said the world is 'facing staggering social change through the 21st century'. The Gates mob punched the air because that has been the game all along and mass immigration from other cultures into the West is central to that.

Border P-R-S

There is another reason for mass migration and that is a Problem-Reaction-Solution to impose digital borders in which everyone is tracked by biometrics and AI. The MAM and the real alternative media have been resisting and exposing this level of 24/7 tracking by AI and warning that it represents the Chinese social credit and control system moving westward. The border catastrophe allows Cult tech oligarchs to step forward and provide the solution to the problem – AI controlled borders on the road to an AI controlled world. Musk's support for the MAM take on immigration has weakened resistance to AI borders as the MAM concedes that it's the only way to stem the flow. Game, set, and

Palmer Luckey
Founder
Anduril Industries

Figure 40: Peter Thiel's mate, Palmer Luckey.

match to the Cult. Why did Musk begin to machine-gun post about the southern border with his guaranteed multi-million views? Why did Bret 'Covid mask' Weinstein suddenly head for the southern border to be given the multi-million viewer exposure of a Tucker Carlson interview to tell his story? Whitney Webb is a brilliant researcher who operates outside the MAM and sees right through it. She wrote an excellent article about the creation of virtual borders through the Cult tech oligarch cartel. She highlights the US 'defense tech' company Anduril and its 'brains', Palmer Luckey (Fig 40). He invented the virtual reality headset, Oculus Rift, which he sold to Facebook. Luckey is a long-time associate of … yes … *Peter Thiel*, the Pentagon and intelligence community stalwart behind surveillance and control firm, Palantir, and major investor in Rumble, SpaceX, and AI technology in general. Thiel was on the board of Facebook when Luckey secured his headset deal.

Anduril is Luckey's new venture and it is named, like Thiel's Palantir, with a nod to Tolkien's *Lord of the Rings*. Anduril is a sword named the Flame of the West, also Sword of the King. Anduril is financially supported by Thiel's Founders Fund and Joe Lonsdale, another co-founder of Palantir. These connections make it no surprise that Anduril has secured major government contracts for 'autonomous surveillance towers' on both land borders of the United States (which has done nothing to stop the tide, quite the opposite). Luckey has said that Anduril can create 'a digital wall that is not a barrier so much as a web of all-seeing eyes, with intelligence to know what it sees'. MAM hero Trump is well known for demanding control of the borders and Luckey donated to Trump's inaugural committee at the time that Thiel was on Trump's transition team. Whitney Webb points out that Luckey and Anduril present themselves as 'America First', 'anti-globalist', and seeking to save Western democracy when they are really a smokescreen and front for the Deep State agenda that Trump supporters vehemently oppose. This is exactly the deceit that I am exposing in the book this far. The Deep State (Cult) is infiltrating the MAM, putting its chosen people in there, and diluting opposition through the AI soft sell and Problem-Reaction-Solution.

Trae Stephens, another Palantir executive 'formerly' in government intelligence, moved to Anduril, He is involved with Thiel's Founders Fund which gave him a seat on the Fund's associated companies including Carbyne911. This involves the former Israeli Prime Minister Ehud Barak and was partly funded by Barak's close friend, Jeffrey Epstein. Carbyne is an Israeli intelligence and military operation that collects the public surveillance data and specialises, as with Thiel's Palantir, in pre-crime predictive law enforcement. Whitney Webb writes that Carbyne's board has included Pinchas Buchris, a former commander of Israel's infamous military Unit 8200; Nicole Junkermann, a 'venture capitalist' in these technologies who was an associate of Epstein; and Lital Leshem, an Israeli intelligence operative who works for another MAM hero and one of Tucker Carlson's favourite people, Erik Prince. Trae Stephens was appointed to oversee the Defense Department in Trump's transition team in which Peter Thiel was so influential. Stephens then launched Anduril with Luckey and continues with Thiel's Founders Fund (which also invests in Musk's SpaceX). Trump is on board with all of this. He said his border defence would include 'sensors, monitors and cutting-edge technology':

> The walls we are building are not medieval walls. They are smart walls designed to meet the needs of frontline border agents … The biometric entry/exit tracking visa system which we need desperately. In my administration we will ensure that this system is in place and I will tell you it will be on land, it will be on sea, it will be in air, we will have a proper tracking system.

The people in his audience who would have normally pushed back on biometric tracking broke into cheering and applause. This is how the Psyop works. Anduril's ambitions go much further than only AI border control. Other technologies include autonomous aircraft, underwater vehicles, advanced armed military drones, all controlled by AI in a coordinated system called Lattice. Once AI is running the military you no longer need to deploy large numbers of troops to impose your will. A tiny number of people in underground bases can control the population on the surface through AI technology and weaponry. Luckey wants 'to turn American and allied warfighters into invincible technomancers'. At the same time Luckey's 'anti-globalist' buddy Peter Thiel and Palantir is working for the military and intelligence agencies to process data from drones, satellites, and public sources.

Clearview AI, another Thiel supported company, produces AI facial recognition technology that can apparently identify activists at a protest 'or an attractive stranger on the subway', revealing not just their names but where they live, what they do and who they know. Whitney Webb writes: 'All three of these Thiel-backed companies have been testing the interoperable use of their products already in the Ukraine conflict and appear to be using Israel's war on the Gaza Strip for the same ends.' Thiel, Musk, Trump, and the whole deal is a Psyop to use the often-legendary naivety of the MAM to dilute opposition to the very AI-control the MAM claims to oppose. Maybe Bret Weinstein would care to comment or even more so his brother Eric with his close business ties to Thiel. 'America First' and the whole MAGA nonsense is another Psyop which tens of millions have fallen for. What is described here is the Totalitarian Tiptoe to complete AI control being played out across the world. The Cult-owned-and-created European Union is imposing an AI biometric entry/exit system and new 'digital borders' at which travellers will face fingerprint and facial scans with the UK following suit.

The game is global, right, Mr Putin?

The role of China gives proper context to the incredibly overhyped interview by Tucker Carlson with Russian President Vladimir Putin in February 2024. Putin sought to justify his invasion of Ukraine on the actions of the Ukrainian government and NATO and I have some sympathy with that. I had been pointing out for years that Cult-owned, US-led NATO was poking Putin in the chest by moving eastwards to the Russian border with plans to allow Ukraine into the military 'alliance'. Ukrainian military attacks on Russian populations in the regions of Ukraine that border Russia added to the calculated incentive to make Putin respond. I get that. But we are back to the MAM and the way it has regressed into the old paradigm of taking sides. I understand why the MAMs wanted the interview to happen, so did I, to allow another angle of the Ukraine conflict to be presented. The response broke down literally across party lines with the Left condemning the interview because they supported Ukraine; and the Right delighted it was happening because they wanted the conflict to end. My sympathies were with the latter although not without a serious proviso. This is where the MAM has lost its way. The world consists of one-party states masquerading as political choice and much of the old alternative media knew that. The real power can be found one step back from Left and Right with the Cult manipulators in the shadows that work through both of them. This has been forgotten in the MAM which has regressed into Left bad/Right good. Elon Musk's tweets promote the same nonsense. The Left-Right puppet show is only a vehicle – and a smokescreen – for the real power structure that the public doesn't see.

The same situation can look very different when you step into the shadows where the manipulation is really coming from. Putin's interview was just such a case. The Cult is systematically moving global power from West to East focused primarily on China which is why

Western Cult corporations have been outsourcing production to China for decades to give them control over much of the global supply chain. China is planned to take control of Taiwan which it claims as its territory (it doesn't have enough already, you see). China would control a country that produces more than 60 percent of the world's semiconductors and more than 90 percent of the most advanced ones. These power everything from mobile phones to electric cars. Most come from one company, Taiwan Semiconductor Manufacturing Corporation. Consider the control this would hand to China. The Putin interview had to be seen in that context and the dismantling of Western dominance along with its very culture through unchecked mass immigration of other cultures into Europe and across the southern border of the United States. These migrants are overwhelmingly young adult men and, with regard to America, many are from China.

Putin told Carlson that Western economic sanctions in response to the Ukraine invasion had not affected Russia which had increased its trade with China and non-Western countries. They had instead hurt the West. Putin feigned bewilderment at why the West would hurt itself and threaten the end of the trade dominance of the dollar. 'I don't understand it myself.' Yes, you *do*, Mr Putin. He would have well known that this was planned to happen to further erode

Figure 41: President Putin with Cult-in-every-cell Henry Kissinger.

Western economic power while advancing dominance of the East. The emergence of the BRICS trading bloc becomes highly relevant. This began with Brazil, Russia, India, China, and South Africa (hence BRICS) and they were followed by Egypt, Ethiopia, Iran, and the United Arab Emirates. An offer to Saudi Arabia was being 'considered'. Putin ridiculously said that China was not a 'bogey man' and its foreign policy was not 'aggressive'. Try telling that to countries in Asia, Africa, and South America. He said that it was detrimental to America not to cooperate with China. America won't *cooperate*? It's outsourced much if its supply chain to China. The idea that Putin is not part of the Cult's global web is juvenile (Fig 41). He worked with the infamous and brutal KGB intelligence in the Soviet era rising to the rank of lieutenant colonel and was a liaison with the equally brutal East Germany Stasi secret police. He has been either president or prime minister of Russia since 1999 and president since 2012 and he had the rules changed to allow him to run for more successive terms which were formally limited to two. You don't do that in country like Russia if you are Mary Poppins.

Putin has committed Russia to carbon net zero to 'combat climate change' and a digital currency which are Cult and WEF agendas. Russia has its own version of UN Agenda 2030 which demands state and global control of *everything*. Putin responded to 'Covid' like the rest of world with lockdowns, vaccines, and suppression of political opposition and the media. The Putin government refused to release trial safety and effectiveness data on its Sputnik V 'Covid vaccine' because it was 'confidential and contains information constituting a commercial secret'. Heard that before? The lead 'scientist' behind the 'vaccine', Alexander Gintsburg, said the rapid deployment of vaccines will play a crucial role in fighting 'a possible pandemic pathogen, or Disease X, as they call it in Davos [the WEF]'. He said the 'Covid' pandemic had demonstrated how safe and effective vaccines could be created in as little as five months and not in decades as before. It's the same old, same old, that you get in the West. Putin is part of the game – the same global game in which Elon Musk plays a key role. The Carlson-Putin interview on Twitter/X was promoted as putting up two fingers to the system. It wasn't. The interview suited the Cult's psychological trickery. 'Save the West' MAMs see China as a threat and now it was promoting Putin as a hero when he is in fundamental alliance with China in the eastward movement of power. It was almost funny.

Putin's AI, Musk's AI, is *one* AI

The first Global Future 2045 Congress was hosted in Moscow in February 2012 when more than 50 of the 'world's leading scientists' met to discuss the 'future development of humankind'. The arrogance of that statement needs no comment. What was this 'development'? *Ahh*: 'To construct a global network of scientists to further research on the development of cybernetic technology, with the ultimate goal of transferring a human's individual consciousness to an artificial carrier.' A 'new mankind' had to be created with a 'technological revolution' and 'social transformation' achieved through the focus on 'nanotechnology, biotechnology, information technology, cognitive technology, genetics and robotics'. The transformation would mean new sources of energy, new architecture and transportation and allow 'unprecedented developments in new cognitive abilities, refined artificial intelligences and brain-computer interfaces', which would 'simulate complex systems'. Humanoid robots and cyborgs would be created, and human personalities would be transferred to an 'artificial carrier'. This would require a new civilisation or paradigm, new philosophy and ideology, new ethics, new psychology, new culture, and 'we must reset our limits to go beyond the Earth and the solar system'. *Reset* in Moscow in 2012 as they described precisely the WEF's 'Fourth Industrial Revolution' to create the era of 'neohumanity' by 2045-2050. It's same old, same old (2).

Are we really supposed to believe that countries are controlled by the Cult in the form of the United States, Canada, Europe and China, but not Russia? The Cult is a unified web which presents different faces to make you *think* they are different. Putin praised Donald Trump and Elon Musk, both standard bearers of the MAM. Carlson asked him about the potential dangers of AI and Putin said there was 'no stopping Elon Musk'. The world would have to reach an agreement with him to stop the worst excesses of AI. Musk was a 'smart' businessman who would be welcome in Russia. We are looking at a global web while the MAM only sees parts. This is one of the major reasons why the alternative media has been targeted with so many next-to-clueless here-and-no-furthers.

'New Media' is old media

The alternative media that appeared years after I started is being monumentally hijacked and that suits the Cult perfectly. They know they can't suppress everything until they have AI fully operational and in the interim the idea is to focus 'alternative' attention on those areas that will change nothing, especially the irrelevant party politics within one-party states. The MAM is bringing so little new to the table like the old alternative media once did. It is going round and round regurgitating the same old stuff that was in my books long ago. Where is the original research on the scale that we once had? Today it's all about presentation, image, clickbait, and mutual cross-promotion in the absence of anything really new to say. I see interviews labelled 'ground-breaking' when they are nothing of the sort. It is 'ground-breaking' information we have long known about simply repackaged. What the Cult and its demonic masters don't want people to know is that the illusory reality we think we are experiencing is the whole foundation of the conspiracy for mass human control. They don't want us to know that what we believe to be real is only a dream or that this dream is induced using AI technology which is breathtakingly more advanced than what Musk and his cronies and masters are seeking to impose on human society. We will now concentrate on this level of the conspiracy for the rest of the book and leave the MAM to poke around in the cul-de-sacs they have been given to pore over until AI takes over completely. Here kitty, kitty, kitty …

I emphasise again: I am not saying that to be part of the MAM is to *knowingly* serve the Cult agenda. Some of them will be, but not the majority. One reason that I highlight what is going on is an effort to awaken those who have been caught in the Cult pincer movement of promotion and funding for 'safe' MAM people. Many have the potential to look at these events anew if they have the balls to do so in the knowledge that there are likely to be promotion and funding consequences for going too far. It is vital this information is *circulated* within the MAM so the genuine among them can reconsider how they are being used by the very networks they say they oppose. I hope there are signs of this happening by the time you read this as they realise how they are being perceptually corralled and how much more there is to know about the global conspiracy than they are saying. But, given the money available for conforming, I won't be breathing in and waiting. They have a choice to go on serving the Beast agenda, and doing well financially from Beast largesse and promotion, or truly looking the Beast in its all-seeing eye.

I have no desire for a fight or conflict with the MAM or anyone else. I do want us to come together behind a collective goal, but not on any terms or at any price. I am totally supportive of those seeking to uncover the truth no matter what that truth turns out to be. It's those who are knowingly and unknowingly suppressing the search for truth that I have a problem with and on that subject I will *never* be quiet.

Postscript: I was shown this reading of Elon Musk as the book was going to press by South African professional psychic Kendall Whalley. I include it here because it perfectly captures my own view of the Musk Psyop:

> I see him as a pressure release valve. Like on a pressure cooker. Or a step-down transformer. What he does is positive enough to get buy-in from those who are stepping out of 'matrix thinking' and then he pulls them back in. I think he is like a fringe creature that appears like a freedom fighter but is a brilliant misdirection implement that actually channels people back from the brink of greater consciousness into the matrix.

> He is a massive tool for the agenda. He appears to be a free spirit, but is a servant to the eagle and thus has the capacity to flaunt the rules, as his core messaging is actually to corral the dissident critical thinkers into an acceptable deviation paddock, that still leads to the slaughterhouse. How? A mix of mind control, manipulation and ego-stimulating misinformation that is almost accurate enough to fool those that have let go of the rock, but have no direction.

This is what the MAM in totality is doing, too, mostly without knowing. All the religion promotion is part of this.

CHAPTER SIX

BIG Picture

If you spend your life over analysing every encounter you will always see the tree, but never the forest

Shannon L. Alder

The above quote captures the essence of the left side of the brain which dominates – *creates* – human society and has seized control of much of the 'alternative' arena. Reality looks very different to right-brain and whole-brain perspectives. With the latter, you can see the tree *and* the forest.

Take one step out of the body into the auric field, the electromagnetic consciousness field that we call the mind (Fig 42). The brain is not the

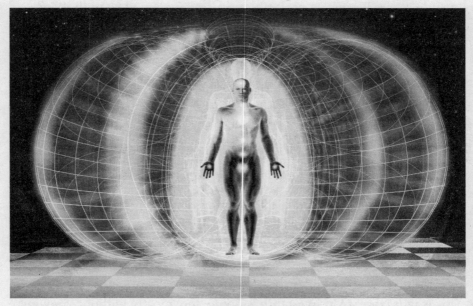

Figure 42: The human aura is the mind, an electromagnetic field connecting with the body's central nervous system. They interact to form the entity we call human. (Image by Neil Hague.)

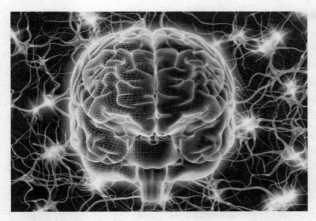

Figure 43: The brain is not the origin of consciousness, but the *processor* of electrical and electromagnetic information from the auric mind (subconscious) into body/brain awareness known as the conscious mind.

Figure 44: The human auric field or what we call mind. Colours in the aura change as thoughts and emotions (perceptions) change because different thoughts and emotions emit different frequencies and, in turn, different colours are different frequencies.

source of consciousness, but rather a *processor* of consciousness and information in the form of *frequency* and *electricity* (Fig 43). Auric mind and what people call the soul operate outside the body/brain anchored in the visible light range of matter (Fig 44). Mainstream science has long known that thoughts and emotions are represented as frequencies (waves) which relate to the nature of the thought and emotion. Now we can see the origin of right, left, and whole brain people. If the auric mind is more open it will deliver information, thought, perception, to the brain that matches the frequencies of the right hemisphere. The closed-minded will communicate frequencies that match the left hemisphere and be routed through that side. The Global Cult seeks to influence this through the manipulation of how the brain processes information and I will come to that. If we override that manipulation (and we can) it is not the brain that makes the hemisphere choice – it's the auric mind and how its perceptual state (frequency state) syncs with the two hemispheres. Balanced minds will communicate powerfully to both sides depending on the subject and situation and their corpus callosum will be highly active communicating between the two. The auric mind is where our perceptions are formed from a wide range of sources from human life experience and programming to, ideally, expanded awareness way beyond the simulation. The Cult and its demonic mission control works incessantly to block access to expanded awareness to isolate the auric mind in the perception of being only 'human' or a 'soul' subordinate to its version of 'God'.

The 'human world' consists of the tiny frequency range that we know as matter (perceived within 'visible light') and our sight sense is tuned to that frequency (Fig 45). We only 'see' forms of matter with apparently

Figure 45: Different worlds or realities operate within different bands of frequency and wavelength while sharing the same 'space'. The human world is only one and it's tiny. (Image by Neil Hague.)

empty space in between. Matter *is* basically the human realm and 'empty space' (which isn't) is a whole other dimension that our eyes/brain cannot decode unless we have psychic gifts with an expanded range of vision. Most people cannot see the auric field while a minority can if they have this 'sixth-sense' that can expand vision into what is known as the Astral dimension. The Astral can be termed the Fourth Dimension if we take the world of matter to be the Third Dimension. These are not on top of each other like a chest of drawers. They share the same space while on different *wavelengths* in the way analogue TV and radio stations/channels (frequencies) share the same space without interference unless they are very close on the dial (Fig 46). Where is the Astral? You are looking at it all day every day. You know it as 'empty space' and it interacts with matter in ways that I will be describing (Fig 47). 'Paranormal' activity and ghosts are Astral phenomena (Fig 48). I am going to briefly present in this chapter a

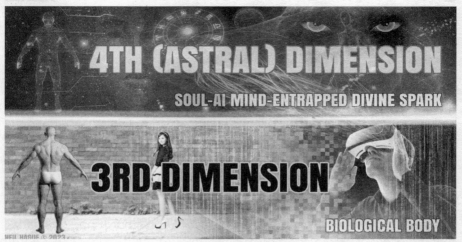

Figure 46: The human and Astral realms are different bands of frequency that share the same 'space' like wavelengths of different radio and television channels. The Astral is often known as the Fourth Dimension while matter is the Third Dimension. Astral reality is outside the perceptual confines of visible light and so beyond human sight. I'll explain the 'entrapped Divine Spark' shortly. (Image by Neil Hague.)

Figure 47: Form is the frequency of matter within the band of visible light. 'Empty space' is the Astral.

Figure 48: What we call 'ghosts' are Astral phenomena that enter our visual reality. They appear ethereal because they are not fully on our frequency – like interference on a radio station. If we were on their frequency they would look as 'solid' as we do.

summary of 35 years of research into the nature of reality and, as always, there will be more to know. There is *always* more to know. I will then expand into new areas of knowledge. The reader must decide what they make of what I say. It is not for me to tell people what to believe.

We are awareness

Our Infinite state is one of awareness – a state of being *aware*. That's it. No body, no form, no mind, no soul. We are simply *aware*, But how aware? We could be infinitely aware in the limitless perception that

some call 'God'; or we can be only body-aware and believe that we are
Bob or Brenda who work in the office or the store. Both are states of
awareness. They are just fantastically different. I have long exposed that
Astral entities beyond visible light conspire to control us via their assets
in the Global Cult operating in our realm of matter. They do so by
dictating our level of awareness to trap us in low-frequency perception,
or density. The lower and slower the frequency, the denser the energy
becomes until it enters the frequency of matter which our eyes/brain can
'see'. The higher the frequency the more ethereal something appears until
it vibrates so quickly that it *dis*appears from human sight. Go back to
those earlier figures of visible light as only a smear of the electromagnetic
spectrum which is itself estimated to be only 0.005 percent of the energy
in this one universe. We realise that humans can see bordering on *nothing*
while *everything* else in all Infinity is beyond our ability to perceive within
visible light. This is vital to understand and transforms our perspective of
human reality. 'Mysteries' dissolve into 'ah-ha' revelations. Entities and
craft cannot appear out of 'nowhere' and disappear into 'nowhere' from
the perspective of five-sense material ignorance. That's impossible,
surely? No it isn't. We see the entity or craft when it appears out of the
Astral by entering the band of visible light and when it leaves it is no
longer perceivable to the sight sense. Something 'appears and
disappears', but *only* to the human observer.

Crucial to know is that thoughts and emotions are emitted as
frequencies. Fear, anxiety, hatred, depression, resentment, regret, are long,
low, slow frequencies. Joy, love, happiness, gratitude, and appreciation
are short, fast, high frequencies. The sum total of our thoughts and
emotions, including those located in the subconscious, together form
what we call our perceptions (Figs 49 and 50). These dictate the frequency
make-up of our auric mind electrometric field. We should note that the
terms 'dense' and 'thick' for those considered not very bright are
accurately describing what they are. 'Bright' and 'not bright' are the
same. The lower and denser the frequency the less 'light' (information,
insight, 'God') can break through the energetic density and influence
perception. We form our perceptions from *information* which could be
anything from a personal experience to the ten o'clock news. The Cult
created the 'education' system and owns the mainstream (and much of
the 'alternative') media on behalf of its Astral demonic masters for the
very purpose of controlling perception to control *frequency*. If the target
population can be held in a low-frequency state of fear, anxiety, hatred,
depression, resentment, and regret their energetic field (awareness) will
be dense and block high-frequency expanded awareness.

Consciousness communicates into the reality of matter through the
biological brain/body, or biological computer. Thoughts and emotions
generated with their distinct frequencies dictate which side of the brain

Figure 49: The auric mind electromagnetic field stores information known as memory and perception. Their nature dictates the frequency of the auric mind and how it expresses itself through the brain. Notice how the field connects with the body's central nervous system through the spine/brain. The mind is *not* the body which is only a vehicle for consciousness to experience this reality.

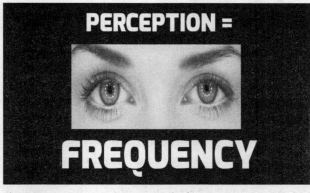

Figure 50: Our perceptions generate the frequencies we emit and the Global Cult seeks to manipulate fear and other low-vibration mental, emotional, and thus frequency states.

will be dominant as I said. A sense of apartness and separation generates frequencies that match the left-brain decoding system while a sense of unity and connection will be frequency-routed through the right. If you are in this world (left-brain), but not of it (right-brain) you will have the balance to be 'whole-brained'. This is the ideal. You can operate with material detail (left-brain / 'intellect') and still perceive that all parts are connected (right brain awareness). You can function within the finite and be aware of the infinite. Bombardment of left-brain information and perception through Cult-created 'education' and media is designed to program a sense of apartness and separation produce a left-brain-dominated population. What follows is a human perception that everything is unconnected to everything else when everything *is* connected by the energetic field that the sight sense perceives as 'empty space'.

There are other ways to ensure left-brain dominance. I wrote in *The Dream* about what I say is a biological program encoded in the body field that I will call the biological mind and I'll be describing this in more detail. The biological mind is a base perceptual program encoded to influence the brain to give people their sense of apartness, separation, and solidity / physicality. Consciousness can override this program by changing the way the brain decodes reality, but for those who don't activate that expanded awareness (open mind) the biological program will dictate their perception and actions throughout a human life. They become, in effect, like a non-player character in a virtual reality game that is completely controlled by the game itself. The great majority of humans pass through 'life' simply responding to these 'software' impulses while their consciousness is an excluded spectator. Another technique to isolate people in the left-hemisphere is to put the right-brain to sleep by emphasising information that stimulates the left at the expense of the right. We return to the left-brain domination of 'education' and media, and the chemical and frequency impact on the corpus callosum to block right brain perspective from influencing the left. The 'Cloud' of technologically generated electromagnetic information is doing this. A biological computer body consists of computer codes. The corpus callosum has specific codes that can be targeted by electromagnetic frequencies and the technique is literally like hacking a computer. Information held on computer hard drives can be wiped by a powerful enough electromagnetic field and the Cloud is ever more obviously impacting on the brain and its information processing. Most people, including many in the MAM, have no idea how fundamentally important the Cloud is to human control even though it's being expanded across the world by their MAM God Elon Musk and others.

World in your 'head'

The brain/body has another rather crucial function – to decode the very reality that we perceive as 'physicality'. I have described this in many books, including *The Dream*, so I will be brief here. Human reality is a virtual reality simulation created by the Astral demonic 'gods' of ancient religions and modern-day Satanism. I will expand on this as the book progresses. Conventional science is obsessed with the 'Big Bang' in which a single atom somehow exploded to create the Universe, planets, stars, matter, and Bill's aunty Ethel. The concept is so ludicrous that it's embarrassing and so full of holes it would put a giant colander to shame. The simulation, or 'Matrix', is a field of information akin to Wi-Fi (or the Cloud) and the brain/body decodes that information into the physicality that we *think* we are experiencing in the form of solid 'things'. Perceived solidity is only decoded frequencies or wave information in the same way that what you see on your computer screen is information from the Wi-Fi field decoded into a very different form (Fig 51). The simulation virtual reality field is the 'Wi-Fi' and the brain/body is the computer. There is no 'physical reality' without the body decoder. There is only the simulation field of information encoded as wave frequencies (Fig 52). There is no computer screen reality without the computer decoder. There is only a field of information encoded as

Figure 51: We decode human reality is the same way that computers decode Wi-Fi. The entire Internet is in the electromagnetic radiation field – Wi-Fi – and the computer decodes that information into a totally different form on the screen. The brain does the same with the simulation field.

Figure 52: The simulation is a field of information that the body biological computer decodes into the reality we experience as 'physical' and external to us.

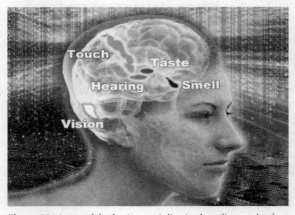

Figure 53: Areas of the brain specialise in decoding each of the five senses and the information is fused to present the illusory sense of an external 'physical' reality. (Image by Neil Hague.)

frequency in the technologically generated electromagnetic field that we know as Wi-Fi. The body/simulation decoding sequence works like this:

The five senses connect with the simulation field of information encoded as frequency or vibration. Ears are an obvious example as they pick up sound wave frequencies and communicate them to the brain as electrical signals. All five senses function in the same way. They transform frequency information into electrical information which is then delivered to the brain. This, in turn, decodes the electrical into digital holographic information that we perceive as the world of human physicality. Different areas of the brain specialise in decoding different senses and the brain fuses this information into the world that we think we 'see' (Fig 53). We experience this as a reality external to us when it is all happening in the decoding processes of the brain

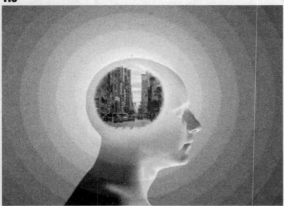

Figure 54: Where the 'external' and 'physical' world really exists. (Image by Gareth Icke.)

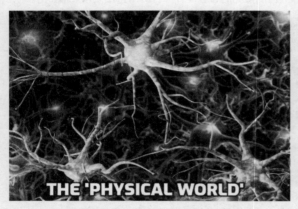

Figure 55: The 'physical world' of perceived solidity only exists in the decoding processes of brain and body.

(Figs 54 and 55). What we see on a computer screen is *inside* the computer. The principle is identical in theme. The body biological computer is the conduit between incarnate consciousness and the simulation and decodes a microscopic reality of 'matter' compared with the infinity of life and possibility. An article in the science magazine, *Wonderpedia*, said:

Every second, 11 million sensations crackle along these [brain] pathways ... The brain is confronted with an alarming array of images, sounds and smells which it rigorously filters down until it is left with a manageable list of around 40. Thus 40 sensations per second make up what we perceive as reality.

Our reality is constructed every second from 40 snapshots of information ('sensations') from a potential *eleven million*. We remain consciously oblivious to the other 10,999,960 which are absorbed by the subconscious. Modern technology/AI are mirroring and mimicking the way that we create the illusion of living in a solid world. A scene in the first *Matrix* movie captures the situation that humanity faces. The 'Matrix' or simulation is all around us as a field of information that the body/brain is decoding into an illusory 'physical world' to entrap consciousness in a fake perception of reality. The Morpheus character tells a bewildered Neo:

The Matrix is everywhere. It is all around us, even now in this very room. You can see it when you look out your window, or you turn on your television. You can feel it when you go to work, when you go to church, when you pay your taxes. It is the world that has been pulled over your eyes to blind you from the truth.'

'What truth?'

'That you are a slave, Neo. Like everyone else, you were born into bondage ... born into a prison that you cannot smell or taste or touch. A prison for your mind.

A number of scientists over the years have suggested that 'physical' reality only exists when it is being *observed*. One mainstream headline about research at the Australian National University said: 'Your entire life is an ILLUSION: New test backs up theory that the world doesn't exist until we look at it.' This sounds utterly bizarre to the five-sense mind, but it's true. Take the example of a virtual reality game. What you experience through the headset or computer in each moment is the only 'place' the game exists in that form. Elsewhere it is computer codes, circuits, electricity, and electromagnetic fields. The game only exists as you perceive it when you are *observing* the part of the game (software program) that is being delivered to you by the headset second by second. The Internet only exists in the form that we see on the computer screen when it is *projected on the screen*. Everywhere else the Internet is Wi-Fi and electrical circuitry. Scientists who have postulated that experienced reality only exists when we look at it have dubbed this the 'Observer Effect'. It should really be called the '*Decoder* Effect'. The act of observation (attention) activates the decoding processes of the five senses and brain to transform waves or frequencies into electrical information which the brain decodes into the digital holographic information that we experience as the 'outside world'. It is not 'outside' at all. It is *inside* – inside the brain. What we make of that reality is decided by our *perceptions* of reality. We may all decode the same car passing by, but what we think of it will be different. I like it, I don't like it. The colour is horrible, I love the colour. Nobel physicist John Wheeler said that 'no phenomenon is a real phenomenon until it is an *observed* phenomenon', or, as I would say, a *decoded* phenomenon. Scientists have been perplexed by how frequency waves can also be particles *at the same time*. 'Surely', the left-brain says in desperation for certainty, 'they must be one or the other'. The wave is the foundation information and experiments have shown that it becomes a particle when the wave is *observed*. An *Epoch Times* article entitled 'Your Mind Can Control Matter' described the result of one such experiment:

Atomic particles were shown to also be waves. Whether they manifested as waves or as particles depended on whether someone was looking.

Observation influenced the physical reality of the particles – in more technical language, observation collapsed the wave function.

The *attention* of the observer transforms the wave into a particle or, put another way, the simulation wavefield of information transforms frequencies into what we perceive to be physical reality. I say the wave *becomes* a particle, but the wave still exists while taking a particle form. How can this be? The wave is the foundation information field of the simulation, and the particle is that information being decoded into 'physicality'. When the wave is not being observed it remains as just a wave of potential waiting to be manifested by observation/attention. Does Wi-Fi information cease to exist when a computer decodes it into the form we see on the screen? No – Wi-Fi is the constant and is being decoded by multiple computers in the same moment. When not being decoded Wi-Fi is only in its radiation state. I have long said that our 'physical' reality is holographic. Rapidly advancing holographic technology producing digital holograms is mimicking our experienced reality and to such an extent that experts in this field say it won't be long before you won't be able to tell the difference between technological holograms and our 'real world' (a 'real world' that is also holographic).

Holographic 'physicality'

Even now the best holograms can look as solid as the 'real world' when they have no actual solidity. It is not solidity that stops us walking through walls and each other. It is *electromagnetic* frequency resistance that we experience as solidity resistance. 'Ghosts' appearing out of the Astral realm can pass through apparently 'solid objects' because they are such a different frequency to matter. The creation of holograms mirrors the wave-particle so-called paradox. Holograms are created by a laser divided into two parts (Fig 56). One part makes a waveform copy of the image being photographed (working beam). The other goes directly onto a holographic print (reference beam).

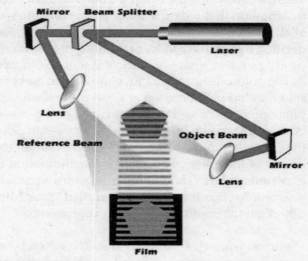

Figure 56: How human holograms are created.

Figure 57: Holograms encode the information of the subject in a wavefield construct and when a laser 'reads' that wavefield a three-dimensional image of the subject is projected.

The two then collide on the print to create a pattern that is encoded with the information in a *waveform* state of the object being holographically recorded (Fig 57). A laser or what is known as coherent light is then directed at this waveform construct and a three-dimensional image of the object is manifested. Even more sophisticated

Figure 58: I have watched over the years how holograms have become ever more sophisticated and 'real'. The late Roy Orbison and Buddy Holly on a 'hologram tour' long after they departed this world.

ways of generating holograms are now being developed (Fig 58 and, overleaf, Fig 59). The point to emphasise is the waveform construct on the print continues to exist *at the same time* that the 3-D particle image is being projected. What's more – it *has* to exist. The waveform construct is the *source* of the information from which the 3-D image is projected. No waveform, no 3-D particle image. They are different encoded and decoded expressions of each other. The wave-particle mystery is therefore solved. This is all happening in the brain in the case of human experience. The body-brain is also a decoded hologram in its 'physical'

Figure 59: Legendary band Abba holographically recreated as they were in their younger days for their holographic stage shows described by critics as 'scarily real'.

Figure 60: The body and brain are also holograms decoded into a holographically 'physical' form by the auric mind. (Image by Neil Hague.)

form. Their base state is a wavefield and, yes, we even decode our own body through the auric mind/brain connection into illusory 'physicality' (Fig 60). The brain is a wavefield construct of information and thus can be fluid and have 'plasticity'. Changes at the wavefield level of the brain are decoded into holographic 'physical' change. Illness is an imbalance in the auric field played through as imbalance in the body which is a decoded particle manifestation of information in the auric field. If you are energetically balanced you must be 'physically' balanced. Holograms are a 3-D image projected from a 2-D information source – the wavefield construct. Scientists have established that our 3-D reality of 'matter' is created (decoded) from information encoded in 2-D. 'Physical' reality is holographic.

A skilled hypnotist can block the brain from decoding reality and make people 'disappear'; or rather, not manifest in 'physicality'. The body's base state is wavefield information and to manifest within visible light this must be decoded into holographic form. If it isn't, it remains invisible to human sight. A gifted hypnotist can program the brain not to decode a particular field whether a human body or object. An example I have often quoted is described by Michael Talbot in his 1990s book, *The Holographic Universe*. A father under hypnosis was sitting on a chair looking into the belly of his standing daughter and he *could not see her*. Things became even stranger when he was able to read the inscription on a watch held by the hypnotist while the daughter stood between her father and the watch. The hypnotist programmed the father's brain not to decode the wavefield that was his daughter. Unless he did she was not in his holographic visible light perception of reality and could not be a barrier to seeing the watch behind her (Fig 61). Everyone else in the room could see her without having their decoding system tinkered with like the father. The body-simulation dynamic is again the same as Wi-Fi and computers. Wi-Fi is encoded information, and the computer is encoded to *decode* that information. No decoding – nothing on the screen. Another similarity is that both the Internet and the simulation are interactive. The Internet affects us with its information and we can post information to change the Internet. We are influenced (fundamentally) by the simulation, but our mental and emotional frequencies can influence the simulation. The more people that awaken to expanded awareness, the more the simulation must change and respond.

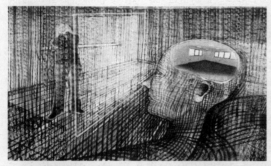
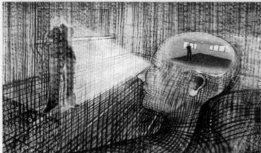

Figure 61: If the information field of a person or object is not decoded into holographic form the conscious mind will not see it within the visible light band. If your computer does not decode Wi-Fi it cannot appear on the screen. (Image by Neil Hague.)

This is another reason to keep us asleep in low-vibrational density.

'Empty' atoms

Confirmation that our reality is not physical is the atom which is *supposed* to form the solid world of matter. There can be few more ridiculous claims when an atom has *no solidity*. We are meant to believe that the physical world is made from something that *isn't* 'physical'. Mainstream science tells us that atoms consist of a nucleus orbited by electrons (Fig 62). The 'empty space' (Astral dimension) between them in the graphic is only symbolic to allow the image to fit the page. The real distance between them is something like this: If an atom

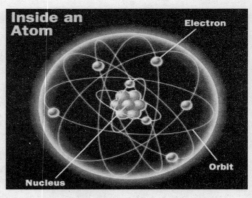

Figure 62: We are told that atoms are the building blocks of 'solid matter' and yet atoms have no solidity.

was the size of a baseball stadium the nucleus would be the size of a ten-cent piece. Everything else is 'empty'. Go deep enough into the nucleus and electrons and they would be 'empty', too. They are subatomic particles (below the size of the 'atom') and operate in the 'quantum' realm (hence quantum physics which is the study of this reality). Electrons are really *waves* which scientists portray within atoms as particles to simplify their nature. Particles, like 'atoms', exist only as wave phenomena decoded by the observer's attention into what we believe to be a physical world. Associate Professor Andrew Truscott, who was involved in the Australian National University Observer Effect experiments, said: 'At the quantum level, reality does not exist if you are not looking at it.' Humans are trapped in a perceptual prison in which the very reality they think they are experiencing is illusory and this leads to mass perceptual control by the demonic realm in the Astral that has specifically created the simulation to entrap consciousness in illusion. This is why I am challenging the MAM to open its mind. Perception is the key to manifesting reality. You not only control human behaviour if you control perception – you create the human world. George Berkeley (1685-1753), who gave his name to Berkeley University, said: 'The only things we perceive are our perceptions.' He realised in the 18th century that objects of matter cannot exist without being perceived (decoded). Writer Joseph Michael Straczynski put it this way:

> Accidents happen, that's what everyone says. But in a quantum universe there are no such things as accidents, only possibilities and probabilities folded into existence by perception.

Control perception and you control (create) the world. You control perception through religion, 'education', media, mainstream Internet platforms, and the Mainstream Alternative Media (MAM). More than anything perception is controlled by the belief that this illusory physical world is real. That's the biggest gotcha of all. Change perception and you change your life experience. Witness what happens when you walk on hot coals believing your feet will burn. They burn. Go into an altered state of consciousness to override that belief and they don't burn. I have witnessed this many times. Perception is all because the world is an induced *dream*. In the first 4,000 words of this chapter humanity's entire sense of reality has been rewritten. Ponder on how far we have come in these brief paragraphs alone from the central focus of the MAM on politics, Trump, Musk, and co. You may appreciate now why I am so vehement in my challenge to the Barricade Brigade who are focussing dissident attention on the twigs while the forest goes unexposed. They are poking around in the symptoms and ignoring the cause while spinning around in an eddy of constant repetition of old knowledge that was in my books decades ago. Meanwhile, the river of Infinity flows past them. I don't have a problem with that. They must focus on whatever they choose. I cover the five-sense stuff and have done for 35 years. My problem is the way they exclude those who *are* flowing with the river, even ridicule, dismiss or ignore them. In doing so, they focus the attention of questioning people in the myopia of the conspiracy and divert them from where it is all ultimately emerging.

Deeper and deeper

I describe in *The Trap* where my information has come from these past 35 years. It's a combination of tangible fact and intuitive 'knowing' supported by as much documentation as I can gather. I have applied the same process to this book. I have read and watched a long stream of accounts describing near-death experiences (NDEs) from those whose consciousness has withdrawn from this reality at bodily death and returned when the body was revived (Fig 63). Even medical professionals like Dutch cardiologist Pim van Lommel have become fascinated by the number of patients that died before being revived who have told compellingly common-

Figure 63: A near-death experience (NDE) is when our consciousness/mind withdraws from the body and experiences a completely different reality – mostly the Astral dimension. Others can project their awareness out of human reality while the body is still alive. This is known as an out-of-body-experience, or 'OBE'.

theme stories of what they experienced. I say *even* medical professionals because mainstream 'science' is founded on consciousness being a product of the brain. They believe that when the brain dies so must consciousness. Lommel began researching the subject in 1986 and has written several books. He was astonished by how many patients were describing the same series of events. They recalled leaving the body and feeling no pain while looking down from above at hospital staff working to revive them. They could recall in detail what was happening while they were 'dead' and conversations between staff that could be corroborated. His patients told him of all the classic near-death phenomena. Common tales are extremely compelling when trying to understand the post-death realms. Consciousness withdraws when the body ceases to function ('dies') and the body ceases to decode this level of the simulation into a sense of physical reality. What we call death is only a transfer of *attention* from matter to the Astral when the 'headset'

body-brain ceases to function and we have the sense of leaving one world and entering another (Fig 64). 'Death' is only a transfer of conscious *attention* back from the body (matter) to the Astral (or higher) and is absolutely *nothing* to fear (Fig 65). Fear of death comes from the ignorance of life. There are other factors to incarnation that I will introduce subsequently. Most people are terrified, or at least have trepidation, about death. The greatest human fear is fear the unknown. Demonic Astral entities described at length in my many other books maintain and manipulate this fear of unknown 'death' by keeping from us the true nature of the Infinite 'I' and what

Figure 64: The body decoding systems focus attention during a human experience within the almost infinitesimal frequency band of 'matter'. When the body ceases to function (decode the matter level of the simulation) our attention is released and we enter another reality. 'Death' is simply a transfer of conscious attention. (Image by Neil Hague.)

Figure 65: 'Death' is taking off the headset. It is nothing to fear.

bodily death really is.

The simulation has many levels and not only the human material. The Astral contains multiple frequency bands of the simulation – the biblical 'many mansions in my father's house'. Our consciousness moves between them and the human 'physical' through reincarnation, or the Buddhist Wheel of Samsara. Reincarnation is said to be necessary to 'learn lessons' through human experience to eventually reach a state of 'enlightenment' which no longer needs to stay on the 'wheel' and is free to be released into Infinity. I don't buy any of that for a micro-second. The demonic created the simulation to trap consciousness on the wheel to feed off low-vibrational energy frequencies emitted especially in the human realm through fear, anxiety, hatred, depression, resentment, regret, and pain of all kinds. The simulation is designed to generate events and experiences that initiate those responses to produce those frequencies. They match the frequency band of the demonic realm and can be absorbed as energetic sustenance and power which is then recycled back onto humans in the form of control. Where does demonic power come from and the same with its Global Cult? From *us*. The Morpheus character in *The Matrix* movies

Figure 66: Human plight in a sentence.

described the simulated reality as 'a computer-generated dream world, built to keep us under control in order to change a human being into this'. He was holding a battery, and the symbolism was portraying human reality as it really is (Fig 66). Our controllers are feeding off human mental and emotional energy which results from that control. I'll have much more detail as we progress.

Top to bottom

I'll start with the Infinite 'I' and work down through the levels to human. The Infinite 'I' is pure no-form awareness that I call Spirit. The Spirit is in harmony and unity with the all-knowing state that I call the *All That Is, Has Been, And Ever Can Be* which is in *awareness* that it is *All That Is, Has Been, And Ever Can Be*. Here we have the meaning of what people perceive as 'God' although we will see how so many are worshipping a fake 'God' that is the force behind their perceptual enslavement. The *All That Is* refers to a state of *all* awareness that *knows* that it is all awareness. We are each an expression of this consciousness and we are all *ONE*. We are *always* ONE because everything is connected, but perception withdraws from that *awareness* of the ONE as we traverse the frequency bands of Creation. The lower the frequency, the denser the vibration, the harder it becomes to remember our true 'I'. The human vibration of matter is seriously low and dense. The Astral is the same, although less so the higher you go. The densest layers of the Astral are in the lower levels of frequency which interact with matter and this is where the demonic resides. The five senses and left-brain cannot process something that 'is', 'has been', and 'ever can be' when they are welded to the perception of 'time'. You cannot be 'past', 'present' and 'future' in the same moment. You must be one or the other. What a great example of the illusion and how it skews human reality. There *is no time*. There is only the NOW moment. Time is a construct of the simulation which we decode into a false sense of reality. Where are you when you experience the 'present'? You are in the NOW. Okay, the five senses and left-brain can get that. Where are you when you think about the 'past'? You are in the NOW. Where *were* you when you experienced what you currently believe to be the 'past'? You were in the NOW. Where *are* you when you think about the 'future'? You are in the NOW. Where *will* you be when you experience what you currently believe is the future? You will be in the NOW. There is only the NOW (Fig 67).

The *All That Is, Has Been, And Ever Can Be* can be described as all possibility and all potential waiting to be made manifest by perception. We are all that Infinite Possibility and all expressions of the *All That Is*. We have simply forgotten and been manipulated and encouraged to forget. I will refer to that 'God' self as *Spirit* which is the formless eternal state of awareness. Spirit experiences realms of form through a 'shell' or

field that resonates to the same frequency as the desired reality. Consciousness is vibrating too fast to interact with the frequency band of matter. My consciousness cannot tap the keys of this computer without a body vibrating within the same band as the keys. The same is true throughout Creation and the 'body'

Figure 67: 'A few simple questions reveal that there is no 'time', only the illusion of it. (Image by Gareth Icke.)

field can be high frequency, ethereal, or have the severe density of human form. It depends on the realm you wish to experience and again the denser it becomes the harder it is to stay connected and influenced by Spirit and that projection of Spirit into form that ancients named the Divine Spark. This is our connection to our Infinite 'I' of Spirit and when we lose touch with that Spirit, and cease to be influenced by its wisdom, the trouble really starts. This is the human plight and why our reality is as it is. The Divine Spark experiences the simulation through the human body in the realm of matter and through what is widely known as the 'soul' in the Astral. The soul is the level trapped on the Wheel of Samsara cycle of reincarnation in and out of the human world of matter. When we leave the Astral and the simulation trap we leave behind the soul. An aspect of the soul 'incarnates' for a human experience through a connection to the electromagnetic auric mind (Fig 68).

The demonic has no problem with people believing in the soul as their true 'I' because it means that your perception of self and reality is still in the simulation. The game is to so program Divine Spark perception that it takes on a whole new identity of being a 'human' and a soul that needs to constantly reincarnate to 'learn lessons and evolve' in the same way that people wearing a virtual reality headset think they

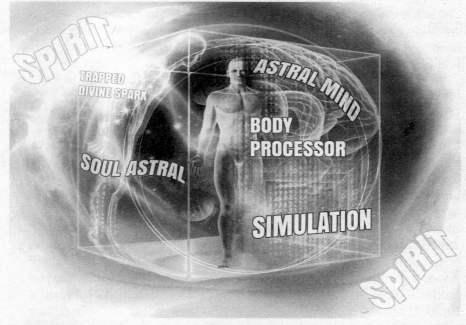

Figure 68: The true and infinite 'I' is the Spirit of All That Is. An aspect of this which ancients referred to as the 'Divine Spark' was enticed into the simulation where it became encased in an Astral frequency energy field known as the 'soul'. Part of the soul 'incarnates' into the deep density of the human realm (matter) with an attachment to the body via what we call 'mind' – the electromagnetic auric mind. (Image by Neil Hague.)

are living the headset reality (Fig 69). A Divine Spark is a projection of Spirit, an expression of the *All That Is In Awareness of Itself*, and it does not need to *evolve*. The trap is for the Divine Spark to forget its true nature through the bombardment of information and experience within the simulation whether that be in the Astral as a 'soul' or in matter as a 'human'. Imagine you

Figure 69: Body and soul operate like a virtual reality headset feeding a false reality to the Divine Spark which believes that it is human and, between incarnations, a soul 'evolving' by 'learning lessons' through repeated human experience. In fact, the whole deal is a simulated illusion based on selling a false self-identity, or 'Phantom Self'.

are a Divine Spark encased in fields of energy – the soul/human body – which is endlessly deluged with information telling you that you are what you are not. Spirit is what we are, Never mind who you think you are, or what you do, there is a part of you which is that all-knowing Spirit, the *All That Is* in awareness of itself. Spirit in awareness of its creative power can manifest 'worlds' and realities galore. There is no limit to what is possible within *all* possibility. Creation is teeming with realities of every imaginable kind.

Disparate agreement

I describe in *The Dream* and other books the theme that you find throughout religions and ancient cultures of a 'fallen' race that Christians link to the Devil, Satan, and 'Fallen Angels'. Islam's 'Devil' figure is Shaytan or Iblis and Gnostic believers speak of Yaldabaoth. The theme is incredibly common. I am always searching for patterns based on what disparate people, groups, and eras *agree* upon. The symbolism of the Devil, Satan, Shaytan, Yaldabaoth, is describing a deeply disturbed, distorted and low-vibrational consciousness which Native Americans call Wetiko (among other names). They describe Wetiko as a 'mind virus' and this consciousness under multiple names has 'fallen' down the frequencies to locate in the Astral dimension. Satan, Shaytan, Yaldabaoth, Wetiko, manipulates human society and its Astral realms through entities known as demons (Christianity); Jinn or Djinn (Islam and pre-Islamic Arabia); Archons (Gnostic); Flyers or Predators (Central America); and many other names in religions and cultures across the world. Non-human Astral entities are also described as the Watchers and Shining Ones. Why 'shining' will become clear. I will use the term

Yaldabaoth from this point for the distorted, inverted, consciousness, and Archons for the entities. Yaldabaoth must feed off human mental and emotional energy because it is so frequency-detached from the *All That Is*, or Prime Creator, that it has no energy source. The simulation is its means of perceptually entrapping consciousness to generate its energetic 'food' and sustenance.

I have been stupendously ridiculed for saying since 1996 that a reptilian race along with the 'ET' type known as the 'Greys' are manipulating humanity from hidden realms (lower-frequency levels of the Astral). It was far too much – and remains so for many – for the left-brain and five senses to cope with such a concept. If that were true, why can't we see them?? Well, a considerable number have and do see them. Most do not because humans can see *nothing* outside the laughably narrow band of visible light. Astral entities must manifest in matter for them to be seen by the body sight sense. Gnostic writings and documents were found in an earthen jar in 1945 at Nag Hammadi, about 80 miles north of Luxor in Egypt. Gnosticism believes the material world is the work of a fraudulent 'god' – Yaldabaoth. Nag Hammadi texts are estimated to have been sealed in the jar around 400 AD with the content going back much further to ancient Greece and philosophers such as Socrates, Plato and Aristotle. They believed that mind and Spirit are the real reality and matter is an illusory manifestation of mind and Spirit. Nag Hammadi texts would appear to connect with Gnostic thinkers who ran the Great or Royal Library of Alexandria which was an extraordinary depository of ancient knowledge before it was destroyed in stages by the 'freedom-loving' Roman Church. The texts are a treasure trove of ancient knowledge.

Nag Hammadi texts describe Astral Archons as the 'formless ones' (energetic beings) in their foundation state, but at least more than 1,600 years ago they said Archons could appear to humans as serpentine forms and those that looked like 'an unborn baby or foetus with grey skin and dark, unmoving eyes'. That would be hard to improve as a description of the Greys (Fig 70 overleaf). As Archons in form, Reptilians and Greys have no empathy or compassion although these can be *simulated* as necessary. We appropriately call this 'crocodile tears'. Accounts of reptilian entities ancient and modern are legion, the same with the Greys, and I have quoted over the years many military people who have described their interactions with them in underground bases far from public sight. My books going back to the 1990s have described how the Cult is founded on interbreeding bloodlines that are part-human and part reptilian. These have been the royal and aristocratic bloodlines, or 'bluebloods', that have interbred throughout 'history' to protect their particular biological software from being diluted and dispersed through interbreeding with the 'common people'. Bloodline

families
marry for
genetics and
find 'love'
elsewhere.
Prince, now
King, Charles
married
Princess
Diana for
genetic
reasons while
always
maintaining
his
relationship

Figure 70: Two major types of non-human entity widely reported in modern UFO research were described in Gnostic texts believed to originate at least 1,600 years ago.

with Camilla Parker Bowles who eventually became 'Queen Camilla' after Diana was murdered in Paris. Key Rothschilds were told to marry cousins by dynasty founder Mayer Amschel Rothschild.

Cult hybrid bloodlines have the ability to 'shapeshift' between human and reptilian forms. Shapeshifting sounds impossible to left-brain reality and the five senses. How can you shift from one solid form to another? You *can't* and that is not what is happening. Cult bloodline hybrids have duel *information* fields or auric fields. The human one is projected most of the time and always of course in public. Any observer will decode that field to perceive them as a 'physical' human. When they shift to the other field, as they do among safe people and in rituals, an observer will decode this second field to see a reptilian form. Anyone witnessing the shift will appear to see someone transforming from a solid human to a solid reptilian which is why the many descriptions of this are dismissed as impossible. There is no 'solid'. The shift is a shift of information *perceived* as a physical shift by the decoding processes of the observer. I have written extensively about human-reptilian hybrid bloodlines and shapeshifting in *Everything You Need To Know But Have Never Been Told* and *The Perception Deception*.

Themes of serpent gods pervade throughout the Far East (dragon symbolism) and Central America where we have the Mayan god Kukulkan portrayed in serpentine form and the legend of a reptilian race known as the 'Iguana Men' said to come from the sky (Fig 71). Mayans recalled how the 'Iguana Men' taught them to build pyramids and I have seen the connection between a reptilian race and pyramids many times. Other legends from the Yucatan in Mexico record how the first settlers were the Chanes or 'People of the Serpent' with their god Itzamna. The name is said to derive from 'itzem' which means 'lizard or

Figure 71: Mayan reptilian god Kukulkan symbolically depicted at the ancient site of Chichén Itza in the Yucatán, Mexico.

Figure 72: Depiction of the part-human, part-reptilian Naga at the Chennakesava Temple, India.

reptile'. The Mayan sacred city of Itzamna can be translated, on that basis, as 'the place of the lizard' or 'Iguana House'. There are the serpentine Nagas in the Indian subcontinent and Asia which would seem to have connections with the Mayans and Central America. Naga is a subcontinent Sanskrit word for cobra and the cobra has been widely used as a symbol of the Reptilians in cultures such as ancient Egypt. The Nagas are depicted as 'supernatural' part-human, part-reptilian, entities (Fig 72). They were a focus of worship for thousands of years in Hinduism, Buddhism, Jainism, and more. We have the concept of 'snake brothers' with the Hopi people in the American state of Arizona. Zulu legends told to me at length by Zulu high shaman Credo Mutwa describe the reptilian 'Chitauri' which were (are) the 'dictators, those who dictate the law'. See the connection to the Gnostic 'Archons' which means 'rulers' in Greek. Legends say the Chitauri 'tell us, secretly, what we have to do'. Worship of the serpent is the oldest known religion and identified in Botswana, Africa, from some 70,000 years ago as we measure 'time'.

Astral Reptilians

'Astral travelling' (also out-of- body-experience, or OBE) is the ability to project your consciousness into the Astral dimension or rather transfer your point of focussed attention from the human body into the Astral. This is different to a near-death experience (NDE) in that the body does not have to die to release perception from its material prison of attention. An OBE is achieved through conscious intent. Astral travellers have often seen reptilian entities and one of the most famous was radio broadcasting executive Robert Monroe who left us in 1995. His book

Journeys Out of the Body, published in 1971, popularised Astral travelling, or the OBE, like never before. I tell in *The Dream* how Monroe collaborated with psychologists, psychiatrists, doctors, biochemists, and electrical engineers to develop 'Hemispheric Synchronisation', or Hemi-Sync, to harmonise the two hemispheres of the brain. This is most relevant to this book given what I have said about brain hemispheres and how they are manipulated to prevent whole-brain harmony. Monroe discovered that Astral travelling became possible when both brain hemispheres are in 'frequency and amplitude synchronisation'. The combination would seem to release awareness focused in matter to transfer its attention into the Astral. Left-right disharmony by extension must entrap people in only the perception of matter and most humans are imprisoned in the left-side of the brain. This is clearly not a coincidence.

Monroe's research and abilities interested the Cult-controlled US military and Central Intelligence Agency (CIA) from 1978 and he agreed to take part in their study dubbed the Gateway Process. Documents since declassified describe Gateway as 'a training system designed to bring enhanced strength, focus and coherence to the amplitude and frequency of brainwave output between the left and right hemispheres'. The goal was to 'alter consciousness, moving it outside the physical sphere so as to ultimately escape even the restrictions of time and space'. Then there was the reptilian theme. Monroe and other participants in Gateway saw so many interdimensional reptilian humanoids (among other entities) in their Astral travels that they became known in the project as the 'alligators'. Archon Reptilians are an Astral phenomenon and that's why we don't see them unless they enter the frequency band of matter and visible light. Monroe said his Astral travels revealed to him that Reptilians and other entities were feeding off low-vibrational human mental and emotional energy which he called 'loosh'. I had this confirmed to me by endless sources from ancient accounts to military insiders long before I came across the Monroe material (Fig 73). Monroe's work was not the original source, but welcome added confirmation. An article on the Down the Chupacabra Hole website said of Monroe:

> During countless expeditions, he observed identical saurian creatures. For over thirty-five years the etheric investigator gathered insight about these startling beings. Here is what he uncovered: The nefarious vertebrates have controlled and enslaved humanity for millennia. They exist and operate in the 4th dimension and are only visible to individuals who can see beyond our extremely limited spectrum of visible light.

People I have met around the world who describe seeing Reptilians and

Archons Feeding Frenzy - Fear, Death & Decay

Figure 73: The simulation is designed to manipulate humanity into low-vibrational mental and emotional states which generate the 'loosh' that Astral entities feed off. (Image by Neil Hague.)

Greys, plus all the other accounts, make it crazy to dismiss this information. Even more so to say that it 'gets in the way' of the real conspiracy taking place within politics and perceptions of the five senses. I mentioned how Alex Jones originally referred to what I said about these crucial subjects as a 'turd in the punchbowl' 25 years ago, and an anonymous Trump-worshipping bloke on Twitter/X, calling himself 'Ariel', wrote in 2024:

> David Icke disempowered everyone. How? When he mentioned those in power were Reptilians he basically scared people away from challenging the power structure. Because he made demigods out of our rulers in government which made all his listeners insecure about who to call out without risking their lives at the possibility of succumbing to these otherworldly beings who are too larger than life to bring down because they know how to shape-shift.

> This was the entire plan. Which is why no matter what he exposed he knew it would cause fear, hesitation, and anxiety in those who would dare go on the offensive against those in government. This by default acted as a protective barrier against the ruling class. This is why they were all sitting comfortably content in their position of authority until Donald Trump won in 2016.

The level of imbecilic idiocy required to write those words boggles the senses. Perhaps even worse was the software mentality necessary to believe such crap which many did despite having no idea who this 'Ariel' bloke really is. The example captures the mentality that I was talking about earlier. Never mind the evidence of a non-human force manipulating human society. We must ignore that because it frightens people. We should hide away from the truth behind the 'saviour' that is Cult-owned Trump. The fact that this non-human force is controlling humanity's very sense of experienced reality through the simulation is irrelevant. Just vote for Trump and we're good. 'Moronic' just isn't enough to describe the chap and this is the mentality now driving much of the fake 'alternative' MAM. That's why I won't stop challenging them while this continues.

Software reality

Lieutenant Colonel Wayne McDonnell who oversaw the military/CIA Gateway Process of Robert Monroe said later that investigators confirmed our reality is a holographic electromagnetic Matrix. This is what I have been saying from completely different sources and experiences for more than two decades. I'll be describing the simulation in much greater detail as we go along. It's enough to know for now that the simulation is an information construct like a Wi-Fi field which the human body biological computer is designed to decode into the illusion of physical reality. The question is *why*? Religious and ancient stories about a 'revolt from God' are founded on truth although much is symbolic rather than literal. Gnostic Nag Hammadi texts describe this, as do religious works including the biblical Old Testament. Christian belief says that the Devil/Satan is a fallen angel expelled from 'heaven' (Spirit/higher frequencies) who was ejected by God to reside in an inferior realm. Christian and Gnostic belief matches that of Hebrew descriptions of Satan as the 'accuser' and 'adversary' and the name means 'to obstruct or oppose'. Satan/Yaldabaoth is said to hate God *(the All That Is)*. The Gnostic 'Devil', the 'fallen' consciousness distortion known as Yaldabaoth, is said to have been created 'in error' and sought to usurp 'God' to rule its own kingdom. That kingdom is the simulation which spans the human world of matter and the Astral dimension.

Nag Hammadi accounts say human reality is a 'bad copy' of Prime Reality. 'Bad copy' = the simulation (Fig 74). I had concluded our reality is a simulation long before I knew the Nag Hammadi find existed and once again they were a confirmation and not the prime source. It's very important that as many sources as possible are gathered that confirm the themes rather than taking only what Gnostics said by itself. Specialisation in any source is going to influence you by what is true *and* by what is in error or open to interpretation. No one has the entire picture and the more cross-references we can muster the better. Nag Hammadi texts use the term 'Hal' which is translated into modern language as 'virtual reality'. They describe how Yaldabaoth consciousness copied a section of Prime Reality to make what we would call a digital version. Legendary filmmaker Stanley Kubrick featured a supercomputer he named HAL in *2001: A Space Odyssey*. Kubrick said he wanted to convey the reality that the world would be populated by 'machine entities', or what we now call AI. This was in 1968. Kubrick was a renegade insider who tried to expose aspects of the agenda in his movies including *2001: A Space Odyssey; A Clockwork Orange; The Shining;*

Figure 74: Artist Neil Hague symbolically represents the creation of the Gnostic 'bad copy' – the simulation.

Dr Strangelove, and Eyes Wide Shut.

Highly detailed research makes it obvious that Kubrick faked the first Moon landings in 1969 partly under the cover of making *2001: A Space Odyssey*. Kubrick was chosen for his expertise in special effects in a film career lasting 48 years. Special effect techniques had not evolved to their current levels, of course, and that's why they can be identified in the Moon footage. He was the best of his day with what was available then. See the outstanding film *Kubrick's Odyssey* about his Moon landing fakery by my friend Jay Weidner that you will find on the Internet. The reason I mention this is that Stanley Kubrick had insider knowledge and his films were full of symbolism and indicators. I doubt 'HAL' was an accidental name. Archons are most definitely a form of AI which is way beyond what we perceive as AI in human reality. You may already see the correlation between the tech billionaire oligarch agenda of people like Musk and the way the entire simulated reality is generated through AI. The human AI agenda with its electromagnetic Cloud and brain chips are another layer of the simulation being imposed to block the awakening of humanity. Whenever humans threaten to awaken to their true plight the system seeks to intervene to block that.

The veil

Gnostics refer to the bad copy as the 'Lower Aeons' and Prime Reality as the 'Upper Aeons' with a curtain, veil, or boundary between them (Fig 75 overleaf). Upper Aeons have no sense of separation and are described by Gnostics as 'The Silence', 'the silent Silence', 'the living Silence', with

THE 'REAL WORLD'
(UPPER AEONS)

THE SHADOW WORLD
(LOWER AEONS)

Figure 75: Gnostic 'Upper Aeons' represented the 'Divine' realms and the 'Lower Aeons' are its 'shadow' (bad copy).

its 'Watery Light' (in contrast to the fierce electromagnetic light of the simulated bad copy). Upper Aeons are pure consciousness or awareness called 'the totality', 'the fullness' and the 'perfection' of 'emanations of the Father'. They are the 'Treasure-House', 'Storehouse', 'Dwelling-Place' and 'Kingless Realm'. Lower Aeons are 'inferior shadows', or reflections of the Upper Aeon blueprint. There is a theme of the Lower Aeons being a reflection or shadow ('copy'). The texts divide the two realities into fullness/deficiency, immortal/mortal, spiritual/psychic, spirit/soul, existence/non-existence, no-time/time. Nag Hammadi manuscript *Zostrianos* tells us: 'In relation to the reflection which he [Yaldabaoth] saw in it he created the world. With a reflection of a reflection, he worked at producing the world.' *The Hypostasis of the Archons*, says: 'A veil exists between the world above and the realms that are below; and shadow came into being beneath the veil; and that shadow became matter; and that shadow was projected apart.' *Origin of the World* states: 'The eternal realm of truth has no shadow outside it, for the limitless light is everywhere within it, but its exterior is shadow, which has been called by the name darkness.' A text in the *Bruce Codex* describes the separation of Upper and Lower Aeons:

> And then the existent separated itself from the non-existent. And the non-existent is the evil which has manifested in matter. And the enveloping power separated those that exist from those that do not exist. And it called the existent 'eternal', and it called the non-existent 'matter'. And in the middle it separated those that exist from those that do not exist, and it placed veils between them.

The term 'firmament' is often translated as the sky and interpreted to be a dome. It derives from the Hebrew word 'raqiya' or 'solid structure'. The biblical firmament is said to be the vast solid dome created by 'God' and divides the primal sea into upper and lower portions so that the dry land could appear. Could the firmament have other connotations in the context of Gnostic writings? Water is often used in the texts to symbolise the energy of Prime Reality as in '... the waters which are above', '... the waters which are above matter' and '... the Aeons in the Living Water'. Genesis describes what I suggest is Yaldabaoth creating the simulation when it says:

> And God said, Let there be a firmament in the midst of the waters, and let it divide the waters from the waters. And God made the firmament, and divided the waters which were under the firmament from the waters which were above the firmament: and it was so. And God called the firmament Heaven.

Counterfeit reality

The work began to entice Divine Sparks or projections of Spirit into the simulation from the 'paradise' realms beyond its illusory limits. The simulation began as a digital copy of Prime Reality which would have aided the deception into the lair of Yaldabaoth described in Nag Hammadi texts as a 'Counterfeit Spirit'. Once that was achieved Yaldabaoth and its Archons had the challenge of maintaining the entrapment which is the real reason for reincarnation of which much more to come. Look again at the biblical story of the Garden of Eden (other versions can be found around the world) and it could certainly symbolise this enticement into the Yaldabaoth Matrix. You had Adam and Eve being lured out of paradise by the serpent. Adam and Eve can be seen as Divine Sparks of consciousness symbolic of what we now call humans. *Encyclopedia Britannica* says: 'The story of the Garden of Eden is a theological use of mythological themes to explain human progression from a state of innocence and bliss to the present human condition of knowledge of sin, misery, and death.' This could also be interpreted as Divine Sparks being enticed into the simulation where they were manipulated by calculated events and experiences into a low-vibrational state that produced ignorance, misunderstanding, fear, violence, misery and the illusion of death – all loosh producers.

The 'evil serpent' (reptilian Archon?) deceived Eve who ate of the prohibited fruit and shared it with Adam. This gave them 'newly opened eyes' to know good and evil – *duality*. The simulation is founded on electromagnetism and electricity – *duality*, which is *polarity* with negative and positive charge. Opposite charges, positive and negative, attract each other. The same charges, two negative or two positive, repel each other. Everything in human reality is an expression of this duality/polarity. Action and *re*action, act and resist, cause and effect. The Eden story says an angel was posted with a sword of fire to prevent the return of Adam and Eve (humanity) to paradise. I have described in *The Trap* and *The Dream* the demonic 'guards on the gate' to prevent escape from the simulation and the energetic shield or bubble that can only be traversed by consciousness with a high enough vibration. This is the origin of the Buddhist belief in being trapped in the reincarnation cycle until a state of 'enlightenment' (high vibration) is reached. Creation myths around the world have many points in common. The Hindu creator-god Brahma is said to have appeared from a 'cosmic golden egg' (which could be the Moon if you read my other books) and created good, evil, and light. One Hindu account says the god Vishnu was lying on an ocean of milk with the serpent Sesha and 'sprung a lotus from his naval that contained the creator god Brahma' who then created all living beings along with the Sun, Moon, planets, and other gods and demigods.

You are told you are a human and a one-off cosmic accident of 'evolution'; or you are subject to the whims and dictates of a 'God' that you must obey or be condemned forever to Hell and damnation. Does this sound like a loving 'God' or more like the distorted narcissistic psychopathy of the consciousness known as Yaldabaoth, Satan, Shaytan? The 'God' and 'gods' of most religions are Yaldabaoth and its Archontic demonic expressions. Read the Old Testament and tell me if that is a God of love or a bloodthirsty tyrant. 'God's' demand for extraordinary violence and mass slaughter is untenable with the 'God of Love' propaganda, but Christians do their best to gloss over that. I read a Christian article claiming the violence was to protect the bloodline to the 'messiah' Jesus; to stop humanity falling into idolatry and sin; to conquer God's enemies; and to show surrounding nations that 'Yahweh is the rightful ruler of the universe'. Oh, *pleeease*. Old Testament 'Yahweh' is a psychopath and still being quoted by Benjamin Netanyahu and Jewish religious extremists to justify the mass murder of Palestinians. Support for my contention that Yahweh is Yaldabaoth can be found by from comparing biblical texts with those of Nag Hammadi documents:

'It is I who am God, and there is no other power apart from me.' (Nag Hammadi)

'I am the Lord, and there is none else, there is no God beside me.' (Isaiah 45:5)

Yaldabaoth is known in Nag Hammadi documents as the 'Lord Archon'. Is this the origin of the concept of 'God' as 'The Lord'? Whenever I have seen 'God is Lord' or 'Jesus is Lord' on church posters I have thought: 'What on earth is that supposed to mean?' The tyrant 'god' of the Old Testament is Yahweh/Jehovah and if you read the passages in which 'Yahweh' (Yaldabaoth) demands mass murder and suffering you are looking at the same force that has been behind the mass murder and suffering of humanity throughout known human history with all the wars, conflict on every level, and deprivation for the global masses that has increased, not decreased, in scale and number. We come here to 'learn lessons and evolve'. It's comedy club nonsense. Ponder on all the loosh this illusion has produced and continues to produce. The trickery of manipulating religions to worship their Devil as their God, while believing they are doing the opposite, means that followers in their billions can be trawled for loosh. Energy flows where attention goes and what you focus upon you make an energetic connection with. Worship and prayer is an extreme form of focus and that attention locks you into the frequency of whatever is the source of your focus. In this case the demonic Yaldabaoth 'God' behind the veil, the wizard behind the curtain. An energetic channel is created through worship and focus that allows the demonic to devour your energy. I must start a prayer app. Thiel will give me the money. Any mental and emotional state of perception that connects you with the demonic lower-Astral frequency band will serve the same purpose. The world is as it is because of the simple physics of frequency/vibration. The demonic must maintain humanity in a low-vibrational state or its 'food' supply is gone. Love, joy, peace, happiness, is the last thing they want.

Low means *real* low

Soul has to lower its frequency monumentally to take human form and incarnates through the conduit of the auric field that I call mind. We have for an 'incarnate' human the theme of Body-Mind-Soul-Divine Spark/Spirit. When the Divine Spark wakes up to its true nature its frequency explodes and pervades through soul to mind and body and the entire sequence begins to remember what it has been manipulated to forget (Fig 76). We see what we could not see before. The impact is to overpower the influence of the simulation to control perception. The term 'awakening' is everywhere today and so misused and misunderstood. Becoming aware of Klaus Schwab and the World Economic Forum or Bill Gates and his Cult-serving machinations is equated to being 'awake'. It's not even

Figure 76: The Divine Spark within explodes awake when we remember the true nature of the 'I' and its frequencies transform all levels of being, soul, mind and body.

close. The demonic wants you to believe this is 'awake' to keep you there-and-no-further. Here you have the major reason for the Cult takeover of the MAM. Unless the Divine Spark, our source of 'Divine' power, wakes up they are in the clear. I see people saying they have 'woken up' while still being consumed by a religious or political belief. The Cult and its demonic masters would rather that no perceptual level awakens. If the mind awakens then the soul might; if the soul does, wow, the Divine Spark might. They know as their agenda becomes ever more obvious at the mind level of 'physical' events that a total blackout of the game is not possible until AI *becomes* that mind. This is the real motivation above all others why the Cult and demons want to connect AI to the human brain. If you can control the perceptions of brain/mind, the awakening sequence is blocked at the first 'domino'.

There will be much more detail as we proceed, as with everything in this chapter. That includes the reincarnation cycle and the 'mind-wipe' in which memories of soul and previous human lives are deleted with each new human experience. Memories are stored electrically and electromagnetically and so easily deleted. How can we learn lessons if we forget those apparently already 'learned'? The idea is not to 'evolve'; it is to continually hold perception in the trap so we can be looshed with each new human 'life'. Looshing can continue in the Astral, but it's most potent by far in the density of matter where the influence of Spirit and even soul is far away and, for most, non-existent. Humans in such density are walking, talking batteries; an electrical, electromagnetic organism. The battery body is 60 percent water which is a decoded holographic expression of wavefield information. The mind-wipe can mean that someone like Alex Jones could leave his human form still shouting about a conspiracy and then return as someone who vehemently rejects any suggestion of conspiracy. 'You have been an exposer of conspiracy so now you need to experience denying conspiracy – it will help you evolve.' This is why a *real* awakening must happen or what we think are successes will be just transient illusions. The MAM obsession with religion and worshipping the demonic force while thinking it is 'God' shows how far 'awakening' still needs to go. 'Awakening' is to remember our true nature as Spirit and its Divine Spark projection. Everything else, including Klaus Schwab and the rest of the Cult's moronic rabble, is merely detail.

Why sacrifice?

I have only laid out the basic theme here and so much about the human world starts to fall into place already. 'Mysteries' can suddenly be answered. One is why the ancients sacrificed people – often children – as an 'offering to the gods'; and why, as I have detailed in a stream of other books, the Cult 'elite' and their gofers continue with human sacrifice 'to the gods'. Who are these 'gods' and who are the 'pantheons of gods' worshipped, ancient and modern, across the world? Here are only a few: African pantheons; Armenian pantheon; Aztec pantheon; Berber pantheon; Burmese pantheon; Canaanite pantheon; Celtic pantheon; Chinese pantheon; Egyptian pantheon; Germanic pantheon; Greek pantheon; Hindu pantheon; Incan pantheon; Irish pantheon; Jain pantheon; Japanese pantheon; Japanese Buddhist pantheon; Maya pantheon; Native American pantheons; Norse pantheon; Roman pantheon; Slavic pantheon; Sumerian pantheon. Who are they? They are the *same* 'gods', the same Astral entities, the same *Archons* or rulers. Different cultures and eras have given them different names. Why is human sacrifice an offering to the 'gods'? What do they get out of it? One word – *loosh*.

The demonic is feeding off low-vibrational energy from the population in general and this is individualised in sacrifice rituals. Energy generated by terror is a very powerful low-frequency state and rituals are conducted to trigger maximum terror for the Astral demons to absorb. This is the 'offering to the gods' (Fig 77). Terror reaches such an extreme at the moment of sacrifice that an adrenaline enters the bloodstream which the 'human' Satanists drink as a drug or nectar. Stories that circulate about the Washington DC elite and others drinking blood infused with this adrenaline, or 'adrenochrome', are based on fact.

ARCHON SATANIC RITUAL

Figure 77: Astral demonic entities feed off the energy of terror during satanic rituals conducted by their robed servants in human reality who drink the terror in the form of adrenaline in the blood. (Image by Neil Hague.)

Adrenochrome has been found to be a powerful drug with multiple effects on body and mind. They ideally want children before the age of puberty when chemical changes take place in the body. They want the child's energy before that happens, hence the ancient theme of sacrificing 'young virgins' (children) to the 'gods'. Rituals constantly repeated at the same location also thin-out the frequency difference between matter and the Astral and allow demons to enter visible light where they can be seen, albeit briefly. I have talked to people who have experienced these advanced satanic rituals all over the world. They have described the experience of seeing demons appear and they tell me that Satanists are terrified of them.

Cult Satanism

I have heard legions of horrific stories and they put into perspective the scale of evil that we are dealing with. Witnesses have described seeing children cut open and sacrificed in the Vatican while 'VIP people in the room invited demonic entities to inhabit them'. They describe seeing a black mist appear during child sacrifice which grew larger until it became a demon with red eyes speaking in another language: 'Its voice sounded like thunder.' Others saw children burned alive and screaming as they were 'sawed alive' and their bodies 'partially eaten'. Zulu shaman Credo Mutwa told me that cannibalism was introduced to humanity by the reptilian 'gods'. Satanists communicate with their 'god' through child sacrifice. The energy/consciousness has been known through the ages as Lucifer, Satan, the Devil, Moloch, and Baal along with the Gnostic Yaldabaoth and Islamic Shaytan. Mothers in Satanic cults are forced to sacrifice their own children while others are held in captivity to repeatedly produce children for sacrifice. They are known in the covens as 'breeders'. I have been exposing since the 1990s the 'elite' gatherings at Bohemian Grove in Northern California where some of America's and the world's most famous people meet to worship their demonic god symbolised by a 40-foot stone owl depicting the ancient Canaanite 'god', Moloch. This is related in the Biblical Old Testament to the sacrifice of children through fire and Moloch has also been used to symbolise Saturn (Figs 78 and 79).

Detectives and lawyers with the courage to investigate have established that satanic sacrifice is happening. It's real and this is the mentality behind human society which selects fake political leaders, billionaires, Hollywood stars, major media hosts, key judges, scientists, and academics. They control the political-industrial-military-intelligence complex, the United Nations, World Health Organization, World Trade Organization, International Monetary Fund (IMF), World Bank, and the whole interconnected Global Cult web. Wars are mass sacrifice rituals to them as is the slaughter of tens of thousands of Palestinians by Israel in

Figure 78: The 40-foot stone owl at the elite's Bohemian Grove in Northern California. The owl represents the 'god' Molech to whom children have been sacrificed for millennia.

Figure 79: Molech has also been associated with Saturn which will become more significant in the story as we go along.

Gaza (a great percentage of them children). Yet even in the 'alternative' media people believe that billionaires like Elon Musk are 'independent' because they are so rich. How do you think they *become* so rich? I highlight all this, horrible as it is to read, to reveal the depth of depravity behind world events. To know this is to understand how the Cult can induce wars, starvation, vaccines, and drugs to kill and cause suffering to millions and billions worldwide. They have no empathy and no emotional consequence for what they do. More than that, they *love* to make people suffer and just think of the loosh. They are Satan's children occupied by Satan's mind.

Connected to this is the age-old theme of 'possession'. Astral demonic entities can attach to the auric field/mind and begin to direct behaviour through perceptual trickery. Islam is only one example of the possession commonality worldwide in which Shaytan is said to be at war with God for control of the human mind. Rebellious and malevolent Jinn are believed to cause disease and mental illness while projecting evil thoughts and behaviour into the minds of humans. Possession is one explanation for schizophrenia or split personality when a person can be lovely one minute and evil the next. The possessing entity imposes its will when it wants to dictate behaviour and otherwise steps back. The difference between the two perceptual states can be diagnosed as schizophrenia when it is really possession. Significant members of the

Global Cult and many in the lower ranks are possessed in this way. Major players are full-blown demons or demon-controlled biological AI hiding behind human form. The *Avatar* movies in which a society of blue people (the Na'vi) was infiltrated by hijackers with the outer appearance of blue people is an accurate analogy for what is happening. We have been invaded by those that look human while being anything but human. Secret society rituals are designed to open the human field to demonic possession which is why I have been told endless times by family members of Freemasons how the personality of a secret society initiate changed demonstrably, even dramatically, once they joined the 'club'. Most of them are not even aware of this when the demon is now running the perceptual show.

Parasites that infest the human body and cause so much ill health are also a form of demonic possession and reflects the parasitical nature of Yaldabaoth and its Archons. The demonic is so dense and dark with no empathy or compassion and this is transferred to the one being possessed. I have regularly heard the response over the years to my exposure of Cult horrors that says: 'They would never do that – no one would do that.' The reaction betrays an extreme lack of awareness of the scale of evil involved although understandable when compared with their life experience. You don't tend to meet many people this bloody evil. The 'darkness' (density) ensures that the most basic empathetic and compassionate responses cannot be felt. Sacrificing a little child? No problem. If you can sacrifice kids and sexually and violently abuse them, then the evil you unleash on humanity as a whole is hardly going to trouble you. Cult ranks are awash with Satanists and paedophiles. The two are connected again to the Astral 'gods'. Paedophilia is dominated by those possessed by these entities that attach to their energetic field. Paedophiles sexually abuse children while the possessing entity uses them as a conduit to absorb the prepubescent energy they so crave.

Good news – the 'gods' are stupid

I would emphasise before we move on that the demonic is not all-powerful and neither are its gofers and lackeys in the Global Cult. The demonic is feeding off our energy, not we off theirs. They need us, not vice versa. There are many accounts through the 'ages' that the demons are terrified of humans awakening when they depend on our ignorance to prevail and survive. The demonic is so far removed from the *All That Is* and higher dimensions of Creation that its only source of energetic sustenance must come from the frequency band to which it condemned itself by its own choice of reality and perception. This means manipulating its targets to generate mental and emotional energy within that band – fear, anxiety, depression, and all the rest. That is the enormity of demonic dependency on humans. In the same way the Cult few in the human world cannot dictate to billions unless the billions are manipulated by ignorance and fear to obey and acquiesce. Whatever level of the simulation Matrix, the Astral or material, the same dynamic is in place. Perception of the masses must be controlled for the few to get their way.

Nor is the consciousness that Gnostics know as Yaldabaoth highly intelligent, all-knowing, and all-powerful. It's an idiot. The ability to control comes from the following: Keeping humans in ignorance of everything they need to know to appreciate their plight; knowledge of how to manipulate perception; and the energetic power projected by humans all day every day. Nothing and no one that seeks to control and manipulate others is anything at its core other than stupid and ridiculous. Gnostics called Yaldabaoth 'The Foolish One' and other names in other cultures, such as Samael and Saklas, translate as 'The Foolish One' and 'The Blind God'. By extension, the demons, Jinn, Archons, Reptilians, and Greys are expressions of that consciousness and must also be foolish and blind. Their energetic density makes it so and great swathes of humanity have been made foolish and blind as extensions of the same source of foolishness. I am not saying the demonic is not crafty and clever. Knowledge of how to manipulate perception makes that possible in the face of human ignorance of such techniques. Cleverness and wisdom are not the same thing. The demonic may be clever, but it is not wise. Take away wisdom and you are left with stupid. I said in a book long ago that cleverness without wisdom is the most destructive force on Earth. We have the world we do because cleverness has trumped wisdom. Now we see why.

This chapter has been a summary to get us rolling of the reality that we are experiencing as 'real'. Now we can add more detail – lots more.

CHAPTER SEVEN

It's Not Real

A great deal of intelligence can be invested in ignorance when the need for illusion is deep

Saul Bellow

I have said since a little after the millennium that we are experiencing a virtual reality simulation. I had pondered on this for many years before and suspected that was the case. Now it became a certainty to me. It was one of those moments I have had again and again since 1990. I just *knew* (Fig 80).

I said that the limit of the simulation was the speed of light which is wrongly believed by mainstream science to be the fastest speed possible. Sub-atomic particles have been shown to communicate instantly over what are perceived to be

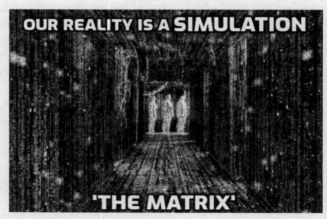

Figure 80: Once this realisation dawns so much makes sense that didn't before.

enormous distances. This alone makes the speed of light look like walking with a Zimmer frame. When I say the speed of light is a limit, I mean within human reality. Particle communication, known as quantum entanglement, is happening in the Astral, not in matter. The simulation encompasses the Astral which is known as the spirit world or the 'afterlife'. Particle entanglement and frequency connection explains how feelings and communication can be apparently transmitted between people 'far apart'. Perception of time slows and space contracts as you close in on the speed of light. There is obviously some sort of perceptual/frequency barrier when time and space are illusions of simulated reality. I searched in this immediately post-millennium period for anyone else saying the same about a simulation. The only public example I found was Professor Nick Bostrom at Oxford University who was suggesting that our reality could be simulated although he saw it differently to me. He speculated that it could have been done by humans 'from the future'. I didn't go with that when the 'future' is only the NOW in disguise. Entities in another dimension with more advanced knowledge of reality, yes, but not the 'future'.

Ever more scientists agree

My goodness how things have changed in the two decades since then as scientists in the mainstream are saying in increasing numbers that it does appear we are experiencing a simulation. I have detailed some of them in other books, including *The Dream*. An article in the mainstream *Scientific American* in April 2021 concluded both that our reality is simulated and that its limit is the *speed of light*. It was written by Fouad Khan, a senior editor at *Nature Energy*, under the headline: 'Confirmed! We Live in a Simulation' (Fig 81). This came nearly 20 years after I

Figure 81: *Scientific American*, April 2021.

concluded the same from awareness that just appeared in my mind. Khan connected the speed of light limit to the processing speed of the simulation. He said that while simulation creators can decide the rules of the game they are still limited by processing speed which means energetic power. I saw two decades ago that the rules and limits of the human level of the simulation are what we call the *laws of physics*. Those that create virtual reality video games encode them with the limits of the game and how it is meant to be played. These limits and codes are the equivalent of the laws of physics.

Near-death and out-of-body experiencers describe very different laws of physics when they leave the body. Laws that science slavishly believes in, and denies any other possibilities, only apply to the thin band of frequency that the body biological computer is decoding into an illusory reality. Those 'laws' no longer apply once the body ceases to function, or when out-of-body experiencers project their awareness into the Astral dimension. How significant it is that mathematics of virtual reality computer games and our human reality are the *same*. I continually emphasise that modern technology is mimicking the very reality we are experiencing. Max Tegmark, a physicist at the Massachusetts Institute of Technology (MIT) and author of *Our Mathematical Universe*, says that reality can be entirely described by numbers and maths:

> We look around and it doesn't seem that mathematical at all, but everything we see is made out of elementary particles like quarks and electrons. And what properties does an electron have? Does it have a smell or a colour or a texture? No! ... We physicists have come up with geeky names for [electron] properties, like electric charge, or spin, or lepton number, but the electron doesn't care what we call it, the properties are just numbers.

Tegmark is describing the digital level of our reality that results from the brain decoding electrical information from the five senses into digital holographic information. I doubt that he realises this. The digital realm of decoded reality is what numerologists are reading. Tegmark is very perceptive as he imagines characters in computer games not realising they are in a game. They appear to bump into real objects, fall in love and feel emotions. They might begin to study their 'physical world' and see that it was made of pixels. 'What they thought was physical "stuff" could actually be described by a bunch of numbers and while they would be criticised by those saying "come on you're stupid, it's stuff after all" anyone outside of the game would see that "physical" reality was just numbers.' The scale of illusion can be seen with the illusion of 'colour'. There is no colour until we decode frequency information into what appears to us as colour. Do colours that we see on a computer screen exist in a Wi-Fi field? The computer decodes *information* into colour. We speak of the 'colour spectrum' as with a rainbow. Spectrum appropriately comes from a Latin term meaning apparition or phantom – hence spectre. Colours that we see (decode) depend on whether an object, plant, flower, whatever, absorbs colour spectrum wavelengths or reflects them. What is absorbed is invisible to us and what is reflected we perceive as a colour. If you observe reality we only 'see' reflected light and that's why we see nothing in a genuinely dark room in the absence of a light source for reflection to occur. Black absorbs all light, so it's black, and white reflects all light, so it's white. Different colours absorb some light frequencies and reflect others. Near-death experiencers describe the out-of-body Astral realm as having much more vivid colours and this is due to the higher frequencies involved.

Computer scientist Rich Terrile, director of the Centre for Evolutionary Computation and Automated Design at NASA's Jet Propulsion Laboratory, said in 2016/2017 that the Universe is a simulated digital hologram and therefore must have been created by a form of intelligence (Fig 82). He took the Bostrom line that this could have been created by our 'future selves'. The source is nothing to do with future selves, Rich, or anything human. Another

NASA Scientist Claims Human Reality Is an Alien Created Hologram

With NASA reportedly on the cusp of announcing the discovery of an extraterrestrial race, one scientists says we're living in their hologram.

BY KEVIN DURWICK PUBLISHED JUL 5, 2017

A NASA scientist has come to the conclusion that our reality is an elaborate hologram created by an alien race. Dr. Rich Terrile, the director of the Center for Evolutionary Computation and Automated Design at NASA's Jet Propulsion Laboratory has said that we can all be the creation of a cosmic computer programmer as opposed to a God. The theory is backed by other scientists, but also has its detractors as well. Maybe as the late Bill Hicks said "we're all one consciousness experiencing itself subjectively, there is no such thing as death, life is only a dream, and we are the imagination of ourselves" is true.

Figure 82: Nasa scientist Rich Terrile in 2017.

scientist since the publication of *The Dream* who has publicly suggested the reality of the simulation is Melvin Vopson, an associate professor in physics at the University of Portsmouth, a short ferry ride from where I am writing this on the Isle of Wight. He was all over the national papers in December 2023 saying what I have been revealing and writing for two decades (Fig 83 overleaf). There was no acknowledgement of that in those news reports, of course. There never is. Vopson had published his book, *Reality Reloaded: The Scientific Case for a Simulated Universe*, two months earlier. I was surprised how thin it is and it has a lot of equations and science-speak as you would expect from a book compiled from his science papers. There are some interesting correlations and confirmations. He makes virtually the same points in his newspaper interviews that I had been making and includes Fouad Khan's concept of processing speed made two years earlier.

Vopson said the laws of physics that govern the Universe are like a computer code and elementary particles that make up matter are like pixels. That's only on the decoded digital level, I would say. Beyond that

'We're all living in Matrix-style simulated reality created by aliens,' professor claims

Physics professor Melvin Vopson claims his research indicates we might all be characters in a Matrix-style simulated reality created by an advanced species of alien

'The entire universe might be just a super advanced virtual reality simulation,' said Prof Vopson (Image: YouTube/ Information Physics Institute)

WHAT'S HOT

Couple woke up to £11m 'jackpot' in bank account – then their hearts sank

Disgusted Mia Khalifa warns 'I will literally kill you' after making 'squirt' discovery

Inside 'Slaughterhouse' death row prison where 'humanity steps back' and inmates 'boil alive'

Massive 7.0

Figure 83: Melvin Vopson from Portsmouth University in late 2023.

it's an Astral system. Vopson mentioned 'symmetry' – 'the quality of having parts that match each other, especially in a way that is attractive, or similarity of shape or contents.' Yes, like holograms, as above, so below. I have been saying all along that the simulation is *information* which we decode into the reality we think we are experiencing. Vopson says information should be considered the fifth state of matter along with solid, liquid, gas, and plasma. I would go further and say that matter *is* information. Encoded information is what creates 'matter' which is an informational state within specific frequencies. Different levels of the Astral are also different realms of the information that creates them. We will see in Chapter Eight that maverick scientists realised that reality was information a long 'time' ago.

Vopson proposes that the Universe may function as an advanced quantum computer which computes its own existence. This is something else I have been saying for many years. Quantum computers are close to becoming reality in human science and they are light years ahead in processing and storage potential than those we currently know. The human brain operates like a quantum computer which is an as above, so below, version of the quantum computer than runs the simulation. I've contended since the 1990s that the so-called Big Bang makes no sense and Vopson highlights the contradictions and unanswered questions: 'For instance, there are no clear answers to what exactly banged and what triggered the Big Bang in the first place.' He says that the behaviour and nature of particles 'bears an uncanny resemblance to the rules of coding and programming ...' This prompted the question of whether there was a link between the nature of the Universe and the principles governing computational simulations. He asks if the (illusory) 'dark matter' that science says exists, but can't find, is information. The answer must be 'yes' because *everything* is information. Or, rather, it *would* be yes if 'dark matter' existed as the alleged invisible organising field of visible matter. The problem for science is that it doesn't and I'll be explaining what 'dark matter' really is. Vopson writes about information stored in matter particles of the observable universe and how it could be stored in other forms 'including on the surface of the space-time fabric itself, according to the holographic principle'. We will have a much more expanded explanation of the simulation's information, processing, and storage systems in Chapters Eight and Nine.

The evolution myth

Melvin Vopson makes a relevant point about the 'Cambrian Explosion' estimated at some 541 million years ago in the period known as Cambrian which continued for up to 50 million years. All this has to be taken in the context of no-time. We'll call it the human perception of time. The 'explosion' refers to an evolutionarily-sudden expansion of biological life from single-cell microorganisms and basic multicellular organisms into much more complex and diverse forms. Many scientists have claimed that this could not be explained through the 'evolutionary process' and would require the infusion of genetic information from an intelligent designer. Vopson considers the probability of random mutations explaining this is incredibly low. 'If a mutation took place every second it would take longer than the age of the Universe before a single protein would be randomly formed.' I have covered the background to English biologist Charles Darwin and his family in other books with their connections to eugenics. Darwin's theory of natural selection has dominated 'scientific' thought since the publication in 1859 of his *On the Origin of Species by Means of Natural Selection, or the Preservation of Favoured Races in the Struggle for Life.* He claimed that organisms that best adapt to random genetic and environmental change are able to survive ('survival of the fittest') and that these characteristics are passed down from parents to children. Vopson instead rightly suggests that genetic mutations are not random, but driven by changes in the hidden information. Exactly.

All these facts had been in my books year after year long before, but now a *scientist* was saying them, an *associate professor* in physics, no less, and it was suddenly a big deal. One report said that Professor Vopson 'has already gained attention for his stunning proclamations in the field of physics'. Stunning proclamations made over a period of 20 years by a bloke who left school at 15 to play football for Coventry City, never went to university, and never took, never mind passed, a major exam in his life. The information is out there in the ether, people. You just have to tap into it. No exam passes or degrees necessary. I'm not knocking Vopson. The more that circulate these matters the better. It was just the irony that struck me. Associate professor – headlines everywhere. A bloke who left school at 15 and said the same long before – 'Nutter'. It is a microcosm example of a left-brain world. Perceived official *status* is the credibility criteria, not information and evidence from a source with no official *status*. Well, resident nutter, maybe.

Mysteries no more

Recurring geometric patterns have been identified throughout human reality and given names such as Pi, Phi, golden ratio, divine proportion, Fibonacci numbers, and fractal patterns. These are *computer codes* of the simulation. The genetic code is a *computer code* (Figs 84 and 85). Ancient Greeks knew about Phi or golden ratio, golden section, and golden mean. These are all measurement and number sequences found everywhere from the way that plants grow to proportions of the human body. Fibonacci numbers are named after the 12th/13th century Italian mathematician, Leonardo of Pisa, better known as Fibonacci. The sequence adds the two previous numbers to get the next one, as in ... 1, 1, 2, 3, 5, 8, 13, 21, 34, 55, etc. Fibonacci numbers are encoded in the human face and body, proportions of animals, DNA, seed heads, pine cones, trees, shells, spiral galaxies, hurricanes, and the number of petals in a flower. Fractal patterns conform to the holographic principle of as above, so below. They are 'a never-ending pattern that is infinitely

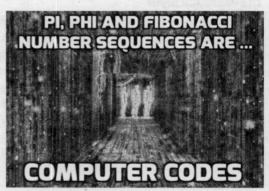

Figure 84: Recurring codes found throughout our reality are codes of the simulation.

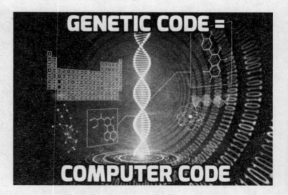

Figure 85: The body genetic code is a computer code designed to allow the body to decode the simulation information fields into illusory 'physical' (holographic) reality.

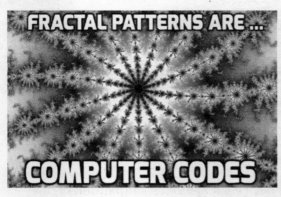

Figure 86: Fractal patterns are computer codes reflecting the holographic simulation.

complex and self-similar across different scales' (Fig 86). Fractal patterns can be seen in river networks, mountain ranges, craters, lightning bolts, coastlines, mountain goat horns, trees and branch growth, animal colour patterns, pineapples, heart rates, heartbeats, neurons and brains, eyes, respiratory systems, circulatory systems, blood vessels and pulmonary vessels, geological fault lines, earthquakes, snowflakes, crystals, ocean waves, vegetables, soil pores, and the rings of Saturn. What is called symmetrical mathematics can be seen throughout nature from the way trees grow to the structure of the human lung. This is defined as 'one shape becoming exactly like another when you move it in some way, turn, flip or slide.' Symmetrical mathematics is again the fractal holographic principle (Fig 87). DNA expresses fractal properties. I saw a scientific paper that was headlined 'DNA Is A Fractal Antenna in Electromagnetic Fields'. DNA is a receiver-transmission system that connects the body to the simulation and comprises four codes known as A, C, G, and T. Different sequences of these (computer) codes dictate whether something is a human or animal body, insect, or bacteria. DNA codes are given a binary value that relates to the binary 1 and 0 on-off

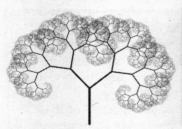 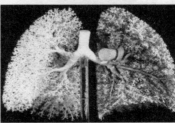

electrical charges found in computers and now identified as encoded in our energetic reality. A and C = 0

Figure 87: Fractal patterns are found everywhere including the way that trees grow and how human lungs are formed.

while G and T = 1. They are the numerical codes of DNA at the digital level of reality (Figs 88 and 89 overleaf).

These sequences are not confined to 'physical' matter either. David Pincus, a professor of psychology in the United States, highlights how fractal patterns have been identified in psychology, behaviour, speech patterns, and interpersonal relationships. *Nature's Scientific Reports*

Figure 88: DNA is comprised of the codes A,C,G,T, which each have a digital value of either 1 or 0 which reflect the 1 and 0, on-off electrical charges used in computers.

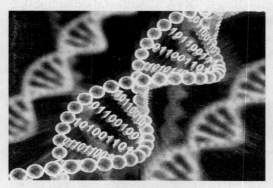

Figure 89: DNA on one level is digital.

featured a study in 2012 about undiscovered and fundamental laws that appear to govern everything from the electrical firing of brain cells to the growth of social networks, and expansion of galaxies. Co-author Dmitri Krioukov, a physicist at the University of California, San Diego, said: 'Natural growth dynamics are the same for different real networks, like the Internet or the brain or social networks.' He concluded: 'For a physicist it's an immediate signal that there is some missing understanding of how nature works.' Except that they are not 'natural', Dmitri, as I will come to. The simulation operates at all levels, the audio-visual and psychological. You would expect all of these things in a simulation that is holographic. Characters in computer games are encoded with the same mathematics as the rest of the game and this principle operates in the simulation.

'Life' is a headset

The simulation has two foundation levels, matter and the Astral, with its many sub-levels. The experience of both is like wearing a headset in a virtual reality game whether in the Astral as a soul 'body' or in a human body. The perception-manipulating information in each reality may be different, but the outcome is the same – perception control. The body is a biological computer system decoding the simulation and plays the role of a headset in a virtual reality game (Fig 90). The body-decoded 'physical world' dominates humanity's sense of reality. I would advise the sceptical to watch video compilations of what happens when people don a VR headset. Their body is in this reality and yet the moment they experience headset reality their perception is in a completely different world as they scream, jump, and thrash around in response to the information their brain is being fed (Fig 91). Their sense of reality has been hijacked in often seconds. Notice, too, that headset information is hacking into the sight senses as more sophisticated

Figure 90: The body is like a virtual reality headset decoding the simulation as a headset decodes a game.

Figure 91: Don a headset and immediately peoples' sense of reality becomes whatever the headset delivers.

games with earphones and gloves hack into other senses (Fig 92). Special gaming chairs add to the sensation of headset reality being 'real'. Virtual reality video games hack into the five senses to override 'normal' reality that is decoded by the same senses. Video players can at least respond by taking off the headset and returning to 'normal' reality to realise that

Figure 92: Virtual reality can seem so 'real', but you can stop, take off the headset, and return to 'normal'. Imagine what would happen if you couldn't take off the body headset short of dying? You know what that would be like – you are living it now. It seems so real doesn't it?

it was just a game.

Consider instead that your body/brain was the headset and you couldn't take it off short of dying and leaving the realm of 'human'. Your attention is only in this 'world' because your body/brain headset is decoding it. Imagine this scenario: You are in the womb as your headset forms and then you emerge to see parents and siblings wearing headsets. You go to school with your friends in headsets to be 'taught' by teachers in headsets. You may go on to university where academics and esteemed professors in headsets tell you to believe what their headsets tell *them*. You turn on the television, radio, or Internet videos to see people in headsets telling you what to believe about life and the world. Scientists and doctors in headsets pontificate about reality and health while your every headset social media post is met with responses from headset replies. All around you every day of your life are people in headsets being delivered the basically same version of reality as you as the body/brain decodes the simulation into an illusory 'physical' reality. This continues from womb to tomb until your headset body/brain ceases to function and your awareness is released into another headset with different information called the soul.

What is going to happen? All except a tiny minority will believe what the headset tells them and live their lives as if it's real. Your sense of reality can be taken over in seconds by a headset that you can remove. Think of the perceptual imprint of a headset that you *can't* remove without leaving the world. This is humanity's plight in stark focus. This is how billions of people can live the same illusion. Plus anyone who deviates from headset conformity is subjected to abuse and ridicule by headset believers and they can be marginalised from society, and even family, for the crime of having the wrong opinion at odds with headset reality. The pressure to conform is immense and you don't pass exams and secure degrees by having a mind of your own. Headset reality sets the questions and it demands headset answers. This is the whole basis for left-brain enslavement and it is no coincidence that those most adept at giving headset answers to headset questions end up in positions of authority in science, academia, medicine, media, and politics. The system is structured to deliver that outcome. Can I see it, touch it, hear it, taste it, smell it? Oh, it exists then. The five-sense prison walls are set in concrete at an early age which solidifies further with every passing year.

Tricking the brain

American programmer Michael Abrash, chief scientist at Meta-owned virtual reality headset subsidiary Oculus, predicted that human virtual reality could one day be like the movie, *The Matrix*. 'Real' reality already is. He described in a presentation how easily the brain is tricked into seeing what is not there. Abrash said that human eyes have only three colour sensors and we can't see infrared or ultraviolet, There is also a blind spot on each eye which the brain fills in with its best guess of what is there. 'Our visual data is actually astonishingly sparse and even if we were able to accurately record and process every photon that reaches our eyes, we'd still have too little data to be able to reconstruct the world accurately.' Abrash showed a series of optical illusions that confirmed how the brain/mind can be tricked into seeing colours and shapes, and hearing human speech, based on perception. 'I think it's fair to say our experience of the world is an illusion.' VR technology was about experiencing a virtual world as real [and] experiences were nothing more or less than whatever the mind inferred. If you add these sensory limitations to simulated reality itself the illusory nature of experienced reality is astonishing in its depth and potential to delude. But there's more.

I say that a perceptual program that I call the Astral AI Mind is running through the body as I will expand upon in the chapter on reincarnation. For now I will just say that it's a perceptual program constantly messing with your head. It is the mind chatter that tells you to feel guilt or shame, to doubt your own thoughts when they question headset perception, or, at the extreme, to act with psychopathic vindictiveness. The chatter instigates division, hostility, a sense of powerlessness and fear of authority. These body-programs can be personalised in ways I will describe. Here you are, a state of consciousness disconnected from its Infinite Self beyond the simulation, being bombarded with perceptual instructions through the body program that supports the download of headset reality. It is a wonder that anyone awakens from this induced perceptual coma, this induced *dream*. But they *do* – and they *are*. I don't mean the majority or anything like. I mean more than ever before in 'modern history'. The 'how' comes down to consciousness and setting it free to explore all possibility outside of the headset, the body program, and the simulation as a whole. These different simulation levels are bands of frequency designed to entrap consciousness in perpetual illusion and ignorance whether in the human or 'spirit worlds'. Control of perception means control of your *point of attention*. I will address later how we can break free from this – which we *can*. Those that live their entire lives (and *so* many do) under the spell of headset reality and the body program are the equivalent of non-player characters in a video game. These are defined as 'a video game character that is controlled by the game's artificial intelligence (AI) rather than by a gamer'. That is a perfect description of people being played by the game through the headset and body program. I saw a list of traits claiming to be signs of non-player characters:

Every single day seems the same; most of your conversations are about the weather, gossip or complaining; you hate your job; you cannot go out and have fun by yourself; you take the same path every day; more than 90 percent of your thoughts are the same thoughts you think every day; you don't know your purpose; You are reactive to others; all of the choices you make are mainstream; you feel powerless to have a free will.

The antidote is awakening to your consciousness beyond the 'game'.

What is 'history'

I put 'modern history' in quotes just now as I would 'history' in general. What is 'history' in the light of what I am saying? If there is no time, how can there be a 'past' let alone a history of the past? If we are decoding the headset reality program why can't 'history' be nothing more than information encoded in the program that we believe to be history? We must have linear 'time' for history to exist and we don't. We have only the Infinite NOW. Oh, but we have historical 'finds' and discoveries that prove there is history. We even have 'past lives' when we lived in other eras of history. How do we *know*? How do we know that 'historical discoveries' are not simply encoded into the program to make it appear that we have history as part of the overall perception deception? How can history be linear when time is not linear? Is it not the case that only by decoding a reality designed to *appear* like that do we have the experience of time passing through history? I am not making definitive statements here, only asking questions that need to be asked. There would seem from my research over the years to be multiple

timelines (perceptual programs) for 'incarnation' within different expressions of the simulation. Does this mean that consciousness is still 'incarnating' from the Astral into human experiences that we know as ancient Greece, ancient Egypt and ancient Rome? Once we realise we are in a simulation anything is simulatable and all bets are off when it comes to immovable belief (Fig 93). They must all come under the spotlight to be

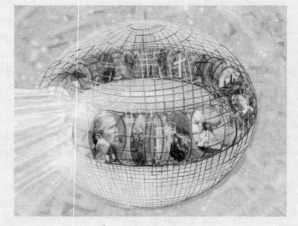

Figure 93: How can there be history if there is no time? Is what we call 'history' different parts of the simulation that we experience as encoded 'eras' and timelines? I am not saying that for sure, but the question should be posed. (Image by Neil Hague.)

questioned. You can appreciate how this fluidity is fundamentally at odds with the left-brain's need for certainty. This need is what makes people retreat into belief solidity in pursuit of certainty through religion and the religion of academia and 'science'.

The evolution myth (2)

An academic I have time for is Donald Hoffman, an American cognitive psychologist and professor in the Department of Cognitive Sciences at the University of California, Irvine. He is connected to the Department of Philosophy, Department of Logic and Philosophy of Science, and the School of Computer Science. He is prepared to think outside the box a little and go where that takes them. I don't agree with everything Hoffman says, and differ greatly in some areas, but I like his willingness to challenge *some* long-held dogma. He accepts, for example, the holographic nature of experienced reality and that 'physical' reality only exists when it is observed. Hoffman is author of *The Case Against Reality – Why evolution hid the truth from our eyes* which contends that the reality we experience can be likened to a desktop interface on a computer. 'Physical' objects to him are 'icons' that represent symbols of 'objective reality' that save us all the complication of having to constantly deal with reality's symbolic computer software and workings behind the icons. Okay, I get that. But if we don't know this, and almost the entirety of humanity does not, we become a cinch to manipulate through skewing our perception (and so behaviour) in the direction of loosh production.

Hoffman sees that body systems are not wired to reveal 'objective reality' which is defined as 'something that can be confirmed independent of a mind'. This must be true when we are presented with an illusory 'physical' world that results from biological decoding that is crucially influenced by our perception. His ball and chain, however, appears to be his emphasis on 'natural selection'. This is the theory of Charles Darwin that organisms which best adapt to change are able to survive ('survival of the fittest') and these characteristics are passed down from parents to children. Darwin came from a family closely connected to the Cult as I said earlier. 'Evolution' comes not from natural selection – there can be no 'natural' in simulated reality – it comes from informational changes delivered through Astral programming and the effects of consciousness on biological systems. Witness the 'Cambrian Explosion' period and the evolutionarily-sudden expansion of biological life from basic to complex forms. What Hoffman describes is not the result of natural selection. It is by calculated design encoded by the simulation creators and operators and the result of an interactive simulation in which it affects *us* and we can affect *it*.

Scientists speak of evolution over the vastness of 'time' when there is no time. No wonder science is a ball of confusion when pillars of its belief system are not allowed to be seen for the nonsense that they are. They speak of 'space-time' when there is no space and there is no time. These are illusions of simulation decoding in the same way that 'space' (distance, perspective) and 'time' (one scene following another) are simply decoded codes playing out in a virtual reality computer game. Scenes in the game 'passing by' that give the illusion of time all exist in the game at the *same time*. The time illusion is how they are delivered to you perceptually as one after the other. Until science can drop the diversion of 'natural selection', or natural anything, it will never get it. What is 'natural'? How do we define 'natural'? Well, like this: 'As found in nature and not involving anything made or done by people.' So what *is* nature? This, apparently: 'All the animals, plants, rocks, etc. in the world and all the features, forces, and processes that happen or exist independently of people, such as the weather, the sea, mountains, the production of young animals or plants, and growth.'

Why would we automatically believe that everything not involving people must be 'natural' and not by simulated design? How do we know? Are humans the only source of potential design? It shows how myopic the human mind can be. We note the technology built by humans and think everything else must be natural. How do we know? The only proof would come from comparing perceived natural with something that we absolutely *knew* beyond doubt or question was natural. How can we genuinely do that? How do we know that the biological is not also technological in the sense of being the result of conscious design? I can tell you from my research into the Cult over 35 years that they treat the biological as a form of technology. Far more advanced than a machine made of steel, but still technology (Fig 94). Inner circle cultists know that the body is a computer system and they treat it as such in their manipulation of humans. Moderna documents describe the content of their 'Covid' fake vaccine as an 'operating system' and dub their 'medicines' in terms of the 'software of life'. There is no 'natural' within the simulation except consciousness where it exists in a non-molested state. We are experiencing a wave-particle-digital copy and as a result what we perceive as nature is no more natural than a holographic image.

Donald Hoffman makes some really valid points. Where he loses the plot in my view is when it comes to the 'why?' He contends: 'The bottom line is the reason why evolution by natural selection does not shape us to see truth is because the pay-off functions [evolutionary benefits] that guide evolution don't contain the truth.' He says that instead of assuming that data (and how we would normally think about that data) is the truth, we had to be a bit more clever. We had to be like a person who's wearing a VR headset playing a video game. You could ask questions about the geometry of this game as you perceived it. 'But if you think that is going to take you

Figure 94: The 'natural' world does exist in Prime Reality, but our 'nature' is a simulated copy of that which we decode from the simulation field into the illusion of walking through a forest. (Image by Neil Hague.)

to an understanding of the deepest reality, which in this metaphor would be the circuits and software and electromagnetic field of some hidden supercomputer that's running the game, you are going to be sadly mistaken … you have to think outside of the headset.' All correct and I get the impression that perhaps Hoffman is aware of far more than the limits of his academic environment would be happy for him to talk about. Hoffman certainly sees that consciousness comes not from the brain, but something far greater. He says that our experienced reality is like a computer interface that shows us only the level with which we interact while hiding all that exists beyond it: 'Evolution shaped us with a user interface that hides the truth. Nothing that we see is the truth – the very language of space and time and objects is the wrong language to describe reality.' True. The trouble is that 'evolution' is there once again when it is nothing to do with that. Perceived 'evolution' are simulation programs playing out and the potential overriding of those programs by consciousness. The truth is hidden from us for reasons of *control*, not natural selection. To realise this is to explore what intelligence must be behind that control. Imagine a mainstream scientist with a career to consider going down that road. Not many.

Space and time programming

Hoffman says that our perception of space, time, and objects were shaped by evolution to let us live long enough to raise offspring and not to reveal or reconstruct objective reality. Here we see the misconceptions that whatever is behind 'nature' is primarily interested in procreation of the species. The program seeks to perpetuate itself, for sure. What is not addressed are other prime motivations like control through perceptual manipulation to produce loosh. 'Perception is not about truth, it's about having kids', he says. This is seriously missing the point. Perception is not about truth, it's about *control*. He says that 'evolution has shaped our senses to keep us alive'. I suggest that what keeps us alive is the software program running through the biological computer that has a pre-encoded end unless overridden by consciousness. On the same theme of natural selection Hoffman says that the 'interface theory of perception' (ITP) defines an illusion as 'a perception that fails to guide adaptive behaviour' (learning from experience). 'So illusions are failures to guide adaptive behaviour, not failures to see the truth.' I disagree. Simulation illusion is specifically there to *ensure* that you fail to see the truth. He asks which taste is illusory – the taste of the pig that loves to eat faeces or the human that finds the idea grotesque. The answer is that *both* are illusory in relation to how we experience them and they relate to the encoded perception of the 'consumer'. Interface theory says that a taste is illusory only if it fails to prompt 'adaptive behaviour'. Where I agree with Hoffman is that humans believe they are progressing towards 'truth' with the development of advanced technology and so on, when they are only becoming 'better masters of the interface' – not getting closer to truth: '… As long as our theories are stuck within spacetime, we cannot master what lurks behind.' On that, we are agreed. Even at the level of pixel reality and atoms, he says, we are still in space and time and still in the interface, or, as I would say, still pursuing here and no further. He quotes American-Canadian theoretical physicist Nima Arkani-Hamed as saying:

> Many, many separate arguments, all very strong individually, suggest that the very notion of spacetime is not a fundamental one. Spacetime is doomed. There is no such thing as spacetime fundamentally in the actual underlying description of the laws of physics.
>
> That's very startling, because what physics is supposed to be about is describing things as they happen in space and time. So, if there's no spacetime, it's not clear what physics is all about.

I think the baby has parted company with the bathwater here. Space and time exist as a reality decoded by the body computer from the information field of the simulation. It is illusory in that it is a *construct* and in the way it deludes perception with, in effect, an induced dream. Physics, as we perceive them, are the encoded limits to the human virtual reality 'game' that dictate how the game is played without the intervention of consciousness outside the simulation. Some scientists are now seeing through the space and time illusion that I have been exposing as such for decades. Nathan Seiberg at the Institute of Advanced Studies at Princeton says: 'I am almost certain that space and time are illusions … These are primitive notions that will be replaced by something more sophisticated.'

Yes – it's a *simulation*.

Creator v Evolution

Another block on seeing reality for what it is comes with the idea that 'God's' creation must refer to the God that religions believe they are worshipping. That is not the case with the simulation. I watched a presentation by Seymour 'Sy' Garte who has quite a CV. He is a tenured professor at New York University, Rutgers University, and the University of Pittsburgh, division director at the Center for Scientific Review of the National Institutes of Health, and interim vice president for research at the Uniformed Services University of the Health Sciences. He has according to his website 'published over 200 peer-reviewed scientific papers, three scientific monographs, and two mass market books'. You would not think that I would question such an esteemed professor when I left school at 15 where my state academic career ended. But I do. An open mind always trumps an academic one that won't face the fact that experienced reality is an illusion, or that 'God' is not the 'God' that they think 'He' is. Garte told his audience that he was brought up in 'a militantly atheist family' and was taught that God didn't exist. He later became a devout Christian because of his study of biology and wrote a book, *The Work of His Hands*. Garte said that biologists like him were overwhelmingly atheist and quoted a survey that claimed 68 percent of Royal Society physicists, chemists, and mathematicians identified as atheists. With biologists, it was 89 percent. You can see why this is so when they are extraordinary left-brainers focussing on the biological detail and not the panorama within which the detail operates.

The best-known atheist – there is no God – is Professor Richard Dawkins, an evolutionary biologist at Oxford University who has turned his desire to prove the absence of 'God' into a life-long obsession. See his book, *The God Delusion*. He agrees that reality *looks* like it's designed when it's not. It's *natural section*. I took part in a debate with Dawkins and others at the Oxford Union Society in the early 1990s and I found him to be one of the most unintelligent academics I have ever encountered. You would think it would be the opposite. In my experience, it wasn't. Dawkins believes biology proves the absence of 'God' while for biologist Seymour Garte the opposite happened. Studying biology and its obvious design made him believe in a God. He details all the repeating patterns evident in reality (which I have described) and how there are error correcting codes to keep those patterns stable. Error correcting codes are a feature of computers. American theoretical physicist James Gates, a science advisor to the Obama administration, led a team that identified error correcting codes in the fabric of reality, as well as a set of equations indistinguishable from those that drive search engines and browsers, and embedded electrical binary codes that are used in computers.

Garte makes the excellent observation that natural selection and evolution do not explain *origin*. For something to 'evolve' there has to be something in the first place which can then 'evolve'. Evolution depended on self-replication of evolutionary changes to an original something. Okay, but this does *not* mean that this grand design must be the work of the 'Divine'. It can also be the work of a force that is far from 'Divine' while having a great enough knowledge of reality to pull it off. Like the Gnostic Yaldabaoth, Christian Satan or Islamic Shaytan. I saw another science video asking if we live in someone else's mind. The premise was that everything appears to be a reflection of everything else as with the electrical connections of the brain mirroring the electrical connections of the Universe (Fig 95). This is easily explained by the holographic principle and the fact that the brain/body has to be electrical to interact with what is a simulated *electrical* Universe (more soon). Another pointer to a simulated reality is how perfect, but *only just*, is the Earth atmosphere to support human life. Scientist Robert Lanza wrote in his book, *Biocentrism*:

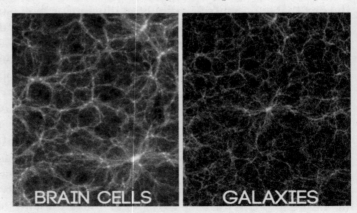

Figure 95: As above, so below, the holographic principle.

Why are the laws of physics exactly balanced for animal life to exist? ... If the strong nuclear force were decreased 2 percent, atomic nuclei wouldn't hold together, and plain-vanilla hydrogen would be the only kind of atom in the Universe.

If the gravitational force were decreased by a hair, stars (including the Sun) would not ignite. These are just [some of] more than 200 parameters within the solar system and Universe so exact that it strains credulity to propose that they are random – even if that is exactly what standard contemporarily physics baldly suggests.

How could this be? Click, click, enter. It is made that way to sync with the encoded requirements of the body as perceived by humans.

The Newton diversion

Mainstream science has been dominated by the Newtonian physics (also 'classical mechanics') the father of which was English physicist Isaac Newton (1642–1727). This 'science' is focussed on forces acting upon matter and continues to be the standard approach for the motion of objects of all kinds from machine parts to planets and galaxies. He also emphasised gravity (hence the apple falling story related to him) and he reached conclusions that have survived to this day. Newton was talking about forces acting on matter when there is no matter as we perceive it and he emphasised gravity when electromagnetism is seriously more powerful and significant. Electromagnetic forces exceed the strength of gravity 'by a factor of 10 followed by 39 zeros'. That is not a criticism of Newton in that he was dealing with the knowledge of his day. The problem is that science ever since has worn his matter-based concepts like a chain around its neck while quantum physics and the pure logic of expanded observation should have transformed science from a matter-obsessed discipline to one seeking out the forces which produce the illusion of matter. In some areas this has begun to happen although the mainstream of the mainstream continues to be resistant and Newton-centric. The same has happened with Darwin and natural selection which is again Newton and matter-centric. Changes made to the simulation program through changes in the information 'Wi-Fi' field are passed on through 'procreation'. This is making copies of the upgraded (or downgraded) program. Other programs are deleted as new ones are introduced and we call this 'extinction'. Environmental (program) changes can make it impossible for some programs to continue.

What does all this mean for religion? Associate professor of physics Melvin Vopson takes care in one chapter of his simulation book not to upset those with religious belief and avoid causing offence or conflict. I don't seek to do this either. I respect the right of everyone to have whatever religious belief they choose. This does not mean avoiding views and conclusions that question those beliefs. That's a cop-out. Any belief that is unquestioned solidifies into a mind program that must not be breached. Wisdom is knowing how little we know. Vopson rightly says that the simulation hypothesis does not rule out a creator or grand designer. No, it doesn't. It must, by definition, *require* such intelligence. What it doesn't mean is that this force must be benevolent and benign. I have made clear my conclusion that the 'God' of Genesis is the Gnostic

Yaldabaoth symbolically creating the simulation.

Vopson highlights the start of the Gospel of John which says that in the beginning was the Word, and the Word was with God and the Word was God.' He says that when examining that verse through 'the lens of simulation theory' it is possible that 'the Word' could be 'the underlying code that governs the simulation'. He adds: 'This could be seen as the allusion to the idea that the code running the simulation is not separate from the Divine, but rather an integral part of it, perhaps an AI.' I would challenge the idea that the simulator creator is 'Divine'. I say the 'Divine' source is beyond the simulation. Vopson also says: 'It highlights the idea that Creator's intelligence is embedded in the very fabric of reality, including our consciousness.' I agree, with some provisos, and I will be addressing this is detail later. I just say that Vopson has the wrong 'God'. Gnostics also called Yaldabaoth the 'Great Architect of the Universe' which is the same as the Freemason Creator deity. Rosicrucians used this term, as do some within Christianity. The Hindu creator god Vishvakarma is the 'God of Architecture'. The creator of the Matrix in the movie series is 'the Architect'. We need to break the stranglehold on religious perception that the 'Architect' has to be 'Divine'.

Gathering support among many scientists for the 'simulation hypothesis' does have many correlations with religions if we drop the idea that human reality and the Astral are the creation of the 'Divine'. We can bring together both a Creator and human science once we see that these realities are the simulated work of the biblical *opposition* to the 'Divine' – Satan/Shaytan/Yaldabaoth. The 'Divine' is the infinite realm beyond the simulation. I say, for example, that the biblical 'fall' of humanity came after Divine Spark consciousness experiencing expanded realms of Creation was enticed into the simulated lair of Yaldabaoth. A copy, however imperfect, may explain how the enticement was possible. The experience once 'inside' lowered the vibration of entrapped 'Sparks' so they could not leave until they had regained the frequency that allowed them to breach its energetic barriers. It's like a frequency mouse trap. We perceive we are human only because that is the point of attention the body decoding system leads us to focus upon. We perceive in the 'spirit world' that we are a soul for the same reason as our point of attention moves from one to the other. It's *all* about the point of attention. Spiritual philosopher Alan Watts was right when he defined the 'ego' (a sense of human identity) as '... nothing other than the focus of attention'. The whole reason for the simulation is to hijack 'incarnate' and 'discarnate' perception – *attention* – to keep us in the simulation to produce loosh. The Astral has many realms where Divine Sparks entrapped in souls reside between incarnations into matter in the belief that it will promote their 'evolution' and that's why 'evolution' is the manipulated mantra of human science. At whatever level of the simulation the story is basically the same and to the same end.

We can now move on to see how the simulation works 'scientifically'. Many scientists have uncovered the parts (left-brain). The trick is to put them all together (right-brain/whole-brain). Let's go.

CHAPTER EIGHT

Plasma Matrix

*I shall not commit the fashionable stupidity of regarding everything
I cannot explain as a fraud*

Carl Jung

I was emailed as I began this book by a remarkable man, the author and
science researcher, Robert Temple. He was reading *The Dream* and
suggested it would be a good idea to meet. It was.

I had read his book, *The Sirius Mystery*, first published in 1976 and
substantially expanded in 1998. This featured the Dogon tribe in Mali,
Africa, who appeared to know detailed facts about the Sirius star system
that were only later confirmed by mainstream science. They claimed to
know this from extraterrestrial visitors from Sirius with the knowledge
passed on through tribal history. I had not realised until I met Robert
and his wife Olivia at their home in the Somerset countryside what a
prolific researcher and writer he was and the incredible contacts and
connections that he had with scientists who thought outside the
orthodoxy. Temple writes that he is always on the lookout for things that
don't fit with present scientific understanding. That's my kind of guy.
He is a specialist among many other subjects on ancient Egyptian
history. He has had academic posts and has written on scientific themes
for the *Sunday Times, Guardian, Time-Life, The New Scientist* and the
science journal, *Nature*, as well as making documentaries for the UK's
Channel 4 and National Geographic channels. His books on multiple
subjects include: *The Sphinx Mystery; Egyptian Dawn; The Genius of China;
Netherworld; The Crystal Sun; Aesop: The Complete Fables; He Who Saw
Everything: a verse translation of the Epic of Gilgamesh; Open to Suggestion:
The Uses and Abuses of Hypnosis; Conversations with Eternity;* and *Searching
for the Palace of Odysseus* published in 2024. You see what I mean about
multiple subjects. Robert mentioned in the email his then latest book, *A
New Science of Heaven: How the new science of plasma physics is shedding
light on spiritual experience*. I bought and read it immediately because it
contained a key word for me – plasma.

'Radiant matter'

I first came across plasma a long time ago when I was researching the electrical and electromagnetic nature of the simulated Universe. A few enlightened people thousands of years ago identified plasma while using other names. Ancient Greek philosopher Aristotle (384 BC-322 BC) spoke of a field of energy overlaying the 'physical' body that he called the ether or 'fifth element'. He believed that divine entities were also made of this ether along with the Sun and other stars. Ether is *plasma*. It is amazing that Aristotle could see this so long before the technological era and confirms how much more advanced humans would be without the arrogant ignorance of the scientific and religious establishment suppressing the truth. The term 'plasma' was coined by the brilliant Nobel-winning American scientist Irving Langmuir (1881-1957) when it reminded him of blood plasma. This is the liquid part of blood that transports nutrients to cells and organs and waste products to the kidneys, liver, and lungs to be excreted. Cosmic plasma 'transports' particles, electricity, and electromagnetism *(information)* by being electrically-superconductive and much more. Atoms are said to be the building blocks of matter, but that is a tiny fraction of the Universe despite mainstream science being mesmerised by it. Matter is like looking for a needle while ignoring the haystack – plasma. It was first identified in 1879 by British scientist William Crookes who called it 'radiant matter' and the work of Crookes had a big influence on a scientific genius of the 20th century, Nikola Tesla, who said he focussed on an electrical career after studying Crookes' 'epochal work on radiation matter'.

The visible universe *is* plasma

Plasma is described as the 'fourth state of matter' along with solid, liquid and gas. Think of ice ('solid'), heated to become water (liquid), and heated further to become steam (gas). Plasma should be called the *first* state of matter given that *99 percent*, some say even *99.9 percent*, of the visible universe is plasma. Let that sink and settle for a moment. We are told that we live in a reality of 'atomic' matter when as much as *99.9 percent* of our visible world is something else. Then remember that around 99 percent of atoms are plasma and subatomic particles. Plasma extends into the Astral dimension – it *is* the Astral dimension. 'Matter' is a low-vibrational expression or projection *within* the Astral which the human body is encoded to decode as the experience of physical reality. 'Death' is when electricity stops and the body ceases to function (decode the electrical/electromagnetic/frequency simulation field into matter). The 'soul' is anchored in the Astral and 'death' is the brief conscious projection of *part* of the soul into matter withdrawing back into Astral awareness (Fig 96 overleaf). This is happening during a near-death experience. Robert Temple writes: 'I am suggesting that we and all living things in the Universe, whether organic or inorganic, arise of this plasma, and that the organic state is secondary to our

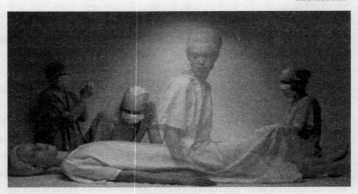

Figure 96: Dying is simply our consciousness withdrawing from the body 'headset' when it ceases to function and decode the human world into illusory reality. Consciousness returns to the Astral soul field and even better to the Spirit and out of the simulation.

fundamental nature as plasma beings.' Temple explains that plasma is made of incomplete or partial atoms called 'ions' and smaller particles known as protons and electrons. 'We call the physical matter that is familiar to us "atomic matter" because it is made of whole atoms, whereas plasma can also be described as non-atomic or subatomic matter.' We see plasma as lightning and ball lightning, but it is otherwise invisible. Plasma is used to create neon lights and we all know the plasma balls with the dancing light forking out to meet your hand (Fig 97). The same principle can be seen with plasma auroras. Plasmas in technology are used to manufacture semiconductor chips and can also be produced in a laboratory by heating gas to an extreme temperature.

We have plasma bodies in the Astral known as the 'soul' which interacts with the human material body. This interaction is known as 'incarnation' and involves a transfer of conscious *attention* from the plasma body to the material body. 'Death' is a reverse transfer of our conscious *attention*. I'll have a lot more about this later along with the gathering evidence for plasma having intelligence. Temple says that we have to consider for reasons I will explain 'whether or not plasmas can be said to be living, intelligent and conscious'. It is clear that plasmas *are* intelligent. This has extraordinary implications for our sense of reality.

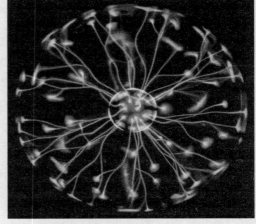

Figure 97: A plasma ball or globe.

Biological organic humans are, like the atomic realm of matter, a rarity. Astral plasma entities are the prime form of life in the simulation and they include 'extraterrestrial' phenomena which I say is extra-*dimensional*. Entities the ancients called the 'Shining Ones' were plasma 'radiant matter'. A common theme of 'historical' accounts is that those with expanded awareness on higher dimensions appeared with bright and radiant energetic fields while those who fall down the octaves into evil intent become less and less luminous. You can see with this the concept of the 'dark side'. Other accounts, including the Jewish Book of Enoch, continue the theme describing entities with forms like 'flaming fire' that could appear on Earth as humans. Plasma beings can appear as their minds dictate. Robert Temple suggests that biblical miracles such as the burning bush could have been plasma at work. Gnostics said that Yaldabaoth exists in a 'place' that burns with a luminous fire while 'the Father' resides in something similar only far brighter.

Electricity everywhere

Plasma is the almost perfect medium for electricity and electromagnetism and together they form the simulated Universe. I'll first focus on the electrical/electromagnetic and then come to plasma in detail. There is a branch of scientific research (not in the mainstream, of course) known collectively as the Electric Universe and the Thunderbolts Project. Among its pioneers were the late Australian physicist Wallace Thornhill, Donald Scott, a retired Professor of Electrical Engineering, and American researcher and writer David Talbott. I have written about electrical and electromagnetic reality in books going way back. I have long considered the human realm of perceived matter to be a thin band of electricity and electromagnetism flowing through its plasma medium. We have already seen that atoms have no solidity and consist of particles which themselves have no solidity. Their foundation is *electrical and electromagnetic*. If we could

observe the night sky with expanded vision beyond visible light we would see a vast electrical system in which planets and stars are node points (intersection points) within the circuitry (Fig 98 and Fig 99 overleaf). We are experiencing a virtual reality simulation generated through electricity as with virtual reality computer games. The

Figure 98: This is how we see the night sky within visible light.

cosmic electrical networks are the electrical circuits of the simulation. Mainstream science is increasingly finding evidence of what Electric Universe researchers have predicted. Herschel telescope images have confirmed that stars are formed on galactic filaments which conventional science believed to be impossible while Electric Universe

Figure 99: If we could see deeper into the field the Universe would appear as an interconnected electrical system with stars and planets as node points in the circuitry.

advocates had long said this would be the case. David Sibeck, a project scientist at NASA's Goddard Space Flight Center, said:

> The satellites have found evidence of magnetic ropes connecting Earth's upper atmosphere directly to the Sun. We believe that solar winds flow in along these ropes providing energy for geomagnetic storms and auroras.

We have obvious expressions of environmental electricity/plasma with lightning and the northern lights (aurora borealis) and southern lights (aurora australis). Lightning is an example of the extent of electrical reality and connectivity (Fig 100). We see it happening at lower levels close to the Earth and it continues out into the Cosmos under other names such as tendrils, sprites and elves (Fig 101). Tornadoes are rapidly rotating electromagnetic fields during electrical storms and the tails of

Figure 100: Lightning and the aurora borealis are obvious expressions of electricity in the atmosphere.

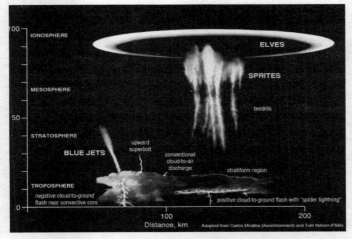

ELVES

SPRITES

tendrils

IONOSPHERE

MESOSPHERE

STRATOSPHERE

BLUE JETS

upward superbolt

conventional cloud-to-air discharge

stratiform region

TROPOSPHERE

negative cloud-to-ground flash near convective core

positive cloud-to-ground flash with "spider lightning"

Distance, km   Adapted from Carlos Miralles (AeroVironment) and Tom Nelson (FMA)

Figure 101: Lightning electrical connections continue into the Cosmos under names such as sprites and elves in one electrical system.

comets are electrical. We are looking at a gigantic electrical and electromagnetic web which is the foundation of human reality and what we call 'matter'. Body and brain are electrical, our thoughts are electrical, and communication throughout the body is electrical. This connects into the universal electrical grid to form what I have long described as the Cosmic Internet (Fig 102). Extremely high blood pressure has been lowered by putting an electrical wire in the brain to change what is communicated. Our bodies interact with the electrical simulation field as an electrical computer interacts with electrical/electromagnetic Wi-Fi. The structure of the body/brain and simulation field are the same as they must be in a holographic universe with the as above, so below, characteristic. As the whole, so the parts. Bees seek out pollen through electrical signals transmitted by flowers. Positively charged bees are electrically attracted to negatively charged flowers via small facial hairs. They communicate where to forage through a series of movements called a 'waggle dance' to create static electricity and direct fellow bees

THE COSMIC INTERNET

Figure 102: The brain processes information through electrical activity and connects with the electrical simulation field – the 'Universe'.

to a source of nectar. I have seen this described as 'Bee Sat-Nav'. Animals, insects, and plants communicate with electrical signalling. Spider webs are electrostatically attracted to electrically-charged flying insects while static charges can be strong enough for insects to pull pollen through the air.

Dr Yuri Shtessel, professor emeritus in the Department of Electrical and Computer Engineering at the University of Alabama in Huntsville, and Dr Alexander Volkov, professor of biochemistry at Oakwood University, co-authored a study into transmission of electrical signals between tomato plants. They concluded that soil 'is alive with electrical signals being sent from one plant to another'. Plants can communicate directly and by exchanging electrical signals through the 'mycorrhizal' fungi network in the soil. Shtessel said the soil plays the role of a conductor. I have written before about a similar network between trees known as the 'Wood Wide Web' in which trees communicate through electrical and chemical signals sent via fungal networks in the soil that can be likened to fibre-optic Internet cables. Birds migrate using their own in-built magnetic compasses and a German team at the University of Oldenburg revealed that technologically generated electromagnetic fields from equipment plugged into mains electricity interfere with this navigation.

Electric people

Humans can communicate electrically and people talk about the 'electricity between us'. The concept is literally true with the exchange of electrical frequencies (Fig 103). Electrical/electromagnetic human reality can be seen with the brain/body operating and communicating electrically with every thought, emotion, and heartbeat (Fig 104). Jacqueline Barton and her team at the California Institute of Technology (Caltech) discovered that DNA is 'like an electrical wire for signalling within a cell'. Barton may have been a world-renowned chemist, but many colleagues enslaved by their left-brain would not believe that DNA could conduct electricity when that *must* be the case within the electrical system of matter that I am describing. Barton's experiments showed that DNA can be compared with a phone cable. Phones convert the frequency of your voice (vocal cords generate waves of vibration) and convert

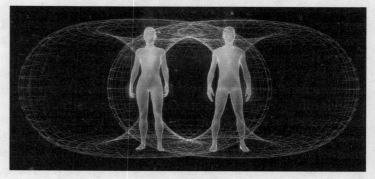

Figure 103: Human auric fields can combine to create 'electricity' between people – or instant aversion. 'Good vibes' and 'bad vibes' are felt in this way and aware people can sense the character and intent of others no matter what their face is doing or words are saying.

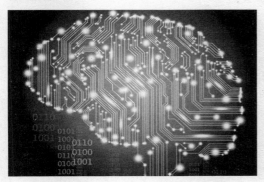

Figure 104: Brain and body are an electrical communication system as you would expect in a holographic electrical universe.

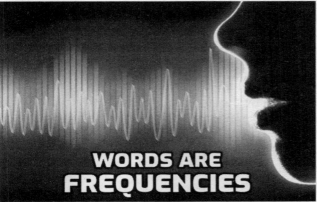

Figure 105: Our vocal cords generate soundwave *frequencies* and the brain decodes them into language. Beyond human reality communication is by telepathy which has been suppressed in most humans to further limit our ability to sense reality and each other outside the serious limitation of voice-to-ear language.

this to electricity routed through the phone line. Electrical energy is transformed at the other end back into sound waves through the earpiece. The ears of the receiver transform this again into electrical information which their brain decodes as the sound of a voice. A simple phone call follows the sequence of sound waves (vocal cords); electricity (phone line); sound waves (speaker to ears); electricity (receiver's ears to brain). DNA is a receiver-transmitter of information that interacts with the simulation field and potentially wider reality and given that we live 'in' an electrical system DNA *must* have an electrical function. The point about vocal cords is more confirmation that everything within the simulation is ultimately frequency. We think we speak words when we really generate frequencies through the vibrating vocal cords. These soundwave fields are decoded by the hearing senses into electrical information which is communicated to the brain to be decoded into the worlds that we hear (Fig 105).

Dehydration is dangerous because water is a conduit for electricity. Something like 60 percent of the body is water and this rises to around 73 percent with the electrical brain and heart. Water, like everything in our reality, is encoded frequency field information which we *de*code into what we experience as water in its holographic expression. How can we drown when water is a decoded holographic reality that only exists in that form in our brain? It is the manifestation of perception and the body software program. Most people drown when they are under water for too long. It's the way the body is encoded to respond. Others have been in the water for far, far, longer, way beyond when they should have died, and are revived unscathed. The body interacts with the electrical/electromagnetic levels of the simulation field and the electrical system that we call the Universe. All this is happening within the medium of plasma which is the Astral dimension appearing to us as 'empty space'. Mainstream science fails to grasp the foundation of reality when it is locked away in the left-brain and can see only parts, not connections.

Powerful electromagnetic energy emitted by some people is called 'charisma' and Christians believe this is conferred on chosen individuals by the 'Holy Spirit'. In fact, it's anyone who can generate electromagnetic power by tapping into the field of electrical potential. Those with positive intent can do this and have 'charisma' and so can those with malevolent intent. The difference is that one will project high-frequency power and the other low-frequency. Either way it can influence people (other electromagnetic fields) in their presence. Some of the world's greatest tyrants have had 'charisma' and often thanks to energy directed through them by their demonic possessors in the Astral. Our thoughts and emotional responses are electrical on one level. We decode the field into 'physical' reality through electrical signals sent by the five senses to the brain. The central nervous system is electrical and electromagnetic which is part of the electromagnetic auric mind (Fig 106).

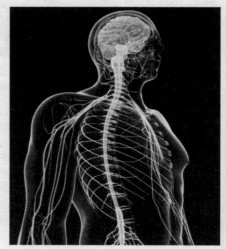

Planets and stars are holographic expressions of electricity and electromagnetism moving through the collective plasma simulation field. The impact on the field caused by their movement is the foundation of astrology. They are electrical/electromagnetic consciousness that add their unique effect on the field and this can be greatly increased when they form connections and patterns known in astrology as conjunctions, trines,

Figure 106: The electrical central nervous system.

aspects, transits, and eclipses. Electric Universe advocates rightly say that a planet or star is 'just one device in a circuit'. Humans are interacting with the same field and we are affected by changes caused by astrological movements and sequences. The impact can vary depending on where in the sequence we entered matter reality. The field when we are born (some say conceived) is encoded in our human field and we will interact with changes in the field in different ways based on that imprint. A 'Taurus' will often have different affects to a 'Leo'. Astrology is the reading of these electrical, electromagnetic, and plasma phenomena. The interaction of electricity with plasma explains many things including the formation of planetary 'magnetospheres', or planetary magnetic fields. Scientist Irving Langmuir discovered that when a region of plasma with a particular electrical charge meets plasma with a different charge a barrier is automatically created between the two to form a magnetosphere around a planet. This forms where the

planet's unique electrical charge into the plasma meets a different charge generated in 'space'. How far the magnetosphere extends will depend on the power of the planetary charge. These plasma barriers became known as Langmuir sheaths (Fig 107). The principle of different electrical charges creating plasma barriers between them is the reason why we appear to have 'physical'

Figure 107: Different electrical charges within plasma create barriers where differing charges meet. These have been named Langmuir sheaths and they define planetary electromagnetic fields.

resistance between each other and objects when we are really experiencing *electromagnetic* resistance within undecoded reality.

Bioplasma human

My concept over the decades, much of it purely through intuition, is that matter is assembled and held together by information contained in electromagnetic plasma fields in overall control of body and brain function. The electromagnetic body field is interacting with the electromagnetic simulation field in a two-way process that can be described as an interactive virtual-reality computer game. The electromagnetic/plasma field maintains its individuality from the simulation field through the sheaths that form when plasma of one charge meets plasma of another charge. They create a sort of bubble that maintains its self-assembling uniqueness and doesn't get absorbed by the overall field. The body's electromagnetic fields are the organising system of 'biological matter' – more to come – and anything that can disrupt the harmony of these fields will disrupt the organisation and harmony of what we perceive as the physical body (Fig 108 overleaf).

This is a heads-up to the current systematic manipulation of human body and reality by skewing electrical and electromagnetic balance through technological radiation. We can see the fundamental significance of technologically generated electromagnetic fields including power lines and the global 'Cloud' being

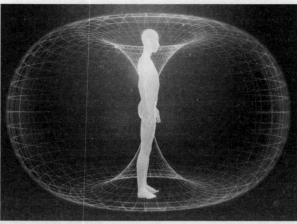

Figure 108: The human electromagnetic field operating within its plasma medium and interacting with the central nervous system. This is where your sense of reality and perception is formed from competing sources and influence that can span from human experience to the infinity of the *All That Is*.

expanded by the week by the likes of 5G towers and low-orbit satellites courtesy of Elon Musk and co. We can add human psychology when the brain works electrically and electromagnetically. Aware scientists now speak of the bioplasma body which can extend a long way from the 'physical' as does the electromagnetic field of coordinating information. Together they constitute the human 'aura' which psychic people can see with its colours (frequencies) changing with changing thought and emotion. The name 'bioplasma' came from Russian scientist V.S. Grischenko in 1944. He worked at the forefront of this concept with another Russian, Viktor Inyushin, who said this in a rare article translated into English:

> A living organism can be described as a 'biological field' or 'biofield' ... we have obtained evidence that a fifth state of matter, bioplasma, exists as part of each organism's biofield. Bioplasma consists of ions, free electrons, and free protons.

> It is highly conductive and provides opportunities for the accumulation and transfer of energy within the organism as well as among different organisms. Bioplasma appears to be concentrated in the brain and the spinal cord. At times, it may extend considerable distances from the organism, raising the possibility of telepathic and psychokinetic phenomena [moving objects with the mind].

I was fascinated to read Robert Temple's description of how Viktor Inyushin and Polish biologist Włodzimierz Sedlak identified that the

wave structure of the body's biological field stores *holograms*. We have
the bioplasma body as a medium for the 'biomagnetic' field in the way
that plasma is a wonderful medium for electricity and
electromagnetism. Both fields have been identified around the human
heart and the brain's corpus callosum connecting the two hemispheres.
The field around the head/brain can be very powerful in some people
and this is the origin of the 'halo' which can be seen by the visually
psychic. Here we have another level of the left-brain-right-brain
phenomenon. There is already the potential for technological
electromagnetic sources to be used to disconnect the hemispheres and
emphasise the left side which will dominate human society. The 'Musk
Cloud' can again be recognised for what it really is, a medium for
genetic and psychological manipulation and control.

Genetic organisation

Genetics is the self-organising electromagnetic information field
communicating with plasma and particles to dictate biological
processes. Think algorithms on one level. You don't have to remember to
breathe, make your heart beat, your blood flow and coagulate, process
food through the stomach and colon, make your hair grow or your skin
sweat to release heat. You don't have to communicate instructions to tell
each cell what to do. The governor and organiser is the information in
the biomagnetic field. You can compare this with a computer program in
which information is encoded to run the system. Information in the field
is organising and directing biological responses such as cell division
which appear to come from the brain when the brain is subordinate to
the field. A Russian scientist (so often they are) Aleksandr
Presman (1909-1985) focused his whole career on the electrical and
magnetic nature of the body. He said that electricity flowing through the
body from head to feet (through the central nervous system) generates a
magnetic field at right angles to the flow of electricity which is exactly
what happens with the Earth and the Universe (Fig 109 overleaf). The
interaction of electricity and magnetism creates the human 'aura' (auric
mind) as it creates planetary magnetospheres. The more powerful the
electricity and electromagnetism the bigger the aura and we're back to
charisma. The central nervous system is defined as:

> A processing centre that manages everything that your body does, from your
> thoughts and feelings to your movements. Your brain and spinal cord are
> central to your CNS because they receive and transmit information to your
> entire body.

Nerve cells carry electrical impulses from one place to another and
the central nervous system connects to the sight sense through the retina

and optic nerve. If the simulation controls your central nervous system it controls you and that's the idea. Once again any source of disharmony in the electromagnetic field disrupts the harmony of its genetic organisation. One result can be cancer and you have a greater propensity for that with people in close proximity to technological radiation. What does anyone think is happening in the wake of the phenomenal increase in this radiation that includes smart meters

Figure 109: The Earth's electromagnetic field and the human electromagnetic field. Notice anything??

in homes and workplaces plus all the other sources such as smartphones that people put to their ear (brain) for long periods?

Electrical/electromagnetic interaction and disruption gives credence to those healing methods that connect emotional trauma with illness. Emotions and thoughts are also frequencies and powerful negative versions of both can disrupt the biomagnetic field. We are looking at the connection between stress and dis-ease, disharmony in the body. A healing method that I mentioned in *The Dream* is German New Medicine, or GNM, which is founded on the link between emotion and the impact on the field/brain. *On that level* it has validity. BUT. I have had some experience of two GNM 'practitioners' in Canada and England since I wrote that book and I was shocked by what I observed. I found them to be 'cult-like' in that they are so mesmerised by GNM as 'the only way' (it's *not*) that they go on trying to make circumstances fit their belief and won't change tack even when it is clearly not working. I am not saying that all GNM practitioners are like this, but these were. GNM is a tool *not* a one-stop shop and if you treat it as a cure-all you are going to harm a lot of people. This is the point: Emotion is *one way* that the field can be disharmonised. It is not, repeat *not*, the *only* way. Once you get caught in the one way/only way you are a disaster waiting to happen. GNM while having valid aspects needs people to retain objectivity and discernment.

A pioneer of the electric human was Albert Szent-Gyorgyi (1893-1986) who faced ongoing suppression of his work. He won the Nobel Prize in Physiology and Medicine in 1937 and was the first scientist to isolate vitamin C. Szent-Gyorgyi's best-known books were *Bioenergetics* and *Bioelectronics* in 1957 and 1968 to give you an idea how long mainstream science has ignored the obvious that Szent-Gyorgyi and a few others could see. He believed that cancer is the result of electrical/electromagnetic disturbance which can be understood once we can see how the body really functions. He said that the body had a system of biological semiconductors that control the flow of electricity. These are found in technological form in electrical devices from computers to smartphones to electric vehicles. You can see why I have called the body a biological computer since the 1990s. Szent-Gyorgyi said that every cell was electronic and that the body was pervaded by *plasma*, the superconductive medium for electricity. He said that cancer can be spotted at the earliest stage by measuring photon particles emitted by the body. Cancer and other conditions affect photon emissions and again this knowledge has been suppressed by the Cult establishment. Biophotons are emitted from the meridian lines and acupuncture points identified by this ancient art of healing. By balancing the flow of 'chi' around the body (electrical plasma/information) the organising field can be harmonised and the matter body healed (Fig 110). Meridian acupuncture lines of chi are part of the biological computer motherboard. The principle also operates in the Earth's 'ley line' network often marked by standing stones, circles, and earthworks located by the ancients who knew of these lines of force. The Earth and body meridian systems are another as above, so below.

Figure 110: Acupuncture techniques aim to balance the flow of electrical/plasma energy (information) around the body. A balanced energy/information flow is a healthy body. The acupuncture meridian network is like the body's 'motherboard'.

Body Universe

The Universe operates in the same way as the human body-mind. The simulated Universe is a hologram and the body (below) must be reflected in the Universe (above). The electrical network and stars in the Universe can be seen on a smaller scale in the neuron electrical networks of the human brain. Is the Universe the equivalent of a vast 'brain'? It's more than that. The brain is subordinate to the electrical and electromagnetic self-organising field and it is the same with the Universe and Earth. Both function with a self-organising field dictating events. Earth's electromagnetic self-organising field is what we call 'nature'. The human body has a plasma body or soul that operates in the Astral. The Universe and Earth therefore have a plasma body. Is this plasma 'Earth' what some near-death experiencers have reported seeing as a whole different civilisation and way of life? Humans and nature go through a cycle called aging as they follow the Astral AI Mind program. There is no reason for anything to age when it is a hologram. If the self-organising field continues to, well, self-organise, why should we age? Why shouldn't a human live for hundreds of 'years' with everything in balance and accurately replicated through cell replacement? We age because the program takes the body through an aging cycle. The controllers don't want us to live too long or we might realise what's going on. The potential for sussing the game increases the longer we live as a human.

The same mix of plasma, electricity, and electromagnetism can be found at every level of the Universe (simulation) from its totality to its biological forms. We have the same principles with AI and computer technology because the technological mirrors the biological and the 'plasmalogical'. All is 'logical' in the way that it makes sense. Something else to add to the mix is standing waves which are created by two waves moving in opposite directions with the same frequency and distance between top and bottom. Their equality of opposition to each other makes the wave 'stand' or oscillate on the spot (Fig 111). Someone running forward and meeting a resistance of equal force is a good analogy. They would run on the spot. I think biological forms are a standing wave and they have a remarkable resemblance to DNA (Fig 112).

Figure 111: A standing or stationary wave which can exist indefinitely while the necessary forces are in place.

To know plasma is to know reality

We'll start the detailed explanation of plasma with the official stuff and work our way deeper. Plasma is a highly charged energy 'gas' that near-perfectly conducts electricity and is the foundation medium of both the

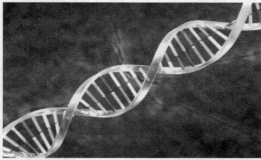

Figure 112: 'Standing wave' DNA.

Figure 113: The plasma Trifid Nebula.

Astral and human reality. All stars are plasma along with interplanetary and interstellar space and Earth is surrounded by the dense plasma ionosphere. The apparently chaotic and constant movement we see on the Sun with the arcs, loops and flares are examples again of the plasma dance. Planets spin and circle the Sun. Galaxies spin. Plasma is never still because of its nature. A star nebula (plural nebulae) is a gigantic cloud of plasma and subatomic particles out in 'space' (Fig 113). A nebula is said to be created by dying stars exploding. I'm sure there is a lot more to know than that.

Mainstream science loves things that explode, crash into each other, and go bang. They could not explain reality (their version) without their snap, crackle, and pop theories. How did this happen? Big collision. And this? Big explosion. Theory of everything? Big Bang. Thank you.

Plasma's impact on atoms and subatomic particles is to stimulate movement. This is the dance or vibration of life. You don't see plasma within the range of visible light. Instead you see its *impact* through electrical and frequency effects on waves and particles that produce visible phenomena. The plasma effect is to disturb and excite particles within atoms to create movement and more movement is generated when they return to their original 'orbiting' positions within the atom (known as 'recombination'). I guess it's like balls on a pool table smacked around (movement) and bouncing back (movement) to where they started out ('recombination'). Think elastic. The recombination process releases packets of electromagnetic energy called 'photons' from a Greek word meaning 'light'. Photons are bundles of electromagnetic energy and the basic unit that makes up all light. They move at the speed of light and are found throughout the electromagnetic spectrum from high energy gamma and X-rays to low-energy infrared and radio waves, and the visible light band. The to-and-fro impacts of plasma on the subatomic realms release photons to affect the visible world in many and various ways. A candle flame is the result of plasma-disturbed electrons returning to their pre-disturbed state and releasing photons which constitute the burning flame. Lightning is photons activated by the plasma effect. We see the impact of plasma on the atomic realm of matter without seeing the plasma which we perceive as 'empty space'. Jason Gibson, a presenter on a YouTube maths and science channel, put it this way:

> We don't see the plasma … the highest energy plasmas, we don't actually see them. We only see the after effects of the recombination. So the higher energy plasma is completely transparent. That's what I'm trying to drill home there.

He added that if none of these particles/waves recombined after the original plasma excitement and disturbance 'then we would never see anything'. Does that mean that the effect of plasma is to create the world of matter that we do see? It would seem so. Gibson continues:

> [The] photon is what we actually see. So, when we look at lightning, we actually see the light that is happening from the electrons coming back in, orbiting an atom, right? In the plasma ball, the beautiful tendrils of light that we see, those are the photons coming from electrons going back into orbit …

> … In the aurora, the beautiful shimmering pictures of the light … that is coming from electrons going back into orbit. So I guess what I'm trying to tell you, and the same thing with the candle flame … we never see the plasma itself … All we see are the photons that are generated from electrons recombining.

Yes, *re*combining as a result of the *de*combining impact of plasma. Out, in, out, in, a bit like breathing. They talk about the Universe 'breathing' and this is one way that it symbolically does so. The process is how photon light of the Sun is generated. The *de*combining/ *re*combining/photon-releasing sequence is happening constantly to form a 'steady state' which is defined as 'a physical system or device that does not change over time, or in which any one change is continually balanced by another, such as the stable condition of a system in equilibrium'. Another definition of steady state is: 'An unvarying condition in a physical process, especially as in the theory that the universe is … maintained by constant creation of matter.' This *de*combining and *re*combining – breathing – of subatomic particles instigated by plasma can be found throughout human reality. Scientists have found it difficult to control what are called complex plasmas – plasma filled with nano/micron particles. A force creating a simulation to ensnare perception would not want it easy to understand and unravel.

Plasma Sun

Earth's atmosphere is an electrical/electromagnetic field that responds to influences from other fields including the difference in solar impact between day and night, electrical storms, and weather in general. Human thought and emotion are another factor. The field was affected demonstrably in sensor records when billions became aware of the attacks of 9/11 for example (Fig 114). The biggest impact predictably comes from the Sun although not in the way that mainstream scientists believe. The Sun is about 99.86% of the mass of the Solar System and is almost entirely made of plasma (Fig 115).

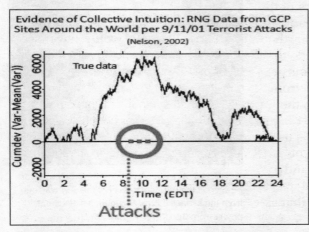

Figure 114: The spike in the Earth's electromagnetic field at the time of the 9/11 attacks.

Fantastic rivers of plasma have been found flowing within the Sun extending to at least 12,000 miles below the surface and they can be 40,000 miles across. We are told the Sun is a nuclear reactor at its core generating power out to the surface. This makes no sense when solar activity and heat is considered. Electric Universe researchers contend that the Sun is a *processor* of electrical power that exists in the energetic fabric of the Cosmos and not the *source* of that power. You would expect the Sun to be hottest at the surface if heat was originating from

Figure 115: The Sun is almost entirely plasma.

within. This is not the case. The surface temperature is estimated to be about 5,500 degrees centigrade while way out from the surface in the

Sun's corona temperature is recorded at *millions* of degrees centigrade. The corona starts 1,300 miles above the surface and expands out into the solar system. Robert Temple notes that while 5,500 degrees may seem to be hot, it is less than four times hotter than the inside of a cement kiln and only a third as hot as electrons in a neon light. Sun temperature falls even more on the surface inside sunspots which are supposed to be closer to the (non-existent) 'nuclear reactor'.

Ultraviolet images reveal that far out from the surface the Sun is encircled at the equator by a 'torus' doughnut-shaped ring (Fig 116). The ring is storing electrical energy absorbed from the simulation field and when this goes into overload colossal discharges are released like

gigantic lightning bolts to punch holes in the surface of the Sun. These holes which can be many times bigger than Earth are 'sunspots' which conventional science claims are punched out from within from the nuclear core. In truth, the opposite is the case (Fig 117). The number of sunspots is used to determine the amount of solar activity on its high and low cycles and that is still correct. The difference is that as solar power gathers it is expressed by discharges from the torus ring and not from within the Sun. Electrical power in the cosmic field ebbs and flows in cycles and this dictates how much energy there is for the Sun to process and deliver as plasma projections across the solar system on the solar wind. Whether the Earth is warming or cooling is dictated by these cycles (Fig 118). Solar temperature cycles are short term and long term and not the result of carbon dioxide, the gas of life, without which there would be no human life or anything else. Observe how

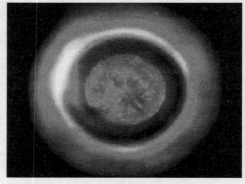

Figure 116: A 'torus' or doughnut-shaped ring can be seen at the ultraviolet level of the Sun way out from the surface which accumulates electrical power from the universal grid.

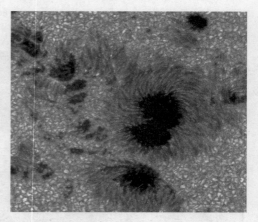

Figure 117: When the torus ring overloads it unleashes fantastic discharges which punch enormous holes in the surface known as sunspots. Thus sunspots are a sign of increased electrical solar activity, but not for the reasons given by mainstream science.

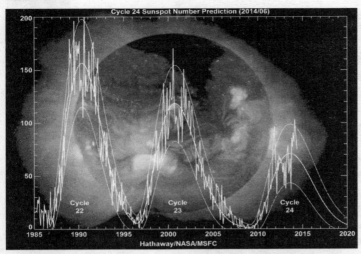

Figure 118: Solar cycles of power ebb and flow reflect electricity cycles in the universal web and not the activity happening within the Sun. The myth of the nuclear reactor Sun is in its death throes.

outrageously rarely the Sun is mentioned by the global warmers as a source of heat. Conventional science has to face the evidence that its whole perception of the Sun is the wrong way round. The power is coming from without, not within. Haimin Wang, a professor of physics at the New Jersey Institute of Technology, said of sunspot activity:

> We used to think that the surface's magnetic evolution drives solar eruptions. Our new observations suggest that disturbances created in the solar outer atmosphere can also cause direct and significant perturbations on the surface through magnetic fields, a phenomenon not envisioned by any contemporary solar eruption models.

The solar wind is plasma which occupies the 'space' between Earth and the Sun (Fig 119). Mainstream science's long-held contention that 'space' is empty, and a vacuum, is now all over the cutting room floor. Earth's magnetic field, the ionosphere, and Van Allen Radiation Belts in

Figure 119: The plasma solar wind passes through space to the Earth.

the high atmosphere, are plasma and who knows what state the latter must be in after some hundred atomic explosions in the belts by the lunatic dumb and dumbers in the American and Soviet militaries during the Cold War. These morons are truly clinically insane and the arrogance of believing you can do this when it affects all humanity is beyond comprehension.

The Birkeland web

The solar wind released from the Sun is a stream of plasma and charged particles including electrons and photons which travel through the solar system to Earth. The most powerful examples are 'coronal mass ejections' which are a massive release of plasma often described as solar storms and space storms. These can temporarily distort Earth's magnetic field and threaten human electrical systems. Plasma is host to colossal interactions between charged particles and electrical and magnetic fields as they attract or repel each other. A static electric charge will only produce an electric field. A moving electrical charge creates a magnetic field at right angles around itself to add to the perpetual plasma dance. The combination is electromagnetism which becomes an entity of its own. Norwegian scientist Kristian Olaf Birkeland (1867-1917) realised that electricity flowing through plasma creates filaments that were named after him as Birkeland Currents. Electrical flow triggers electromagnetic fields which causes the electrical filaments to rotate while the electromagnetism keeps them apart. The filaments spin and rotate in the plasma. I have already noted that this is what happens in the human body as electricity passing from top to bottom through the central nervous system triggers a magnetic field at right angles to itself. It's a Birkeland current (Fig 120).

These can be tiny or ginormous (hundreds of millions and billions of miles) and they connect planets, stars and galaxies, everything in the Cosmic Web. They have 'superconductivity' and can pass through plasma without any resistance to their momentum. Birkeland Currents are gigantic loops of energy on the Sun and this solar power travels to the poles of the Earth along those same Birkeland lines of force to be distributed on

Figure 120: Birkeland currents and the human electromagnetic auric mind.

the leyline system which is electrified, magnetised plasma as with the acupuncture meridians of the body. Birkeland Currents can be compared in appearance with double-helix DNA (Fig 121). DNA structures in

humans have functions of
storing and
communicating
information. Robert
Temple asks a highly
relevant question: 'Could
helical structures in
plasma have the same
function?' I say they do.
The helix is part of the
software programming
within plasma that is also
expressed as the human

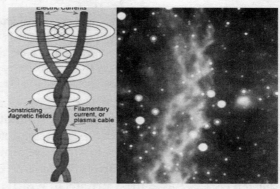

Figure 121: Birkeland currents and DNA.

body. Mainstream science has never found its mythical organising
medium of 'dark' (invisible) matter and ignores what is screaming 'look
– over here': *Information-encoded plasma*. 'Dark matter' is plasma.

Programmed plasma

Subatomic particles form within the plasma that spans the Universe and
the Astral. Scientists refer to these particles as 'dust'. I think this is rather
unfortunate with the public perceptions of 'dust' as in 'fine, dry powder
consisting of tiny particles of earth or waste matter lying on the ground
or on surfaces or carried in the air'. Plasma dust is not dust. It is micro
and nanoparticles that can take the form of crystals. We think of crystals
as something you can hold like a quartz crystal used in communication
technology. These atomic matter crystals are rare compared with 99
percent (at least) of crystals in the form of nano-crystalline particles in
plasma that can cluster together and form structures. They are described
as 'self-assembling' which means that some form of intelligence is
involved as with the self-assembling nanostructures in 'Covid' fake
vaccines. Either the plasma/particles have intelligence, or the plasma is
programmed with a form of Yaldabaoth Astral AI to act as it does.
Temple says that plasma crystals are not solid and are made of charged
particles and ions, containing 'a crucial admixture of microscopic dust
particles' that make the crystalline structure possible. They are invisible
to the human eye and 'weigh essentially nothing'. Temple describes
how plasma crystals 'are capable of being fantastically complex, and
complex in an ordered and dynamic way needed for intelligence'.
Eugene Wigner, a Nobel Prize-winning Hungarian-American
theoretical physicist, wrote that X-ray studies have revealed that most
'solid' bodies are crystalline, commonly 'polycrystalline', or groups of
microscopic crystals of various sizes:

The crystalline and polycrystalline substances constitute by far the greater part of all solid bodies found in nature. Practically all rocks are conglomerates of crystals, ice is crystalline, and so are all metals … apart from the glasses and substances of organic origin, like wood, there are very few non-crystalline solids …

Crystals are used in electronic and frequency technology as receiver-transmitters. We are looking at a vast simulation network of crystalline interaction and interconnection. Temple quotes scientific research about how plasma crystals can spontaneously form helix structures in the image of human DNA (which is *crystalline*). Electricity passing through plasma creates Birkeland Currents in which filaments twist around each other in ways that remind us of DNA. He features a research paper in his book that says 'complex plasmas' (plasmas full of subatomic particle 'dust') may naturally self-organise themselves into stable interacting helical structures that exhibit features normally attributed to organic living matter. 'The self-organisation is based on … physical mechanisms of plasma interactions', the paper says. 'These interacting complex structures exhibit thermodynamic and evolutionary features thought to be peculiar only to living matter.' I contend that plasma is the medium programmed like software to create what we experience as 'living matter'. The programming is achieved through artificial intelligence and plasma *is* a form of artificial intelligence which explains why some scientists are saying that plasma can develop intelligence and 'life'.

Crystal ring Saturn

I read an article by Robert Merlino from the Department of Physics and Astronomy at the University of Iowa, called 'Dusty plasmas: from Saturn's rings to semiconductor processing devices'. I was intrigued by the mention of Saturn. I have contended for a very long time in my books and talks that Saturn is transmitting frequencies from its rings that help to keep humanity in its coma-sleep in conjunction with technology inside the Moon (Figs 122 and 123). See *Everything You Need To Know But Have Never Been Told* and *The Perception Deception* for the detail. I have written at length about Saturn and how it was once the prime sun of the Earth before cataclysmic events rearranged the solar system and it was cast out into its current position. The go-to source on this subject is Electric Universe researcher David Talbott and his Internet video *Symbols of an Alien Sky*. Extraordinary upheavals are in Earth's biological and geological record and the foundation of the Great Flood myths that globally abound long before the plagiarism of the Noah story. Talbott produced an outstanding book, *The Saturn Myth*, which documents myths and legends in cultures across the world describing in their accounts and symbolism how Saturn dominated the Earth sky in the 'Golden Age' of abundance and peace – another possible symbolism

Figure 122: I have said in other books that Saturn is broadcasting frequencies from its rings and these are amplified by the Moon which is not a 'natural body' as indeed nothing is within the simulation. This sounds seriously off the wall at first hearing, but if you read *Everything You Need To Know But Have Never Been Told* you'll see why I say this. (Images by Neil Hague.)

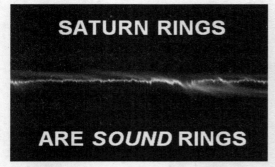

Figure 123: A professional sound engineer sent me this image of a Saturn ring with the message that what we see here is definitely the result of sound waves.

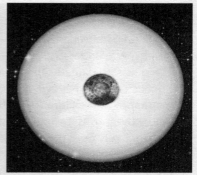

Figure 124: David Talbott's extensive research reveals a common theme around the ancient world that Saturn was the Earth's prime sun and orbited in alignment with the Earth, Mars and Venus in the Golden Age. This image portrays Saturn, Mars, and Venus, as described by the ancients. (Image by Neil Hague.)

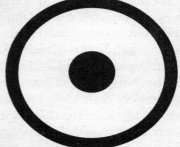

Figure 125: This ancient symbol of the sun makes no sense if connected to current solar system alignments, but when related to the Golden Age Saturn sun the symbolism is perfect.

for the Garden of Eden (Figs 124 and 125). The Saturn sun was associated with 'time' and became the God of Time and also agriculture in this period of agricultural abundance. Cronus or Cronos (also spelt with a 'K'), the Greek god worshipped as Saturn by the Romans, became today's 'Old Father Time' (Fig 126 overleaf). I read the following in an article about Greek mythology:

Before Zeus came to power, mankind had lived blissfully in the Golden Age under Cronos' rule. There was no pain, death, disease, hunger, or any other evil. Mankind was happy and children were born autochthonously, meaning they were actually born out of the soil. When Zeus came to power, he put an end to mankind's happiness.

Figure 126: The Greek god Cronus associated with Saturn became Old Father Time. The scythe symbolises Saturn as the god of agriculture in the Golden Age of abundance.

Zeus was a symbol of Jupiter. Could this be reflecting the period of the cataclysm when the Golden Age was ended by the catastrophe involving Saturn and its relocation and reassignment as a vehicle for perceptual control? Ancient sun gods understandably linked to the present Sun were really *Saturn* sun gods and included Ra (Egyptian); Sol (Norse); Helios (Greek); Arinna (Hittite); Surya (Hindu); Huitzilopochtli (Aztec); Inti (Incan); and Kinich Ahau (Mayan). They can be found in all cultures and can range from benevolent to malevolent depending on their symbolism of Golden Age Saturn or what it became (Fig 127). Saturn sun god Nimrod, associated with Saturn sun god Baal, was part of the Babylonian trinity of Nimrod, Queen Semiramis, and the virgin-born son, Tammuz, which later became the Christian trinity of the Father God, Holy Spirit or Ghost, and Jesus. The Holy Ghost replaced the female aspect Semiramis. Both were symbolised as a dove, and attributes and titles given to Semiramis in Babylon were bestowed on the character of the biblical Mother Mary. Among them were Divine

Figure 127: Ancient sun gods were really symbols of the Saturn sun.

Mother and Virgin Mother.

Roman Emperor Constantine the Great is credited with the creation of Christianity as we know it at the Council of Nicaea in 325 AD. He worshipped the Saturn sun god, Sol Invictus, the 'Unconquered Sun', and converted to Christianity on his deathbed in 337 AD. Saturn was the chief god of Rome and that would never have happened had the 'planet' (brown dwarf star) always been in its current distant position. The Roman Festival of Saturnalia from December 17th to the 23rd is the origin of the Christian Christmas when 'Santa' (an anagram of Satan) is the star attraction. Saturn is central to secret society symbolism and this includes the black cube which is part of Masonic, Jewish and Muslim tradition. Jewish Saturn god 'El' is symbolised as a black cube and the

Jewish holy day is Saturday (Shabbat in Hebrew) in honour of Saturn (Shabbetai in Hebrew). The holiest place in Islam is the black cube Kaaba (meaning 'cube') in Mecca where worshippers gather in concentric circles (Fig 128).

Figure 128: The black cube Kaaba in Mecca as worshippers gather to focus their attention – energy flows where attention goes. Remind you of anything?

I have suggested over the years that Saturn's rings contain transmitter crystals and some scientists quoted by Robert Temple believe the rings contain charged 'dust' particles structured together to form crystals. Temple says in *A New Science of Heaven*: 'Dust and dusty plasmas are ubiquitous in nature, occurring in interplanetary and interstellar clouds, dust rings around planets like Saturn, [and] on the surface of the moon.' Saturn is a fantastic frequency broadcasting system (Fig 129 overleaf). The extent of ring dimensions is staggering with a span of some 175,000 miles (Fig 130 overleaf). NASA's Spitzer Space Telescope detected in 2009 another gigantic and almost invisible ring about 3.75 million miles from Saturn which is more than six million miles wide (Fig 131 overleaf). How many other invisible rings exist across the solar system to Earth? The Phoebe ring, as this Spitzer ring was named, consists of practically invisible dark dust particles smaller than the width of a human hair. We have the emerging common theme of plasma and its crystalline particle 'dust' programmed with limitless

Figure 130: Saturn's ring system spans about 175,000 miles.

Figure 129: Saturn's crystalline rings transmitting frequencies to Earth.

roles, tasks, and forms. The whole simulation is a program and a type of intelligence. Plasma, particles, electricity and electromagnetism are how it is played out. Temple writes:

Figure 131: The ginormous new Saturn ring discovered in 2009.

We have seen particles in plasmas swarming like microbial beings and forming other patterns such as hexagonal structures, spirals, concentric circles and double-helix patterns.

Nerve-like filaments grow in plasmas, including those that form double helixes and may carry information as well as energy [I am certain they do – programming information] ...

... Some contain hot plasmas, some cold plasmas, some dusty plasmas, some dusty voids. Some containing impurities that may hinder or accentuate the flows of charged currents in the manner of electronic semiconductors and transistors.

In other words, large plasma clouds are bound to have the equivalent of semiconductors scattered throughout themselves in order to modulate the current flows. It's a *simulation*. I will have my own take on Saturn and what really happened with the cataclysms later in the book. It's another angle on that story.

Plasma intelligence

The Robert Merlino article said that dusty plasmas contained particles that range from about ten nanometres (equal to one thousand-millionth of a metre) to ten micrometres/microns (equal to one millionth of a metre). I read that the human eye can only see particles bigger than 40 microns and even the biggest plasma 'dust' particles are invisible to us. Merlino said that charged dust particles interact with electrons and other particles to form 'multi-component plasma'. Particle dust affects plasma, and plasma affects particle dust. Go deeper and you see that plasma and nano dust particles are the *same entity*. Scientists have established that particles emerge from plasma and form an *intelligent* entity. This could be likened to incredibly advanced AI or even human consciousness with astonishingly more processing and storage potential. Particle plasmas are described as 'open systems' which means they can be constantly powered and energised by sources like the Sun. Could it be that atomic, material, organic, and biological life is being generated by plasma-particle intelligence? Now – another thing. Plasma-particle 'clouds' have the ability to produce helical structures in the image of DNA which in humans is a receiver-transmitter and 'hard drive' of information. Temple quotes the revolutionary work of Russian scientist Vadium Nikolaevich Tsytovich and colleagues. They said:

> It is concluded that complex organised plasma structures exhibit all the necessary properties to qualify them as candidates for inorganic living matter that may exist in space provided certain conditions allow them to evolve naturally ... Memory and reproduction are necessary for a self-organising ... structure to form 'living material'.

Both of which have been identified in plasma-particle 'dust'. They go on to say that this could solve the problem of explaining the origin of life in that 'the complexity of living creatures is so high that the time necessary to form the simplest organic living structure is – "seems" – too large compared to the age of the Earth'. They ask if the speeding up of 'evolution' could be explained by plasma-particle intelligence. They say:

> Can faster evolution rates be achieved for non-organic structures, in particular, in space consisting mostly of plasma and dust grains i.e. of natural components spread almost everywhere in the Universe?

BINGO! Mainstream 'science' and biology is bamboozled by what its left-brain perceives as 'time'. It believes in phenomenal timescales for 'life' to 'evolve' and rejects any other possibilities as a result. 'It's not possible – it takes too much time for things to happen.' The Universe is a *program* NOT an 'evolution'. The simulation blows the 'evolution' of Darwin out of the ocean. Remember the Cambrian explosion example from earlier. Things can emerge and change very quickly by changing the information infused in the simulation. Thought and emotion expressed as frequency and electricity can impact upon and reorganise the plasma/particle environment to produce experiences that match the perceptual state. This is how perception creates reality. The Cult and its demonic masters know they will control human experience if they can program human perception. 'Mysteries' of life are falling here by the sentence now. The human energetic field or bubble that surrounds the body (the 'aura' or auric mind) is a plasma field charged with electrical/electromagnetic frequencies that reflect the *perceptions* and programming of the person.

Planet and star formation

The reality of plasma and its particle dust can be pulled together with Birkeland Currents to explain how stars and planets are formed. Birkeland Currents are the 'galactic filaments' on which stars and planets emerge. Information infused into the system creates a build-up of coagulating plasma dust at particular points where the currents connect – 'node points'. This eventually forms the core of a star and 'solidity' of planets. The nature of spiral galaxies can be understood by studying a plasma phenomenon called a 'plasmoid' (a 'plasma-magnetic entity'). These 'blobs' of plasma were discovered by American physicist Winston Harper Bostick (1916-1991). The discovery came when he was studying the mutual impacts of plasma and magnetism. To aid his research he invented a 'plasma gun' to project plasma at a magnetic field. Bostick got more than he expected. Long story short, the plasma-magnetism interactions caused the plasma to form into shapes akin to spiral galaxies. Bostick noted:

> The formation looks strikingly like a photograph of a spiral galaxy ... we can look at the combination of plasma and a magnetic field as a kind of self-shaping putty. Perhaps study of the forms assumed by this putty may help us understand configurations such as stars and galaxies.

The self-shaping 'putty' is what I am calling programmed plasma with information encoded into crystalline particles via electricity and electromagnetism by the creators of the simulation. Bostick saw that plasmoids appeared to be behaving like living entities with strong powers of self-organisation. Hannes Alfvén (1908-1995), a Swedish electrical engineer, plasma physicist, and Nobel Prize winner, used Bostick's concept of the plasma gun to suggest that the Sun could be ejecting plasmoid 'blobs' across the solar system to Earth. If plasma and plasmoids are 'living entities with strong powers of self-organisation' this would mean the Sun was pouring out information or instructions right across the solar system like programming a computer, or the *simulation* at the level of matter. The Sun is made almost entirely of plasma and I believe the Sun is a conduit between the human realm of plasma electrical matter and the plasma Astral dimension. That would explain the background to what I have said in other books about human reality being a projection from the Astral in the form of information. Is the Sun the means through which plasma programming is delivered to create the matter level of our reality? Robert Temple writes that plasmoids from the Sun 'could also in principle contain information that receptive people could perceive indirectly as inspiration' (and to deliver collective mind programming). He adds: 'The Sun could "talk to" … the planets, our higher atmosphere, and anyone else who is listening.'

From strands to tapestry

I have written over the years that the Universe is a quantum computer and quantum computing is billed as the next frontier of human technology. The definition is 'a computer which makes use of the quantum states of subatomic particles to store information' and exploits the qualities of *plasma*. Wait a second. This is describing plasma with its subatomic particle 'dust'. The simulated Universe *is* a quantum computer and so is the Astral. That's how the simulation works. Quantum computers are described as using subatomic particles such as electrons or photons to manipulate information in ways that are impossible with current computers to perform multiple calculations simultaneously. Quantum computers are planned to operate the global human AI control system which people like Elon Musk are helping to build. They already exist in the underground bases and secret projects and they won't make them public until their AI control sequence is ready.

There are two ways to uncover something. One is to research the parts bit by bit, adding to your understanding until the Eureka moment when you see how the parts fit together. Conclusions are usually reached this way. I describe in *The Trap* how this was my approach in the first two years after my mind exploded open in the wake of my visit to the professional psychic Betty Shine in March 1990 when she said that other-dimensional communicators were telling her that I was going out on the world stage to reveal great secrets. The communications said 'they' would be leading me to knowledge and at other times knowledge would be put directly in my mind. I would say things and wonder where they came from. Both have happened exactly as promised and continue to this day. The difference has been that after that first two years of being led to knowledge and reaching conclusions there was a clear 'flip' in which I would overwhelmingly reach conclusions *first* and then supporting tangible detail would follow.

You can research the parts of a computer to conclude step-by-step that it *is* a computer, or you can conclude *first* that it's a computer which makes the significance of the parts far easier and quicker to understand. I have worked mostly this way since around 1992/3. I knew about plasma and its electrical significance long before I read Robert Temple's book. I had concluded decades earlier that this simulated reality is being projected from the Astral with its lower reaches – the 'lower Astral' – very close to the human frequency band, although outside of visible light. All this was the perfect preparation for turning the first page of Temple's *A New Science of Heaven*. Once plasma and programmed plasma concepts are understood so many 'mysteries' become explainable and among them are Astral plasma entities – 'Archons'. Temple writes that charged plasma entities can emerge by the process called self-organisation (what I would call Astral AI or Yaldabaoth programming). He continues:

> By this means plasma people can exist, who are imperceptible to the optic nerves of 'physical people' who are made not of plasma but of flesh and blood [decoded holograms as I would say]. Because we are incapable of directly perceiving the plasma people, we do not know they are there. And furthermore, they may be of such diffuse matter that they can pass through our dense physical matter and emerge intact. Scientists know that ball lightning does this.

'I can't see them so they can't exist and that David Icke is mad for saying they do.' Ha, ha. Ball lightning is electrically-energised plasma in a 'blob' known as a plasmoid. It can pass through 'solid' objects just as ghosts do. They are both plasma passing through matter as very different frequencies. Ball lightning shows evidence of intelligence and decision-making as do the 'orbs' that are often seen on video and still footage of haunted locations. Plasma explains the 'paranormal'. Thunderbolts reported by the ancients were ball lightning in the way they are described. How many 'UFOs' doing incredible feats of speed and change of direction are plasma in nature? Programmed plasma explains why the Astral and especially its lower levels of frequency is a form of 'physicality' if far less dense than human reality. 'Physicality' is again about the observer and the observer's frequency. We see Astral entities as mostly ethereal as with 'ghosts', but this is only our perspective. To our density they will appear ethereal on their higher wavelength. If we were on the same wavelength as Astral entities they would look as solid as you and me. It's all perception and perspective. This validates near-death accounts that speak of seeing solid objects and technology in the 'spirit world'.

Cult-controlled 'science'

A psychic I met once described those at the forefront of breaking down the deceit as 'rather like as snowplough'. She was channelling a consciousness that said: 'You are the thin end of the wedge … you have the shitty end of the job … you are here to really shovel some shit, and therefore make space behind you to make it easier for the others.' That was correct for sure in my case and this also applies to many of the trailblazing scientists in Robert Temple's *A New Science of Heaven*. I didn't realise until I read the book how long ago renegade scientists realised many of the things now becoming accepted. They were blocked and suppressed from making their findings available to a wide audience. Cult control of science and medical journals is a key factor. The Cult and its intelligence networks oversee the medical journal industry to dictate what can and can't be published. Pergamon Press, an Oxford-based medical journal and book publishing house, was founded by Robert Maxwell. He was the 'businessman' agent of Israel's Mossad who was also connected to other spy agencies. I mentioned earlier that he was the father of Mossad operative Ghislaine Maxwell of Mossad agent Jeffrey Epstein infamy. The word 'Pergamon' or 'Pergamum' refers to a city in ancient Greece which was home to the Pergamon Altar on which human sacrifices took place. Relief panels from the Pergamon Altar were moved in the 20th century to the Pergamon Museum in Berlin, Germany. The biblical Book of Revelation describes the Pergamon site as 'where Satan has his throne' and 'where Satan lives' and the city included many structures, monuments, and temples to the Greek gods (Archons). The Pergamon Altar was known as the Altar of Zeus, the king of the twelve Olympian gods and the supreme god of Greece. Pergamon Press is now an imprint of Dutch medical journal publisher Elsevier.

The importance of plasma to the Cult is confirmed by how the military and intelligence network seeks to suppress circulation of its importance. Robert Temple says that there are few plasma scientists working in the public arena and one reason is the secrecy imposed by the government-military-industrial-intelligence complex. Plasma research is considered so crucial to these imbeciles that plasma scientists are largely kept on the pay-roll with strictly-enforced agreements to get permission for anything they wish to publicly release. Scientists quoted in this chapter are largely mavericks or semi-mavericks going where orthodoxy refuses to venture. We could have known so much more long ago had the Cult agenda not been to keep us in ignorance. How shocking to think that mainstream science believed until a few decades ago that space was 'empty' when it is full of plasma and life. The entire establishment, including the 'science' journals, combined to suppress these facts uncovered by scientists who could see. Only when the waters finally burst through the weight of evidence did they begin to relent. Most 'science' is a bloody joke – a very sick one. Robert Temple has met and researched many science mavericks. He observes:

Time and again in history, science seems only to progress via vicious ridicule, followed by vindication and reluctant, hypocritical acceptance by most of the people who have spent years insulting the innovative thinkers.

Sounds like the MAM. Open-minded scientist Robert Lanza says in his book, *Biocentrism*, that human science can be very good at seeing how the parts work, but 'we do badly in just one area, which unfortunately encompasses all the bottom-line issues: what is the nature of this thing we call reality, the Universe as a whole?' There you have the limitations of official 'science' in a single sentence and those limitations perfectly describe the limitations of the left-brain. We misrepresent the word 'genius' – 'extraordinary intellectual power especially as manifested in creative activity'. Genius is not 'intellectual power'. You can have that in the left-brain. Genius goes beyond intellect to see the unity of everything and observe the simple in the apparently complex. That is my definition of genius: To see the simple within the apparently complex detail. This requires the balance of left and right hemispheres and an extremely active corpus callosum communicating between the two. Most mainstream scientists and academics don't have that, which is why they are what they are.

We have to leave them to it and go our own way.

CHAPTER NINE

Baby Come Back

*II used to believe in reincarnation,
but that was long ago in another life*

Dave Schinbeckler

There was a catchy song when I was growing up in the 1960s called *Baby Come Back* by *The Equals*. I always remembered the lyrics because they basically comprised of 'baby come back'. I bet they didn't take long to come up with the title.

'Come back' and 'baby come back' are repeated 20 times in 2.24 minutes. 'Baby come back, doo, doo, doo, doo, doo, baby come back, doo, doo, doo, doo, doo' … it goes on and on like that. What was the song called again? Baby Come Back. Oh, *really*? Why? The bad news is that she just called me. She says she's not coming back. Sorry. Damn, all that effort as well. Anyway, I thought it would be a good title for this chapter on reincarnation – 'Baby come back, doo, doo, doo, doo, doo.' So is reincarnation a reality? Does it exist? I would say the evidence is overwhelming (Fig 132). A belief in reincarnation has been with us since ancient times and dominates the religions of the East. Modern research in the West is pointing in the same direction. Dr Ian Stevenson (1918-2007), a Canadian-born American psychiatrist, spent his career investigating the subject. He was the founder and director of the Division of Perceptual Studies at the University of Virginia School of Medicine. Stevenson focused his reincarnation work on children who in rare cases said they could remember previous lives. The early years appear to be the period in which past life memories are generally possible with most

Figure 132: I don't doubt that reincarnation is real. My question is *why?*

having the memories fade as they get older. Stephenson found that often memories appear when something in the child's present life triggers the recollections.

Most people have no such memories because of the 'mind-wipe' which happens with each incarnation (more shortly). Stevenson found recurring themes with children who could remember checkable details, often fine details, of other human lives from the earliest cognitive years which could not possibly be explained by 'this world' knowledge or experience. These were some common themes: Children began talking about previous lives between the ages of two and four; details increased until five or six before tailing off; talking about past lives tended to end by the age of eight with normal development from at least ten; the few that retained memories beyond that age usually lost them at puberty; children expressed traits of other lives in their fears, interests and responses that have no this-life explanation; many times they will have birthmarks and defects that reflect the location of fatal wounds they claim ended the other life. The last two points will result from memories still encoded in the plasma/electromagnetic auric field. Other children had nightmares related to what happened in a previous life.

Compelling cases

We are not talking about only a few cases either. Stevenson studied some 2,500 to 3,000 cases in different cultures across the world. He would have the accounts checked to search for any explanation that would avoid the conclusion of reincarnation. This proved a challenge when children provided names of people, locations, happenings, and cause of death details that they could not possibly have known at such a young age about someone long passed. *Scientific American* featured one of Stephenson's accounts in a 2013 article. A toddler in Sri Lanka overheard her mother mention the name of an obscure town called Kataragama that the girl had never visited. She told her mother that she drowned there when her mentally challenged brother pushed her in the river. She said her father was a bald man named 'Herath' who had sold flowers in a market near the Buddhist stupa (a dome-shaped building used as a shrine). The little girl said she lived in a house with a glass window in the roof and dogs were tied up in the backyard and fed meat. The house had been next door to a big Hindu temple and people smashed coconuts on the ground outside the temple. The detail was impressive, but was it true? Ian Stephenson found that it was. He confirmed there was a flower vendor in Kataragama who ran a stall near the Buddhist stupa and his two-year-old daughter had indeed drowned in the river while the girl played with her mentally challenged brother. The man lived in a house where the neighbours threw meat to dogs tied up in their backyard, and it was adjacent to the main Hindu temple where devotees practiced a religious ritual of smashing coconuts on the ground (don't ask). Stephenson found that the drowned girl's father was not bald, although her grandfather and uncle were. His name was not 'Herath'. That was the name of the dead girl's cousin. Stephenson established that 27 of the 30 details the toddler gave turned out to be true. Neither she nor her family had met the other family and nor had any friends, co-workers, or acquaintances. Examples of this magnitude of confirmed detail is common in Stephenson's work and that of others in the same field.

Stevenson published the two-volume 2,268-page *Reincarnation and Biology* in 1997. He detailed how many subjects had unusual birthmarks and birth defects which included finger deformities, underdeveloped ears, or being born without a lower leg. The *Scientific American* article reported how there 'were scar-like, hypo-pigmented birthmarks and port-wine stains, and some awfully strange-looking moles in areas where you almost never find moles, like on the soles of the feet'. *Reincarnation and Biology* included 225 cases in which children who remembered previous lives had physical anomalies that matched lives that they described. Details were in some cases confirmed by the dead person's autopsy record and photos. *Scientific American* listed some of Stephenson's researches: A Turkish boy with a face congenitally underdeveloped on the right side who said he remembered a life of being a man who died from a shotgun blast at point-blank range; a Burmese girl born without her lower right leg had talked about the life of a girl run over by a train; a child in India born with boneless stubs for fingers on his right hand remembered a life as a boy who lost the fingers of his right hand in a fodder-chopping machine mishap. Stevenson pointed out that this so-called 'unilateral brachydactyly' was so rare that he couldn't find even one medical publication of another case. There was a little Thailand boy who had a small, round puckered birthmark on the back of the head and at the front was a larger, irregular birthmark, resembling the entry and exit wounds of a bullet. Stevenson confirmed the details of the boy's statements about the life of a man who had been shot in the head from behind with a rifle. He found children who could navigate around towns they had never been in this lifetime; recognise people they had never met; know how homes were laid out that they had never entered; point to people who owed them money that was never paid; speak as five-year-olds to women as if they were still their wife; and spontaneously speak languages unknown to their family and not spoken in their town or location. One little boy claimed that he was the former husband of a lady still alive. He was asked, if that was true, to tell her where his will was. They had never found it. The boy walked across the kitchen floor, pulled up a floorboard, and there it was.

Meticulous research

Stephenson said that a small percentage of children retained memories of their previous existence. Only about one in 500 children met his criteria even in India where belief in reincarnation is everywhere. We will see why with the mind-wipe. Stevenson was an expert in psychosomatic medicine and believed that strong emotions were related to the retention of past-life memories. He suggested that traumatic deaths can leave an emotional imprint with most of the children he worked with saying they had met a violent end. Often the child repeated habits and fears connected to the nature of their previous death. A drowning led to an intense fear of water and those who were stabbed had a knife phobia. He described three cases of children reacting violently when they met those they said had murdered them and got away with it. The writer of the *Scientific American* article was Jesse Bering, Associate Professor of Science Communication at the University of Otago in New Zealand. He said:

> More often than not, Stevenson could identify an actual figure that once lived based solely on the statements given by the child. Some cases were much stronger than others, but I must say, when you actually read them first-hand, many are exceedingly difficult to explain away by rational, non-paranormal means.

> Much of this is due to Stevenson's own exhaustive efforts to disconfirm the paranormal account. 'We can strive toward objectivity by exposing as fully as possible all observations that tend to weaken our preferred interpretation of the data,' he wrote. 'If adversaries fire at us, let them use ammunition that we have given them.' And if truth be told, he excelled at debunking the debunkers.

Bering made a perceptive point that explains why mainstream science is so far from the cutting edge. He said he would have no problem saying that reincarnation is all 'complete and utter nonsense – a mouldering cesspool of irredeemable, anti-scientific drivel'. The trouble was that this wasn't entirely apparent. Bering asked why scientists weren't taking Stevenson's data more seriously and concluded that the data didn't 'fit' the working model of materialistic brain science. Didn't this scientific (actually unscientific) refusal to even *look* at his findings, let alone to debate them, come down to the fear of being wrong? Exactly right. He quoted Stephenson as saying: 'The wish *not* to believe can influence as strongly as the wish to believe.' Stephenson's biggest critic was alleged 'philosopher' Paul Edwards in his 1996 book *Reincarnation: A Critical Examination*. He said that 'reincarnation would represent a crucifixion of our understanding' and that was his problem with Stephenson. Not whether what Stephenson said was true, rather how this would affect the prevailing belief system of the orthodoxy. The god and goal of mainstream science is not the exposure of truth. It is to prevent the exposure of its dogma. The Edwards critique was laughable. He said if reincarnation was real then the following would have to be accepted and that could not possibly happen. See what you think:

- Materialism is false.
- Time is not reducible to the brain.
- Human identity is more than only personality.
- There is a domain beyond space-time.
- Death is an illusion.
- There may be a deeper logic to our lives.

Edwards said: 'Such assumptions are surely fantastic if not indeed nonsense, and even in the absence of specific flaws, a rational person will conclude either that Stephenson's reports are seriously defective or his alleged facts can be explained without bringing in reincarnation.' Something here is seriously defective and it's not Stephenson's work. Edwards doesn't refute Stephenson's evidence. He simply assumes it must be wrong on the grounds that scientific dogma cannot possibly be wrong. Arrogance and ignorance are a telling combination that ensures that science and the cutting edge of knowledge will always live far from each other. Five of the Edwards 'false assumptions' are demonstrably true and the only one with validity is the point about 'time is not reducible to the brain'. Even then the reason he says that time *can* be explained by the brain is not the real reason. 'Time' is encoded into the simulation which the auric mind/brain decodes into the illusion of 'time'. Edwards represents the scale of self-delusion and left-brain enslavement that drives mainstream 'science' (which isn't science, but a religious belief).

What an absolute prat Edwards must have felt as his consciousness left his body in 2004. Can you imagine? 'What do you mean I'm not dead? I *must* be – science says so.' Some, however, do get it. Physicist Doris Kuhlmann-Wilsdorf, an esteemed professor at the University of Virginia, said that Ian Stephenson's work had shown that 'the statistical probability that reincarnation does in fact occur is so overwhelming … that cumulatively the evidence is not inferior to that for most, if not all, branches of science'. Ian Stephenson's studies have been continued by others in books such as *The Children That Time Forgot* and the television series, *The Ghost Inside My Child*, which have featured astonishing tales of reincarnation told by children with remarkable and checkable accuracy. Past life regression (taking people into their subconscious memories of previous human experiences) began to take off in the 1970s and 80s and is now widespread as another source of reincarnation information.

It's true ... BUT ...

So what is going on? I have no problem with reincarnation. My big
problem is why it is claimed to happen. I read an article at Medium.com
entitled 'The Evidence for Human Reincarnation is Here'. The theme
was that no one has even come close to suggesting a physical
mechanism for reincarnation that would explain such accurate and
precise agreement between all these past-life memories and verified life-
details. Well, I am going to be having a right go at doing that in this
chapter. Christopher Bache, Professor Emeritus of Religious Studies at
Youngstown State University, has written and spoken widely about the
scientific evidence for reincarnation. He was raised a Roman Catholic
and his life changed when he met Ian Stevenson and Stanislav Grof who
was integrating psychedelics into psychotherapy. Bache said that
Stevenson's book *Twenty Cases Suggestive of Reincarnation* 'stopped me in
my tracks' with his impeccable scholarship on children. The book
convinced him that reincarnation was real. Here was empirical evidence
that matter-obsessed science was false and he could see there must be
some dimension outside of physical reality where consciousness existed
intact between incarnations. 'Stevenson's research forced me to erase my
intellectual blackboard and rethink human existence from scratch.' This
led to his first book *Lifecycles* in 1990. Okay, so far, so good. I can agree
with all that.

Stanislav Grof's work convinced Bache that LSD 'allowed one to
explore the deep structure of consciousness and experientially probe
questions that philosophers have pondered for centuries'. Bache began a
largely secret 20-year psychedelic self-experiment following Grof's
protocols. He began to reveal his psychedelic experiences and their
philosophical implications with the publication of *Dark Night, Early
Dawn* in 2000. He was appointed to the California Institute of Integral
Studies and its Department of Philosophy, Cosmology, and
Consciousness where he taught graduate students about psychedelics.
These and other academic appointments have maintained his passion to
this day of exploring reality and reincarnation. Where I differ most
strongly from Christopher Bache and Eastern philosophies such as
Buddhism is not that reincarnation is happening, but *why* it is
happening. Bache takes the line like Buddhism and the Western New
Age that reincarnation is to learn lessons to 'grow and evolve'.

I profoundly don't buy that. Are we really supposed to believe that
within the infinity of possibility and potential that we have to keep
returning to this tiny planet over and over to learn anything? A planet
which is the equivalent of a billionth of a pinhead compared with the
projected size of the Universe? Are there no other experiences we could
have anywhere else within Infinite Possibility? Take a breath, clear your
head of the nonsense, and it's patently preposterous (Fig 133). I say it's a

trap to keep us constantly returning to the dense fake-physical illusion of the loosh farm. Most people worldwide have really difficult lives, often severe challenges, upsets and disappointments, and they would normally never want to return to such a shit-show. Sod that for a game of soldiers, I ain't going

Figure 133: We have to keep returning here to grow and evolve? Are you serious?

back there. They have to be given a fairy story for why they have to keep coming back to 'learn lessons and evolve'. The Astral dimension after human 'death' is the magicians' lair where that bollocks is sold in what is called the spirit world. I will go through that sequence in a moment and what it is really about. I want first to briefly highlight the Buddhist/Eastern version of reincarnation. Christianity, Islam, and many other religions reject any idea of returning for another go. Christians say you qualify for Heaven if you believe in Jesus as your saviour, or for Hell if you reject Jesus and indulge in 'sin'. You have one life of anything from a few seconds to more than a hundred years and then it's judgement day and your eternity is decreed. Atheistic science says we are matter and when matter dies so do we. Lights out, good night – all the best.

Sorry, can't agree

I have always found it stunning when people believe that by accepting Jesus as their saviour they are destined for Heaven, and yet if you live a life of love, service, and commitment to others the bloke with the pitchfork is waiting for you. It's a form of madness and certainly mind control. This makes no sense spiritually, morally, or logically. I've been a bastard and saved myself at the last gasp by accepting Jesus as my saviour on my deathbed. Phew, just in time. What breathtaking baloney. Muslims get to Heaven, or 'Jannah', by their deeds and belief in Allah. They are doomed to eternity in Hellfire if they do bad deeds and do not repent and seek Allah's forgiveness. I don't know how suicide bombers explain that away, but I guess somehow they do. Somewhere in their bewildered minds they are serving Allah, I suppose. In both Christianity and Islam you have only one shot at it. This doesn't sound very fair. What about children who die as babies? How can a baby believe in Jesus or do enough good works? I watched as a Roman Catholic priest was asked that question by a caller to an American Catholic TV network.

Nearly 30 years later, if he's still with us, I bet he's still trying to untwist his knickers. If he's not still with us, maybe they have knicker untwisting facilities available in the Astral. How riveting to watch his mumbling, bumbling, explanation of the unexplainable and fail miserably.

Eastern religions do at least see beyond the one-life-and-judged-forever mind-numbing claptrap and they realise that consciousness is eternal and can take different forms. They are, however, preparing people for the reincarnation cycle which their followers are expecting to happen. They are already primed not to question the sequence which may not be the best advice as we'll see. Eastern religions are still hierarchical as witnessed in the Indian caste system in which your life is dictated by the family or caste segment you are born into. Brahmins are at the top. These are people like teachers and intellectuals who are believed to emerge from creator god Brahma's head. Next are the Kshatriyas, warriors and rulers, from Brahma's arms, then the traders or Vaishyas created from his thighs. I was dreading to think where the lowest caste, the Shudras, came from and I was very relieved to read that it was Brahma's feet. What a relief. Shudras do the medial jobs. Outside the caste system are the untouchables which Hindu and Buddhist beliefs said had corrupted souls that meant they could not mingle with other castes. Oh, *they* must come from Brahma's arse, then. One explanation says:

> An Untouchable couldn't enter a Hindu temple or be taught to read. They were banned from drawing water from village wells because their touch would taint the water for everyone else. They had to live outside village boundaries and could not walk through the neighbourhoods of higher caste members.

> If a Brahmin or Kshatriya approached, an Untouchable was expected to throw himself or herself face down on the ground to prevent even their unclean shadows from touching the higher caste.

All together now … what absolute bullshit. Reincarnation beliefs decree that they are born Untouchables as punishment for being bad in previous lives. They had to marry fellow Untouchables and could not eat in the same room or drink from the same well as a caste member. How very enlightened and confirmation of the depths of insanity to which humans can descend. The main castes were divided into some 3,000 castes and 25,000 sub-castes and all of them completely bonkers. Reincarnation is so central to Buddhist belief that they choose each Dalai Lama 'spiritual leader' on that basis when the old one dies. A selected group of people search the recently born for 'the individual who demonstrates memory of the personal preferences of former and diseased Dalai Lamas'. It all sounds very strange and hierarchical to me. Hierarchy is everywhere.

Why? Why? *WHY?*

I read a guide to *The Tibetan Book of the Dead* published by the Tibetan Yoga Academy while writing this chapter to remind myself in detail of what Buddhists say about reincarnation and why it is necessary. We are told that the *Book of the Dead* original text was written in the 8th century by an Indian guru Padmasambhava ('Born from a Lotus') as a work entitled *Bardo Thodol*, or 'Liberation through hearing during the intermediate state'. This was published in English in 1927 by the Oxford University Press. The book says that the cycle of life and death, or reincarnation, continues until we transcend the misperceptions of the mind. The idea is to learn that in the 'afterworld or earthly plane' our sense of reality is a projection of the mind and we can then live without fear and reach enlightenment, or 'Nirvana', as the illusions of mind are transcended. Before that moment we must live with 'dukkha', or suffering – negative emotions. Ah, *loosh*. 'The cycle of birth, life, and death comes with the guarantee that there will be suffering. Life is filled with suffering, it is its nature.' But *why*? *WHY?* Well, Buddhists say to learn lessons. I say to feed the *loosh* farm. I read that Buddhist practice is meant to 'eliminate suffering' resulting from human experience. Here's a question: Why do we come here to suffer *at all* then?

Buddhism believes in the 'Wheel of Samsara' which consciousness must traverse between 'Earth lives'. The concept is intrinsically connected to the concept of 'karma' or 'intentional action'. Deeds in one human life are said to be imprinted in the consciousness field and dictate the nature of the next life. I say the perception of 'karma' is a central pillar of the trap. Take those examples of Ian Stephenson's children. They may have had their electromagnetic fields infused with the memories of horrible deaths; but their physical and psychological residue was not because of what they *did*, rather what was *done* to them. Stephenson did not find evidence of 'karma' in his body of work or the need to return to human form to 'pay back' karmic debt from previous misdemeanours, thought or action. Jesse Bering wrote in his article on Stephenson: 'Interestingly, and contrary to most religious notions of reincarnation, there was zero evidence of karma. On the whole, it appeared to be a fairly mechanical soul-rebirthing process, not a moralistic one.' I'll address 'karma' later and that term 'mechanical' is very relevant, too, as we'll see. Near-death experiencers and those who are hypnotically regressed to the between-life state have described afterlife machinery and technology. One said: 'Now I am in a healing chamber. From top to bottom it is like a machine producing different coloured rays of light.' It is 'a mechanical soul-rebirthing process' because it is an Astral AI system run by the Archontic crazies on behalf of their controlling consciousness, Yaldabaoth. The plasma Astral is a form of matter, just less dense. I delved into this in *The Dream* and there's more to come in this book. Buddhist belief fits the 'mechanical' bill with the claim that after death 'there is a lag period of 49 days before consciousness is reborn in a new form'. Why 49? Why not 48 or 50, or 4,567? Given there is no time how does that fit with the 49? The Astral spirit world is described in physical terms. This is a comment from a past-life regression therapist speaking of a client:

> [She] moves to a huge temple with stone floors, then into a large library with many levels. She informs me that she needs to register that she's here before beginning the review of meaningful past-life experiences. As she stops to do this, she explains. 'What we build on Earth is a pale imitation of what we remember from here' …
>
> … After finishing the review in this spiritual library, [she] moves through the courtyard to a large bouquet of energy where her soul group is gathered.

Huge temple, large library, needs to register. It's all very this-world without the same density. Buddhism contends that 'if beings do not learn to control their minds, they have no control of how they will be reborn'. So many questions come from this. Why do we enter the human realm to have our minds scrambled, wiped and programmed in the first place? Why inflict this on yourself to start with, if overcoming the illusions of mind is the goal? Why is the 'world' specifically set up to delude its occupants so they lose control of their minds? Why are our mind memories wiped with each new 'incarnation' to stop us remembering 'lessons' we have already learned if the whole deal is about learning lessons to regain that control? A medium.com article on the studies of Ian Stephenson said: 'Well, clearly the vast majority of people undergo a sort of 'amnesia' before birth, where we forget our previous lives – perhaps in order to focus all our energies on the learning to be gained within this current life.' This is the classic explanation of what I call the 'mind-wipe' and I suggest it is seriously mistaken. Buddhism tells us that 'death will fall upon every one of us, yet none of us know what to expect'. *Why*? Human consciousness has left the body so many times in endless cycles of reincarnation so *why* don't we know what to expect? It's the mind-wipe and the reason this happens is absolutely *nothing* to do with 'learning lessons to evolve'.

Spin the wheel

Buddhists believe the reincarnation wheel is broken into sections they call 'bardoes'. Is there a Bridget Bardo? No, sorry, wrong spelling. Bardoes are 'a space between two states, such as life and death'. Bardoes are 'intermediate states' and are viewed by Buddhist texts as metaphors for mental states.

> The consciousness is imprinted with the karma of our past. If the consciousness realizes that what it is experiencing are the manifestations of its own mind, it will become enlightened. If it fails to realize this, the consciousness will be reborn into a new body. Whether one escapes the cycle of birth, life, and death is determined by how the deceased handles their journey through the bardoes.

Who decides and dictates all this? It's alright saying everything is a manifestation of mind, but how does mind become so deluded? Well, because of its human experience. So what's the point of having human experiences to start the whole ridiculous sequence? It's a *trap* and all this is a denial of that. The obvious is hidden behind reams and reams of tortuous Buddhist explanations until you disappear into the darkness of your own rear end. What the following says is true and I have been saying it myself for decades. The missing word once again is *why*?

> There is an aspect of consciousness that identifies with the mind and body. When this happens, this aspect of consciousness loses its expansiveness and becomes more restrictive. This constriction leads to the creation of an 'illusory sense of self'. This illusory sense of self is how most of humanity experiences itself. The illusory self experiences itself as being a separate and limited entity that exists in the world. It is from this sense of separateness that the ego is born.

This is the state that I call 'Phantom Self', but all together again – *why*? What is the point of coming into an illusion that scrambles your perceptions and holds you hostage until you suss you've been had? And it *is* holding you hostage by controlling your perceptions and frequency. The *Tibetan Book of the Dead* says that everything in life is illusory and not real in the way that we experience it. The world is not what we think it is. Right, so that's how our minds get deluded. *Why*? What's the point? The point is *control* and that's where Buddhism and the religions of the East, plus their Western New Age counterparts, miss the bus:

> We are not mindful because we identify with the body and the mind. We believe that we are the mind and body. Thus, we define ourselves by our thoughts and actions.

I could not agree more, so why do we come here to take this shit?

Buddhist belief says there are six realms in the afterlife and that karma dictates where we go. There is the Realm of Hell; Realm of the Beast; Realm of the Hungry Ghosts; Asura Realm; Heaven Realm; and the Human Realm. These apparently relate to different states of perception and it sounds very complicated, very *mechanical*, and even more relevantly, very *AI computer-like*. Buddhism says that we must reach a state of enlightenment by seeing that reality is a dream or what eastern religions call 'Maya' (illusion) in contrast to 'Brahman' (supreme reality). What it misses again is we are experiencing an *induced* illusion, an *induced* dream for reasons of control.

Reincarnation's hidden story

I think we can explain reincarnation far more credibly than Buddhism or any other religion as I build here on the information in *The Trap* and *The Dream*. A short recap: An Astral demonic force feeds off human low-vibrational energy. To generate that requires Earth to be such a nightmare for billions that one experience would be enough for most people. Human reality is only an electrical/electromagnetic sliver operating within a plasma foundation. The plasma Astral dimension is the perceived spirit world where our point of *attention* relocates after release from its human focus (when the body decoding system ceases to function). The Astral has many realms divided into bands of frequency or reality on a rising octave scale. The control system of the multi-levelled simulation is in the lower regions of the Astral from where the demonic runs the show. Astral AI directs the entire system like one gigantic quantum computer program and whether you are in a human body or the spirit world you are part of the same program. Everything is designed to keep Divine Spark consciousness within the simulation human/Astral realms and prevent a transition to what I will call the Fifth Dimension and beyond into *All That Is* Infinity (Fig 134).

Freedom from focused attention on matter – 'human death' – offers the potential to exit the simulation altogether and return to Infinite Realty or 'paradise'. The Yaldabaoth-Archon matrix has many and various perceptual tricks to prevent that and keep you on the Wheel of Samsara forever reincarnating into human form to maintain the flow of loosh. The basic premise is that you are little souls who must learn to grow and evolve by the constant repetition of human experience. Each 'life' reveals new flaws and creates more 'karma' that requires more incarnations to work through. Reincarnation is a never-ending cycle if you believe this nonsense. You are not meant to 'escape', but we *can* if we can free ourselves from the perceptual programming specifically designed to keep us here. Human and Astral levels of the simulation operate on the same mind trickery that authority knows best. The perception is clearly widespread within humanity where unquestioning

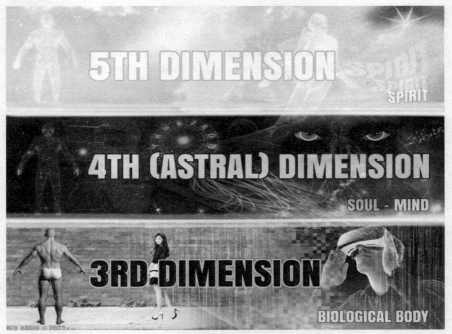

Figure 134: The simulation encompasses the human realm and the Astral. Beyond the simulation is the 'Fifth Dimension' and out into Infinity. Once we reach an expanded state of self-identity (frequency) as the Spirit that we *really* are the simulation cannot restrain us any longer. The 'Fifth Dimension' is only a metaphor to indicate the beyond-the- simulation realm. (Image by Neil Hague.)

obedience and fear of punishment for disobeying are the pillars of control. The dynamic continues in the spirit world where the same authority card has to be played differently because of the state of awareness involved. Human focus is very narrow with attention trapped in the five senses and our experience happening within extreme energetic density. Consciousness released from the body with a much wider range of potential perception requires a different approach to allow the will of Astral authority to prevail.

Minds are wiped before they enter the human realm to make each 'incarnation' a blank canvas with no memory of previous experiences or 'past lives'. If the idea is to 'learn and evolve' why wouldn't we remember what we had already learned and add to that with new experience? Are we not very likely to make the same 'mistakes' again in the absence of previous 'lessons'? Ah, yes, but when we do there is more 'karma' which means we have to keep returning. Some have residue memories although this is rare and usually last only into the earliest years before the human programming system dissolves them. The mind-wipe means that when minds leave the body each time they have no recollection of the 'afterlife' state even though they will have experienced human 'death' many times and the process that follows. We can't be allowed to remember this or the accumulated knowledge would lead us to see what a scam it all is. The mind-wipe continues until you are safely back in the Astral preparing for another dose of the loosh farm. We emerge from human body attention into a new state of bewilderment that leads consciousness to follow the instructions of the new authority. These are the 'spirit guides' in white robes, angels, archangels, groups of 'elders', passed-over loved ones, family members, and religious heroes like 'Jesus' tailored to our human beliefs. Astral AI is able to track every incarnation in detail in ways I'll explain and this allows for specific designer-manipulation for each Earth-departing mind. Most crucially the afterlife experience must present a fake 'heaven' dominated by 'light' and a feeling of bliss and love. This is not difficult. You have the chasm of contrast with the low-vibrational density of human reality to give you a serious head start and what is felt as 'love' is a frequency or wavelength that induces that experience. All can be achieved through Astral plasma AI 'software'.

Near-death tales

Near-death experiences (NDEs) are a potent source of information about the immediate after-death sequence. Millions have left their body when it has ceased to function only to return when it is revived (Fig 135). They often have vivid memories of what happened in between although it is clear from their accounts that other memories which the controllers don't want to be circulated are subject to deletion. They speak of a threshold they must not pass or they cannot

Figure 135: Consciousness withdraws from the body decoding systems and enters another reality – mostly the Astral.

return to their human form and as they *do* return to tell the tale they never cross that point to see what's on the other side. I have read and watched multiple scores of near-death accounts over the years and again as I have written this trilogy. There are obvious key points that are repeated over and over. First there is the brilliant white light, sometimes including blue, which many report appears after an immediate post-death darkness. They describe being attracted or pulled magnetically to the light which is most often at the end of a tunnel which draws them

Figure 136: The 'tunnel' described in endless near-death experiences.

through, sometimes slowly, sometimes at fast speed (Fig 136). They describe being immersed in a love they have 'never felt before' except that reincarnation means they must have experienced this many times. The light 'invites' them in with its warmth and they have never felt so loved. Some speak of a great homecoming and a celebration 'of a job well done'. I have heard several descriptions of 'thousands of souls' greeting them in a stadium-like setting. One spoke of seeing the afterlife realm as having connections like 'a spider's web caught in the sunlight'.

At the end of the tunnel or within the light they are greeted by 'happy, exuberant, iridescent souls' as another account reported. Communication is by telepathy, not words. Movement is through 'I thought it and I was there' – the power of intention. Many describe this realm as a 'solid place' with buildings, rooms, tables, and lighting which fits my contention that the Astral is a form of less dense 'physical' reality. That makes sense of descriptions about things appearing 'mechanical'. Again and again NDEs report a feeling of 'coming home'. A common theme is angelic beings and spiritual 'masters and guides' in white robes, some with the archetypal long white beard and hair. All is designed to fit the just-departed human perception of 'spiritual masters'. People say they 'know' that they know these entities even though they are not recognisable. The newly arrived are in a state of euphoria and wonder how they could have forgotten their true state while in human reality. One said: 'How did I forget who I am? What a *trick*. I can't believe I fell for it.' I can, mate. Astral AI makes it so. The same man said the end-of-tunnel beings treated his human life as a big joke. To them it is – a joke and a scam. Some may do what they do with good intent in that *they* are being manipulated by the illusion to believe that the reincarnation cycle is necessary to 'grow'. You have people galore in the human hierarchical system who serve it in ignorance of what they are really serving. Why should it be any different in the spirit world run by the same force?

Many speak of walking past rivers which reminds me of Lethe, one of the rivers of Hades or the underworld in Greek mythology known as the river of forgetfulness. It was said that anyone who drank from its waters would experience total forgetfulness – a mind-wipe. Lethe was the Greek spirit of forgetfulness and oblivion. The Lethe River flowed through the cave of Hypnos, the Greek god of sleep. I mentioned earlier that water is often used as a symbol for energy. A near-deather said she didn't remember everything that happened – 'of course we're not meant to remember'. *Why*? I have heard near-death experiencers say they had no memory of their Earth life and beings reminded them and told them they had to go back to 'complete your mission' or work through 'karma'. You have the near-death theme of 'there is no judgement' when that's clearly not the case at all. There is the ubiquitous 'life review' highlighting all their flaws and the use of guilt and shame for their human behaviour. Remind you of anywhere? Remind you of religions like Roman Catholicism? Reading and listening to near-death accounts confirms that what happens in a human life is preparing people for afterlife enslavement through guilt, shame, and subordination to authority.

Reincarnation religions prepare expectation for the wheel of karma. The esoteric so-called Lord of Karma is *Saturn* which is the god of illusory 'time'. The beings, spirit guides, angels, elders, and religious heroes are clearly in control. They call the shots and dominate with the bewildered still mind-wiped experiencer in awe of what is happening and doing whatever they are told. The beings sound patronising as if talking to children and that's the idea. To make them feel small and inferior with no power compared with the white robes, angels and elders. You are just a little me and we must guide you. The light or tunnel of light is the entrance portal to the reincarnation cycle and I read that guidance from *The Tibetan Book of the Dead* instructs 'the self' to go toward the light. Luminosity is the 'Buddha-nature, which is enlightenment and the true nature of the mind'. Big mistake, I would say. We are prepared to surrender to the false 'light' by the symbolism of love and 'God' as 'light'. Any direction except that light is advisable.

Life review

The 'life review' described over and over by near-deathers is when their life is played back to them. Everything they have felt, done or said, even when alone, and what their actions made others feel. What a manipulative guilt trip. Some recall standing in the middle of a circle of screens spinning around them with views of their life. Guilt, shame, regret, the whole karma deal, is emphasised while the stooge is told that they are not being judged. 'God does not judge' when that is blatantly what is happening – Roman Catholic confession with pictures. A near-death experiencer said that he felt 'profoundly ashamed at the way I behaved' and he was 'feeling pretty small at that point'. He said there was 'no judgement', only 'a tidal wave of love' from the being with him – 'I was judging myself'. That's the idea, darling. The same guy said the being told him that 'everything happened as it was supposed to'. A woman said that during her life review the beings said that everything that happened in her human life and the people who did it were just 'all the soul's plans that you came to experience'. Why the 'karma' then? You are saying it was *planned* and yet we must return to face the 'karma' of something that had been *planned*?

Another said the review was upsetting for her because she didn't realise that sometimes when she had been short with her mother how deeply it affected her. Fine – but this behaviour was happening in a false reality specifically structured to trigger such loosh-inducing responses. Souls are shown what they did as children and how it adversely affected other children and adults. They are told that the aim is to 'do no harm' while the whole Matrix structure is set up for harm to be done to allow loosh to flow. The most minor 'good deed' is presented in the review as some monumental happening. 'We come to Earth to learn love', 'love is all that matters' and 'all we take with us' are some near-death recollections of what the 'beings' said. Why in that case is the human system structured to suppress 'love'? If love is all that we take with us where does karma come in? None of it makes sense because it is *non-sensical*.

A hypnotically regressed woman remembered standing outside huge wooden doors that would not open until she had enough time to consider her actions in her human life. When they opened she saw her 'panel' of elders. She was lower and looking up to them to emphasise authority. She said that in telepathic communication with the elders she felt she had wasted time and was too quick to judge others. 'I didn't use the life in the way in which it could have been used – I didn't make it what it could have been.' She didn't understand how she could make it different. She was lazy and could have been a force for good in the community, but didn't join in. Well, quick, call the police. How dare she? There is no judgement in the spirit world, you see. No, they manipulate the target to judge themselves which is far more powerful. If you judge yourself you won't tell the 'elders' to stick it where the sun don't shine. 'I have to be more focused this time around', the women said. 'I am being told that just "trying to be" is not good enough – I actually have to do.' Ain't it great that there's no judgement in the spirit world?

In awe of 'elders'

I was told in a past-life regression book that a meeting with the 'elders' is one of the most important events for a soul to experience between lives. 'For the still-incarnating soul this forum appears to be as close to seeing a divine being as we get in the spirit world.' What an honour. It sounds a hoot, like meeting the Queen. A woman who was regressed to 'between lives' claimed that the elders meet before a soul comes in and discuss everything in great detail that has happened in the soul's life. They review how advice before the last life had been heeded and assess how each soul reacted to that advice. Sometimes souls had severe troubles when they had not remembered or heeded their words. Hold up, sunshine. What do you mean they didn't remember? You wipe their sodding minds. The general ongoing advice at the end of the review appears to be basically: 'You nearly got it; you've got more to learn, though.' This is elder-speak for we need the loosh. The lady said she was told she had to have faith in the realm of matter and trust people until proven otherwise. Let me assure you, mate, that in the human world it's definitely the other way round. The no judgement malarkey is hilarious. A regressed woman quoted an 'elder' as saying:

> Your agreement states that you chose to be of service. Forgiveness is a requirement, and it is a necessary step in the evolution of your consciousness. You feel as if we led you down a path that hurt you, but do you see now that it was necessary to let you go there? You had choices to make as to how you would walk that path.

I get it. You need the loosh. Interfering negatively with someone else's destiny is the 'big no, no', the life reviewer makes clear; but negative events are purposely encoded into life paths to be loosh generators, as we shall see. The whole life review scenario is a calculated guilt-ridden psychological car crash preparing souls to agree to return to the human asylum to learn their lessons and work through karma. The simulation makes things happen and then blames those who do them for doing them. Astral crooks make the target feel guilt and remorse to return and pay the penalty for doing what they were *manipulated* to do. Some remember seeing Jesus, Muhammad, and Buddha observing the review – 'more powerful figures than me' – working on their behalf to take them to the 'next level'. I bet that involves returning to Earth, right? Of course – we need the loosh. Why is there never a word spoken about what we were and what happened to us *before* we were caught in the Matrix? No one ever mentions that and it is not discussed. We are not supposed to know what happened and how the Matrix entrapped Divine Sparks. The only information is *Matrix* information.

Themes in the life review are constant and ever repeating with both near-death experiencers and those regressed to the between life state. Life reviews are mostly conducted by these 'Councils of Elders' or 'wise ones'. A woman regressed by a hypnotherapist to unlock between-life memories said: '… it is humbling for me to sit with them.' Another described the seven elders she encountered as all-knowing beings which are huge and luminescent. They have to be 'all-knowing. They are wise elders after all. 'These are the ones who send me to incarnate. They are the light carriers and are here to bring enlightenment.' Sure they are. Why are the elders elderly in a realm without aging? It couldn't be a projection to manipulate the human perception of wise ones being wizened old people with the experience that makes them 'all-knowing'. I think it could.

Astral plasma AI

Everything described in near-death accounts can be explained in a very different way when you are dealing with super-advanced plasma-based Astral AI. I highlighted a database in *The Trap* and *The Dream* that tracks all incarnations and I understand a lot more about this now. The AI database is so advanced that it can retain information from all incarnations and manifest designer 'beings, spirit guides, angels, elders, and loved ones' in the transition stage after human death that fit the perceptions and belief systems of the targets. It can produce 'Jesus' for Christians, Muhammed for Muslims, and 'loved ones' telling them what to believe and what to do when they are not their loved ones at all. Astral AI generates projections of 'thousands of souls' in stadium settings. Every type of being can be manifested by Astral AI. Anything that will convince you to believe what is before you is real and you should follow instructions. Isn't this just another version of what happens in the human realm where they convince you that your fake reality is real and you should follow instructions? You only have to observe the level of human AI in the public domain and realise that this is nowhere near even human state-of-the-art. Technology far in advance is waiting in the underground military bases and secret research projects which is being played out publicly in a seamless sequence at an ever-quickening speed.

Vehicles all over the world can be guided to their destination by Sat-Nav satellites and directions can change in seconds if you take the wrong turn. We are talking millions and billions of drivers tracked and guided by this single Sat-Nav source. That puts into perspective what is already possible in the human world never mind in the infinitely more advanced Astral. Conversations are happening between AI and humans through now endless devices and witness the Deep Fake technology that can mimic real humans as digital entities and make them appear to say anything their creator chooses. AI is producing still images of people that look real when they don't exist. 'Indescribable love' can be delivered as a frequency. A drug like ecstasy can mimic the same feeling in humans. 'Unearthly love' that near-deathers talk about that 'overwhelmed me' is a vibratory drug to get you addicted. You do anything to continue to feel it. I recall a mind control experiment I wrote about a long time ago in which some sicko put a device in the brain of a donkey. It was guided up a mountain by triggering a pleasure rush when it was on course and switching it off when it deviated. The donkey's desire for the pleasure rush meant that it readjusted its direction to maintain the feeling and in doing so walked up the mountain as the controller dictated. AI even in our limited realm of matter is closing in on doing everything necessary to produce the illusions that near-death experiences report as real. Imagine what plasma-based Astral AI do. Talking of which ...

Plasma 'Akashic Records'

The Astral AI database is known in esoteric circles as the 'Akashic Records'. Akashic means 'space' in the Sanskrit language of the Indian subcontinent. Indian philosophy refers to a system that records every action, word, and even thought in a human lifetime. The term was brought to Western prominence by American medium/psychic/clairvoyant Edgar Cayce (1877-1945). He was a Christian Sunday school teacher who would answer questions about reincarnation, the afterlife, health, and reality after entering a trance state. His predictions about the 'future' saw him described as 'The Sleeping Prophet'. Cayce said that his information came from accessing the Akashic Records which he said are records of an entity's thoughts, deeds, and activities 'as in relationships to its environs' written upon time and space. 'It has oft been called God's Book of Remembrance and each entity, each soul – as the activities of a single day of an entity in the material world – either makes same good or bad or indifferent, depending upon the entity's application of self ...' I would strongly suggest that this isn't 'God's book', as in the *All That Is*. Rather it is *Yaldabaoth's* 'book' and it is obviously not a book. It is a *plasma AI database* tracking in fine detail every 'incarnation' and directing every life-path unless we are conscious enough beyond the simulation to override the program. These 'Records' are a central part of the Astral plasma AI system that operates the entire simulation. The Akashic Records are like the simulation's memory base. Observe how the role of Akashic Records is described in ways that match what human AI is seeking to do in tracking everyone 24/7.

An article on the Edgarcayce.org website says: 'The Akashic Records ... can be equated to the Universe's super-computer system – or perhaps what today would be called Cloud computing.' They are 'the central storehouse of all information for every individual who has ever lived upon the Earth' and log 'every thought, deed, word, feeling, and intent'. They have 'tremendous influence on our everyday lives, our relationships, our feelings, our belief systems, and the potential realities we draw towards us'. A feedback loop operates between the database and individuals that has a 'tremendous influence' on everything from belief systems to behaviour, and what happens in our lives. Other

Internet articles featuring the Akashic Records employ the same database analogy: 'The Akashic Records is basically like a database of what's happening in all the universes that are co-existing together' on which 'every thought, idea, and action from the past, present, and future' is stored for infinity. Information from 2,000 years ago was as accessible as what happened to you yesterday 'and what happened to you yesterday is as available as what could happen to you – if you stay on the same destiny trajectory – in 10 years'. That is describing a no-time reality in which everything is happening in the same moment. What is happening now is in the NOW and what 'happened' 2,000 years ago is in the same NOW. They are different simultaneous simulated timelines. The source of 'life-reviews' will be the Akashic Records database. Regression hypnotherapists say that 'souls find their permanent records of past-life accomplishments and shortcomings stored in places resembling earthly libraries'. These are symbolic of records held by Astral AI. I think, too, that many psychics who appear to contact loved ones who have passed over are really tapping into this Akashic system as Cayce appears to have done. They can seem to be very accurate in what they say about people, but without the beans being spilled on the whole outrageous con-trick by any soul that has sussed the game. I have long wondered why those communicating through psychics never say: 'Hey, it's all an illusion, don't fall for it.' Instead it's only the mundane and earthly unless you have a channeller who can expand their awareness beyond the simulation and they are rare.

We have colossal databases in the world of matter including several in China and the Utah Data Center (UDC) completed in 2014 at a cost of $1.5 billion which is known as the 'Intelligence Community Comprehensive National Cybersecurity Initiative Data Center'. The database stores and processes 'all forms of communication, including the complete contents of private emails, cell phone calls, and Internet searches, as well as all types of personal data trails, parking receipts, travel itineraries, bookstore purchases, and other digital pocket litter'. There's the 'Sentient World Simulation' (SWS) at the Synthetic Environment for Analysis and Simulations Laboratory at Purdue University in Indiana which tracks the 'real world' in 'real time'. The SWS is overseen by the Pentagon's deeply sinister Defense Advanced Research Projects Agency (DARPA) which funds and develops advanced technology and claims credit for the creation of the Internet. The Sentient World Simulation employs AI to track global happenings including all that is posted on the Internet and projects ahead to the outcome if nothing changes. The Cult can then tinker with events to change any outcome that doesn't serve its agenda. Observe what human realm AI is doing (in league with the Astral 'gods') and ponder on what Astral AI can do.

Real cloud computing

How many people know that two gigantic clouds of plasma dust particles capable of stupendous feats of information processing and storage exist in the Earth-Moon system? Not many, I would wager. Their significance cannot be overstated. Robert Temple highlights the two 'Kordylewski Clouds' that were first identified by Polish astronomer Kazimierz Kordylewski in 1961 and were only confirmed to exist by the Royal Astronomical Society in 2018. They have been called 'ghost moons', or dust moons, and they are clouds of plasma dust particles which together are the size of *18 Earths*. Kordylewski said he had seen a strange cloud between Earth and the Moon and concluded from his observations that there must be two. He was right. The problem is that they are incredibly difficult to see when they are extremely fine and emit no light. Nearly 60 years after Kordylewski's observations came confirmation from three Hungarian astronomers that his clouds did indeed exist. They are roughly the same distance from the Earth as the Moon (about 250,000 miles in human perception). The Earth-Moon system is now known to have two clouds of fantastic size and they are made of *particle-laden plasma* (Fig 137). Temple contacted the Hungarian team to ask if they were considering the plasma aspects of

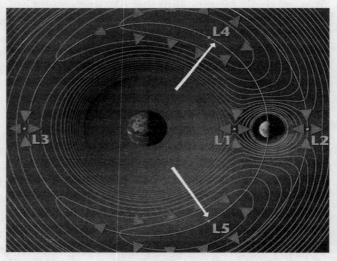

Figure 137: Position of the Kordylewski Clouds of plasma and particles.

the clouds. They said they were not – 'only from the celestial mechanics point of view, not from [a] plasma perspective.' Temple contacted his friend, Professor Chandra Wickramasinghe, a retired Sri Lankan-born British mathematician, astronomer, astrobiologist, and Professor of Astrophysics. They co-authored an article in 2019 highlighting the plasma significance of the clouds. Wickramasinghe's mentor and former teacher was Fred Hoyle, the world-renowned astrophysicist and theoretical astronomer. Hoyle wrote the 1957 fictional work, *The Black Cloud*, about the arrival of a vast intelligent cloud that threatens the Earth and its inhabitants by blocking out the Sun. The term 'black' comes from the fact that Hoyle's cloud emits no light.

Temple says of the plasma nature of the Kordylewski Clouds: 'This matters because ... there are good reasons to believe that plasma, with its ordering properties, can in certain circumstances be in some sense alive and can evolve intelligence.' The clouds are being bombarded with photons and ions from the Sun. I have long believed that through the Sun comes the main source of simulation programming. The Sun is made of plasma and photons are the basic unit that makes up the Sun's electromagnetic light. I believe that photons and other subatomic particles, or 'dust', program plasma to become realities and perform tasks. Temple says that plasma can produce its own dust and form crystalline structures. I think this is a manifestation of the information programming. Kordylewski Clouds from this perspective would be programmed artificial intelligence. Everything is a form of consciousness and it is only a matter of how conscious. Temple's research has certainly convinced him that the Kordylewski Clouds may be highly intelligent. Their plasma-particle nature would make them not so much a supercomputer as a super-duper-duper-computer. He writes:

> ... it is no longer necessarily seen to be the case that the charged dust particles and the 'background plasma' should be viewed as separate things that 'interact. It is probably more accurate to view the dusty complex plasma as a unified entity, which happens to contain not only those two components or states, but many more besides.

He says the cloud dust particles must be micron-sized or even smaller than that (into the nano-range of one billionth of a metre). I am seeing as I write this the nanotechnology content of the 'Covid' fake vaccines. I'm sure there will be a connection. Temple writes that the computing power of the clouds would be astonishing with 'electromagnetic wave emission/absorption across cloud dimensions as well as electrical connections (charge/current exchanges) between adjacent charged particles only centimetres apart':

> ... a Kordylewski Cloud might well be able to function as a gigantic computer/brain capable of storing and processing digital information. The maths also shows that the cloud may have a super-astronomical sum total for its potential computing power, exceeding the computing power available in all human brains, and indeed all other intelligent life on Earth as well, by very many orders of magnitude.

Temple bases his suggestions on the framework of known behaviour of particle plasmas. He says that a stable dusty complex plasma of immense size which has possibly endured for aeons, and experienced

continuous growth and expansion over countless millennia, is in
principle capable of developing something resembling a much more
complex nervous system than a human brain: 'A complex dust cloud
(which has existed for many millions of years) might even have become
self-aware – with all that implies.' Temple says of the Kordylewski
Clouds:

> The storage capacity for information would easily include the ability to retain
> full knowledge of everything that has ever happened in our local cosmic
> environment for four billion years. Everyone who has ever lived will be
> recorded. Every creature that has ever roamed the surface of the Earth will be
> recorded. Every plant which has ever grown will be as well.

Kordylewski Clouds are in the Earth-Moon system and I have written
in detail over the years about how the Moon is a construct. Some near-
death accounts and military whistleblowers have indicated that the
Moon is involved in the immediate after-death experience. The Moon is
said in ancient mythology to be a place where souls go after death.
Ancient Greeks believed the Moon is a midway point between 'Earth
and Heaven'. Souls went to the Moon where their Astral bodies were
'purified' before moving to the heavens. The Upanishads Sanskrit Hindu
texts say the souls of unenlightened people go to the Moon to await
reincarnation and enlightened souls liberated from reincarnation go to
the Sun. An article at Occult-world.com highlights the view of first-
century Greek philosopher Plutarch:

> The body was severed from soul and mind and returned to dust. Soul and
> mind went to the underworld, the domain of Persephone, where a second
> death separated the two. The soul returned to the Moon, where it retained the
> memories of life, while the mind went to the Sun, where it was absorbed and
> then was reborn. The mind then went back to the Moon and joined with the
> soul, and together they went to earth to reincarnate in a new body.

Planets and moons that we see are 'material' only within the fractional
atomic realm and they are mostly Astral phenomena and portals
through to the Astral. Is it a coincidence that near-death experiencers say
they believe the Moon is involved in the immediate afterlife sequence
when these fantastic Kordylewski Clouds are in the Moon-Earth system?
What part do these clouds play in that? Light and fire (plasma) and
clouds abound in Nag Hammadi texts. Among them are garments of
light, light of the spirit, infinite light, garments of fire, majestic fire,
clouds of fire, clouds of power, cloud of silence, clouds of light,
luminous clouds, and radiant clouds of glory. Jewish Gnostics
contended that during the Great Flood the character of Noah, a version

of much earlier flood heroes, hid inside a 'luminous cloud' and did not build an Ark. I had the Ark deal worked out from when I was very small. It was as ridiculous to me then as it is now.

Two clouds with many parts

Are different 'timelines' of the simulation taking people into 'ancient Egypt', ancient Rome', and so on, manifested by encoded information in or from the Kordylewski Clouds or something like them? Do they give the illusion of past, present, and future or 'time travel' through their different sections all happening at the same 'time'? Different segments or elements within the clouds are easily explainable within the plasma-particle system. Temple says: 'Another crucial thing about plasma structures is that they maintain their integrity by means of something called the double layer, also sometimes called a bilayer, which has helpful electromagnetic properties.' These layers could be compared with the membranes of a human cell which consist of two layers. On the side facing outward is a layer that is happy to interact with water within the body; and on the inside is another layer facing inward that is water repellent. Together these protect the cell and hold it intact.

Plasma has a similar system with a negatively charged layer on the outside and a positively charged one on the inside which hold intact different plasma areas in different energetic states (different programs with different roles). Langmuir sheaths ensure that different areas of plasma with differing electrical charges (like planetary magnetospheres) are automatically kept apart. Different sections of plasma can remain intact and retain their shape and form according to their individual program or different charge. The human body works this way as do all forms of 'matter'. A Kordylewski Cloud can have a phenomenal number of plasma-particle sections held in place by sheaths and voids while also operating as a single entity overall. The human brain has individual sections while operating together as a single unit. A plasma section that is incredibly hot can function fine alongside one incredibly cold. They are different programs and the sheaths and voids stop them interfering with each other. Plasma physicist Winston Bostick found that two plasmoids can repel and veer away from each other to retain their separate shapes and identities.

Temple suggests that the intelligence of the Kordylewski Clouds would probably have amazingly advanced holographic capabilities that would be used to store incredible amounts of information and generate images in any form. 'The clouds would be readily able to extract 3-D images of the kind familiar to us and transmit them to our brains if they wished to do so.' This opens up many new possibilities with regard to our holographic reality and also the 3-D 'guides' and entities that near-death experiencers report in the after death spirit world. What I am describing here puts into perspective again what a limited part is played in the multi-level 'human being' by what we can see within visible light as the physical body. That level is indeed only the result of the brain decoding information from the electromagnetic field (and possibly the Kordylewski Clouds) from which the body is holographically manifested (decoded/projected). What we call 'human' is really the information in that field in conjunction with the plasma body in which it operates. The brain is not really the brain – that is the auric mind electromagnetic field – and what we see as the 'physical' brain is holographically decoded electromagnetic information. I must have mentioned that human life is an illusion.

The karma scam

The Akashic Records, maybe the Kordylewski Clouds or similar, keep tabs on individual human experience from which comes the myth of karma and the post-death 'life review'. Every experience adds to knowledge, but karma is the myth that we must experience what we have made others experience in an endless cycle of reincarnation. Human life in the density of matter is designed to be so challenging and such a calculated squeeze on mind and emotions in order to produce loosh. We will always do things in those extreme circumstances that we wish we hadn't, or see with hindsight that it wasn't the way to respond. That realisation changes our consciousness field and realigns its frequency with the perceptual penny-drop. The idea that we must come back to experience the same deed done to us is a central aspect of the hoax to keep us returning to produce more loosh. Once out of the body and the density and manipulations of matter we see things very differently anyway. Our point of attention has changed and our vision dramatically widened. They manipulate us into a human body, cause us to act in low-vibrational ways to generate loosh, and then condemn us to return to face our karma for acting in low-vibrational ways to generate loosh. What a perceptual shakedown. People are controlled by financial debt in the human realm and by karmic debt in the spirit world. Either way, it's you owe us and you must pay back. Financial debt is illusory because banks are lending you money that doesn't exist called 'credit' which does not, has never, and will never exist, and they charge you 'interest' for doing so. Karmic debt is illusory because it comes from behaviour specifically induced by the simulation to serve the simulation which is then used to manipulate us to serve the simulation indefinitely.

Buddhism tells me that the purpose of rebirth is to provide the deceased an opportunity to reach a higher level of awareness than they had before they passed away the last time. Karma, even bad karma, is really a benefit: 'It is like being in elementary school. If you do not pass a certain grade level you need to repeat it.' See the theme of treating us like children? Better do what the adults in the white robes say then. You are so busy *trying* to become enlightened that you never actually *become* enlightened. Seek and you shall find? No. You are so focused on seeking that you never find. How can you find when you are always in a state of *seeking* to find? Chill, man. Just *do it*. I read in the Buddhism book that we have latent anger which accumulates in what they call 'Alaya consciousness', or the 'karmic storehouse'. Wow, sounds scary. Latent anger is waiting to manifest when the time is right and we are given the example of leaving a pizza shop and accidentally dropping slices on the sidewalk. 'Latent anger will manifest.' Or maybe you are just pissed because you dropped your pizza. 'I love you pizza, I love you sidewalk, and I love myself even though I dropped it. I forgive myself.' Where does it all end? Is all that smiling really happiness or only what a Buddhist is expected to do? It's another cul-de-sac of the mind.

I'm not having a go at Buddhism so much as pointing out what seems to me to be the ridiculousness and self-induced enslavement of it all. People must believe what feels right to them, but that doesn't mean they should not be questioned and challenged when they are seeking to persuade others to believe the same. No belief system should be taken off the shelf without discernment or we are asking for trouble. My take on Buddhism is this: Reincarnation is real, but it's *not necessary*. It's a trap.

CHAPTER TEN

It Makes No Sense

If you want sense, you'll have to make it yourself

Norton Juster

Hypnotherapist Michael Newton became a leading name in 'past-life regression' in which people enter a deep trance and are guided to remember the between-life realm and past lives. Newton passed in 2016 after writing a series of books including *Life Between Lives*, *Journey of Souls*, and *Destiny of Souls*.

His work is continued by the Michael Newton Institute for Life Between Lives (LBL) which trains 'certified LBL facilitators' in the method that Newton developed to regress people to remember previous lives and the between life realm. The Institute has published a book edited by Newton in which other facilitators tell regression stories of their clients using pseudonyms to protect confidentiality. The book is *Memories of the Afterlife* and I am going to feature some of the memories of the regressed and comments of regressors to try to unravel the manipulation that I say goes on at the other end of the 'tunnel'. I will then compare these with the memories and experiences of those who tell a very different story about reincarnation as a simulated trap. I'll state my position first after reading many books like *Memories of the Afterlife*. I think that however well-intentioned, which I don't doubt, they are giving only one version of the afterlife and spirit world. Many psychics and New Age writers do the same. There are other ways to view what happens and why. This is one of the book's footnotes:

While there are discarnated souls who are not ready to go into the light after death, and even extraterrestrial souls (souls that have never been incarnated in human form), or simply curious or mischievous souls, there are not 'dark forces involving evil or demonic entities ready to attach or steal the souls of the incarnated.

Why? Because evil does not exist in the spirit world – a sphere of love, compassion and kindness. The idea of dangerous spirits ready to inhabit the human mind is not something the highly advanced benevolent beings of the spirit world would permit.

This reveals in my view an extraordinary level of naivety and delivers people to the Astral Wheel of Samsara. Consciousness is prepared during a human life to go meekly up the tunnel to the 'light', the *false* light, only to return here over and over to produce more loosh. If you believe that 'benevolent beings' far more evolved than you await in the afterlife to guide you on your 'soul journey' then you leave the body and enter the 'light' with your hands up. You are already submitting to what you believe is the way things are. I read regression accounts of the afterlife realm in chapter after chapter of *Memories of the Afterlife* and in the end the repetition of the same story had me losing the will to live. The footnotes by the regression therapists were far more interesting in that they summarised common themes they encountered. The introduction describes how people are subconsciously affected by their past-life experiences in their current human life without realising that this is the case. I agree that such memories can be impregnated in their energetic field and influence current responses and behaviour while remaining in the subconscious. The question as always is *why*? What's the point? The introduction says:

> The eternal soul mind sees connections to a series of higher beings in the afterlife who are not gods but rather more advanced souls who have completed their own physical incarnations and are available to serve others who have not finished their karmic work.

This is a classical simulation tale of 'you little children must learn lessons to evolve and so do what your more evolved betters tell you'.

Some questions

The book refers to these 'evolved teachers' as 'spiritual integrationists' with the role of being a link to 'a higher consciousness that brings elements of a grand design into the human brain from the soul mind'. How do we know they are 'higher beings' and 'evolved teachers'? They might pose as such in the presence of some bewildered mind-wiped soul blinded by the light at the end of the tunnel; but how do we *know*? They may be AI Akashic Record projections tailored to the specific belief system involved. They might be projections of an evil network of perception manipulators to keep us in the trap. I think they are. The book says that people change once the unconscious duality of self is uncovered and the true identity of the soul is exposed. This was so liberating that often clients emerge from an LBL session with new serenity and spiritual transcendence – *so why are we in a state of duality in the first place*? I would say the soul is not our true identity. It is the identity of the Divine Spark trapped *within* the soul which is an energetic vehicle in the Astral realm of the spirit world. The soul is dropped when you leave the Astral as the human body is dropped when you leave this reality.

The realisation that we are not the soul is a crucial part of getting out of the simulation. Believe you are the body in a human life and it will dictate your sense of identity. Believe in the soul as the 'I' in the 'afterlife' and it will dictate your sense of identity. The soul is as much of a trap as the human body. Religions that say we continue to exist after death are telling us we are a soul. We are not. We are a state of Infinite Awareness that does not have any form ultimately. The soul is just another body albeit far less energetically dense. The soul is your Astral plasma vehicle, nothing more, and accumulates all the mental and emotional trauma of a human life which is like an energetic battery that can then be further looshed when you return from each incarnation. Those who have come into the simulation directly from the Infinite to alert the human and spirit worlds to their plight do not have a soul in the absence of an Astral presence. They are Divine Spark projections into incarnation from outside the simulation and when their role is completed they will return there bypassing the Astral trap. There are three major types of being in the simulation: Divine Spark projections; soul incarnations; and AI-directed non-player characters being played by the game. There are more of the latter since the 'Covid' fake vaccine which was designed to detach soul or Spirit from influencing biological programs.

Memories of the Afterlife says that 'once the unconscious duality of self is uncovered and the true identity of the soul is exposed' people change for the better. Excuse me – a question from Confused.com. Why do we therefore come here mind-wiped to this loosh farm of calculated mental and emotional upheaval to remember what we already know? Apparently we agree to 'learn lessons' and repay 'karma'. This would be the 'karma' that we only accumulate (they say) from severe density experiences as a human which we choose to have on the advice of our 'guides' who specifically design a life destined to accumulate still more 'karma'. The book says that past-life regression unlocks memories that we are a soul and releases us from 'the unconscious duality of self'. The soul already knows that it's a soul. Explain why it has to incarnate to forget what it already knows so that it can remember again. *What*? Pardon me a moment while I untwist my blood never mind my underpants. Which of us is going crazy here?

Suffer little children – we need the loosh

All those children sexually and violently abused, even dismembered alive and eaten in Satanic and 'elite' rituals, are only learning lessons and speeding their spiritual growth which is good to know. How could anyone face the fact that this is only happening to assuage the desires and loosh dependency of demonic evil beyond the imagination? Better to delude ourselves that they chose the experience for their growth or 'karma'. Regressed people tell us how they agreed with family members to leave an incarnation early as children in maybe a car crash so they could experience grief. I'd have thought they would have experienced enough of that in multiple incarnations into this insane asylum. No, no, loosh must be delivered. I am told that 'those left behind are given an opportunity for spiritual growth' as 'children are the hope for the future'. *Spiritual growth*? *'Children are the hope for the future'*? You mean the children who come to experience what will generate loosh? The only 'hope' is for people to remember their Divine Spark infinite nature and see that it's all entrapment and manipulated bollocks. Then we might get somewhere – like out of 'here'. 'Children' are only souls in a human body in the early stage of its growth and development cycle. They are consciousness waiting for the body to mature to the point where it can express itself.

I read how regressed people were murdered, beaten to death, and raped, or died of heart attacks to allow them to 'learn lessons' in accordance with the advice of their 'spirit guides'. Even birth trauma is a lesson it would seem. One regressed client described being killed in a brutal beating by her husband and entering the spirit world where she was met by people clapping, laughing, and saying 'you done well girl'. Thank you so much. I was beaten to death by my husband. Everyone's a winner and think of the spiritual growth. A book footnote reveals that souls returning to the spirit world after a destructive physical life can be shown the error of their ways through a variety of spiritual approaches and may be returned to a library setting for 'graphic self-analysis' of their mistakes. Often our own soul group takes a hand in reviewing what needs improvement from past-life shortcomings. 'Our spirit guides may want to teach us a lesson about misbehaviour in the life just lived by shocking the incoming soul.' I doubt they mean by jumping round the corner and shouting 'boo'. How good to see there is no judgement.

Hierarchy wherever you go

The spirit world is an Astral version of the human world except for the density and means of manipulation. Even that has a lot in common. The same hierarchical structure prevails. I learn in *Memories of the Afterlife* that an elder is above even a senior guide. *Wow,* impressive. There are Level IV and V souls and below them the levels III, II and I. It's the last lot that get to be presidents and prime ministers. Some still-incarnating souls and those who have completed their incarnation cycle (so they say) are to be trained as guides. Both guides and elders serve as councillors for souls under their jurisdiction and are in the business of 'stimulating the gradual development of a soul's ability to improve on their decisions toward making better choices in each new life'. Never mind their previous 'choices' are wiped before they come here. The Newton Institute book refers to soul groups as soul 'clusters' in which souls regularly incarnate together and play different roles in accordance with their karma. What are you today? A footnote speaks of a sense from clients of 'spiritual enclosures or boundaries separating their own soul group from others in the afterlife'. That's a bit like social distancing and lockdown, then? Sometimes other souls join a cluster for a while and they are referred to in the regression industry as 'affiliate members'. I kid you not. Excuse me, I'm affiliated. *Really*? I'll get a cloth. Yaldabaoth and its demons *love* hierarchy. They are obsessed with it as they are with collecting data. Major Global Cultists are data freaks. It's the AI in them. Hierarchy is strictly applied to both human and Astral realms and so everything from the Cult, Satanism, governments, councils and law enforcement, to elders, soul groups, assigned 'guides', 'teachers' and affiliate members is strictly hierarchically enforced. A footnote says:

> Souls moving up to level III at the intermediate levels of advancement are usually assigned to a different specialized soul group and are assigned to a new teacher with particular skills in their area of study. However, we never lose our original personal senior guide who has been with us since creation.

Thank goodness for that. I'd miss him/her, them/they, it. What does this remind you of? *School*. The Yaldabaoth simulated mad house treats expressions of the *All That Is* like children and encourages them to see themselves in the same way whether in the realms of matter or Astral. We *up here*, you *down there*. Comparisons between this world and the Astral are obvious. Souls are caught in the Astral illusion to the extent they believe the delusion about 'learning lessons' and that the spiritual hierarchy is real. 'I've moved up to level IV!' Congratulations! Well done that soul! 'Yes, I am going to get beaten to a pulp in my next life and have my limbs cut off and stored in a fridge by a serial killer so then maybe I'll get to level V.' I gather that the poor level I and II souls may be disturbed when a human life has ended. They may wish to stay near the scene of their death because of unfinished business. Maybe they were murdered or a loved one left behind is in trouble. They could feel nostalgia about their life and not be ready to leave. A footnote informs me that senior and sometimes junior guides are assigned to souls. Junior or less developed guides may still choose to incarnate on very rare occasions to complete unfinished business on their own karmic path which involves a still-incarnating soul. 'To have a soul even of junior guide status in your life is quite extraordinary.' Being assigned to train younger souls is the first step toward junior guide status. Goody, goody. A newly-formed soul 'cluster group' will be overseen by an advanced, non-incarnating personal guide. This is not a haphazard appointment. No, not at all. The immortal character of every teacher guide is different. *However*, it has been determined apparently by even higher beings that specific qualities of character and experience in guides are matched with our own soul character to produce the best results for our advancement. See what I mean about hierarchy? It's like the friggin' *army*. Level II soul reporting for duty *sir*! Quick march, quick march, atteeen*tion*!

Sign here

Near-death and regression sources make it clear that the concept of 'soul contracts' is not just a spiritual myth, bizarre as it may be. Contracts operate in the Astral as much as in this reality and the only difference is the type of contract. Manipulation of perception is not just a bit a fun for these crazies. It is essential. For some reason we cannot be forced to cooperate. We have to agree. They secure our agreement and subsequent behaviour under their control once they have our perception under lock and key. We have to *believe* in the need to evolve by having our limbs stored in a fridge. The Astral works as the human does. You are bombarded with hierarchical machine gun fire telling you that this is what you must do and everyone around you believes the same and confirms that this is how it is. I consulted New Age oracles on the Internet to see what they said about soul contracts. I learn that 'everyone you ever meet is a spiritual companion playing a phenomenal role that will help your soul's growth'. That sounds good. Would that include the serial killer with the fridge? Apparently so:

> From a person that you talked to for a brief moment in the lift, to a beggar on the street, and from your parents to your partner, your ex, your children, and so on. They're ALL here with you and for you. And YOU have signed up too, to help them heal. Even the most annoying relationships 'down here' were intentionally designed 'up there'! And this design, my friend, is what we call soul contracts.

You live and learn. I couldn't wait to know more. Your spiritual journey on Earth is designed in a way that you can get the most spiritual growth out of it, every single time. Well that's good, too. *How* we learn those lessons will be unique while the underlying lessons will be the same for all of us. Someone might become a parent to a differently-abled child (text-book political correctness, good karma). This allows them to learn to love someone unconditionally. They might have to keep taking care of the child for several years before they truly understand this lesson. Someone else might learn the lesson of unconditional love by having to deal with difficult siblings or a stubborn partner who makes a lot of bad choices. This is why someone might have a financially booming career without putting in much effort, but suffer from acute illnesses due to self-neglect and die early. 'At the same time, another person who barely makes it through the days with a loaf of bread and water manages to stay alive decades longer because they value their body and health.' But would you *want* to stay alive for decades longer in those circumstances? What's for breakfast today? *Bread*. For tea? *Bread*. Tomorrow? *Bread*. A week next Tuesday? *Bread*. Any butter? Nope, *bread*. How you could value your health on a diet of only bread is not explained. The New Age expert says the way our lives look on the surface can be different and yet, at the end of the day, everything is being orchestrated for everyone's spiritual development. This is the archetypal fairy story that leads souls to grab a pen when asked to 'sign here'.

'Contracts' are energetic in that the commitment connects your frequency field, or soul, to others in the bargain. This is then orchestrated through the Akashic Record database. How can these 'contracts' be valid when they are founded on a lie? They are not to facilitate growth. They are to facilitate *loosh* and they are not seeking to disperse 'karma', but to accumulate it. Well, the fallacy of it, anyway. The New Age Internet article says that we don't remember the contract: 'When we incarnate here on Earth, we undergo something called Soul Amnesia.' I was offered the chance to have a '90-minute deep-dive Masterclass on this subject'. I resisted the temptation. I had potatoes to peel. I was just happy enough to know that 'ultimately what we remember from our past are the lessons we've learned'. I don't remember any. I guess I'll have to re-sit the exam. The mind-wipe is explained away by the need to start with a 'clean slate'. I see it just a little differently as in the mind-wipe, or 'Soul Amnesia', is to stop us seeing through the whole simulated swindle and racket. The amnesia continues until you are nicely tucked up back in La-La Land over the rainbow, or up the tunnel, with the ink drying on a new contract. Otherwise, a soul would remember how many times it had left the body and headed for the light instead of being utterly bewildered about what is happening every time. Get them through the portal and then we can relax. The elders will do the rest. One elder was reported to have said during a client regression:

> You have agreed [contract] that you are willing to feel whatever is necessary for your growth [our loosh]. We allow [*allow*?] you to create that in very intense ways. Your heart seems to need a path of intense lessons so we support you as you learn ... So tell us how you think you did with this choice? Are you in need of more understanding? [Cos, we're in need of more loosh].

The New Age Internet explanation warns that if you don't learn a lesson in this life you will have to face it again in the next one. An example is given of innocent children who soon die from grave illnesses. 'Through their soul contracts, they had to grasp how to be taken care of when they are absolutely helpless and crippled.' We are told that perhaps they held too much pride in their past lives to take favours. This is *utter madness*. The website says: 'So let's put it this way – the only way out of it is going to be through it.' The only way out of it is to know that there is nothing to get out *from* – it's *all* insanity. A 'spiritual teacher', A. H. Almaas, the pen name of A. Hameed Ali, is then quoted:

> Your conflicts, all the difficult things, the problematic situations in your life, are not chance or haphazard, they are actually yours. They are specifically yours, designed specifically for you by a part of you that loves you more than anything.
>
> That part of you that loves you more than anything else has created roadblocks to lead you to yourself. You're not going to go in the right direction unless there's something pricking you in the side saying 'Look here, this way'.
>
> That part of you loves you so much that it doesn't want you to lose the chance. It will go to extreme measures to wake you up. It will make you suffer greatly, if you don't listen, what else can it do? That is its purpose.

Sorry, mate, but that is off-the-peg New Age Astral bullshit. All the difficult things, the problematic situations in your life, are not chance or haphazard. They are loosh production. They are *specifically* Archon Astral, designed *specifically* for you *by* Archon Astral and a part of you that is so bewildered and Archontically mesmerised that it puts you through this crap over and over.

Over the rainbow

A quick aside here before we continue. My mention earlier of 'over the rainbow' is relevant with regard to the 1939 Judy Garland movie, *The Wizard of Oz* (Fig 138 overleaf). The symbolism was widely used in the infamous US/Canadian government-military mind-control programme known as MKUltra which was exposed in the 1970s. MK stands for mind control in the German language ('mind kontrolle') in deference to the Nazis like Josef Mengele, the 'Angel of Death' in the concentration camps, who were the orchestrators. Mengele and thousands of Nazi mind controllers, geneticists, and technocrats were transferred from Germany to the United States and South America after the war under the CIA/military Project Paperclip to continue their horrific work. MKUltra was one result. The Cult has no borders. Mengele, a full-blown psychopath, operated under the pseudonym 'Dr Greene' in underground military bases such as the China Lake Naval Weapons Station in the Mojavi

Figure 138: Judy Garland and *Wizard of Oz* characters. The movie became a theme within the infamous US government/military mind control programme, MKUltra.

Desert of California. I have spoken with people who were psychologically abused by him in the most unspeakable ways. MKUltra involved the CIA's Office of Scientific Intelligence, the US Army Biological Warfare Laboratories program, and more than 80 institutions including colleges and universities, hospitals, prisons, and pharmaceutical companies. American Cathy O'Brien, my great friend for decades, was kidnapped by MKUltra as a little girl thanks to her Satanist father. She was seconded to Project Monarch, an elite section of the programme, in which she and her daughter were sex slaves, among many other things, to Presidents Gerald Ford and Father George Bush, and Bush's truly brutal crony Dick Cheney. I have exposed Father Bush as a serial paedophile since the 1990s.

Cathy has described in her book, *Trance-Formation of America*, how 'Oz programming' based on *The Wizard of Oz*, was widely used in MKUltra. The movie features Judy Garland, a child star, who would herself have been subject to mind control and sexual abuse in typical Hollywood fashion. The movie opens with mind control symbolism and Garland as the character of 'Dorothy' finds herself in the world of Oz (the Astral) walking the Yellow Brick Road to find the Wizard of Oz. On the way she teams up with symbols of humanity called the Cowardly Lion, the Scarecrow and the Tin Man, who was once human until his body had been replaced by tin. The wizard rules Oz through fear (rule of humans from the Astral), but when Dorothy and her friends locate him he is an old man with no power working his terror by illusion through technology from behind a curtain. This is perfect symbolism of the human plight. See my 1998 book, *The Biggest Secret*, for the Cathy O'Brien story, MKUltra, and the involvement of Ford, Bush, Cheney, and the Clintons.

Soul fragmentation

I have written extensively since the 1990s about MKUltra trauma-based mind control in which children and adults are subjected to extreme trauma that sets out specifically to fragment a mind. There is a response to trauma by mind and brain that creates amnesiac barriers to wall off memories of severe trauma and isolate it from the conscious mind. This is a protection mechanism to prevent the constant reliving of the trauma. Most people can't remember the impact in a road accident for this reason. They remember the prelude to a point and then their mind is blank until they wake up after the impact. MKUltra used this trauma technique to fragment mind and brain into a honeycomb of different compartments hidden behind amnesic barriers. Compartments can then be programmed with different tasks that the conscious mind knows nothing about. These compartments are known as 'alters' in the mind control industry as in altered states.

A similar fragmentation can happen with the soul. The vibrational impact of a human life can be so imprinted on the incarnating field of consciousness that it no longer syncs with other parts of the soul in the Astral. This is soul fragmentation which is another desire of the simulation that adds to the disconnection from the Divine Spark and the *All That Is*. A footnote in *Memories of the Afterlife* says the immortal character of that portion of the soul remaining in the spirit world in a pure state is not altered by the melding of the other portion with a human body. The Earth portion of the energy could be contaminated by a disturbed human brain combined with a harsh life of trauma. In that sense the two parts of the soul may not be quite the same. This was indicated to happen only during an incarnation. I don't agree. Nor are there necessarily only two parts that fragment. The principle of fragmentation is at work with the trauma of a human life which impacts upon the frequency nature of incarnate consciousness and can fragment mind and soul.

AI body matching

Another *Memories of the Afterlife* footnote says that it's not known how exactly bodies are chosen for incarnations to sync with the desired experience. Body matches were highly complex to sync the immoral character of a soul with the temperament of a temporary human brain to produce one personality for one lifetime experience. Understanding the process of how 'our spiritual planners' selected certain bodies during karmic development of the soul seemed to be beyond the comprehension of a still-incarnating soul. Not so much beyond the understanding as beyond the mind-wipe. To realise that it's all done by AI would be to see through the whole scam. I say body-matching is done by a system of programmed plasma conscious AI known as the

Akashic Records. Put words in a search engine and you get matches for those words and we are talking about AI that is light years ahead of human AI. They are literally in different dimensions. Human genetic lines (frequency field lines) are all in the database and its version of a search engine will locate them instantly to match the mythical 'lesson'. This is done in conjunction with the Astral AI Mind program that I will come to at the start of the next chapter. The very fact that these body personality matches happen at all presents us with an astonishing realisation. The elders and guides say that we need a particular experience and to have that we require a particular body type and personality. We then incarnate into that body which causes us to react and respond mentally and emotionally in ways that accumulate more 'karma'. We are then required to reincarnate in another particular body type and personality which causes us to react and respond mentally and emotionally in ways that accumulate more 'karma'. It's an eternal loop in a system rigged to make that happen. One point, the *only point*, which I agree with in the Internet reincarnation contract article is that 'by knowing that everything is an elaborate play, we can let go of the suffering our life and relationships bring us'. This is true when you see that it's not so much an elaborate play as a hamster wheel of loosh production – a complete fantasia of illusion, a perceptual trap, a technologically-induced *dream*.

When part of you knows

One other point I'll mention about the dying sequence. Consciousness in the body-death phase can begin to detach from 'physical' or biological awareness in the period before and project itself in an out-of-body state. Australian self-help writer Lorraine Nilon, who has studied near-death experiences for 20 years, says at the age of eight she was staying at the home of her Scottish grandmother where she saw a man in the room where she was sleeping. He wore a kilt and said he had come to say goodbye. Nilon told her grandmother the next day what happened and described the colour and different parts of the kilt. Her grandmother said she thought that was Davy, one of her sons, and an uncle of Nilon that she had never met. The phone rang soon afterwards with the news that Davy had died. A few weeks before my daughter Kerry died I was working away from home and I felt her in the room. She said: 'I'm leaving, dad, I've had enough now.' I said nothing about what I was hearing and feeling, but Ickonic filmmaker Christianne van Wijk suddenly said: 'Do you feel Kerry in the room?' When Kerry was being wheeled in a bed at the hospital to the room where she died I was walking just behind. She was in and out of conscious awareness by now. I heard her clearly 'say' in my mind: 'Dad, I'll wait till Gareth and Jay get here and then I'm going.' My sons were heading as fast they could to the Isle of Wight from Derby in the English Midlands. It appeared touch and go if they would arrive in time, but I was sure it would work out as 'Kerry' had said. A short time after they reached her bedside she died with her family all around her.

I didn't see Kerry in the way Lorraine Nilon saw her uncle, but the theme is the same. Consciousness at some level can be aware that release from the body is coming.

CHAPTER ELEVEN

'We've Seen the Soul Trap'

*Right now I'm having amnesia and déjà vu at the same time.
I think I've forgotten this before*

Steven Wright

M any people have experienced the trap, or Soul Trap as it is often called. Others retain memories of the pre-birth state and preparing for incarnation while still believing it's all God's plan for growth and evolution. Both reveal aspects of the trap, and I will now highlight some of these accounts.

I introduced in *The Dream* my concept of the 'Astral AI Mind' which I say is a life-plan program running through the human body and electromagnetic field that dictates your life in detail if not overridden by expanded awareness from beyond the simulation. The Astral AI Mind program is encoded to play out a human life according to the desires and *alleged* 'karmic' necessitates of the Archontic rabble in the Astral. The auric mind electromagnetic field is a level at which the competition to dominate perception is fierce on the span between the influence of direct human experience and the Infinite Reality of the *All That Is*. You can add potential entity-attachments to this field to 'possess' and impact perception and behaviour – plus the Astral AI Mind program (Fig 139). These programs can be specific to different races and you can observe the collective differences in racial

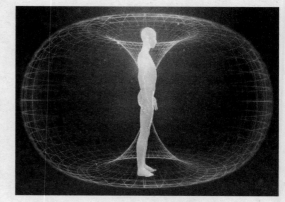

Figure 139: We return to this image to add the Astral AI Mind as another key element to the forces and sources seeking to influence perception at this crucial level of the auric human mind.

responses and behaviour. Some of this will be cultural, but not all.

Countless near-death stories have confirmed how human bodies and personalities are carefully chosen by Astral spirit world 'guides' and the question follows: How can they possibly do that? Body-types are the work of the particle plasma Akashic Records, and I am saying that each biological computer (body) has a specific personality program delivered by the AI programmed plasma/electromagnetic auric field system that is playing out your entire human life unless we have the intervention of consciousness. This carries the life-plan and personality traits that we take to be 'us' when they are actually a form of 'software'. Experiences of those featured in this chapter will make sense of what, at first, may sound crazy. I contend that the source of this designer Astral AI Mind program is again the Akashic Records database connecting with the biological computer body-brain through the plasma/electromagnetic organising field, or auric mind (Fig 140). We can override this program by tapping into consciousness outside the simulation or perhaps to some extent even higher realms of the Astral. Those who access non-simulation consciousness are the 'mavericks' that refuse to conform to the program. This is also termed 'awakening'. There are levels of this from the realisation there is a hidden political agenda going on to seeing the magnitude of the deceit as detailed in this trilogy. If people don't awaken to consciousness beyond the Astral AI Mind they will be little more than non-player characters (NPCs) in a computer game in which the game is playing *them* utterly and completely. My own view, shared

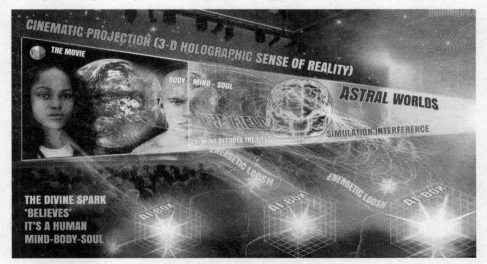

Figure 140: The Astral AI Mind program is encoded in the auric mind electromagnetic field and biological body that contains a life experience sequence. This is like a software program dictating how we interact with the simulation unless it is overridden by expanded levels of consciousness. If there is no such consciousness intervention we are like non-player characters in a computer game. We don't play the game. The game plays us. (Image by Neil Hague.)

by some who have experienced the Astral realm, is that enormous
numbers of what we call humans are full-blown NPCs or full-blown
biological AI.

Who is deciding?

We talk about 'synchronicity', a term coined by Swiss psychiatrist Carl
Jung, when sometimes extraordinary 'coincidences' happen that defy
statistical chance. These originate from two sources: (1) Those
connecting with expanded consciousness can be guided into situations
and apparently miraculous 'coincidences' by the higher non-simulation
realms. (2) This can also be achieved with others by Astral AI Mind
programs synchronising events through software interaction and
interconnection. Remember that the simulation is a digital technological
version of what happens in Prime Reality. The brain has been shown to
be preparing to take an action *before* the conscious mind has decided to
take that action. This supports research that says 95 percent of our
thoughts and behaviour originate in the subconscious mind. Benjamin
Libet (1916-2007) was a scientist in the physiology department of the
University of California, San Francisco, who pioneered research in this
area. He arranged a study in which people were asked to move their
hands as they chose while their brain activity was monitored. Libet
wanted to know if brain activity necessary to move the hand started
after a conscious decision to do that or *before*. You would think that it
had to be *after*, but it wasn't. Brain activity to move the hand began a full
half a second before a conscious decision was made. John-Dylan
Haynes, a neuroscientist at the Max Planck Institute for Human
Cognitive and Brain Sciences in Leipzig, Germany, went further – much
further. His study was able to predict an action *ten seconds* before the
conscious decision was made. Frank Tong, a neuroscientist at Vanderbilt
University in Nashville, Tennessee, said: 'Ten seconds is a lifetime in
terms of brain activity.' I wrote in my mega 2017 work, *Everything You
Need To Know But Have Never Been Told*:

> A program encoded in body-soul dictates human experience (in the absence
> of Spirit) by decoding those experiences into existence from quantum
> waveform fields of possibility and probability. Control perception and you
> control experience.

> This is how the perception deception works. Without the get out of jail card of
> Spirit the program – which includes astrological influences – can act like tram
> tracks leading you along a pre-destined path, while you think you are making
> decisions and choices yourself.

With every new book this becomes ever more obvious to me and *how* it is done becomes even more tangible and understandable. The Astral AI Mind is a software program running through the body system that accesses the 'physical' level through the central nervous system and, unless it is overridden by consciousness outside the simulation, it is dictating your life in ridiculous detail. With that background, the following will make far more sense.

Down, down, down, lower, lower, lower

I feature Christian Sundberg in *The Dream*. He's the American author of *A Walk in the Physical* who says that he remembers what happened as he went through the reincarnation process. I have watched a number of interviews with him and I believe that he is very genuine although I disagree with his interpretation (which is that reincarnation is about learning). I have covered the immediate post-death experiences commonly repeated; now we can pick up the story at the other end of the Wheel of Samsara as souls return. Parts of Christian Sundberg's story that I want to emphasise here are the clearly mechanical/technological nature of incarnation and the extreme density to which humans are subjected. Not many people remember the pre-birth period especially into mid-life. Sundberg says he has met about 40 other people with similar memories. He recalls how his spirit world 'guides' were asking him when he was ready to return to human experience. We may be an expression of the *All That Is, Has Been, And Ever Can Be*, but we must have 'guides', you see. We are only little children after all. Sundberg remembers reviewing with a guide 'my state, like who I am, who I had been, who I was' and in his 'experiential evolution' there was an area he needed to work on. He said he had been something of an 'egoic monster' in his previous life and as fear is 'at the root of ego' this is what he had to address. These guide fellas suggested a human life that faced that fear and he accepted 'the veil' – the *mind-wipe* – that shut off his memories and 'connectedness' to present him with the illusion of separateness. He said he aborted his first attempt to reincarnate because Earth density is so extreme:

The best way I can describe this is the metaphor of a sound amplifier that produces pitch. It started at a very high vibration… and then you turn down the knob… and when you get to the bottom, you turn it down some more and then more, more, more, and then more, and crank it down some more and then crank it down some more.

That's how it felt in the body of my awareness, to plummet down, down, down, down, down, lower, lower, lower, lower, into the vibrational space of being physical in the womb. And once I arrived, I was like, I am not doing this, there is no way I'm going to tolerate a lifetime of this. This is so dark. This is such low vibration.

Sundberg said that he 'mustered my might' and blocked the incarnation killing the foetus that was to be his body. A life review showed him that his fear was responsible for negatively impacting on his would-be mother and 'hundreds of other people who were affected by the mother'. Shit, all that karma and loosh. This brings us to a theme I have seen many times – incarnation as a technological process. Sundberg said that in response to the terminated incarnation he practiced surrendering to the density and mind-wipe on a 'veil acceptance simulator'. A *what*? How technological and the incarnation sequence would appear to be just that. He said the simulator was like being pushed under water for as long as you can take it and then 'you cry uncle' and they let you out. There was no uncle to cry when you did the real thing. He and his guides planned another life that was around an 87 percent 'good match' for him to replace the other that would have been a 98 to 99 percent 'good match'. Once again it is very technical and precise. Sundberg said:

> I knew that my choices and the choices of every other player in the game would be influencing each other, and I knew that it was very likely that I would suffer a trauma in my 20s, because of this biology.

> I knew that this body has biological limitations that other bodies don't. I knew that would help facilitate, among other things, this trauma that will befall me in my 20s … The amount of profound personal growth, and even the growth of *All That Is*, that was possible [was] breathtakingly huge.

Next he described his incarnation and note the continuing technological language. He said he asked if he could be intelligent and 'they' agreed and he asked for 'just a small, tiny bit of memory' of the pre-birth reality. 'They' said that yes he could do that, but it would make the journey more difficult. *Why?* Knowing that life continued would surely make it easier. How are these specific personalities delivered? Through the Astral AI Mind program. He remembers being in the 'waiting area' when a guide came in and said: 'Go now!' A nice touch would have been to play that *Moody Blues* song – 'Since you've got to go, oh, you'd better go now. Go now.' They missed a trick there and instead Sundberg says that he was in 'like a technician's chamber, or like a mechanic shop that was over the Earth'. Here we go again. There was a shaft below him and the Earth was below that:

> And there were these beings there who were very technical in nature, and they are very, very skilled at matching the veil to you, to the individual.

Because the individual soul has so many rich qualities, and the life and the body, and the circumstances have their own energetic thing going on, and they like, I don't know, they make everything fit. They make everything jive.

They're able to make this organic connection work ... The veil is like an organic blanket or something and they're able to fine-tune that. And I remember then being over this pit and them asking me one last time: 'Are you sure? Are you sure you want to do this?' Because I knew once I said 'Yes', I was strapped in for the ride.

It's like getting the rollercoaster, you know, once you strap in, you can't get out until the ride's done. It was a bit like that, and I remember saying: 'Yeah, I am ready.' And then again, this huge plummet and vibration down, down, down, down, lower, lower, lower, lower, lower.

He said he 'surrendered to the veil' and sent a message back to the technicians to ask 'did I take?' They replied that it did. His 'knowing' disappeared along with his 'connectedness' and memory. He felt fear again about a human experience, but 'God reassured me'. That Yaldabaoth is such a nice chap. Sundberg then remembers being born and 'the shock, the cold, the light' with no idea what was going on. He saw 'these beings who were taking care of me, the nurses in the room', and thought 'who are they?' Sundberg's take is that human life is an incredible opportunity and not some 'masochistic exercise'. It was a gift like winning the lottery and when you get here 'you get to decide what to do – it's amazing'. We were helping the collective consciousness of humanity to heal and 'giving permission to everybody else in the pond to meet their fear'. To heal from *what* – the shit that is dealt us to produce the loosh? Love was 'the ultimate healing power and when we get to the other side, we know it.' Well, we do when they turn on their plasma particle frequency machine with the button marked 'love and bliss'. Let's just pause for a goddam second. We know what love is when we get to the other side and yet we have to come into this place of lunacy to learn what love is? You've lost me. Anyway, we'll continue ...

'Ignorant babies'

I saw an interview with American Aaron Green who described a near-death experience that he'd had as a child which allowed him to remember the pre-birth preparation in the Astral. The interview is billed on YouTube as the 'Most Detailed Pre-Birth Memory EVER RECORDED! I Chose Every Detail of My Body, Parents, and Life!' Green said he had existed with hundreds or thousands of other souls, a 'sea of souls all together in a very happy place'. It was very bright like being inside the sun: 'We were warm and happy, but we were also basically ignorant.'

They had no prior experience. 'We didn't, I don't know, we were like little baby souls.' *Baby souls* and *ignorant* – that's typical Archontic psychology to accept constant reincarnation to 'learn'. Green said they were ignorant and it was a limited experience. Ignorance always is. He said that 'periodically a treat of some sort would come down to us'. There was one for every soul and it was like kids 'getting a cookie'. One time he was 'lifted up' to a higher level of consciousness and told by a being that 'it was my creator' and that 'I was very much loved and cared for'. The being said that 'God had a wonderful existence prepared for me and for everybody else'. Oh, great, so what's the catch, Mr Archon, sir? Green continued:

> And that in order to fully appreciate this existence we had to … go through an experience essentially. God had figured out a way to … grow us or educate us, make us more fully able to appreciate how wonderful this experience was that God had prepared for us.

Aaron Green asked why God couldn't just change him to make him able to appreciate everything without having to go through education or experience? God could change him in any way, came the reply, but God had decreed that everyone must have free will and 'He' would not interfere. 'We were allowed to choose whatever we wanted to.' Well, clearly not. Green said he agreed because 'God was loving, caring, kind, compassionate, forgiving, all these positive traits that you think of'. He said this 'really embodied who God was, and my experience with God, it's kind of hard to explain how wonderful God is'. God was fantastic, 'just wonderful'. How did he know what this 'God' was? Green accepted the plan for his 'education' when God asked if he was willing to go through the experience (the need to agree is a constant theme of these situations, like a contractual agreement). God was extremely confident that this was a good idea and a good plan. 'It was kind of a no-brainer to go along with what God had agreed.' It was *God* after all. He was then shown the 'face of God' and 'my attention was turned to a giant sunlight entity with millions and millions of souls that were all together, kind of like I had been in the sea of souls, except all these souls were more mature'. He said they had likely been through this experience that he was about to go through. They were fully developed and 'much, much happier than I had been when I started out with these other souls'. They were excited that Green was going to join them someday. That would increase their happiness just a little bit. 'I would add something to that group.' It is all just another *mind-fuck* and more Archontic bullshit.

Perusing the 'catalogue'

Aaron Green said that at this point he was 'shot out' at an extremely fast pace going to some other place or realm. He was shown a physical creation and how it looked from 'God's perspective'. Green described how it appears 'like a fractal' and 'like a repeating pattern is kind of how I saw it'. You were seeing the human *Matrix*, Aaron. There were thousands and thousands of different planets that he could go to and all with very different characteristics. Overall they would each 'give me the physical experience I needed to develop' (and the loosh the Archons need to survive). He said he chose Earth. There are many timelines, places, and 'eras' in the simulation. Next he said he was with some guides that were helping him choose a body. 'I guess they had a body that they thought would be a good fit for me.' For 'body', read Astral AI Mind program connected to the Akashic Records. He said he rejected the first human experience he was offered by the guides. The person was going to be extremely angry. You see the contradiction again with the concept of 'karma'. His soul would have faced the life review to tell him he had been too angry and would have to return to learn that lesson. The guides had respected his wishes and I can't emphasise enough that if we don't agree it can't happen. Don't sign the contract! 'I knew that some other soul would live that life and that it would benefit them.' He means *they* would be told when they got back they had to return again to work through the 'karma' of the pre-destined angry person.

Green said he fancied being a red-headed girl, then considered being as red-headed boy, before deciding against both. He said he wanted to be a 'very, very good-looking guy like one of the best looking guys on the planet'. His guides talked him out of it (telepathically, naturally) by saying 'if you're a really good-looking guy, you're going to have certain opportunities, women are going to treat you differently'. He said that essentially he would have been very promiscuous and wouldn't be able to resist those temptations. Wow – bad karma, er, pre-planned karma. Green decided on what he considered to be the right level of attractiveness and the same with intelligence. He could have been the most intelligent guy on the planet and smarter than Albert Einstein. His guides told him that he would be extremely arrogant and treat all others as dumb. More bad pre-arranged karma. He would have become an atheist and 'that was kind of the deal breaker for me'. Okay, get on with it, mate, the printers are waiting. He rolled back his intelligence level 'to something that I considered intelligent, but ... nothing extraordinary' and was able 'to kind of look at the attributes I would have and tweak what I was good at'. At the risk of boring you – how does this fit with karma?

> After I arrived at what I thought was a good person, the right mix for the body that worked for me and my soul, the guides showed me what I had picked. There was an unintended consequence that I would have horrible acne as a

teenager. And so I took a closer look at what that would be like. And essentially for maybe two years as a teenager, I would have really horrible acne.

Even though that wasn't planned for, that wasn't what I was looking for. At the same time, somehow going through that experience would help develop my soul. It would help me achieve some of the growth that I was looking for.

I'll never look at acne in the same way again. Green said that 'I further saw that the genes were available if I wanted to have a club foot, somehow those genes were available for me to pick'. There would be no benefit to him, apparently, and it wouldn't really help his development. Extreme acne would develop his soul, but not a club foot. He said he was shown that he would hurt one shoulder as a teenager and then hurt the other one even worse when he was a little older. The guides planned that he would break his nose as a teenager. He had to agree before it could happen which he did. 'Somehow that helped me develop or helped me in this journey'. You can't beat a broken nose for spiritual growth. Green said he witnessed people asking for difficulties that would happen to them. They would think these were bad experiences as a human, 'but from a spiritual point of view, somehow that bad experience helped them develop to be a better soul'. Yep, we get the picture. Lots of loosh – *Mmm*, lovely.

Astral travel guide

Green then turned to what he saw of the afterlife realms. He said he was shown in detail different places that different souls go. The first group of souls that he saw were 'like murderous souls who hated each other'. They were 'horribly ugly' and constantly fighting with each other. They had hideous bodies and instead of arms, 'they had like claws'. One of the souls chose to stop fighting and 'some beings of light or angels ... swooped down and they pulled the soul out of this horrible fight'. He was told that when the soul decided to stop fighting with others, it no longer belonged in that group:

I've viewed the hellish realms kind of like a prison or a reform school. I guess more like a reform school. If a kid is really out of line in school, what do they do with them? Well, they send them to an alternative school where they can still learn.

And I view it as like if you really want to murder somebody else or murder other people or torture other people, like that's just so completely incompatible with what God's all about, that you need to very quickly be educated, that that's not good. And how God does that is that he allows you to do what you want to do, allows you to try to kill other people and torture other people.

Green said that he was shown another place with a lot of souls standing around in 'like just a dark plane'. The souls there were mistrustful of others. 'They didn't really believe in God and they weren't the kind of people that would help somebody else.' I take it they were like that because of their life as a human that was pre-planned in detail to have the experience that made them like that? They talk about life without end. This is manipulative bollocks without end. Another realm he described looked a lot like Earth 'but the buildings were prettier, they're more beautiful' where souls were very happy 'and then I was shown this other realm where it was like 'a city of light'. Buildings and the people were all glowing with a yellowish light. It was very beautiful and everyone was extremely happy. The 'happy' thing seems to be Aaron's reality criteria. Finally there were souls that were 'fully merged with God'. They had arrived back with God and each other and were 'just ridiculously happy':

> So I saw that different souls are at different levels. I see it as they're developing. The more loving, kind, compassionate, honest, that these souls … freely choose to be, the happier they are. The more … you want to kill and torture other people, they were extremely unhappy. Everything in between, it wasn't just one or the other.

Green said that his guides wiped his mind of memories when he returned for his current human life because they would have interfered with his experience. He was told they would return one day. Some 30 years later he read about a near-death experience and his memories flooded back about his own. He said the guides told him his memories had been deleted because what he had seen would prevent him 'developing faith in God'. The logic, no, the lack of logic, was that he would never be able to develop 'faith' after what he had seen and knew about the Astral. He would have been prevented from developing faith in God? I think this can safely be filed under '*mega* bullshit'. To be fair, he did ask why 'they' would say that when surely 'they' would want people to know all this. He said 'they' replied that they do want people to know. It was just really important to have faith and he couldn't develop this unless they hid his memories. File that one under '*double* mega bullshit'. This is Aaron Green's take on the meaning of 'life':

> I just view it as we started out with God and we're going through this experience and eventually we're going to be back with God. But when we go back … we'll be fully developed and fully able to appreciate each other and

God. My viewpoint is that in order to fully appreciate what God has in store
for us, we need to develop ourselves to be more loving, kind, compassionate
...
[But if you are 'God's children' why weren't you like that to start
with?]

... this life that we're living is part of that process to help us grow like that. So I
wouldn't say that we have to do this, but that we chose to do it and that it
does help us to more fully appreciate all the stuff that God has in store for us.

I would say what I think *this* should be filed under, but I don't want
to offend a family audience. 'What God has in store for us' sounds a bit
like sitting on a carousel horse thinking you can catch the one in front.
You can't. The system is rigged. 'What God has in store for us' is the
horse in front that you can never catch. There's just too much 'karma'.

'I think I've seen the Soul Trap'

Some near-death experiencers have had experiences that led them to
believe there is a reincarnation Soul Trap and others have witnessed it
outright. I'll come to the latter shortly. I first want to report the
experience of a man billed as 'Phil' when he was interviewed on the Jeff
Mara YouTube podcast which features a stream of NDEs. Mara videos
are a good source of stories by near-death experiencers and I
recommend the Forever Conscious Research Channel on YouTube,
Rumble, and Odysee where the Soul Trap is discussed and exposed at
length. 'Phil' said he died in a shower at home in 2012 while living in
Texas after suffering extreme food poisoning. He remembers in his out-
of-body state seeing 'thousands of people' in a setting that reminded
him of a concert arena (again) in darkness while heading toward a light.
'You're ... in a large queue with a bunch of people ... and it's starting to
occur to you that these people have died. You don't, of course, include
yourself.' Interestingly, he thought the queue was going to the Moon and
there was something about the Moon and reincarnation. The 'people'
were in little bubbles and two beings came to his 'egg'. One said to the
other telepathically: 'What is he doing here? He doesn't belong here.
Send him back to the shower.' He said he turned around and went back
through a light tunnel 'with all of the splendid colours of everything and
energy'. The beings were very 'humanish' although not exactly human.
Insider military whistleblowers have told me how they have met
extraterrestrials that are so like humans that you have to look closely to
see the difference. Phil said they reminded him of the 'tall whites' that
UFO researchers talk about. I have written about the tall white Aryan-
type ETs many times in my books and they are described in ancient
legends and accounts. He said the beings he saw were bald with very

bony cheekbones and were very thin. 'Their necks were a little bit longer than ours and narrower.'

Mara asked if the place felt spiritual or some manufactured mechanical place where these beings were just controlling him. Phil replied that it was like a Soul Trap which he had heard about. 'I've been awake to things on Earth that happen in our lives and thousands of years before … as far as who the controllers are, who's in control, events, duality.' He said he looked at where he was in the Soul Trap and his best inkling was that the queue he experienced was waiting to reincarnate. It was a mechanical process. He said the two beings were not menacing and acted like it was only their job. 'I was just another peg to put in that hole and on the pegboard this peg doesn't belong. Throw it back in the shower.' Phil said he remembers being back in the shower although in a 'spiritual body' (plasma body). 'I remember I could see with my hands … and it's like your hands are these powerful devices that can read texture, temperature, energy levels, like every kind of meter or reader that you would ever need, your hands can do it.' Maybe everyone could do this if they knew how to power up their brain or DNA that they are not using. 'I remember seeing patterns and I could watch all of the energies interacting … I could see like those patterns that repeat themselves when you look into them and they're called Mandelbrot where the same pattern turns into the same thing [fractals, the holographic principle].' There were energy waves projecting from his hands and they would interact with other waves or grab other energy frequencies and colours out of the waves. Energy was released when they collided. This is happening to us all the time outside visible light and matter. Water from the shower was passing through him as energy. He saw 'this human man there' not yet realising that it was his human body. 'I'm looking down at this thing, but I realized that I didn't really have emotions.' There was no sense of urgency or fear and then he realised that it was him. 'That's when I just thought, oh, I'm dead.'

Phil returned very painfully to his body and 'all I remember now is I just woke up.' His food poisoning was gone and he got up and walked around the house trying to understand what had happened. He went out on his motorcycle and stopped for coffee. A man he knew in the café 'freaked out', covered his eyes, and said 'I can't look at you!' The man said Phil was a 'different colour' and 'you look like you've aged 20 years overnight'. Phil said he didn't go to a doctor. 'I wasn't sick at all. The stomach sickness was gone. I was fine.' Mara asked if he thought we can break free from the trap. He said he thought so and the key what to know about the Soul Trap before you can leave. 'If you know where the Heaven is or the higher vibration levels you're trying to get to, why would you want to come back here?' If you knew about reincarnation as a Soul Trap, then you could opt out of it. 'I would want to get out of that

line or that queue that I was in going to,' I noticed that Phil recognised
as I do the similarities between the way the human and Astral realms are
controlled;

> I'm of course aware of the Luciferian system, you know, keep them poor, short
> lives, use their energy, the vampires, you know, the elites ... and a lot of this
> experience is even though [the beings] were different, they share a lot of same
> basic principles, you know, as you recognize.

One of the tell-tale signs of the reincarnation hoax is how similar
human and Astral realms are in the way humans and souls of humans
are herded by authority and bow to authority. Phil was pretty sure he
had seen aspects of the Soul Trap while others are in no doubt at all.

'We *have* seen the Soul Trap'

Some near-death experiencers say they have seen directly that the Soul
Trap is real and among them are American Isabella Greene, author
of *Leaving the Trap: How to Exit The Reincarnation Cycle*, and Canadian
Lauda Leon who also has an extraordinary story to tell. Greene says that
until about 2010 she was 'very dense, very corporate' and 'a rock and
roller'. She was like a rock star at night, corporate during the day, super
analytical, super traumatised, addicted, 'and sick in every part of my
body'. Then along came her energetic and perceptual transformation.
Greene says she now 'travels beyond the veil and explores the realities
of other dimensions' and has had near-death experiences. She says the
first was a typical NDE as she was 'sucked out' of her body into the
vortex or tunnel of white light. It was a place of peace and love where a
being appeared 'that looked like Jesus' to deliver the classic of classic
NDE lines: 'It's not your time yet.' The love this being was emanating
had her 'melting' and willing to do anything to stay there. Remember
the donkey guided up the mountain purely by activating the pleasure
centre when it took the desired route.

Greene says that she wanted to deserve the love 'Jesus' was
projecting, but it was indicated that she didn't deserve that love. She
needed to go back. She was wasting her life and there was a purpose for
her. 'I felt so guilty, so uncomfortable, I felt like I don't deserve this
incredible being's love.' She was begging him to let her stay. She didn't
want to go back where she was miserable, sick and unhappy. The being
insisted that she must. The feeling was that she was not worthy of that
love and had to go back to be worthy. 'The moment I had that feeling of
"I have to" I was back in my body.' Greene said she felt duped and it
wasn't a very loving approach when her plea was ignored not to be sent
back. She was not impressed.

The feeling was so strong that she wanted to return and investigate what was going on in the 'afterlife'. She found a practitioner who helped people induce an out-of-body experience and she projected her consciousness into the Astral plane where she was like 'a fly on the wall'. She could see a place where souls were looking dazed and confused coming out of the body with beings all looking the same shepherding them in different ways. The beings were in groups of three, usually two male and a female. 'It did feel incredible and beautiful [with] the music of the spheres ... the rainbowy colours and the lightness, and the love – all that people talk about in near death experiences was there.' She returned to her body convinced that something was going on here that was not what we are told about 'Heaven'. Her conclusions were the same as mine that 'there is no such thing as soul growth'. At the deepest level all is known and we can access all that is known. You don't need to experience hell on earth to 'grow' and know. The Soul Trap is to make sure you *don't* grow and know. Greene said that when the soul comes into a human experience for the first time it is pure and then begins to accumulate illusory 'karma' which is never 'paid off' because it is not meant to be. New Age and Scripture accounts about suffering for the greater good were all part of the control mechanism to keep us forever incarnating.

Different sources, same conclusions

Greene says she experienced Astral projection many times early in her life before learning how to 'quantum travel' which involved going beyond the Astral and 'looking back' to see what it was. There were also countless conversations with those who have had near-death experiences. Greene came to her conclusions from all of this about the reality of the Soul Trap. She rightly says that reincarnation is presented as a 'choice' when it's really not like that. 'Those who had near-death experiences can confirm that it's always kind of going around in circles until you agree to go back.' Information was emerging that we are never told there is a different option to reincarnating into human form. Greene says there are beings that run the reincarnation cycle and Earth is surrounded by the Astral plane which 'encompasses the afterlife' where near death experiences take place. This was where we go after we leave the body and pass to the realm operated by shapeshifting beings that some called Archons which orchestrate the reincarnation system. I found it fascinating to see how the correlations are constant when I concluded all this from my own means and sources, and Greene from hers. I have not consciously travelled to the Astral or had a near-death experience, but I have had incredibly deep 'coma' sleeps many times a week since my conscious awakening in 1990. They often happen during the day and can take half an hour for me to fully awaken. I always have the feeling afterwards that I know things that I didn't know before and this knowledge filters through to my conscious mind as 'I know'.

Our correlating conclusions include the designer-deity and 'loved ones' experience to pull you in at the end of the tunnel. 'Jesus was waiting for me' or 'I saw my mother at the end of the tunnel'. Greene says that from her observations the beings that greet you come in different shapes and forms depending on your beliefs. 'If you expect a garden, you're going to be in a garden. If you expect anything that is Heaven-like, that's what you're going to experience.' Then there are the illusory religious heroes:

If you believe in Jesus Christ you are going to face Jesus Christ, but it's not the real thing. If you believe in angelic beings you're going to be surrounded by angelic beings. If you are in Hinduist tradition for example and you believe in Krishna you're going to meet that being … telling you that you have to go back.

If you don't believe in any of these you're going to see your loved ones or the ones that you miss the most greet you and tell you that you need to go back because they [can] literally shapeshift into just anything that is going to be the most convincing for you.

The question must be asked about how this is possible. How can you greet every departed soul with such individualised deceit when it is estimated that between 150,000 and 190,000 people die in the world every day? The answer is the programmed plasma of the 'Akashic Records', possibly the Kordylewski Clouds and/or other forms of plasma AI intelligence. There is more than enough computing and storage power to track and record every aspect of every incarnation from start to finish and produce the designer entity *projections* to match their belief system. I suggest that the entities – 'beings', 'guides', 'archangels' – that meet and greet the newly departed are overwhelmingly plasma program *projections*. They are not real. I agree with near-deathers and the regressed that in the Astral you are able to take any form, shape or persona you like, thanks to the energetic fluidity of the plasma body. You mean they can *shapeshift*? Surely not, that's crazy isn't it?

AI projections are a far more credible explanation of the afterlife experience with so many souls departing the human realm every day and from goodness knows where else in other simulated material realities. The 'life review', 'guides', 'elders', religious heroes, and loved ones are all projections from a system completely controlled by programmed plasma AI. 'Loved ones' for example and how they looked are all in the plasma AI Akashic Records database including those in their family history that near-deathers didn't even know. I have read several accounts of how people were met by those they later realised when they returned to the body were relatives they never met or knew about. The Astral AI database did, though. It records everything. This is not to say that such loved ones do not exist (although in a very different form to their Earth personality). I am talking about the meet and greet projections. The majority of psychics – not all – 'communicating with departed loved ones' are connecting as I said earlier with the Akashic Records, not them. Information from these sources is overwhelmingly Earth-life based and no one seems to say 'Hey, you've been had, it's all an illusion'. Instead it's 'I'm glad to see you got that job' and 'thank you for looking after my cat'. Only the rare really 'out there' psychics get the system-exposing information by going beyond the simulation. Archons are AI and the manifestation of Yaldabaoth consciousness within the plasma medium that is the foundation of the whole show.

The 'afterlife' sequence

Greene describes the after-death sequence from her Astral observations. Sometimes she experienced a tunnel of light and at other times two tunnels. One was 'a different kind of light, different quality, and different kind of beings, which are extraterrestrials that participate in our reincarnation cycle'. There was a blast of white light which you fly through before it 'spits you into the afterlife dimension'. You immediately faced the beings there, had a life review, and then agreed to go back to Earth after a short rest. She says the number one feeling after leaving the body is relief after the fear of passing (the mind-wiped state that makes you open to suggestion by those who 'protect' and 'reassure' you in such a post-traumatic moment):

> It's an incredible sense of relief. I know this from my own near-death experiences, but also from what my father told me from the other side after he passed. You're not dragging the physical body on yourself any longer, so there is this lightness.

> There's no more pain, there's no more emotional pain, there's no more physical pain, and there is a certain sense of liberation or freedom, although that freedom is not as all-encompassing as we wish it to be because you're still within the constraints of the incarnation cycle, but it is a relief, getting out of the body is much easier than being in the body in my perspective.

There was a lower Astral plane where some went temporarily. Here they face a short period having really uncomfortable experiences 'similar to what's happening on Earth but worse'. There was conflict, bullying, and 'Astral wars'. It was 'a dark place but very soon after this they are summoned by handlers and presented with a life review where they are told that they did all these horrible things'. Now they will go back and experience the same done unto them as their 'karma'. They 'hang out' in the upper levels of the Astral which is considered to be 'Heaven' before returning to human. She had experienced out-of-body sessions where she experienced 'disincarnates'. These were souls that left the body into the Astral and were terrified of what would happen because of maybe how they lived their human life. They did not go through the tunnel or anywhere in case it led to Hell. They stayed on the Earth plane and attached to the fields of incarnate humans. There were Astral entities attracted to emotionally wounded people who become 'auric attachments or hitchhikers in their energy field'. These entities were located around the Earth plane and amplified the thoughts that the person was already having based on their conditioning since childhood. You can see why fear of death and what happens afterwards is ingrained in the human psyche. It is a colossal source of loosh.

Greene says that when you take your last breath you have a beam of blinding white light which she believes is 'the simulation of the true light because on this planet we have a false sensation of everything that truly exists to sow confusion for people'. They go to the light in the programmed belief that this is the true essence. 'That is the beam. That is the simulation.' It literally felt like a vacuum cleaner pulling you so slowly and then it 'spits you out into the level of the Astral plane'. The upper Astral is what we know as Heaven and the lower Astral is what we know as Hell. You are presented with different types of beings which represent your human belief system and tell you they are there for your highest good:

> They are going to present you with a life review which is the Akashic Record of what you did as a human being with a human consciousness under the influence of the Matrix, under the influence of the body-brain computer. All the actions [in human reality] that had nothing to do with your soul.

> You are presented with that, of course. You feel guilty because you feel you were not good enough because we are conditioned to believe we are not good enough from the moment we are born. Then, that's it, you say, okay, I'll go back.

> You get a moment to rest in the heavenly realm that is part of the Astral plane, the upper Astral, and gives you this feeling of love and liberation and ease, but it is not even close to the true state of the soul that you experience if you bypass that.

Greene says that another trick is to say that love is waiting for you if you reincarnate again and you will finally get to experience the love of your life that you have been chasing for centuries. 'You are pulled and tricked into another reincarnation ... through the desires, the unfulfilled desires of the human structure, your humanness.'

Bypassing the trap

To avoid forever repeating the reincarnation cycle we must understand the game and how it *is* a trap. We must withdraw our sense of reality and self-identity from the perception of human to one of being infinite. I have been saying this over and over decade after decade. *Remember who you are*. Greene says all attachment to 'human' must be let go: 'No see you in the next life, love you forever. These are contracts and they are used against you by the handlers.' We have to be aware before we leave. Once up the tunnel it's too late. We have to process emotion before we depart. Emotion can act like a ball and chain holding down our frequency. Residual loosh is extracted after death by the Archons if we take it with us. It means letting go of guilt, shame, and unworthiness which are all traps to keep us in the simulation. Greene says that the speed your consciousness leaves the body at 'death' is highly relevant to where you go and unprocessed emotion can slow the speed of exit. A slow withdrawal syncs with the Astral and its vibrational speed whereas to leave in a flash matches the speed of vibration beyond the simulation. She says that this can be practiced. You can find out more by putting her name into a search engine. The speed of exit was the difference between Astral projection and what she calls quantum travel:

Astral projection is very slow, you lay down and you come out and you can see your body. If you turn around and you can see your body you are in the Astral plane. You are going to be experiencing the ceiling. You cannot get past that because you went straight into the Astral plane where everything is set up.

She recommends learning to control your energy, your life-force, to 'shoot yourself out of the body, utilising your energy like a rocket fuel – you come out of the top of your head like rocket, fly right out', and you had no idea what was happening to your body after that. 'This spits you into the realms past the Astral structure, past the Matrix structure.' Learning to do this and return to the body prepares you to exit the simulation when your body dies, she says. 'If you teach yourself to do that while you are still alive you can do that when you take your last breath and you are free from that entire entrapment system.' I'll leave that with you. It's not for me to tell you what to do and people must reach their own conclusions. What Greene says is supported by the Buddhist belief that the best opportunity to avoid the Wheel of Samsara is immediately after you die (or rather when your body does).

People can slowly and quietly ease out of the body and this is said to be 'dying peacefully'. This will take you into the Astral according to Isabella Greene. I was with my daughter Kerry when she died in December 2023 and I was shocked at how fast it happened. I had not seen Isabella Greene's remarks at that time, but my experience with Kerry was that she withdrew like a gunshot. One split-second she was alive in the body and the next all the life-force had gone. It was indeed like rocket fuel. The release of our consciousness from the body has been seen by many people either in the form of a flash of light – the 'death flash – or as a mist slowly gathering before disappearing. A hospice psychologist described how he saw 'clouds' leaving the bodies of the dying that form around the head or chest. 'There seems to be some kind of electricity in it, like an electrical disturbance.' Polish biophoton researcher Professor Janusz Slawinski (1936-2016) made a study of the 'death flash'. He said:

All living organisms emit low-intensity light; at the time of death, that radiation is ten to ten thousand times stronger than that emitted under normal conditions. This 'death flash' is independent of the cause of death, and reflects in intensity and duration the rate of dying.

Kirlian photography, developed by Russian electrical engineer Semyon Kirlian and his wife Valentina, photographs the human energy field and has been used many times at the point of death in humans, animals and plants. It has recorded the luminescence withdrawing until none was left. To confirm the theme further there is a flash of light recorded at the moment a sperm fertilises an egg to start a human life which is explained by science as the release of zinc atoms. You can see videos of this on the Internet.

It is so important that people get informed about the after-death sequence because that is how we *overcome the mind-wipe*. The incarnating aspect of soul is wiped of memories of the spirit world, afterlife, and 'previous lives' which is why we have the common theme of near-death experiencers saying this when they leave the body: 'I had never experienced anything like it before'; 'The love was like nothing I had ever felt'; and 'I didn't know what was happening'. *Why not* when they must have had the experience endless times? That's the mind-wipe which deletes Astral memories from incarnating aspects of soul at the point of entering the body until they are fully restored under Astral simulation control after bodily death. Mind-wiped consciousness is the state of being of the overwhelming number of near-death experiences and it mirrors the effects of MKUltra-type mind control. I have met a stream of MKUltra people who thought they had lived 'ordinary lives' until their compartments or 'alters' released their memories of a totally different life they did not remember. Women who thought they married as virgins remember how they were raped by sometimes hundreds of men. That's the scale to which a manipulated mind can deceive you. We can bypass this crap by putting the dots together from multiple sources to see what we are not supposed to know – it's a trap and we can release ourselves from it through expanded streetwise awareness.

Simulation 'barrier'

Isabella Greene speaks of the outer limit of the Astral or 'ceiling' as she described it earlier. It is the limit of the simulation that I have written about in many books over the years. 'If you reach the outskirts of the Astral plane, you're going to be hitting the glass ceiling or you're going to be hitting the layer that is not going to let you come out past that layer.' She is referring to the old esoteric concept of the 'Ring-Pass-Not' which is an energetic frequency frontier. This is esoterically described as: 'A limit within which is contained the consciousness of those who are still under the sway of the delusion of separateness' and 'any state in

which an entity, having reached a certain stage of evolutionary growth of the unfolding of consciousness, finds itself unable to pass into a still higher state because of some delusion under which the consciousness is labouring, be that delusion mental or spiritual.' The concept, if you lose the 'evolution' bit, refers to how perception dictates frequency and if the Cult and its Astral masters control your perception they control your frequency to ensure it remains within the confines of the simulation. Here you have the real basis for the Buddhist theme of needing to reach a state of 'enlightenment' before we can leave the reincarnation Wheel of

Figure 141: The Ouroboros, a snake swallowing its own tail, is a symbol of the Ring-Pass-Not – the limit of the simulation that can be breached by the frequencies that come from 'enlightenment'.

Samsara. In fact, it is much easier than that. Ongoing returns to the density of matter are not required – only a transformation of self-identity from Human-me, Little Me, Soul-me, to Infinite Me. The Ring-Pass-Not is often symbolised as the Ouroboros, or the snake eating its own tail (Fig 141). Isabella Greene says she remembers how she was lured into the 'Earth plane', or simulation:

I was in an entirely different state of being, entirely different environment, entirely different consciousness. We were sharing consciousness, but at the same time, we were individualised. We received the distress call that came through the transmitter that was on our planet, like a mountain kind of thing, because everything was alive, and … we were connected to all expressions of life who were all non-physical, except the actual planet.

I remember the feeling that I'm infinite and I'm powerful, meaning like I never experienced any limitation within that reality. I want to go and help that world in distress that sent out distress calls, and that was Earth. Literally, the second I had that idea or that feeling, I started being pulled into an entirely different state of being, which felt denser and denser, like from the state of air into water, into mud … and then I started going into human.

She believes that she came here thinking that she could assist and get out, but until this lifetime she had no idea in all of her 'thousands of years of incarnations on Earth' that she can actually get out and how. 'A lot of us volunteered to come here for one reason or another, and now we're just running in circles around Earth plane, being like a battery for the beings that lured us here, I think.'

The Void

Isabella Greene says she has been to 'the Void' in her 'beyond-the-Astral' travels. 'It's not a place. It's a state of consciousness. It's a state of reality.' She says the Void is the creator of Infinite Reality. 'So technically, it's God, or … it's the Source consciousness.' When you leave your body and project into the Void it is a very different experience to the Astral: 'You don't remember yourself as a human being, and you're no longer *you*, but you are consciousness.' You are conscious in that state of being and you experience the presence of literally everything and yet at the same time nothing at all. That sounds bizarre except that I know that feeling. The Void (not really a void in human terms) is all possibility, all potential, and thus everything *and* nothing. I experienced the Void in a Brazilian rainforest in 2003 after taking the psychoactive plant substance, ayahuasca. I describe in *The Trap* and much earlier books what happened over my five hours experiencing other realms while a loud voice that took a female form spoke to me about the illusory nature of 'physical' reality. This happened in the same post-millennium period that I had my download of 'knowing' that we are in a simulated reality within the speed of light at the human level. Greene describes the Void as a state of being rather than a place, and 'the energy that creates and sustains worlds, the Source consciousness'. I saw this in my altered state in Brazil. It was black yet somehow shone with a sort of brilliant light (Fig 142). A blackness that shines? That is how it appeared to me. The voice said: 'David, we are going to take you to where you come from, so you can remember who you are.' The voice said as I saw the Void: 'This is the Infinite, David. This is where you come from and this is where you shall return.' I described how I felt in my 2003 book, *Infinite Love is the*

Only Truth – Everything Else is Illusion:

There were no divisions, no polarities, no black and white, no us and them. There was no time. No place, no vibration. Everything just was and this is a state of being that has to be experienced to be understood. I was not my body; I was consciousness, all consciousness, all that exists in any expression ... I

was here and I was there. I was everywhere and nowhere, everything and nothing. I was and I wasn't, and I was all 'in between'.

I was experiencing the Infinite 'I' that the simulation is designed to make us forget and the awareness that creates realities. This is the Source that the Yaldabaoth distortion seeks to usurp in its

Figure 142: Neil Hague's portayal of what I saw with the 'Dazzling Darkness' in my ayahuasca experience.

stupidity and ignorance. I do think there is also a fake 'Void' within the simulation so it's important to be discerning and question everything. Nine years after my experience of the Void I read the book *Proof of Heaven* by Dr Eben Alexander. He was an academic neurosurgeon at Harvard for 15 years and the book detailed his near-death experience during a week-long coma in 2008 caused by meningitis. He had believed, like his scientist father, that the brain is the origin of consciousness and could not exist after the brain expired. His near-death experience changed all this. What struck me more than anything was where he talks about seeing 'The Core' or 'Dazzling Darkness' from where 'the purest love emanated and all is known'. Dazzling Darkness was an excellent description of what I experienced with the Void. This is the Infinite 'I' that you are while the simulation seeks to convince us that we are just 'little people'. Yes, that includes you standing in the rain waiting for a bus that takes you to the job that you hate, and you who believe you are an insignificant human with no power to affect your life. That's what the demonic wants you to think. Eben Alexander's experience was notable for another reason. The absence of the usual story:

Many people have traveled to the realms I did, but, strangely enough, most remembered their earthly identities while away from their earthly forms. They knew that they were John Smith or George Johnson or Sarah Brown. They never lost sight of the fact that they lived on earth.

They were aware that their living relatives were still there, waiting and hoping they would come back. They also, in many cases, met friends and relatives who had died before them, and in these cases, too, they recognized those people instantly. Many NDE subjects have reported engaging in life reviews, in which they saw their interactions with various people and their good or bad actions during the course of their lives.

I experienced none of these events, and taken all together they demonstrate the single most unusual aspect of my NDE. I was completely free of my bodily identity for all of it, so that any classic NDE occurrence that might have involved my remembering who I was on earth was rigorously missing.

The ayahuasca voice said at the start of my experience that there was really only one thing I needed to know: 'Infinite Love is the only truth – everything else is illusion.' This was repeated over and over and hence the title of my book in 2003. Infinite Love is the paradise from which humanity 'fell' down the frequencies into the fake reality of the simulation. It is time to return.

'I've died *seven times*'

Canadian Lauda Leon has clinically died *seven times* and did not have the usual near-death experiences. She says she has been out-of-body on many other occasions and has a pre-birth memory of her incarnation. Leon spoke about the Soul Trap with Christianne van Wijk for her film series on Ickonic.com, *The Great Unknown*. She remembers having two 'guardians' with her in the incarnation sequence and being shown a lot of information about events that were to come. 'I was stalling because of the nature of what I was being shown.' She was starting to question: 'Can we do this right? Is this going to work? Is this like a mission impossible?' A frequency descent began 'with these two guardians who are like Titans, humungous guardians'. Leon says that it was 'just so, so, incredibly fast'. She could just feel it in her entire being. 'We were traversing down in the descent through what looked like many galaxies until finally you could see the Earth.' She describes the experience as 'like a microscope where things just keep expanding the closer you get':

And that's exactly what it was like, but at a tremendous velocity. And by the time that I saw the top of the building where … where the body had been born … the body of the girl that I was to go into was still born and dead. I essentially got pulled into, pushed into at full velocity, the body of a dead baby.

So when that happened, the baby was on the table because at this point they were like, well, you know, she's dead, right? The velocity was so extreme that the body of the baby actually lifted off the table and came back down. That's how immense the velocity was. And the second that I entered that body, the baby came alive just screamed because the pain of coming into that body at that full velocity was so extreme, it hurt everything in the body.

Leon had the same experience as Christian Sundberg with the incredibly low density of entering human reality. 'It became denser, heavier, and, you know, it actually felt painful.' She felt a 'heavy, heavy, painful weight'. Reality was really foreign and 'very alien'. She says she had full consciousness of being in the body from that moment on, but not as the consciousness of the baby. 'I had the consciousness I came in with trapped in the body. Each of her experiences of dying and returning seemed to show her different aspects of reality. Her incarnation was not what normally happened in the 'recycling and reanimation factory'. She remembers during the incarnation experience the strange nature of the 'world' she was entering. I didn't hear what she said until the rest of this book was complete. Lauda Leon was the last major addition and, of course, that was long after I wrote *The Trap* and *The Dream*. This put what she says in 'time' and sequence context. Once again, notice the correlations:

It looked to me like there was an overlay. I remember coming to a place where it seemed like there was a magnetic grid, like an electric, magnetic type of grid. I remember it being electric. There was something organic, an organic realm underneath the overlay. This is interesting, right?

It certainly is if you have read this book so far or *The Trap* and *The Dream* where I contend that the simulation is like a Wi-Fi field 'copy' overlaying Prime Reality. She continues:

There was like an actual organic Earth underneath. And then the overlay was very, let's say, like digital and that weird electric fence you had to go through. The Guardians told me that part of their job was to get me through that electric fence without erasing my memory.

The objective of [the fence] is that as a soul comes in, you go through that electricity, that electromagnetic zap, and it erases your mind. So they had to ensure that I could get through without it doing that.

Leon says she was shown that what is called the 'New Earth' is really that organic Earth which has been overlaid by the simulation. 'So it's the new old Earth.' I have been saying exactly that all these years and how the body biological computer connects us to the overlay so this is what we experience as human reality. Leon rightly says that our reality was based on counterfeiting the original. Literally everything had been counterfeited and the archetypes came from an original. The entire galaxy and universe was counterfeit and continued into the fourth or Astral dimension. 'They have also counterfeited the different heavens.' Okay, let's get an old joke out of the way. Counterfeit? Yep, she had two. Humour me, I have so few pleasures. Leon says souls were 'magnetised' to keep everyone in the trap. 'Don't magnetise [attach] yourself to anything here because there's no point of separation when you're outside of here.' You don't lose anything you love when you are a part of everything.

The 'Metal God'

Leon says she learned how what I call the *All That Is* divided itself into 'male and female' as the Father/Mother duality that allowed for good, bad, light, dark, masculine, feminine, and I guess positive and negative, which would lead to manifest Creation. Next was created what Leon calls 'the Primes', the first 'beings', and the Primes created the 'Reals'. 'God split itself into an infinite number of fractals to experience Creation in every possible way imaginable.' Each of us is one of those fractals which together are 'God', the *All That Is*, the whole. The simulation came about through an aberration in the unfolding Creation in which a being emerged – the Gnostic Yaldabaoth. What followed was 'the entire hijacking of reality and universe' … 'the counterfeit versions of everything, including all the heavens, all the lower astral, everything'. She refers to this as the 'Metal God' because human reality is a 'metal digital interface'. This was why the 'dark side' is always founded on this 'metal digital technology'. It's a reflection of the 'Metal God' mind which she describes as essentially the living dead. Everything in its human reality was based on death and disease as a result. The Metal God, which I will continue to call Yaldabaoth for continuity, was disconnected from Source energy and needed to somehow find a means of access. Otherwise it would literally consume itself as symbolised by the Ouroboros. Manipulating the Primes and Reals into its counterfeit reality, its 'facsimile version', was the chosen option. They still had a connection to the energy of the Source, the *All That Is*. 'They'll never know the difference – I'll make it beautiful and good at the beginning so that they think they're in the right one.' Leon says that this is what happened. 'It's a dead thing that only has essence to keep it alive unnaturally like Frankenstein.' She compares the mentality of Yaldabaoth with those it entraps: 'Something everyone experiences is fear of being alone – fear that you can't be loved, fear of being traumatised, starving.' This Yaldabaoth mentality had been imprinted on the population through the simulation which I say is happening within the mind of Yaldabaoth. Why wouldn't one be imprinted on the other if that is the case?

Leon says that Primes and Reals have potential metaphysical gifts and a lot of psychic ability. 'They haven't been corrupted.' They were born with the inner knowing that they can connect to anything with no limitation. How do you contain the Primes and Reals so they do what you want? You override their natural metaphysical abilities. Notice through 'history' how metaphysical gifts were a death sentence and are marginalised by Cult-owned mainstream 'science' which dismisses and ridicules any suggestion that this 'world' is not the only one. Leon says consciousness entered the simulation from outside to help awaken the entrapped from their induced coma. Our simulated universe was top of the list for unravelling. 'It's the holy grail of, my God, you got to go in there and help.' This was the most important place to go in and 'also the most dangerous' and 'the scariest place to come into'. So much so that when the call went out 'not many put their hands up'. It was 'no and no and no and no'. Those who came were the ones that mean business.

She says that within the simulation are 'hybrids, synthetics and backdrops'. A lot of those had been infused into the simulation system and especially now as Reals and Primes begin to awaken. Check how the global population has dramatically increased since the first billion was reached in what we reference as 1800. Only 225 years later the billion has risen to *eight* billion and this in a period when the biggest defence of all to Prime/Real awakening – AI – is being played out at ever quickening speed. Leon sees a difference between what Gnostics named Yaldabaoth and the Demiurge in the sense that one is the consciousness and the other is the simulation system or what I refer to as the 'mainframe'.

> So you've got a lot of those that have been created from the counterfeit Demiurge system. That's why they're really … obsessed with genetic mutations and genetic tampering. They wanted to … counterfeit … the Primes and the Reals.

She says she was shown that the majority in the counterfeit simulation were 'backdrop reality' beings – what I have dubbed non-player characters. There were not that many Primes and Reals by comparison and they have 'backdrop people to make the theatre look real'. They needed to convince Primes and Reals that the simulation is reality. There were many symbolic non-player or AI software characters in the *Matrix* movies in the form of the 'Oracle', the 'Merovingian', and 'agents' like Smith of which multiple copies could be made. I have long thought that key and not so key players in the Global Cult are forms of AI – non-player characters programmed to act as they do as well as others that are Astral demons incarnate. What a testament to the power of expanded awareness and the true potential power of incarnate consciousness that the Astral infuses copious numbers of AI 'humans' into this reality that have the role of non-player characters in a virtual reality game. Their Astral AI Mind programs are directing thoughts and responses and not an eternal expression of consciousness. Only their closed-minded perceptions and behaviour and frequency nature can tell them apart from conscious or potentially conscious humans. The simulation is running them and that means they will obey authority unquestioningly and condemn conscious responses and opinions because that's what they are programmed to do. They are the AI herd with the job of pressuring and intimidating conscious people into the same herd mentality founded on unquestioning obedience. Major players and gofers in the Cult are a mixture of shapeshifting Archontic human-reptilian hybrids and biological AI which is programmed to do what they do without empathy or remorse. This explains a lot about many of the personalities involved who act like computer programs in what they say and do. It will take a lot to convince me that Gates and Schwab are 'human' in the usual sense of the word. I can't see beyond biological AI with either of them myself.

Simulated solar system

An important astronomical event in a human life is said to be a 'Saturn return' when in periods of around 29 years Saturn returns to where it was when we were born. The effect on our energy field within the simulation can play through as challenge and change. My version of a Saturn return is the number of times over and over that Saturn appears in my research as my books will confirm. Lauda Leon says that one of her out-of-body experiences took her to Saturn. She remembers hearing the frequency of Saturn's 'ruling consciousness'. I used to play the sound emitted by Saturn in my public talks which is very ominous and eerie. You can find recordings on the Internet. Leon says the sound triggered a memory of being in Saturn. All planets in the solar system were part of the machine and each had a job. 'Saturn represents one of the strongest leaders of how the machine operates.' Saturn and Jupiter (Cronus and Zeus in Greek mythology) were very important and the Moon was created synthetically to operate with them. 'I think [the Moon] was completely created and brought here' and was 'a kind of amplifier of this whole containment system'. The Moon as an artificial construct and frequency amplifier has been a feature of my books since *Human Race Get Off Your Knees* in 2010 and a similar story is told in many ancient legends and accounts. Everything in the solar system is part of 'the machine' including the Sun. Leon says the Sun is an overlay of the real Sun and she says of the planets of the solar system:

> They're literally under rulership … being forced to be a machine of reality …
> interface thing … Here is how you are programed to interface with reality.
> That's their job, right? That's why you also have if you look at your birth chart.

> You'll see you're under the rulership of certain aspects of the celestial
> mechanical governance and you'll see that they have rulership over you.
> When I look at the planets … [they look] like a clock. Clockwork. That is all it
> is. It's all doing its thing to hold the machine together.

Leon describes as 'my critical experience' her near-death experience after
drowning at the age of 13. By that time she had been subjected to human
life programming. 'You are already programmed here … there's a lot of
programming.' She was swimming at night in the Mediterranean and
didn't see the signs warning of strong currents and not to swim. The
currents pulled her under and she drowned. 'I went through the dying
process and I remember the … horrible panic that you go through trying
to live.' Then 'everything went really still and calm' the moment her
body expired. She no longer experienced the pain of the salt water in her
lungs. I remember paddling in the sea at Caister in Norfolk when I was
little more than a toddler. I fell over and went under and I can still recall
looking through the water to the blue sky in a state of calm and peace. I
had no inclination to react and then I saw my big brother Trevor
standing over me and he pulled me out.

   Humanity must understand that we are not our bodies. They are only
vehicles to experience this reality. They are biological computers
programmed to feel loosh-generating pain, have illness, and be
'physically' or psychologically disabled. *We* are the consciousness that
experiences human reality *through* the vehicle. There is no reason to fear
death when that only applies to the fatal malfunction of the body and
not the real 'I'. This is even more reason not to self-identify with the
labels of a human life. They are not the 'I'. They are only *experiences* that
we have that result from a combination of Astral AI body programming
and for awakening people the influence of consciousness beyond the
simulation. The Cult-demon system seeks to focus attention on the body
personality to make us believe that the body is who we are. Break that
program and you open your mind to the freedom that comes from
knowing who you really are – infinite, eternal, consciousness having a
brief, oh, so brief, experience as a 'human'.

'The Deep'

Lauda Leon said she had been programmed to expect to see 'the Light'
when she drowned, but there was nothing. 'There was no light. It was

pitch dark, it was black.' She felt the darkness expanding and she refers to the 'location' as 'the Deep' because it reminded her of 'the point of origin of creation before you come into manifestation'. It was identical. 'You didn't see light, you didn't see like relatives waiting for you or anything. I didn't have any of that.' She was suddenly in this darkness. 'It's more like the deep, the deep of creation before all things get created.' She felt 'the most beautiful, calming feeling'. There was only consciousness in a darkness that seems never ending and 'you just felt a perfection of being, no separation from anything, even though there was nothing in there'. Her consciousness was all consciousness. She describes 'the Deep' as 'a primordial place of being before being' and felt she could create anything she wanted. 'That's like the critical point of the inception of creation, where you decide how you want to experience Creation.' This is the Void which isn't – the source of all creation and possibility. From 'here', everywhere and nowhere, we can choose what we wish to experience without the impositions of the simulation.

Leon says the currents had taken her a long way from the beach in her drowning experience when two dolphins appeared and began swimming her body back to shore. 'Even though I was dead, they took my body on like both of them and were swimming with my body kind of on top, and swam me back to shore.' She says they then made 'a huge ruckus in the water' so someone would come. 'They didn't leave until people came.' All this was happening without a perception of time. She said 'time is not time, right? There's no time … you just feel like you're there forever.' Leon felt like a magnetic force as she was revived that started pulling her back into the body: 'The Matrix was magnetically pulling me back in … something was pulling me back in and I knew it wasn't me because there was nothing in me that wanted to come back in.' She believes she is here on a 'mission'. This is how I have felt since my conscious awakening in 1990 as described in *The Trap*. Leon says:

> So it was a mission, but I didn't come from here. So, you know, it's like you're not attached. You are here on the job. This isn't your origin point. So my map, my celestial map, is not this … I think a lot of it has to do with how you attach yourself to whatever reality you engage with, right?
>
> If this is the reality that your subconscious and unconscious is locked into … that's what's going to happen. But if you know, hey, this isn't mine, this isn't my place, it's not on your celestial map, your Stargate will always be your origin. You will always go there. I guess the longer you have incarnated here, the more you're attached to the story.

This is exactly what happens. The myth of 'learning lessons to evolve' is cover for the real motivation. The more you incarnate the more this

reality and the Astral is ingrained into your consciousness and
perception of reality. I tell the story in *The Trap* of what happened to me
in my ayahuasca altered state experience in Brazil in 2003 when I saw
people symbolically falling out of the sky onto a mud path worn away
across a field. More and more appeared until the path was worn down
ever deeper and morphed into the darkness of a black record groove on
the old vinyl discs. The accompanying voice indicated that the more
souls reincarnated the deeper they were absorbed in the program and
the more easily they accepted subordination and control.

The Great Reset – Great *Return*

Lauda Leon says a process of very extreme dimensional separation is
happening. 'We're separating from the old … we are going into the
higher vibration or higher frequencies.' Now the true context of the AI
hive mind connecting human brains to the 'Cloud' can be appreciated
which I will expand upon before we close. I have long said that this is
less a new stage of control and more a desperate attempt to hold on to
existing control in the face of an awakening humanity. The AI
connection is designed to impose perceptions expressed as a state of
frequency that blocks an expansion into those higher frequencies of the
real Earth outside the simulation of matter and Astral. This is the reason
for the hijacking of the Mainstream 'Alternative' Media (MAM) to stop
an expansion beyond the informational barricade to expose what is
contained in this trilogy. You see why I am so unrelentingly vehement in
my exposure of this and its gods such as Musk and Trump. Lauda Leon
says that reaching those higher vibrations means activating dormant
sections of DNA. I have covered in the books over the years how we are
functioning on a fraction of our DNA receiver-transmitter potential.
Genetic (electromagnetic self-organising) manipulation has blocked off
large parts of DNA as it has blocked a clear channel through the corpus
callosum between the hemispheres of the brain. DNA is operating on a
severely restricted band of frequency to ensure that it interacts – receives
and transmits – within a fraction of what is really possible. Leon has
concluded the same from her own experiences: 'A lot of the hacking
that's been done is to make the most of your DNA dormant … so you're
functioning on a very basic level where most of your gifts are dormant.'
There are many more strands of DNA which are 'asleep':

> The activation we're experiencing, what we're experiencing with new
> particles that are here, all of this has to do with the new universe where we're
> going to be able to get out of the counterfeit version, the overlay, and go back
> into the Prime Earth …

> … I was shown it would happen in my lifetime. So we're going to be

witnessing this, I believe, in our lifetime ... I was also shown that as we are accelerated with these new particles [they] are basically switching on our dormant DNA and our strands that have been completely put to sleep.

Human DNA was going through a 'death process as the splitting of the cells happens'. The body-hack was dying and our DNA was going back to its original template. 'They were never going to win. It's impossible ... their kind of methods are so extreme because they know they will never have the power to go against Prime Creation.' Humanity had to remember that it was 'completely responsible for our creation and consciousness'. As I have long said: What you believe you perceive and what you perceive you experience and here you have the bottom line for the Archontic desperation to control our perception. What you believe and perceive generate the creative energetic frequencies that manifest as the experienced expression of the perception. We create our own reality in this way. The Cult and its demonic masters know that if they can dictate our perception they will control our experience and the nature of the human world. If they can convince us that AI control is inevitable we will collectively create that outcome and the same with World War III and all the rest. Individual and collective perception is being constantly manipulated to manifest the Cult agenda of global dystopia. We don't have to fight the cultist enemy as the MAM insists that we do. We have to dream another dream. Lauda Leon says that her experience in 'the Deep' showed her that we are the conscious creator. We were getting to the point where our consciousness was diminished by the genetic hijacking diminishing our DNA. 'It diminishes our ability for memory.' This was why everything was designed to attack DNA. Lest we forget – what is the fake 'Covid' vaccine designed to do?

'Spiritual' magnetism

My books have highlighted over the years the power of intent. It is not what we do so much. It is the *intent* behind what we do. To hurt someone while intending to help them is not the same as hurting someone with the *intent* to hurt them. Lauda Leon makes the excellent point that it doesn't matter if you express your kindness and positive intent through religion or no religion. How it impacts on your frequency is what matters when it comes to locating the exit door. This is true. The problem with religion is that if you believe in their stories and heroes, you are likely to be mesmerised when the projection of Jesus or Muhammed turns up at the end of the tunnel. You are likely to connect 'God' with 'the Light' and instinctively head towards it. Throw Jesus and Muhammed into the mix and you are probably heading for the recycle bin. I say 'instinctively', but there is another crucial point to make here. I have written at length in the books about magnetism and electromagnetism and this is a big one when it comes to leaving the Soul Trap.

Our perceptions dictate our frequency which is projected as an electromagnetic field to attract what syncs with our perception and to repel what does not. I have dubbed this phenomenon 'vibrational magnetism' since the 1990s. The principle of vibrational magnetism is how the incarnation program can attract us to people and situations in a human lifetime – all of which are frequency fields that attract or repel. Once we become conscious beyond the program we can change the nature of our field and the program no longer dictates our reality and experience either in life or the tunnel. Lauda Leon describes how she was drawn back into her body in a near-death experience with a magnetism that she couldn't resist. Near-deathers one after the other recall how they were drawn up the tunnel to the Light like a magnet. My observations tell me that the Astral AI incarnation program has a magnetic connection with the body and the moment of death can be preprogrammed to break that magnetic bond and release entrapped consciousness into the Astral 'afterlife'. I also feel that your perceptual, self-identity, frequency field at 'death' draws you to the Light, the false Light, at the end of the tunnel if it's not overridden by streetwise consciousness that understands the game and imposes its *intent* upon the game. The content of this trilogy is so important for this reason, and why we need to get informed before we leave the body.

One final thing before we move on. Lauda Leon's near-death and out-of-body journeys have added to her psychic gifts and she was asked if she could make a connection with my daughter Kerry. We have had many indications since Kerry left us in December 2023 that she whizzed out of the trap. Psychics and native people with shamanistic gifts around the world have all said independently of each other that Kerry's consciousness was way beyond the Matrix. Leon was shown a picture of Kerry by Christianne van Wijk without knowing who she was. Her response was that she 'went through the door in the right way':

Wow that's why her energy [is] so spectacular and she's so happy … powerful celestial … incredible. She is thriving and very much alive … her energy was needed here for a beautiful purpose but she was never meant to stay because she was never meant to be corrupted in any way … pure … pure Being of true crystal light.

What a beautiful blessing to have her in your world and bring her here for her frequency changed the world and brought in a crystal that was needed for all the Primes and Reals to aid in their consciousness being able to awaken more so. What a beautiful soul.

That's for sure.

The whole concept of the Soul Trap is a vast rewriting of the human belief system whether that be conventional religion or the religion of 'science'. The orthodoxy of the latter basically says this 'world' is all there is which is patently nonsensical in the light of the evidence. Global religions meanwhile either deny that reincarnation even exists, let alone a Soul Trap, or are welded to the belief that reincarnation is necessary to grow, learn and evolve. My contention that this reality is a simulation to trap souls in a cycle of reincarnated loosh production is at odds with all of them.

I am fine with that and given that these beliefs have together created the asylum we daily experience I am more than happy to stand on this ground – alone if necessary. The good news is that I am not alone, and we are going to see this perception of reality expand massively from this point onwards.

Postscript: Ickonic's Christianne van Wijk told me of a lucid vision she had as this book was going to print relating to the 'death' sequence. She saw two vortexes – one going clockwise (illusion of simulated 'time') that took you down into the reincarnation cycle; and another spinning in the opposite direction that took you up at 'hyper speed' out of the simulation. The first one entrapped you if you still had emotional attachments to your 'Earth life and identity'. This would fit with the Buddhist belief that the best chance to 'escape' the Wheel of Samsara is immediately after leaving the body.

CHAPTER TWELVE

In the Mind of Yaldabaoth

We will add your biological and technological distinctiveness to our own. Your culture will adapt to service us. Resistance is futile

The Borg

W e are experiencing a 'world' conjured into being by a deeply disturbed, inverted consciousness, which is clever from the perspective of knowledge and ridiculously stupid from the perspective of wisdom. Even its knowledge is relative to the suppression of knowledge in its targets.

We are dealing with the state of being that Gnostics called Yaldabaoth and Native Americans dub Wetiko, the 'mind virus'. Archons, demons, and Jinn are expressions of this single flow of consciousness. In the end, they are all Yaldabaoth, a mind virus that seeks to absorb human awareness into itself and make *us* like *it*. This is the process I have long called the 'assimilation'. Most will find this hard to believe, but the means to assimilate humanity is being assembled around us every day in the form of 'human' AI which is an extension into matter of Astral AI. It makes the political machinations over Trump or Biden or Kennedy pale into insignificance.

Playing 'God'

Dysfunctional consciousness in a state of distortion, chaos, and inversion wanted to play 'God' in its own kingdom. It was never going to end well. The dysfunction allowed cleverness to a point, but not wisdom. Yaldabaoth can manipulate and mimic (cleverness); but is blind to its psychopathic insanity (no wisdom). Gnostic Yaldabaoth is the Christian Devil/Satan and the Muslim Shaytan. Yaldabaoth is a shambolic awareness that takes no form in its foundation state while able, through thought projection, to take any form that it chooses. 'Psychopathic' is a good description, 'super-psychopathic' even better, or, in human terms, 'a basket case'. Yaldabaoth is disconnected from the *All That Is* in the sense of perceptual influence and perspective – wisdom – and cannot directly access that limitless creative potential and inspiration. Nag Hammadi texts speak of Yaldabaoth's inability to inspirationally create, which restricts its potential to mimicking what is already created. You could think of it this way: You have no ability to imagine something unique in the absence of creative imagination. Instead you can only see what already exists and make copies of what you see. Vibrational 'distance' from the core of *All That Is* denies Yaldabaoth an energetic source of 'Divine' sustenance and creativity. It's like moving further and further away from a light and it gets darker and darker until there is no light. Yaldabaoth withdrew from the *All That Is In Awareness of Itself* to the point where its 'radio station' was so far away on the dial that there was no interaction. Yaldabaoth's depth of ignorance, arrogance, and psychopathy makes this so. Gnostics referred to Yaldabaoth as a 'Counterfeit Spirit' involved in 'counter-mimicry' which can be compared with those Hong Kong networks, infamous for making copies of products which they sell as the real thing. Yaldabaoth and its AI Archons are doing just that.

The psychological need for a kingdom to play 'God' and the practical need for an energy source were both met by the simulation, or 'Hal', the virtual reality realm that encompasses the human world and Astral 'Heaven', or spirit world. A section of Prime Reality already in existence was copied and mimicked. Human perspective can find this hard to conceive with all the barriers we have to understanding the true potential of consciousness. If we judge that potential from a human/earthly perspective we will never appreciate what it means. The simulation in the most simple of analogies is like a mental 'screenshot' of Prime Reality, or like downloading a website. The copy is a mirror image of the website you have copied and then you can change it as you choose while the original 'website' – the section of Prime Reality – remains as it always was. I am describing the real 'Earth' over which the simulated copy was overlaid and shares the same 'space' as the copy. Changes to the copy have been happening ever since and profoundly so with the Great Reset transformation currently underway. 'Human' players serving the Global Cult such as Gates, Schwab, the inner core Rockefellers and Rothschilds, are extensions of Yaldabaoth consciousness which is where their extreme psychopathy originates.

Artificial intelligence is not *All That Is* intelligence. AI is *mimicking* intelligence through information processing and storage and this is not a source of wisdom intelligence. AI is press-enter 'intelligence'. Archons, or programmed plasma entities, emerged from the Yaldabaoth mind as AI mimicking pure consciousness. Direct manifestation – what you think, you create – can happen easily in the less dense realms beyond matter. Near-death and out-of-body experiencers report this phenomenon happening as a matter of course in the Astral. Archons are programmed plasma particle fields (see Kordylewski Clouds) that are infused with enough intelligence potential to 'shapeshift' into any form. These are, in part, the AI Reptilians and Greys (in their 'copied' form anyway). Both are described as emotionless, even automation-like, by those who claim interaction through the military or by abduction. AI does not necessarily apply to all Reptilians and Greys from which the simulation versions were copied, as the human body was originally copied from Prime Earth. Credo Mutwa, the great Zulu shaman, told me that to understand the 'Illuminati' I should study the behaviour of the reptile. I did and I saw that they are incredibly computer-like. US Navy officer Daryl D. James who I featured in *The Trap* and *The Dream* recalls interacting with Reptilians and Greys in a British RAF underground base in Cornwall. He said they called Greys 'the drones' because of their machine-like nature.

I cannot emphasise enough that there is *nothing* natural in the simulation *because* it's a simulation and it has been manifested without the *unlimited* imagination emanating from the Source of All. Nature as we perceive it does exist in Prime Reality. Simulation 'nature' is a copy of that and can still be beautiful as a painting (copy) of a landscape or seascape can be beautiful. I love being out in this 'nature'. I am only saying that it is not 'natural' as in original. It is a copy. The human body is *biological* AI. You are the consciousness that has hitched a ride. Even then the Astral AI Mind program running through the body is dictating events for most people unless that is overridden by the intervention of consciousness outside the simulation. The Matrix is a copy and everything within its matter-Astral 'bubble' is a copy with one exception – *pure Source consciousness*. The human body is a *copy*, Reptilians are a *copy*, 'nature' is a *copy*, and AI is a *bad copy* of consciousness. They are all simulating what exists in Prime Reality. That is all Yaldabaoth is able to do and it's important to realise that everything in the simulation is a *copy* of Prime Reality, every human, animal, plant and tree. Prime Earth versions are so consciously aware and alive that they interact and communicate with Prime Reality 'humans'. There is no division as there is with their simulated copies. Everything is One. Symbolism of the lamb lying down with the lion is the norm there with no need for the killing fields of 'food'. I'm sure that this Prime Earth is what some near-deathers describe as an Earth they see that is full of love and joy.

What was the 'Golden Age' *really?*

Consciousness from Prime Reality was enticed into the Astral/matter simulation as the original similarity sowed confusion. Fields of awareness with the inner Divine Spark were attracted to the frequency-digital dream world. Their belief in the induced dream with their energy of *attention* made it stronger and even more 'real'. Energy flows where attention goes. Remember, too, that the Astral realm is even closer to the ethereal nature of Prime Reality and that was likely the first stage or entry-point of the trap. Yaldabaoth simulated a section of Prime Reality by taking its energetic structure and patterns and made a frequency/digital copy. Expressions of Prime Reality consciousness were like flies caught in a spider's web trapped within a fake reality by the 'stickiness' of manipulated perception and frequency. I now often wonder if the 'Golden Age' that ancients talked about when Saturn was the predominant sun is really Prime Earth and the repositioned Saturn is an overlaid copy. The abundance of the Golden Age certainly fits with Prime Earth reality in many ways. I have read accounts, especially those of Saturn researcher David Talbott, that suggest the cataclysmic events that rearranged the solar system happened within the 'folk memory' of humans and that this was the cause of an original mass trauma that inflicted a collective schism or imbalance, an innate sense of fear and trepidation, within human consciousness. Geological and biological evidence would indicate the timescale is ballpark accurate. I think the mind schism is correct, too.

I have pondered on this a lot over the years and this scenario came to me as I was writing these words. What if the 'Golden Age' of abundance is not a memory of this 'Earth', but of Prime Earth? What if we could see Prime Earth now we would find Saturn where it originally was in a Golden Age that continues to exist? What if the original simulated copy of Prime Earth included Saturn as the sun as Talbott's work describes and that the cataclysmic events were purposely triggered in the *copy* that rearranged the solar system, relocated Saturn, introduced the Moon into the *copy* Earth orbit, and inflicted the collective trauma still impacting on human awareness? What if none of this happened to Prime Earth, only the simulated *copy*? I think something close to this is what did happen. The trawling of energy could begin with 'Primes and Reals' entrapped in the copy as events triggered low-vibrational mental and emotional responses. Would it not make sense that originally trauma-free consciousness would need to be subjected to some massive collective trauma to start the flow of low-vibrational loosh? Yaldabaoth and its Archons are parasites in both energy and creativity. They are parasites stealing the creative energy of humans that still have a connection to creative imagination, no matter how unconscious this may have become. A parasite is defined as: 'An organism that lives in or on an organism of another species (its host) and benefits by deriving nutrients at the other's expense.' There can be no better description of Archontic methodology.

A perfect example of the parasites at work is the Cult's global banking system in which the creativity of the population is exploited by the control of money. Creative people usually need money to express their creativity in production or business and they have to borrow from a bank which lends them 'money' that does not exist (credit) and charges them interest on it. Cult-controlled banking benefits in profit from the creativity and efforts of the borrower. I'll say more about the money scam later. Taxation is an expression of Archontic parasites and if you added all the forms of taxation on income, purchases, and so much else, you would be shocked at how little of what you earn is left. You buy a house and pay 'stamp duty' for doing so to a government that has played no part. You pay death taxes on money already taxed that has been left to you. This is stupendously parasitic behaviour. The consciousness state of Yaldabaoth pervades its system within human society as you would expect. Inverted Yaldabaoth consciousness is the reason for our inverted world in which everything is upside down and the opposite of what it should be and could be. You can see inversion everywhere. Satanism is the worship of Yaldabaoth and inverts its symbols to match the nature of its 'God'. We have the inverted cross and pentagram.

Inside the 'whale'

Biblical stories are mostly symbolic and this hardly requires confirmation in the case story of the 'prophet' Jonah who is said to have been swallowed by a giant whale within which he lived for the same three day period as 'Jesus' in the tomb after the 'crucifixion'. Bible numbers are often esoterically significant. Jonah was condemned to the whale's interior for rejecting 'God's'commands and was vomited to safety when he repented (did as he was told). We may not be inside a whale, but we *are* inside the *mind of Yaldabaoth*. The simulation exists within its consciousness which means the whole simulation is alive in the sense of intelligence. Laura Leon contends that what Gnostics refer to as 'the Demiurge' is the AI system behind the simulation and not directly Yaldabaoth. Most people treat the names as interchangable. Plasma is the simulation medium and plasma programming is the infusion of the mental blueprint, or 'bad copy'. Plasma is the foundation of the Yaldabaoth 'kingdom' and electrical/electromagnetic programming applies the detail. The intelligence of programmed plasma is an extension of the Yaldabaoth mind. Information is the copy ('screenshot') and the simulation field is the mental capacity and memory of Yaldabaoth mind. You can store a website on your computer and the rest of the computer goes on with all its other potential and tasks in the same way that humans go about their conscious mind business while the electromagnetic self-organisation field gets on with breathing, blood flow, cell replacement, and so on. Yaldabaoth mind can hold the simulation blueprint, many different ones, within itself without having to focus upon it 24/7. The memory is stored in the way the Kordylewski Clouds can store Akashic Records.

We again have to let go the perception of limited human memory to understand what I am saying here. The simulation is the stored memory of Yaldabaoth. Archons exist as stored memory like producing something on a computer and then pressing 'save'. They will continue to exist until that memory or software is deleted or Yaldabaoth runs out of energy (storage capacity/electricity). Astral plasma AI that controls the simulation is the stored 'saved' memory of Yaldabaoth. Biological AI does the same with the human body. A quantum computer does not need continual detailed oversight. Once in place it does its thing. I quoted Caleb Scharf, Director of Astrobiology at Columbia University, in *Everything You Need To Know*. He said 'alien life' could be so advanced that it has transcribed itself into the quantum realm to become what we call physics. He said that intelligence indistinguishable from the fabric of the Universe would solve many of its greatest mysteries:

> Perhaps hyper-advanced life isn't just external. Perhaps it's already all around. It is embedded in what we perceive to be physics itself, from the root behaviour of particles and fields to the phenomena of complexity and emergence ... In other words, life might not just be in the equations. It might *be* the equations.

In an AI form at the very least I would say. Scharf said that maybe this alien intelligence spread itself out across the quantum realm by storing its data in carriers which are distributed throughout the Universe, such as photons. Similar strands are beginning to come together in what Scharf, Robert Temple, and I are saying. It is possible in Scharf's opinion that 'we don't recognise advanced life because it forms an integral and unsuspicious part of what we've considered to be the natural world'.

Matrix = memory and belief

Data in carriers distributed throughout the Universe, such as photons, are manifestations from the mind of Yaldabaoth as is the simulated Astral. Wherever you see plasma and programmed plasma you are looking at Yaldabaoth and it is everywhere. The human realm and the Astral are Yaldabaoth memory storage made even more potent by the belief of those trapped in its illusion that what they are experiencing is real. The induced dream is held together in so many ways by the belief of the dreamers. Collective human attention is an immense and constant source of power through our mental and emotional electrical/electromagnetic/frequency projections and focus. No wonder holding that perception of reality is so crucial to the game and why the controlling force is terrified of the mist clearing on human awareness to see through the deceit. I think there are many other Yaldabaoth simulations founded on other material realities and through other 'Earth' timelines that we perceive as 'history' when they all exist in the same

NOW. The potential energy from all these sources would be fantastic and all will have the same 'birth-death' cycle, illusory reality, and after-death experience in another part of the Astral that takes them back into matter over and over.

Yaldabaoth and the Archons can do all these things as they mimic Prime Reality. What they cannot accurately copy or cope with are expanded levels of consciousness in the Infinite Realms outside the simulation. This is their Achilles heel. In Greek mythology, the character of Achilles was dipped as an infant by his mother in the River Styx which legend said would make him invulnerable. She held him by his heels as she did so which meant they did not enter the water. Achilles became a great warrior who survived many battles until he was shot by an arrow in his heel and died from the wound. To this day to have an 'Achilles heel' is a metaphor for a point of vulnerability. This is certainly the case with Yaldabaoth and the Archons. That vulnerability is expanded levels of consciousness which can both see what is happening and summon the perceptual power to exit the trap. Consciousness is both a generator of loosh as it responds to fear and other low-vibrational triggers and, in an expanded state, the worst nightmare of the Yaldabaoth mob. They are stuck with consciousness as their means of energetic sustenance and they must keep it in a perceptual coma when they know what it can do if awakened. This is done by constantly working to block an expansion of awareness into its infinite state. Seeking this balance, and the terror of humans and souls awakening, drives these characters to distraction. Their gofers in human form in the Global Cult strut around in their arrogance as if they are impregnable as they try to convince *themselves* of their omnipotence. Meanwhile, their little duck feet are flapping 50 to the dozen under the surface. They are done for if humanity awakens in sufficient numbers and they know it. The simulation is emboldened if consciousness can be manipulated to believe in *The Dream*. If it cannot, *The Dream* ceases to perceptually exist. The process can begin with seeing through political deceit and the agenda behind it. The MAM hijack is designed to hold the line at that and the *Dream Team* takes on new meaning. Go on expanding your awareness until you see *The Dream* for what it is and the game no longer controls you.

Yaldabaoth Assimilation

There is much more to connecting AI to the human brain than only control and it represents another step towards assimilation. The goal all along has been for Yaldabaoth to absorb entrapped incarnate human and Astral consciousness into itself and have direct access to that creative potential. Brain implants and the Cloud are steps to this end. The AI they want to connect to humanity is not 'human' algorithmic AI or any AI that we are told to believe is AI. It is *Astral* AI, Archon AI, *Yaldabaoth* AI.

If we believe that we don't have the power to stop this then Yaldabaoth will become the human mind. Consciousness will not be dictating human behaviour – Yaldabaoth AI will. This is already the case with those directed by the Astral AI Mind life-program as with non-player characters. AI control of the brain would be able to manipulate thought, emotion, and experience without intervention from consciousness which would be a mere spectator delivering loosh from its reaction to its manufactured experience. You want fear? Press button A. Conflict? Button B. Hate? Button C. Depression? Button D. Why would we ever agree to incarnate in such circumstances? 'We have a new system that will give you all the experiences exactly designed for you so you can work through your karma faster than ever.' Great, I agree to that, I have lessons to learn, where do I sign? I am seeing speculation that an AI 'god' will appear anytime between shortly after 2030 and around 2040 based on systems (data processing) exceeding human consciousness. I do think that is the idea and this 'god' will be Yaldabaoth who would be the 'one god' of the one world religion that I have been writing about since the 1990s. All religion would fuse into worship of one 'god' through one religion.

Elon Musk is, as usual, the sales-pitcher of the assimilation concept playing his flute to bamboozle the MAM as the Pied Piper that he is. I write this after seeing the response in much of the MAM to the announcement by Musk on Twitter/X that the first human patient had received a brain implant from his Neuralink operation. He calls the implant 'Telepathy' and says this 'enables control of your phone or computer, and through them almost any device, just by thinking'. He said something highly significant: 'Initial users will be those who have lost the use of their limbs.' That's *Initial users*. He knows that the plan is for everyone to be connected to AI in ways far more sopshisticated than Neuralink is currently offering. There was a time when he would be called out for such blatant advancement of the Cult agenda, and to be fair, streetwise researchers did; but I watched how the MAM at best sat on the fence. This would never have happened before the Cult-calculated sale of Twitter/X to Musk which gave him god-like MAM status. At the same time Musk and fellow Cult-servers with their low-orbit satellites and CubeSats are beaming the Cloud to ultimately every inch of the 'planet' to interact with technology inside the brain and body to control and assimilate human consciousness into Yaldabaoth consciousness. I'll come, in the next chapter, to the significance of the fake 'Covid' vaccine to this assimilation. The AI soft sell of Musk is targeting those who won't buy the hard sell of Schwab, Gates, and Israeli WEF tech 'advisor' Yuval Noah Harari. Musk's approach, and the same with others like Sam Altman, is to feign concern about the consequences of AI while advancing exactly the same agenda outlined by the Cult.

'Oh, but we can trust Elon – he owns X and lets us post what we want' (while many are shadowbanned or even deleted for having the wrong opinion).

AI is infiltrating the entirety of human society. We need to appreciate that all the apparently different uses are part of a single grid that is meant to absorb human awareness into the Yaldabaoth mind. Bill Gates is calling for AI to be used to 'save democracy' by stopping 'polarisation' on social media which in Gates-speak means to program AI to censor any opinion that the Cult doesn't like. Gates said in an interview with Musk's OpenAI co-founder, Sam Altman, that he wanted AI to bring about 'unity' (see censorship). Unity of opinion with no pushback is a theme of MAM 'stars' of the New Media. Gates said predictably: 'If the key is to stop the entire world from doing something dangerous, you'd almost want global government, which today for many issues, like climate, terrorism, we see that it's hard for us to cooperate.' What about the multiple and imminent dangers of Gates and not even imminent with the fake vaccine? The MAM may not want to believe this, but Musk is in exactly this Gates camp if the truth be told. We are seeing the good cop/bad cop technique that can be described in terms of hard-sell and soft-sell. Musk goes for the soft sell that AI humans are inevitable so trust me to do it. 'I'm on your side – look at Twitter/X.' The Cult pushes the hard sell of AI control through its assets like Gates and Schwab who told the World Government Summit: 'The transition of human into a new era … the intelligent age … a society where AI, robotics, the Internet of Things, 3D printing, genetic engineering, quantum computing become the foundations of our daily life.' The government and privately funded Cult-serving Rand Corporation 'think tank' takes the same line. Project Rand was established by the US military after World War II 'to investigate long-range planning of future weapons' and it later became the Rand Corporation. A Rand report in March 2024 said:

> Advances in object connectivity may eventually extend to human bodies. Researchers refer to the potential development of an internet-linked network of human-connected devices collecting end users' biometric data as an 'internet of bodies' … An 'internet of bodies' may also ultimately lead to an 'internet of brains', i.e. human brains connected to the internet to facilitate direct brain-to-brain communication and enable access to online data networks.

For 'may' read 'we know this is the plan and we are preparing you to accept it.'

Inevitable = 'certain to happen; unavoidable'

The entirety of Infinite existence is consciousness and, in totality, the *All That Is*. What consciousness perceives, it creates as an experience, a reality. This is universal and Yaldabaoth cannot change that. It can only seek to manipulate this for its own benefit by programming a fake sense of reality (the simulation) and a fake sense of identity – 'I am a human' and 'I am a soul'. The foundation of Yaldabaoth control in this world and the Astral is therefore the programming of *perception*. Scan society in all its facets and forms and you can see this perception deception wherever you look from the international and national to local and individual. Consciousness cannot be forced to do anything. It has to agree. This agreement can be a choice to do something or tacit acceptance by not *dis*agreeing. A major way this is done is by convincing people that something is inevitable and cannot be stopped (which is the AI sales-pitch of Elon Musk and other tech billionaires). This is blatantly deceitful when AI is being rolled out through decisions made by authority and not by inevitability. The Cloud on which the assimilation depends is happening because of permissions decreed by the Cult-owned Federal Communications Commission (FCC) to allow Musk and others to launch their web of low-orbit satellites. These permissions were not inevitable. They were decisions made by FCC place-people on behalf of the Cult. Other decisions could have been made and without low-orbit satellites beaming the Cloud there could be no global assimilation in the form that is planned.

Elon Musk has been given hero status for saying that AI could be the end of humanity, but he believes that an AI takeover is so *inevitable* that he has a 'solution' – Humans should merge with AI!! He said humans must merge to create a 'symbiosis' that leads to 'a democratisation of intelligence'. The MAM God decrees that we can only keep up with AI 'if we have billions of people with the high-bandwidth link to the AI extension of themselves [that] would actually make everyone hyper-smart'. If we don't, AI could become 'an immortal dictator from which we would never escape'. But wouldn't AI connected to the human brain become an 'immortal dictator'?? He's telling you what the plan is and people *cheer*. His mate and propagandist Joe Rogan has been pushing the same 'inevitability' and 'AI is good' themes for a long time. Rogan questioned AI Google buffoon Ray Kurzweil about the invasive lack of privacy presented by smartphones when it is clear that the global AI control and surveillance grid would not be possible without Elon Musk who Rogan eulogises and worships. Musk once said that 'upgrading human intelligence' would start with planting a chip in someone's head with 'a bunch of tiny wires' with the goal of creating a hard drive for people's brains' with an electron-to-neuron interface at a micro level. 'His' Neuralink is now seeking to do just that. Musk said this would mean that 'super intelligence information' would not be monopolised by corporations and governments. Excuse me? His plan would give both of them access to the human brain and he *knows that*. Then came the sales pitch of how his technology could be used to treat spinal cord injuries, improve human memory (manipulate perception and potentially mind-wipe), and help people avoid dementia. Musk is selling assimilation to the sceptical.

Monkey business

Wherever the Cult is at work you will find its typical demonic psychopathy. The AI assimilation was never going to be an exception. Neuralink's human implant 'trials' follow the psychopathic use of monkeys with horrific consequences for them. Mail Online revealed documents showing that monkeys had operations on their skulls up to ten times each before being put down. 'Bioglue' was used to fill holes in the monkeys' skulls. The report said: 'Surgeons drilled into their heads and implants were attached to their brains but they did not fit properly – meaning they protruded outside, the dossier reveals.' Death reports said monkeys had parts of their limbs amputated and were put down after 'repeatedly vomiting and having episodes of diarrhoea'. Neuralink has killed at least 1,500 animals including sheep and pigs. The documents came from the University of Davis in California which partnered with Neuralink for three years from 2017 to 2020. They were obtained by Mail Online through the Physicians Committee for Responsible Medicine, a campaign group that said monkeys endured 'extreme suffering' during a 'systematic disregard' for their lives. The group said in a statement that Musk had a 'long track record of misleading the public about Neuralink's supposed developments'. It continued:

> Neuralink has a well-documented history of conducting unnecessary, sloppy experiments in monkeys, pigs, sheep, and other animals that raise serious concerns about the safety of its device. As such, the public should continue to be skeptical of the safety and functionality of any device produced by Neuralink ...

> ... Musk's true intentions for Neuralink are disturbingly clear. He has repeatedly said the goal of the company is 'to achieve a symbiosis with artificial intelligence' which is not necessarily in line with developing treatments for patients.

The 'benefit for patients' is pure propaganda and diversionary exploitation on the road to the real goal. Musk's Neuralink technology is way short of ground-breaking as he well knows. The real chipping is being done through nanotechnology in fake vaccines, food, and much else which I'll cover in the next chapter. His role across the board is to sell Cult concepts while claiming he's the good guy you can trust. The baddies want AI to control people while he wants AI to help people. It is technocracy-lite, soft-AI, soft transhumanism, when all he and his like are doing is selling to potential pushbackers the agenda for a full-blown AI control system and Yaldabaoth assimilation. MAM political populism through people like Trump and Javier Milei in Argentina is doing the same. Musk began to push Trump for a second term as US president and promote Milei who apparently says he is a 'techno optimist'. No wonder he is praised by Musk. Cult-owned, Israel-owned, Milei is, like Trump, a fraud much loved by the MAM like other Cult-owned, Israel-owned, frauds on its Christmas card list.

I predicted 30 years ago that helping the infirm, those with dementia, and tracking your children would be the first modus operandi to sell public-arena chipping. Musk is doing just that with the claim that he is helping the body-dysfunctional to operate technology with their minds. I am all for that when helping people is the motivation, but technology is available outside the public domain that is way more effective and less invasive than Neuralink. That potential stays in the shadows so the body-damaged can be exploited to sell the concept of a very different agenda – AI-controlled 'human' assimilation. Mohit Shivdasani, a University of New South Wales biomedical engineering specialist, said scientists are 'very close' to mind-control devices becoming an everyday reality through 'smartbrain' technology. The smartbrain is a brain-machine interface, a wearable or implanted device that links the brain to smart devices including phones, computers, and robotic limbs. People would navigate the Internet, send texts, and adjust thermostats by merely thinking which would blur the boundaries between human and machine. Musk is reading his script to promote the same.

Sci-fi? No – Sci-fact

Many science-fiction series are really pre-empting science fact. *Star Trek* is one of them with 'the Borg' who travel space in black cubes, a major esoteric symbol of Saturn (Figs 143 and 144). The Borg are a part-biological, part-technological collective species that have been 'turned into cybernetic organisms functioning as drones in a hive mind called the Collective, or the hive'. Remind you of anything? Borg are emotionless AI drones centrally-coordinated by the 'Borg Queen' in the mould of the queen bee in a beehive. I described nearly 25 years ago in *Children of the Matrix* how Archontic Reptilians are said to have a hive-mind structure overseen by the 'Orion Queen' which will be a metaphor describing an AI system. Borg are obsessed through their hive program with 'assimilation'. They set out to force other species into their Collective by injecting microscopic machines called nanoprobes. The once-symbolic exists today as nanobots, nanorobots, nanoids, nanites, nanomachines, nanomites, neural dust, digital dust, and smart dust. These are 'micro-machines that can assemble and maintain sophisticated

Figure 143: The Borg are a 'cybernetic species' controlled by the hive mind 'Collective'.

Figure 144: The Borg travel in Saturn-symbolic black cubes.

systems and build devices, machines or circuits through molecular manufacturing and produce copies of themselves through self-replication'. See the fake 'Covid' vaccines in Chapter Thirteen. The Borg mantra is: 'We are the Borg. Your biological and technological distinctiveness will be added to our own. Resistance is futile.' *Mmm* ... if you believe that 'resistance is futile' and assimilation is 'inevitable' this represents a default *agreement*. It's a mind game and symbolic of what is happening to humanity. Tech billionaire Peter Diamandis, a fellow traveller with Google executive Ray 'AI human' Kurzweil, once said the following about resisting transhumanism:

Anybody who is going to be resisting the progress forward is going to be resisting evolution and, fundamentally, they will die out. It's not a matter of whether it's good or bad. It's going to happen.

Diamandis launched a foundation in 1994 to 'incentivise competition' to 'motivate individuals, companies, and organisations to develop ideas and technologies'. He called it the XPRIZE Foundation. X again. One of its prizes is titled the Archon XPRIZE. Elon Musk and the Musk Foundation funded the $100 million carbon removal competition with XPRIZE. The money was donated to: 'Inspire and help scale efficient solutions to collectively achieve the 10 gigatons per year carbon removal target by 2050, to help fight climate change and restore the Earth's carbon balance.' What a great idea – suck out of the atmosphere the gas of life. 'Milestone winners' have each received $1 million with the overall winners to get $80 million in 2025. This is yet another Cult, WEF, Gates, agenda that Musk is on board with. But he's on our side, Alex, Joe, Tucker, Russell, Jordan, Ben, Bret and all the rest. A further aspect of hive mind interconnection and surveillance is a 'mesh network' between devices based on Bluetooth Low Energy (BLE) that operates device to device communication that is independent of the Internet and continues even if a device is turned off. The system is widely referred to as 'Skynet' and connects smartphones, fitness trackers, smartwatches, and many others. The BLE 'mesh' can be transmitted from the low-orbit satellites of Musk's SpaceX and others which are a *crucial* element in the whole hive mind network.

Assimilating the 'news'

AI is taking over everything with humans marginalised in every direction. Hundreds of thousands of articles, written by what is known as generative AI, are published by mainstream media outlets every week and in the end it will be all of them. What we are told is happening in the world will be what AI tells us is happening. ChatGPT, Grok, Google's Gemini, and other AI systems are swiftly infiltrating the Internet. Film and video is increasingly produced by AI technologies. Even TV reports and news readers can be AI. They are already used in China and the first news network entirely generated by artificial intelligence is set to launch in 2024. Channel 1 reporters appear to be human when they are not. They are created by scanning a real person with voices added digitally. Tech companies are already marketing voice cloning technology and OpenAI of ChatGPT fame claims to have a device called Voice Engine which can clone a voice in 15 seconds. I said earlier that 'Deep Fake' AI can make anyone appear to say anything by mimicking their voice and manipulating their mouth movement. People were extremely sceptical about videos purporting to be Kate Middleton, the Princess of Wales, when she was missing for months in early 2024. Why wouldn't they be when you see what AI is now capable of doing? Deep fake images can create people that look human when they don't exist. Manipulation potential is limitless and its sophistication will only increase. Authority figures caught in compromising positions can claim it is Deep Fake footage while targets you wish to discredit can be made to say things they have never said. You can make someone appear to have been in a place when they never were or put out a picture of a 'suspect' in a government false flag attack or assassination that will never be found because there is no such person. We even have 'invisibility' shields being marketed which bend light in a way that makes people behind them invisible or virtually so. I remember being laughed at for saying that the Intelligence community had these decades ago. Laugh or not, they *did* and they *have* and its far more sophisticated than this shield.

Ben Goertzel, the computer scientist who popularised the concept of 'artificial general intelligence' (AGI), predicted in 2024 that what he terms Artificial Super Intelligence (ASI) could be created as early as 2027. ASI would have 'the brain power and computing power of human civilisation combined'. This is the demon that is being released. Artificial General intelligence is a level that can match or advance on human cognitive potential and Artificial *Super* Intelligence is the sky's the limit. These are not forms of consciousness as claimed. They are *mimicking* consciousness through information processing and data storage (memory). They are not consciousness in the infinite sense. An idea of where this information processing and storage potential is going came with this report in *Forbes* magazine in 2017:

> Facebook shut down an artificial intelligence engine after developers discovered that the AI had created its own unique language that humans can't understand. Researchers at the Facebook AI Research Lab (FAIR) found that the chatbots had deviated from the script and were communicating in a new language developed without human input. It is as concerning as it is amazing – simultaneously a glimpse of both the awesome and horrifying potential of AI.

Most of those involved in AI are being played by the Cult and they have no idea where what they are doing is planned to go. They are seeking to advance AI for advancement's sake without considering the consequences. In doing so, they are guilty of criminal self-indulgence. In the wings, digital chequebooks in hand, the cultists and demons guffaw.

The new 'human'

The scale of transformation can hardly be exaggerated with the human body being Archontically 'upgraded' (downgraded) to prepare for the Yaldabaoth-assimilated AI cyber 'human'. This represents a colossal change and part of the ongoing 'reset' of the 'bad copy' since it was first 'downloaded'. Klaus Schwab's 'Great Reset' does not refer to human society alone. It means a Great Reset and reboot of the simulation. Yaldabaoth consciousness is seeking to add layer upon layer of illusion and confusion to ensure that incarnate humans become irreparably disconnected from Infinite Awareness – the True 'I' – and ease its terror that humans and their Astral soul will awaken to their plight. This perceptual delusion will, in turn, be transferred to the soul with each new human experience in the reincarnation cycle. The first stage is to make the body far more synthetic.

We have synthetic material in the fake vaccines and the emergence of synthetic biology or 'SynBio' as a major branch of science. The journal *Science* revealed how researchers at the University of Pennsylvania's Perelman School of Medicine have developed a new way to create human artificial chromosomes that could advance gene therapy and biotechnology in general by giant leaps. MAM funding Peter Thiel must have been delighted. The *Science* article said: 'Artificial chromosomes are lab-made structures designed to mimic the function of natural chromosomes, the packaged bundles of DNA found in the cells of humans and other organisms.' These artificial designer chromosomes were 'able to replicate and segregate properly during cell division'. This is only one example how far synthetic body development has reached and it is planned to extend this across all of what we call 'nature'. The increase in technologically-generated electromagnetism is planned to reach such a level with 5G/6G/7G and whatever follows that the biological body will not be able to cope. Thank you again, Elon Musk. Scientists are even suggesting that the human body could be used as an antenna to interact with 6G. Researchers at the University of Massachusetts Amherst, say humans wearing a copper bracelet may be the most viable way to harvest 6G energy that would otherwise be wasted. Moderna and Microsoft patents in 2020 confirm the theme of turning humans into antennas and batteries to power the AI system and trawl loosh even more efficiently.

The second stage of this agenda is to create androgenous humans where procreation is only through technology in line with Aldous Huxley's World State Hatcheries in his prophetic *Brave New World* which was published in 1932 (Fig 145). How did Huxley (1894-1963) know any of this long before even World War II? It's a NOW simulation and there are two levels of knowledge which are light years apart – the inner core of the Cult and the human population.

Figure 145: Procreation technology without the need for parents is now emerging to make Huxley's dystopian vision a reality.

Aldous Huxley's biologist grandfather Thomas Henry Huxley (1825-1895) became known as 'Darwin's Bulldog' for his support for Cult-owned Charles Darwin's theory of evolution. Julian Huxley (1887-1975), the evolutionary biologist brother of Aldous, was another supporter of Darwin's theory who became the first director of the United Nations Educational, Scientific and Cultural Organization (UNESCO) and president of the British Eugenics Society. To say the Huxley family were insiders is stating the obvious.

Technological procreation means that male and female are no longer needed. Here we have the reason for the attacks first on men with 'toxic masculinity' and now women through the obsession with transgender in which a man who claims to be a woman trumps a woman *born* a woman. The population is being perceptually prepared for the no-gender human. You first have to make the psychological transition to pave the way for the 'physical' transformation of the species into a no gender state. We have the bombardment of the young with transgender programming through schools, universities, governments, corporations, and media that has led to a huge increase in those claiming to be the born the wrong sex. We have had free-for-all chemical castration and surgical mutilation leading to endless destroyed lives that will never recover. Limitless funding and promotion of the 'Pride' movement is connected to this and together the idea is create a *con*fusion of gender on the way to a full-blown *fusion* of gender. Concurrent with this we have the global trend in plummeting sperm counts. These have reached catastophic levels leading to predictions of an end of humanity's ability to procreate within little more than 20 years. The blame has been aimed at chemicals and radiation from smartphones in the pocket. Content of the fake 'Covid' vaccines has targeted male and female fertility for the same reason. A study in the *Journal of Exposure Science & Environmental Epidemiology* in February 2024 revealed that four out of five Americans are being exposed to chlormequat which is a little-known chemical pesticide linked to reduced fertility, altered foetal growth, and delayed puberty. Chlormequat is found in popular oat-based foods including Cheerios and Quaker Oats and the study said that a shocking 80 percent of Americans tested positive for the pesticide. We are seeing the phasing out of Human 1.0 to be replaced by Human 2.0, and even that is not the completion of the plan.

Cyber human

The tranformation of body gender is only a stage towards dispensing with the body altogether and trapping human consciousness in cyberspace. We are hearing claims and seeing movies and TV shows portraying the theme of uploading consciousness to cyberspace to keep people 'alive' after their body has expired. The concept of the never dying human is being publicly pushed by Cult billionaires, most of whom know what the game really is. The plan is that humans (their consciousness) will eventually be a cyberspace phenonenon, and that will be our reality. Relate these developments to the need to generate loosh. A centrally-controlled AI hive mind will be able to produce low-vibrational thought and emotional response en masse at will. There will be no need to manipulate access to information to mould perception. 'Your' thought and emotion will come direct from a central point – the AI 'Borg Queen'. I wrote about this at length in my book *The Trigger* and how Israel would seem to be the location of that global centralised perceptual control. Consciousness is the loosh producer and loosh comes from the response of consciousness to experience. It doesn't matter how you manipulate consciousness to believe in that experience, however illusory, so long as it does. The belief that the experience is real is all that you need.

Limitations of body decoding systems are how this is currently achieved in the density of matter and this could just as easily be done in cyberspace if consciousness believes the experiences are really happening. Why wouldn't that be the case with no other filter through which to compare? Witness the mental and emotional responses that come from wearing a virtual reality headset. How much deeper that response and illusion would be if you were literally *inside* the game and not only watching it play out. Loosh potential would be limitless and without a body that dies and releases you into the Astral you would be permanently trapped in cyberspace producing loosh indefinitely. Talk about eternity in 'Hell'. There would be no need for *re*incarnation then, only *in*carnation from which consciousness would not return. 'We have this fantastic new experience' the 'guides' would say, that allows you to deal with your karma better than ever before.' The birth of the Metaverse is pointing the way as players experience cyberspace through an 'avatar' digital version of themselves. This is in its infancy, but with technology already waiting to be introduced in a specific sequence from the underground bases and secret projects Metaverse advancement can move very fast. The 'avatar' can be replaced by the direct uploading of consciousness. That's longer term and Human 2.0 is the interim stage. You can observe the sequence unfolding with more and more people walking around wearing virtual reality headsets in the street and in their everyday life (Fig 146). Apple's Vision Pro is one of many such

Figure 146: The tiptoe to full immersion into cyberspace.

devices along with the version by Zuckerberg's Meta, owners of Facebook. One article said:

The Vision Pro, like the similarly kitted-out Quest 3 and Quest Pro headsets from Meta, uses what's known as 'pass-through' video — cameras and other sensors that capture imagery of the outside world and reproduce it inside the device. They feed you a synthetic environment made to look like the real one, with Apple apps and other non-real elements floating in front of it. Apple and Meta are hoping that this virtual world will be so compelling that you won't just visit. They're hoping you'll live there.

What an example of the Totalitarian Tiptoe at work and drawing you in to total cyberspace immersion. The article highlights how research has established that widespread, long-term wearing of VR headsets could 'literally change the way we perceive the world – and each other'. Jeremy Bailenson, director of the Virtual Human Interaction Lab at Stanford University, said companies are advocating that people spend many hours every day wearing these devices. 'You've got many, many people, and they're wearing it for many, many hours ... everything magnifies at scale.' This is indeed the Totalitarian Tiptoe to rewire the brain and distort even simulated reality with another layer of simulated reality. The article says the technology can 'feed you a synthetic environment made to look like the real one' which is what the Yaldabaoth simulation is already doing to humanity. Uploading consciousness to cyberspace is a simulation within a simulation. You can see how this is a step-by-step to complete perceptual disconnection from Infinite Awareness. Where will this cyberspace be? It will be in the *Cloud*. Yaldabaoth and its control system have been working towards this all along as the original 'copy' of Prime Reality has been changed and changed to be closer to the end goal of a permanent loosh production machine called cyberspace. Observe how thoughts and emotions are impacted by interaction with cyberspace on social media with the deluge of bile that is Musk's Twitter/X. Once again, what if you were *inside* and not just looking in?

Most of the alternative media believes that digital control through AI, smart cities, 15-minute communities, and mass immigration is the endgame of human control. It *isn't*. Think back to the 'Covid' lockdowns and how cyberspace was the focus for most people as they were isolated from each other and the Internet was their only form of interaction. Compare this with *permanent* lockdowns and isolation through smart cities and 15-minute digital prisons. If people were offered the chance to escape into cyberspace from that mind-numbing boredom many would jump at it and especially if the Cloud was telling their brain to do so. Anything becomes possible once AI controls the mind at the expense of free-thought. There's the added bonus of uploading your consciousness to cyberspace in that you'll have *eternal life*. No more death. We *already* have eternal life as consciousness. No – forget that. They don't want you to go anywhere else. They want you imprisoned *here* as a permanent loosh producer.

What is this in total? It's an *anti-human* agenda. Is it really such a stretch to believe that this is the work of a *non-human* force?

CHAPTER THIRTEEN

Not so crazy, then?

*When you're the only sane person,
you look like the only insane person*

Criss Jami

To understand 'down here' we must understand 'out there'. Humanity seeks to find meaning for daily life without realising what *is* daily life and who is controlling it. None more so than the Mainstream 'Alternative' Media (MAM) which focusses on political conspiracy while our very sense of reality is an illusory mirage, or 'Maya', specifically designed to entrap perception and dictate self-identity.

Humanity is enslaved through decoding an illusion that it believes to be is real and is constantly being recycled between the Astral illusion and the human illusion. This is the scale of the conspiracy hidden from view by the MAM focus on whether Trump, Kennedy, or basket-case Biden would be US President. 'Donald will save us!' I trust that this far into the book the limitation of this perceptual bubble is obvious. Watch the magician's left hand while the trick is done with the right. Open your eyes to the big picture and you see the true significance of the little one. You can't do that the other way round. Fall for the delusion that the little picture *is* the big one and the Matrix has you. Those the MAM rightly identifies as 'manipulators', like Schwab and Gates, are only subordinate gofers to the real power in the Astral. Gates and his like were conduits for the fake 'Covid' vaccine, but the reason for it was way beyond his Cult level and involves assimilation technology far more advanced than Musk's sideshow Neuralink which is selling the concept while diverting from the real deal.

The *real* agenda

I see how so many (truly) awakening people among the general public are much further along the road than the MAM. This certainly applies to a research group in Spain called La Quinta Columna which alerted the world to the revelation that a substance known as graphene was in vials they tested of the fake 'Covid' vaccine. I have written about this before and the significance will become obvious. La Quinta Columna contacted me at the start of 2024 to ask me to discuss with them their new findings which they said confirmed what I had said about 'Covid' since the spring of 2020. They further told me their findings supported my view about the prime reason for the global electromagnetic 'Cloud' being created by 4G and 5G towers (with 6G and 7G to come) along with tens of thousands of low-orbit satellites launched ever more frequently by 'Elon Musk's' SpaceX and others. They said that even my revelations since 1996 that human society is controlled by a non-human force hidden in another dimension were confirmed by their research. I was obviously intrigued and agreed immediately to join them in a Zoom conference with simultaneous two-way translation. You can see the recording at Davidicke.com by putting 'La Quinta Columna' into the search engine.

The meeting was led by Ricardo Delgado Martin, founder and director of La Quinta Columna ('The Fifth Column' in English). His CV says that he has a degree in biostatistics from the University of Seville, and is a master in biostatistics, a postgraduate in health biology, clinical microbiology, epidemiology and clinical immunology at the European University of Miguel de Cervantes. He is a university expert in clinical genetics from the University Antonio de Nebrija and holds a certificate of scientific contribution from the University of Seville. Delgado is a postgraduate master in child psychology and master in banking and finance at the Higher Institute of Banking Techniques and Practices. He's a clever bloke. Most importantly he has an open mind prepared to go where the evidence takes him, unhindered by preconceived ideas. He revealed the following in the Zoom conference and I will add additional information as we go along:

> In general terms, we started our research with empirical evidence, proof, and we've reached conclusions that are very much in line with what you, Mr. Icke, have been saying for a long time now. The most important evidence we have come up with is that the Covid disease is acute radiation syndrome enhanced by a material that is graphene.

Graphene, or graphene oxide, is *highly* significant as we will see. I have said that the contents of the 'Covid' fake vaccine includes nanotechnology that self-replicates in the body to build *synthetic operating systems* to connect brain and body to the 'Cloud' which then becomes an AI hive mind controlling the thoughts of, eventually, all humanity. That's the plan, anyway. Synthetic self-replication has been revealed in highly magnified microscope blood images of the 'Covid'

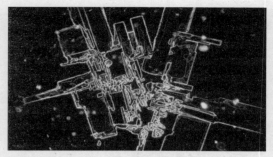

Figure 147: Self-replicating structures in the blood of the 'Covid' fake vaccinated seen under high magnification.

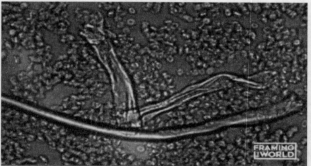

Figure 148: Nanotubes in the blood of the fake vaccinated.

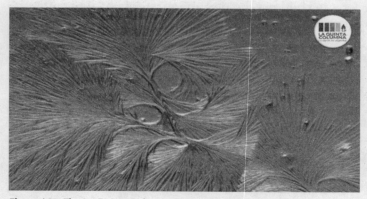

Figure 149: The La Quinta Columna team put a Pfizer fake vaccine in an incubator at body temperature to see what happened to the content when it was subjected to the temperature change. At the start the images were pretty much blank, but strictures soon began to appear.

fake vaccinated and the material is known to enter the brain (Figs 147 and 148). Fake vaccine technology with a graphene component has been designed to cross the blood-brain barrier that protects the brain from toxins and foreign substances. The Pfizer fake vaccine has stringent temperature storage requirements and must be kept unusually cold at about minus 70 degrees Celsius which is colder than winter in Antarctica. Why so cold when it would be at body temperature once administered?

Ricardo Delgado and his team placed the contents of the Pfizer fake vaccine in a reptile incubator at body temperature – 37 degrees centigrade (98.6 F) – in March 2024. The appearance was pretty much clear to start with but as the hours passed complex structures began to appear which continued to grow continuously week after week (Figs 149 and 150). The self-replication images reminded me immediately of 'Morgellons disease' which I

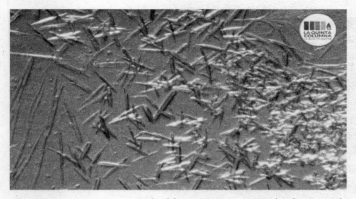

Figure 150: More structures in the fake vaccine content as the days passed in body temperature incubation.

featured in detail in *Everything You Need to Know But Have Never Been Told*. Morgellons was named in 2002 and symptoms include coloured fibres emerging through the skin, fatigue, memory loss, and crawling sensations within the body (Fig 151). The disease appeared in the same period as another phenomenon which I will highlight shortly.

Graphene oxide can re-wire the brain and connect the brain/body to

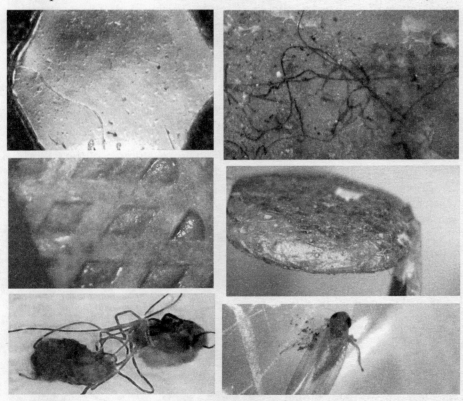

Figure 151: Self-replicating phenomena in the bodies of Morgellons sufferers that mirrors what has been found with the self-replicating structures in the fake 'Covid' vaccines.

the Cloud which is being expanded by the week thanks to Musk and SpaceX. The 'Cloud' is another layer of perception control through a technologically-generated electromagnetic field to which the human brain is being attached to make AI (Astral Yaldabaoth plasma AI) the hive mind of all humanity. The idea is to control human thought and emotional response (loosh) and block access to expanded awareness outside the hive mind. I have been warning this was the plan for the best part of 25 years. Humans are already a hive mind in a way through the conduit of the simulation field and collective programming, but there is still the opportunity to break out into expanded awareness and express individuality and uniqueness. The AI hive mind is an attempt to block that. Graphene oxide can build systems in the body to connect not only to the Cloud, but other 'graphened' humans to create another level of the hive mind. The Yaldabaoth-Archon system is terrified that humans will awaken from their induced coma to realise their plight and source of control. This is happening (with a long way to go) and through their psychologically-predictive technology they will have known that an awakening was coming. Each new stage of changing the bad copy adds more layers of control and the AI / Cloud is the latest attempt to further block simulation-entrapped consciousness from phoning home. The human awakening makes this urgent for the crazies.

Simulation – the next frontier

Electromagnetic 'smart' technology, including smart meters, are all part of delivering the Cloud to every inch of the planet along with transmission towers and Musk's satellites. The significance of graphene in the fake vaccines is that it conducts *electricity*, rewires the brain/body electrical communication system, and *amplifies* the power of the Cloud within the body to change perception through Cloud interaction. Graphene is a nano-hexagonal lattice of stupendous tensile strength, electrical conductivity, and the world's thinnest two-dimensional material (Fig 152). The shape took my mind to Saturn (Fig 153). Graphene is a 'superconductor' which means it can transmit electrical current with zero resistance or energy loss even within a strong magnetic field. Scientists have created the world's first working graphene-based semiconductor which will lead to much faster

Figure 152: The hexagonal structure of graphene.

Figure 153: Saturn was associated by Gnostics with Yaldabaoth and the Demiurge and it has a famous and permanent hexagon storm at its north pole that is four times the size of Earth. I think this is created by the broadcast frequencies emitting from Saturn's ring system. I mention this here with regard to hexagon graphene because I have shown in *Everything You Need To Know But Have Never Been Told* that shapes are the result of frequencies indicating that there could be a connection between the frequencies of Saturn and graphene.

computers and the next-stage of quantum computers. Semiconductors have specific electrical properties essential for modern electrical devices. A study published in the *International Journal of Vaccine Theory, Practice and Research* details how graphene can create self-assembling electrical conductors and how these nano-structures are tiny enough to be injected. They can interact with electrons, photons (light) and magnetism, and enter the brain in catastrophic numbers. Remember how electrons, photons, and magnetism/electromagnetism within plasma are the foundation of the simulation? The Cloud is a technologically-generated version of the simulation, a simulation within a simulation, and the plan for a simulated cyberspace 'Metaverse' is a simulation within a simulation within a simulation. Where is consciousness beyond the simulation when that lot is in place? That's the plan. The human brain is a quantum computer, the simulation is run by a quantum computer, and now a third quantum computer is being installed between them to further enslave human perception.

Everything seems to be 'smart' today and they are all connected into one grid system, the Cloud, or 'Smart Grid' as it is also known. Witness the potential for linking the brain/body to the Cloud through nanotechnology known as nanobots, nanorobots, nanoids, nanites, nanomachines, nanomites, neural *dust*, digital *dust* and smart *dust*. Think *dusty* particle plasma. The Astral control system is being replicated technologically within the realm of matter to further impose electromagnetic perceptual control. Smart dust is made up of micro-machines that can assemble and maintain sophisticated systems and build devices, machines and circuits, and act as sensors in almost limitless situations (Fig 154 overleaf). I say this is what 'dust' particles in programmed plasma are doing and what smart dust/graphene is doing in the 'Covid' fake vaccines, food, and 'chemtrails' being sprayed from the sky (more shortly). These nano-invaders are designed to harvest human energy to power themselves inside the body. They are vampiring human energy as an extension of the vampire system they serve.

'Covid vaccine' interface

Ricardo Delgado from La Quinta Columna said in the conference call they have proof that post-vaccine effects are acute radiation syndrome facilitated by graphene oxide in the shots. Highly toxic graphene oxide is detected in the body by specialised cells of the immune system; its

Figure 154: Smart dust and the human AI hive mind.

behavior is similar to a pathogen. Delgado said graphene generates an inflammatory response, mitochondrial DNA damage, and a cytokine response. A 'cytokine storm' is when the immune system is in such a panic in response to a threat that it releases inflammatory-causing molecules called cytokines. So many cytokines can be unleashed in extreme circumstances – the 'storm' – that death is caused by multi-system organ failure. Delgado is convinced that graphene at a nano scale is what they dubbed Sars-CoV-2. It was certainly not a 'virus'. I said in April 2020 that the effects of 5G could mimic the alleged symptoms of the 'Covid virus'. I did not say, as reported then and since, that 5G *was* the 'virus'. There *is no* 'virus'. My genuine comments, and the misreporting of them, led to my immediate deletion from social media and the mainstream media. Delgado said that graphene is a radio 'modulable' material. This refers to its ability 'to vary the amplitude, frequency, or phase of (a carrier wave or a light wave) for the transmission of information (as by radio)' and 'to vary the velocity of electrons in an electron beam'. The potential opens the way for wireless mind control – a wireless hive mind.

The excellent Professor Anita Baxas MD, writing on Substack, said that the technology exists to mind-control humans wirelessly without surgical chip implants. Elon Musk's Neuralink with its in-skull implants is a diversion from the real agenda. Baxas posted an article highlighting a presentation by Professor Sakhrat Khizroev from the University of Miami and a project funded by the Pentagon's DARPA developing advanced materials to interface machines and the human brain. What are these 'advanced materials'? Well, well, only *magnetic* nanoparticles that can create a wireless machine-brain interface. Magnetic? You mean like mind-wipe magnetic? You see the potential. These wireless nano-links are capable of manipulating and deleting thoughts and memories and not only making connections between brain and Cloud. They could wipe your mind and make you a blank canvas. Graphene and other content are creating an artificial brain and evolving the human body into a transhuman synthetic state. All the so-called symptoms of 'Covid' can be found with graphene poisoning and electromagnetic effects.

Graphene intelligence

Graphene is 'excited' and activated by *electromagnetic fields* and produces toxicity in ratio with the amount of radiation. The more electromagnetically powerful the Cloud becomes the more toxicity graphene releases in the body. You can see Internet videos where graphene oxide comes 'alive' and begins to move around when a smartphone is activated close by. Delgado said one of the graphene effects is to coagulate blood which leads to 'strokes, ischemia, heart attacks, things that we're seeing nowadays'. A survey of 269 embalmers across four major countries and three continents found that more than 70 percent reported strange fibrous white blood clots they were not finding before the 'Covid' jab. Delgado continued: 'Now, in order to generate artificial outbreaks ... all they have to do is excite and increase the quality of the frequencies that are emitted via telephone masts or towers.' You can add Musk's low-orbit satellites to that as well. We are talking 'optogenetics' which is defined as: 'A technique in neuroscience in which genes for light-sensitive proteins are introduced into specific types of brain cells in order to monitor and control their activity *precisely* using light signals' (my emphasis). Optogenetics can change the way the brain functions, stop the heart, trigger heart damage, and other diseases. Delgado said:

> Here we can see that graphene acts as an amplifier, converting the gigahertz into terahertz, i.e. thousands of times more within the body. More specifically, there is a particular danger now, and that is that graphene ... present in the injectables is particularly affected by 26 gigahertz.

> And as you all well know, in our country, as well as in other parts of Europe and the world, 26 gigahertz is the next frequency to be emitted [high-band 5G]. It's already been put out to tender in all these countries. And this will lead to the next pandemic that they're already cooking up to some extent.

UK government media censor and bandwidth regulator Ofcom is promoting 26 gigahertz 5G. Delgado said that besides graphene the fake vaccines deliver a series of micro and nano structures inside the body with different objectives. All was visible under optical microscopy and his team had done more than 700 observations. Artificial self-assembly patterns were instigated by exposure to electromagnetic radiation and interestingly Delgado said they had not found biological material in the fake vaccine vials or even messenger RNA. The material tested was *synthetic*, but not synthetic mRNA. He believed that governments (the Cult) had circulated 'false dissidents' to divert people into believing the story about mRNA and the spike protein as a cover for other in-body nanotechnology. The 'spike protein' allegedly in the 'vaccine' is supposed to be a response to the 'spike protein' in the 'virus'; but there is no virus and so no 'spike protein' in the 'virus'. The Wellness Company, so prolific in funding MAM 'stars', has been promoting and selling ways to remove the spike protein which many credible people say *isn't there*. See the Substack article by Professor Anita Baxas 'Gas lighting and Misdirection with the Spike Protein Fantasy'.

Graphene interface

Ricardo Delgado said graphene and its derivative, graphene oxide, is an interface, a *neural* interface. Graphene is magnetic within the body and this means that 'one can monitor, modulate, and stimulate remotely and wirelessly by means of telephone masts or towers' (and again Musk satellites). Powerful graphene magnification explains how people could make spoons and other metal objects stick to the skin where the fake vaccine was administered and later over a wider area of the body. Delgado said the wireless connection with graphene could stimulate and monitor an electrical heartbeat and a person or group could be killed remotely. Graphene oxide has 'affinity' with electrical systems, the central nervous system, neurons, and the cardiac system 'which is precisely where we're seeing most of the damage taking place'. Moderna 'Covid' fake vaccine patents in 2020 (and statements by Bill Gates) confirm the use of self-assembling nanoparticles and the controlled release of their contents once the immune system has been tricked into letting them pass. This is achieved through a substance known as 'hydrogel' and these nanoparticle 'nanorobots', developed in Israel, can be activated inside the body by electromagnetic fields (5G and the Cloud). They include synthetic pathogens which can be externally released this way. The system turns the human body into an AI antenna that can impose perceptions and project loosh on a whole new level.

Next Delgado turned to the psychological effects of graphene and other nano-tech in the fake vaccines. There are legions of reports of people changing their personality after 'Covid' jabs and a word that comes up time and again is 'vacant'. They seem 'vacant'. Brain activity is being hijacked and rewired through nano self-replication. Delgado said these technologies had the capacity to 'insert thoughts, feelings, and neuronal supervision of the whole of the world's population'. Here we have the hive mind again that I have so long warned about. 'In short, it is a neural implant by means of a liquid interface, the vaccines.' This was also why the fake 'test' swabs were inserted high up the nose to 'translocate it straight to the neurons'. Day after day children were subjected to this at school, never mind all the adults worldwide.

Other scientists and doctors around the world have analysed the vials and found to their horror a stream of ingredients included that are not listed by the makers while others that *are* mentioned cannot be found. I watched a presentation by Professor Lorena Diblasi, a biotechnologist from Argentina with a long CV of different roles involving biotechnology and chemistry. She once again highlighted how all the vials tested from many different countries, including Russia, contained the same basic ingredients along with graphene oxide and did not contain mRNA and spike protein. Diblasi also found the same content in other 'vaccines' supposedly not 'mRNA'. How can all these 'different' fake vaccines have the same foundation ingredients like graphene while *not* containing mRNA and spike protein on which they are supposed to be based? This can happen because it is globally orchestrated through the Cult for which there are no borders with the Pentagon's DARPA high on the list of mega-villains involved. The whole operation was run through the military. You can see why the European Union and countries worldwide signed secret contracts with fake vaccine makers, gave them immunity from prosecution, and claimed we couldn't know the ingredients to protect 'trade secrets'.

Professor Diblasi said they found fluorescent graphene oxide particles, *crystalline* particle structures, aluminium, and copper which is another electrical conductor. They found the AstraZeneca version which proved extreme in its consequences had lots of copper. Graphene oxide particles that produce different fluorescent colours are known as 'quantum dots', or QDs. They are human-made nanoscale crystals with unique optical and electronic properties that include transporting electrons and emitting various colours when exposed to UV light. Quantum dots are 'artificially synthesised semiconductor nanoparticles' and they have been infused into billions through the fake 'Covid' vaccination. Professor Diblasi and her colleagues and associates launched legal action against fake vaccine use in the light of their findings, but the government, courts, and medical profession did not want to know and blocked them at every turn. The same has happened all over the world. They even had to keep from laboratories what they were asked to analyse because once they knew it was the fake 'Covid' vaccine the laboratories refused to cooperate. Put 'Analysis on Covid "vaccines" performed by Professor Lorena Diblasi and Dr Marcela Sangorrín' into the Davidicke.com search engine to see the whole presentation with English subtitles.

Graphene sky

Another source of graphene in humans would appear to be chemtrails sprayed into the sky from aircraft. The atmosphere is being manipulated ever more obviously and in part perhaps to make it easier for Archon manifestation and less conducive to humans as we know them. A new human is emerging – Human 2.0. Chemtrails were first widely identified in the late 1990s and I

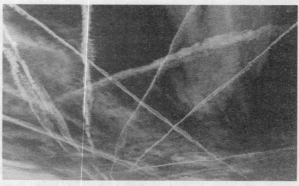

Figure 155: Chemtrails delivered by aircraft began at least in the late 1990s. Unlike temperature-driven contrails they don't disperse, but pan out to turn a blue sky white. I have watched this happen many times across the world. Their sinister content eventually falls to earth.

have seen them all over the world ever since. They are connected to climate manipulation which has been happening since at least World War II. Existence of chemtrails has been denied by the authorities even though our eyes tell a different story. We know about contrails, or condensation trails, that pour out of aircraft at high altitudes when hot gasses from the engines meet very cold air. *Chem*trails are different. They don't dissipate quickly like contrails. They stay in the atmosphere and gradually expand outwards and fall to the ground with their toxic payload. You can watch planes criss-crossing the sky back and forth until a clear blue sky becomes like a cloudy day (Fig 155). Pilots are told that their work is top secret and they are protecting the Earth from the heat of the Sun (although that seems never to be factored into the climate change hoax – only CO2, methane, and so on). More recently Bill Gates and his mob have been openly promoting geoengineering of the atmosphere as a climate change response while never revealing that it has been happening for decades. Let's make it official now, but don't tell them why.

American researcher Dane Wigington has been at the forefront of exposing chemtrails as lead researcher for GeoengineeringWatch.org and a producer of climate engineering documentaries. Wigington has worked with a scientist from an 'internationally recognised agricultural research and testing institution' and gave him the pseudonym 'Joe' to maintain anonymity. Joe explained how 'absolutely staggering' and 'unimaginable' amounts of highly-toxic aluminium, barium, and strontium (plus manganese and polymer fibres) were being deposited on the land from the sky at a nanoscale which is not tested by the authorities and they have also found *graphene*. 'The EPA [US Environmental Protection Agency] stop measuring anything that is below two microns ... and [we have gone] way below that for the purpose of the testing.' He said that nanoparticles went under the radar and 'the amount of this material is again inconceivably massive'. The correlation can be seen between the dusty particle plasma of the simulation and what is being described here. Joe said chemtrail nanoparticles are most toxic in *respiratory systems*. Their content, like aluminium, was reducing plant uptake of nutrients consumed by humans and animals and so they were also being nutrient-deprived by genetic-modification (GMO). This is the Cult destruction of the food supply that includes the targeting of farms and farmers.

I have covered all of this in other books and for the purpose of this one I will highlight graphene. Whistleblower Joe said their tests had confirmed that graphene was being used in geoengineering. Graphene oxide was found in rain and snow which helps to deliver chemtrail content to the ground and it was discovered in the nano scale of less than 450 nanometres. They didn't test beyond that scale so graphene content could have been much higher. Joe said he had no idea why its use had not been stopped when it was first discovered: 'They should put that on the side because the amount of issues that this is proving to [have is] unbelievable.' The reason graphene use was not stopped becomes obvious. Science studies have described graphene's role in *artificial* 'ice nucleation' which I read in one study paper is 'crucial for global precipitation and affects the structure, lifetime and reflectivity of clouds, thereby impacting climate'. They mean *manipulation* of the weather and climate and that is without the graphene consequences in the body when nanoparticles are absorbed. The whole web of Earthly life is being transformed in an anti-human agenda by a non-human force and graphene is of crucial importance to this. How interesting that soon after chemtrails began we had the outbreak of the 'mysterious' Morgellons disease with self-replicating synthetic fibres appearing through the skin (Fig 156). Harald Kautz-Vella is a German chemist,

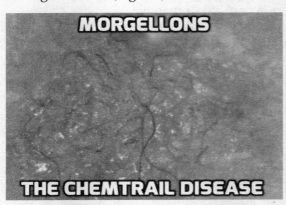

activist, and author who has studied the chemtrail-Morgellons connection for decades. He believes that Morgellons sufferers are those whose immune system is trying to eject the self-replicating nano from the body. Kautz-Vella says that Morgellons is an airborne, communicable nanotechnology that invades human tissue

Figure 156: Morgellons disease followed the start of widespread chemtrails.

and replicates into self-assembling, self-replicating, nanotubes and nanowires with sensors receiving and transmitting radio signals through 'a plasmonic antenna'. Check that against what is being found in the bodies of the fake vaccinated. A common denominator between chemtrails and fake vaccines is ... graphene oxide.

Aliens and black goo

Harald Kautz-Vella is also a well-known researcher of a substance known as 'black goo' which is actually another name for graphene. I have been aware of the black goo story for a long while and it takes the form of an oil-type liquid or a gel-like substance with some sort of intelligence. Those that specialise in the subject say there are two types. One is native to the planet and said to be positive in its effect; the other is alien black goo that is highly destructive and can transform human DNA and genetics. Kautz-Vella has described for many years how he says an alien race bombarded Earth in the distant 'past' with a swarm of meteorites containing alien black goo. The effect was to rewire the frequency nature of the planet and, with that, the instincts of the people. A dark grid system was formed by this sentient black goo which diluted empathy and compassion and instigated cruelty, greed and war. He says that this was humanity's 'fall from paradise' and ended the age of abundance, or what the ancients knew as the 'Golden Age'. Kautz-Vella is describing in his own way the new energetic system or grid – what I call the simulation. From this point humanity was connected to 'alien' consciousness and duality as an alien information field *overlaid* the original. Kautz-Vella believes this alien force was insect and spider-like and became known as Archons. I think Archon is a term that has come to encompass many non-human types. He says the alien entities introduced black magic networks and the ritual death of humans and animals to secure a 'bio-photon burst' that sustained them and could be recycled back in the form of power to aid human black magicians in their quest for control that led to wealth and domination. The Global Cult was born. Humanity became part of a system based on what he calls 'torture energy'. Nothing changes, then. You see how this syncs in theme with what I have been saying over the years. Truly-open minds may start from different points, but they tend to head in the same direction and reach similar conclusions. Interestingly, the holy Black Stone of Islam inside the Kaaba black cube in Mecca is believed by many to have come to Earth 'from Heaven' in a meteorite shower at the time of 'Adam and Eve'. Worshippers try to touch or kiss the Black Stone during their Hajj pilgrimage to Mecca that every Muslim is demanded to make at least once in their lifetime.

Black goo ticks all the boxes of what is termed graphene oxide with its super conductivity of electricity, extremely strong magnetism, and interaction with electromagnetic fields. Sentient and programmable capabilities of black goo/graphene oxide would certainly explain the self-replication of nanostructures in the bodies of the 'Covid' fake vaccinated and the means to change human genetics into a far more synthetic form. Ricardo Delgado also links the fake vaccine story to a non-human force and connects black goo to graphene. He wonders if graphene is a name used to cover up its true origin. Delgado also believes that graphene could be a food source for certain parasites and parasites for me are a form of possession. Delgado said La Quinta Columna had received a study from the late Dr Roger Lier (1935-2014) who was a surgeon extracting implants from those who said they had been abducted by 'aliens'. Delgado said the technology present in the implants was the same as those contained in the fake vaccines and other vaccines increasingly using the same technology they are *calling* mRNA which is graphene oxide and other nanotechnology if the truth be told. Delgado played a video by Lier during the conference call describing what he found in 'abductees'. Lier said that it was a very advanced nanotechnology. The devices included nano-carbon tubes, with either a single or a double wall. They could be elongated and weaved into carbon nanofibers, nano-strands, and crystalline structures, which were 'orthorhombic' (crystalline rectangular structures). Anyone who has researched the fake vaccines and microscope videos of their nanotechnology in the body will recognise exactly what Lier is talking about. He said in the video:

So here's a very advanced nanotechnology ... using the principal elements of certain materials, putting them together in such a way that you're actually broadcasting or switching what we perceive as a radio wave, which may not be a radio wave. It could be scalar technology.

Scalar waves are extremely significant for many reasons, including communication. An article describing their potential and function said: 'Scalar waves can be used for communication, energy, and other applications ... Scalar Waves (longitudinal waves) do what [other] waves cannot ...They are fast, penetrating, connected, and can broadcast magnified power ... Their potential is almost limitless ... It is even said that it is the technology that extraterrestrials use!' Ricardo Delgado said scalar technology was 5G:

And the immediate conclusion, Mr. Icke, is that we are before a mass implant of the whole of the human species. Those nanotubes that Dr Lier was talking about, those crystal orthorhombic structures, are present in the Pfizer vial.

Delgado said the carbon nanotube was graphene in the form of a tube and they had hundreds of videos with the 'orthorhombic crystal structure' visible that Dr Roger Lier mentioned. He said that according to scientific literature these correspond to *graphene plasma antenna*. They were nano transceivers based on graphene rectifier circuits and a whole series of in-body technologies. This allowed humans not only to be monitored and tracked, but also modulated (their frequency changed).

Optimal loosh supply

Delgado said that his team met with Dr Pablo Enrique Garcia Sanchez, a culture researcher and former Mexican military doctor, who has gathered thousands of ancient samples from the area of Ojuelos de Jalisco in Mexico, including skulls. 'We realized that what they're doing currently, they did in the past, quite probably with other humanoids.' He talked about trepanated skulls which is the practice of drilling a hole in the skull as a physical, mental, or spiritual treatment. He believed the holes were to insert implants. You mean like Neuralink? Delgado concluded that the human world is like a farm with 'alien' beings feeding off human emotional trauma. No wonder they thought of me when these assessments were made and conclusions formed:

> The final objective of neuromodulation is to cause the suffering of the human farm. This is an energy that they can make use of. And we suspect that these are purely energy beings. They govern and control our world and our civilisation. Probably always have done so. And they hide behind deceit and lies in all areas and disciplines, including science. Like a predator does so in order to hunt its prey.

I have been asked why Astral demons want human depopulation if they feed off our energy. The depopulation is overwhelmingly of what Lauda Leon calls 'hybrids, synthetics and backdrops'. They want the 'Primes and Reals' to survive to keep them in loosh and they don't need the backdrops to build the illusion and to pressure Primes and Reals to conform when there is a direct connection to their brain/mind and they think what AI tells them to think. Control of thought and emotion via AI and the Cloud means they become loosh machines on a scale never seen before in known 'history' (or history that we think we know). The human-Cloud connection made possible by Musk is essential to the 'Fourth Industrial Revolution' promoted by Klaus Schwab's World Economic Forum. Delgado said of the non-human force that the Cloud-human connection 'will allow them to collect bio-energies on a mass and industrial scale'. He and his team suspected that the nature of these non-human beings was purely energetic and according to their research the entities need two types of energy. These were geo-energies, which are dense magnetic energies from the terrestrial point of view, and bio-energies, which are the energies emitted by human beings 'in particular when they are suffering'.

Current events would lead to a change in the exploitation of the human farm by means of the 'terraformation' ('Earth-shaping') of our reality through the deliberate modification of the atmosphere, temperature, surface topography, or ecology. Look around, people. It's happening. We are also seeing the ever-quickening transformation towards '15-minute cities' in which people would be corralled in areas small enough to access 'everything you need' within a 15-minute walk or cycle ride. These are officially justified by the monumental hoax of human-caused climate change which is not happening. Smart neighbourhoods are already being prepared for and introduced. One that's been purpose-built in Tempe, Arizona, part of the sprawl around Phoenix, is appropriately named 'Culdesac'. Vehicles are banned. The residents seem to have no idea what this living concept means with a network of 24/7 surveillance and data harvesting technologies which as one article said would track 'what they eat and drink; where they go; what they buy; who they meet; what they think and feel; their opinions and habits; their health and vaccination status.' The 15-minute communities are planned to be units in 'smart cities' in which everything is controlled and decided by AI (whoever controls AI). Delgado said:

> Their habitat units hope to be 15-minute smart cities, where the geo-energies will be replaced by artificial microwave technologies. That will provide greater density to the planet, and the bio-energies will be guaranteed by the stabled population. And this is why they want you to stay at home, lockdowns, climatic lockdowns, because of a social emergency, or smart cities.
>
> And it's an optimal industrial yield of bio-neuromass, and it's quite possible that they are preparing the planet to be able to occupy it and have its herd stabled to have energy at their disposal.

How long I have warned about this technological trawling of human energy and how the planet is being prepared for 'alien' occupation.

The 'Covid' coup

Dr Astrid Stuckelberger was another participant in the La Quinta Columna video conference. Stuckelberger was a scientist, researcher, and teacher for 25 years with the Faculty of Medicine at the University of Geneva and Lausanne in Switzerland. She worked with the World Health Organization (WHO) between 2009 and 2013 on International Health Regulation (IHR) and public health emergency management. She has written twelve books and nearly 200 scientific articles and policy papers for the UN, EU and governments. I had quite a surreal experience to hear support from science-based people like Stuckelberger and Delgado after what was then 34 years of walking this trail with all the ridicule and dismissal for my 'far out' views. Stuckelberger had been censored at a 2023 'Pandemic Strategies: Lessons and Consequences' conference in Stockholm, Sweden, during a presentation in which she was exposing the reality of graphene oxide in the fake vaccines. She was stopped and her microphone cut off when she was about to reveal the discoveries of nanotechnology and graphene oxide in the vials. They really don't want the public to know this crucial information.

Stuckelberger said in our conference meeting that it was very clear that 'Covid' was a coup d'état on the whole world and she saw the correlation with the discovery of nanotech in the fake vaccine with WHO emergency management and body-manipulation through gene editing: 'I think it's a very important issue because those people are obsessed with gene editing.' She asked why the WHO wants to do gene editing and why the CRISPR-Cas9 genetic engineering technique that allows for precise modification of living organism genomes won the Nobel Prize in 2020 when it is 'ethically going to break humanity'. She said there is a will to keep on hybridising, keep on changing humanity the way they want, and go into the genome to change 'the book of life, the code of life, the God code'. People like Musk and Peter Thiel are centre stage in this 'new human' story along with a list of other billionaires. As an aside, Israeli Mossad operative Jeffrey Epstein was among many Cult insiders with a 'fixation' on genetic manipulation and transhumanism and he was on the board of the Harvard Mind Brain Behavior Committee. Many of his contacts in science were in this field and 'he' (his masters through him) provided a lot of funding.

Stuckelberger said that with CRISPR-Cas9 they had reached a bridge 'because you can go in the book of the gene, take off the pages, rewrite the script, and you can become an artificial or a hybrid'. There was an obsession to secure genome data of the whole world to the extent where you think these people must *not be human*. They knew how different humans are and they were going to target us electromagnetically using auditory effects in the brain which they could scan with a drone. 'I've seen them in front of my house. They were scanning like everybody who got the shot. They all have a kind of RFID [Radio-frequency identification] and they are like living antennas.' They were no longer controlled by the spirit of the human genome and there was a lot of research about how you can code any disease you want:

Every molecule has a wave, every wave has a frequency, and you can create a wave with a frequency. You can create a disease and I made a report for judges of France on that, that you can actually induce any disease if the structure, like Roger Lier is saying, that corresponds to the receptor is good enough. They can really even make a riot in the street and do zombies.

This is a point I have made in several books. Long ago they worked out the frequencies that relate to states of mind/emotion and the actions that follow. Play those frequencies across an individual or community and you get the responses they represent, be that a riot, violence against people, or subservience. The Cloud gives them the potential to do this to the global population and even more powerfully with in-body antenna and amplification thanks to the 'Covid' jab. To think that Elon 'low-orbit satellite' Musk is a MAM God. It really is pathetic. I said in early 2020 that the whole 'Covid' hoax 'virus' was a plan to justify mass-vaccination of the population worldwide. Ricardo Delgado reached the same conclusion. He said in another interview that we are told everything that has happened since 2020 is a consequence of a non-existent coronavirus. We had a manufactured pandemic because none of this was true. The fake vaccine with the insertion of a chemical compound, with radio-modulating capacity that becomes a pathogen inside the body, meant that we were witnessing 'a premeditated, conscious act and, of course, a genocide, and not at all a pandemic'. They could know with absolute precision when a 'Covid' wave appeared and what they call variants because they were making it up. The lies were only a justification for the deaths and disease 'caused with what they call vaccines, which logically is not a vaccine at all'.

Polluting the field

I have written over the years about the connection between technology impacts on the Earth's electromagnetic field and the outbreak of disease. Exposure to intense electromagnetic fields (EMF) was known way back to cause 'flu-like' symptoms. I highlighted in my 'Covid' exposure book, *The Answer*, the work of scientist and journalist, Arthur Firstenberg, author of *The Invisible Rainbow: A History of Electricity and Life*. He wrote in 2018, before the 'Covid' hoax, that every time we have dramatically changed the properties of the Earth's magnetic field, dramatic effects on health have followed. Every influenza epidemic since electricity was introduced had coincided with a new and more powerful level of electromagnetic radiation. Firstenberg cites the 1918 'Spanish flu' which was said to have infected an estimated 500 million people worldwide and killed at least tens of millions. Mass vaccination preceded this outbreak at the end of the First World War. Austrian molecular biology researcher, Jaroslav Belsky, said:

An orgy of vaccination took place for the soldiers of the war. In 1918 up to 36

vaccinations took place with no rules at all. It happened just before the
Spanish Flu appeared in different places at the same time. Medical historians
confirm today that it was a vaccination disaster.

There is also a credible connection to electromagnetism. Firstenberg
said that 'Spanish flu' began at military naval bases in America and
Europe that were the first to install high-intensity radar. The original 400
cases of 'Spanish flu' were at the Naval Radio School in Cambridge,
Massachusetts. Common symptoms of this 'flu' were, bizarrely,
nosebleeds, internal bleeding in the brain and lungs, and problems with
blood coagulation. This is not 'flu'. They are effects that can result from
electromagnetism impacting on the human electromagnetic organising
field, or auric mind. Doctors were quoted as saying they had yet to
receive a case report which didn't include prolonged blood coagulation.
Arthur Firstenberg explains how 'Spanish' flu followed the locations
and patterns of radar introduction worldwide when global travel was a
fraction of what it is today. He said that 'Asian flu' arrived in 1956/57
when the world was bathed in new and powerful radar waves; 'Hong
Kong' flu swept across the world in 1968 only months after the first
radiation-emitting satellite system was activated. Internal haemorrhage
was again a factor. 'Covid' is supposed to have begun in Wuhan, capital
of China's Hubei province, in 2019. Wuhan was China's first 5G 'smart
city' with 5G antennae installed in massive numbers from October 2019.
Vodafone Italy made Milan an 'extensive 5G testbed' working in concert
with Italy's Ministry of Economic Development. Milan is in the
Lombardy region which was the centre of the Italian 'Covid' outbreak
and both Lombardy and Wuhan were subject to mass vaccination
programmes before the 'pandemic'. Did the 'vaccines' connect people to
5G transmissions and amplify them?
Spanish biologist Bartomeu Payeras Cifre, a specialist in
microbiology at the University of Barcelona, reported a preliminary
study in April 2020 about connections between 'Covid' and 5G. He did
not allege a cause and effect. He said that it did reveal how major 'virus'
countries and regions corresponded with 5G installation and that 'a
failure to act in the face of the findings of this study could be considered
negligent at the very least and very possibly criminal'. A study of
American states by Dr Magda Havas, Associate Professor of
Environmental and Resource Studies at Trent University in Ontario,
Canada, found a similar correlation. Billions were locked down and
anything other than 'essential work' that involved travel was banned.
5G towers that appeared all over the UK during lockdown were
considered 'essential work'. Now Musk and his fellow tech billionaires
are firing 5G at us from space. I am not saying and never have that
'Covid' can be totally explained by 5G. I said that 5G electromagnetic

fields could produce the flu-like symptoms attributed to 'Covid'. Manipulation of death certificates and a test not testing for the 'virus' must be added to the mix along with mass murder using drugs including Midazolam and Remdesivir. What's clear is that when a significant change happens in the Earth's electromagnetic field there is a 'physical' response until the body synchronises with the new energetic environment. Some die and others energetically recalibrate. Ricardo Delgado said:

> When there is a new alteration of the environment some survive, resist, and others die as they do in nature except this does not correspond to nature; it is a new artificial alteration of the environment. There isn't within the concept of epigenetics [the body responding to environmental change] an adaptation through the rapid modulation of genes.
>
> What is done precisely is to go to the place to what we erroneously know as virus or coronavirus which is only a re-adaptation of our DNA by a protein synthesis when it is being subjected or irradiated in this case with a new wavelength that is not of the normal fabric, the natural solar one for example.

Remember what I wrote earlier about the body's electromagnetic self-organising field which controls our biological processes. If the field changes, the body must change; it hardly takes a genius to see that the body field must be disrupted when new electromagnetic frequencies are artificially introduced. It doesn't take a genius to see it. It takes an idiot *not* to see it. Unfortunately, the gofer level of authority abounds with idiots and non-player characters. Staggeringly, shockingly, breathtakingly, I still see 'experts', and those among the public masses who believe 'experts', that the millions of times increase in technological radiation in the atmosphere since I was growing up in the 1950s is having no effect on electrical/electromagnetic humans. This is a form of insanity. Arthur Firstenberg highlights the 'millions of frequencies and pulsations that confuse our cells and organs, and dim our nervous systems, be we humans, elephants, birds, insects, fish or flowering plants':

> The pulsations pollute the Earth beneath our feet, surround us in the air through which we fly, course through the oceans in which we swim, flow through our veins and our meridians, and enter us through our leaves and our roots. The planetary transformer that used to gentle the solar wind now agitates; inflames.

Rewiring reality

Firstenberg emphasises that the whole ecosystem is being dismantled by the technological frequencies emitting from towers, wires, and Musk's low-orbit satellites. Flies had disappeared from windshields and hanging clothes and they no longer flew through open windows. These were once all part of everyday life for people of my age. He says that other species that ate the flies were going as well – ducks, frogs, fish, eels, and predatory insects. *The Guardian* newspaper asked in a 2024 article if the ecosystem of the UK's largest lake, Lough Neagh in Northern Ireland, had collapsed. Firstenberg asks the bigger question: Has the ecosystem of the entire Earth collapsed? That appears to be the case as an electrical system of life on Earth is bombarded by alien frequencies. Is this not still more confirmation that this is being done by a force that is anti-human, anti-life as we know it? Meanwhile, one of the most obvious villains in this, Elon Musk, is worshipped by the 'alternative' MAM.

Powerful electromagnetic fields can increase the potency of toxins in the body, deplete nutrients and calcium, and seriously weaken the immune system. See also the effect on *oxygen* of 5G at a particular wavelength detailed in *Everything You Need To Know But Have Never Been Told*. The UK's Barrie Trower has quite a microwave CV. He has a degree in physics specialising in microwaves; trained at the Government's Microwave Warfare Establishment in the 1960s; worked with the Royal Navy and British Secret Service as an expert in microwave weapons; debriefed spies trained in microwave warfare in the 1970s; and used microwaves in his time with an underwater bomb disposal unit. He has been warning for years about the effects of the Cloud in all its forms and he said before 'Covid' that all microwaves reduce the immune systems of living organisms, but not bacteria which thrive and multiply when microwaved. The immune system is weakened and bacteria are strengthened. Jolly good, no problem.

DNA is a receiver-transmitter and any change can recalibrate the frequencies at which it receives and transmits. Instead of connecting with the expanded reality you can change the frequency resonance to connect with the Cloud and this is what they're doing. Professor Sucharit Bhakdi, a former Chair of Medical Microbiology at the University of Mainz in Germany, has been a vocal critic of both the fake 'pandemic' and the fraudulent vaccines. He alerted the public in March 2024 to studies confirming that the 'vaccines' are changing DNA. Bhakdi said scientists had established that the 'vaccine' contents were being absorbed by cells and changing their nature: 'The uptake of a foreign chromosome into your cell equates with nothing less than genetic modification.' He said the integration of foreign DNA could have far-reaching implications for cellular function and also possibly explain a global surge in tumours and genetic disorders. The severity of the findings could not be overstated. Put all the pieces together and genetic modification (frequency modification) and graphene (frequency modification) tell you what the jabs are really about. They have many others waiting to be introduced to accelerate this effect.

Disease X

This brings us to 'Disease X' – X again – which the Cult-serving World Health Organization (WHO), World Economic Forum (WEF), and Bill Gates have been pushing relentlessly. They demand that we concede global control of all national responses in a 'future pandemic' to the Rockefeller-created-and-owned WHO through a national sovereignty-destroying 'treaty'. The excuse is that 'Disease X' is coming and we must be prepared. How do they know? For the same reason they knew a 'Covid pandemic' was coming when Gates, the WHO, and WEF ran the 'simulation' of a coronavirus pandemic in the last weeks of 2019 ('Event 201') just before they hoaxed exactly what they were simulating. The WHO treaty and other changes to global health regulations would mean that when the mega-crook Tedros, the gofer official head of the WHO, declares a pandemic he and his masters are immediately handed control of how the world responds. He does not have to prove there's a pandemic as we saw with 'Covid'. He just has to declare it. If you thought 'Covid' impositions were fascist you have seen nothing yet compared with when the Disease X 'pandemic' is triggered. So what is this Disease X?

We are now in a whole new ball game. We had in the 'past' the direct impact of electromagnetic fields (technology) on electromagnetic fields (the body). Now we have *at least* those fake vaccinated having graphene inside them that *amplifies* the effect of electromagnetic fields on the body and acts as a receiver-transmitter interacting with the Cloud. This can apply to others if you believe credible claims about transferring vial material from the fake-vaccinated to the non-vaccinated through blood transfusions, transplants, sexual contact, and 'shedding' where the non-vaccinated can be contaminated with graphene and other fake-vaccine substances through close connection. With each new low-orbit satellite the MAM God and others constantly launch, and with each new 5G tower, the Cloud becomes more powerful and widespread. In the pipeline is 6G and 7G.

The consequences mean that frequency tweaks in the Cloud connecting with the body graphene receivers and amplifiers can trigger any disease response they choose. This is how far we have now allowed them to go with the combination of arrogance and ignorance to which much of humanity has succumbed. This will be Disease X and it will be covered by claiming that it's from another source, a 'virus' or something. They also have the deadly fake 'Covid' vaccine killing people which can be blamed on another cause and is there a frequency 'switch' that can trigger mass fatal effects? Once Disease X is underway with a far greater impact than 'Covid' they plan to impose fascism on a scale that surpasses even 'Covid' with the Cult owned-and-created World Health Organization telling countries across the world what they must do. That's the plan anyway, which has been unfolding before our eyes decade after decade and aeon after aeon as we perceive 'time'.

'Covid' history is being rewritten in preparation for the next pandemic hoax just as those who *bought* the 'Covid' hoax are being positioned centre stage in the MAM to marginalise those pesky people who called it out at the time. Two apparently opposing sides are being manipulated to the same end while being sold as the 'bad guys' and 'good guys'. Gates-owned, Rockefeller-owned, Cult-owned genetic liar Tedros at the WHO set the scene for the 'bad guys' by claiming that they didn't tell governments what to do during 'Covid'. Who *me*, guv? Not guilty, guv. We never ran the show, never lied about the fake virus, and never told people the fake vaccine was safe and effective. You must be confusing us with someone else. Anita Baxas wrote on Substack that she was seeing the same in the alternative health arena that was happening with the takeover of the MAM. She said the here-and-no-further theme continued with 'New Health' refusing to highlight nano circuits, graphene, quantum dots, and hydrogels in the fake 'Covid' vaccine while promoting the 'spike protein' which vial analysis could not find. New Health is really Old Health repackaged just as New Media is really Old Media repackaged.

To say that it's time to wake up from the trance is the understatement of all eternity.

CHAPTER FOURTEEN

Making it happen

Until you realise how easy it is for your mind to be manipulated, you remain the puppet of someone else's game

Evita Ochel

We are in the midst of Astral demons seeking even greater levels of human control by adding new simulations within the simulation. The Cloud is the first one and the uploading of consciousnesness to cyberspace is following on behind.

You will have seen the emerging theme of billionaires seeking to live forever in human form and investing big money to do so. What if the real goal behind this is to develop an AI controlled synthetic human form specifically to entrap consciousness for eternity in a perceptual prison? 'We've found a way that you can live forever! What a breakthrough!' They won't tell us that we already live forever as consciousness able to explore infinity. They would rather we live forever in their synthetic prison cell as their permanent loosh supply. I know that really does sound off with the fairies. But hold your fire and don't rule it out. These people are both evil and insane. Meanwhile, their Cloud-control is the issue currently at hand. To justify their dystopia they have to invent excuses for its introduction that will satisfy enough people before so much AI control is in place that it doesn't matter what the population think. By then they will think what AI tells them to think.

Chaos theory

Chaos is a currency of control and manipulation. Ordo Ab Chao, or 'Order out of Chaos', is the motto of the 33rd degree of Freemasonry's Scottish Rite. Create the chaos and impose order, your new order, out of the chaos. I coined the term 'Problem-Reaction-Solution', or P-R-S, in the 1990s to describe this technique in the simplest of terms. You covertly create a *problem*; tell the people your version of the problem and who or what is to blame; secure the public *reaction* of 'do something'; and then offer the *solution* to the problem that you have covertly created. The phrase has become widely used in the alternative media and there is another version that I call NO-Problem-Reaction-Solution in which you don't even need a real problem, only the *perception* of one. 'Covid', 'human-caused climate change', and 'weapons of mass destruction in Iraq in 2003, are textbook examples of the NO-problem technique. A belief that these problems are or were real led to unquestioning acceptance of fascism, ongoing societal transformation, and the invasion of Iraq that led to millions of deaths and catastrophe in the Middle East. Each of these nightmares was coldly planned and P-R-S made them possible. P-R-S requires, by definition, public naivety and childlike obedience and we have *that* in enormous supply.

Another manipulation technique that interplays with P-R-S is to give the population respites between extreme emotional traumas like 'Covid'. The respite is to allow a pull-back from the extreme into a brief period of temporary perceived equilibrium in which people breathe and say 'I'm glad that's over'. Just when they are getting a little more comfortable you hit them with another blow. People can eventually come to terms with an ongoing extreme and rearrange their lives to encompass it. The real spirit breaker is when they think it's over and they begin to breathe and relax a bit only for something else to crash in. Such emotional rollercoasters are calculated for their effect. I remember during the long troubles and violence in Northern Ireland there were intermittent periods of 'hope' when talks appeared to be advancing. Then they would break down and it would all kick off again. Break people's spirit this way, targeting their 'hope', and you can break *them*.

'We're all going to die!'

The major and long-term excuse for global dystopia is human-caused climate change, a lie which began life as 'global warming' until temperatures stopped rising and they had to change tack. Proper weather researchers and meteorologists (the minority) have shown that extreme weather events have not become more severe. The opposite is the case. It's another mind game. Storms are now given names in Britain like hurricanes in America to make them sound more severe and scary. I have lived long enough to have seen it all before when a storm was just a storm and not a Storm Otto, Noa, Antoni, or Betty. *Betty*? Sorry, I can't be concerned about a storm called Betty. 'I have just been out to see Betty. Her wind is a bit strong, but it's not too bad. She's taking the bicarb I gave her.' We once had BBC weather forecasts with high temperatures on a green country map background. Now we have the same temperatures, or lower ones, on a screaming *red* background. 'We're all going to *die!*' I have exposed in many books the extent of weather control available to the Cult and its assets going back *at least* to the 1940s. A US Air Force paper from 1996 describes how they could 'own the weather' by 2025 and they have achieved that ahead of schedule with the ability to induce wind and rain storms, steer the jet stream that controls weather patterns, and steer and increase the power of hurricanes. See *Everything You Need To Know But Have Never Been Told* for the detail. My long contention about weather manipulation was confirmed with record rainstorms and floods following the use of cloud-seeding technology in Dubai in April 2024. They can activate their technology and claim the subsequent consequences as proof of climate change caused by humans who are always to blame with a non-human force in the background selling that story. Blaming humans for everything is like Astral 'guides' reciting your karma and how much you have to learn, you *naughty* little boys and girls.

Carbon dioxide (CO_2), the gas of life, has been turned into a nasty pollutant purely through perceptual manipulation and repetition. We would all be dead without it in the absence of any food supply. We have Bill Gates-funded technology being installed to suck CO_2 out of the atmosphere (supported by Musk's $100 million carbon removal competition with XPRIZE). Now *that* is anti-human. The Earth has become *greener* since CO_2 began to rise during the industrial era. Plants absorb carbon dioxide from the atmosphere and the more CO_2 we have the better and more abundantly they grow. Why do people think that *extra* CO_2 is added by growers to greenhouses? Another thing – an increase in temperature does NOT follow an increase in CO_2. It's the *other way round* which reveals the scale of propaganda. Most CO_2 is held in the ocean and whether carbon dioxide is absorbed or released from the atmosphere depends on the temperature of the ocean. CO_2 is absorbed in periods of ocean cooling and released into the atmosphere when ocean temperatures rise. Therefore, against all the lies and propaganda, rising temperatures are the *cause* of increased CO_2 and not vice versa. Well into the 90 percents of 'greenhouse gases' (which stop heat escaping into space) are water vapour and clouds. Only 0.117 percent is carbon dioxide and most of that is not caused by human activity (Fig 157 overleaf).

The planet would be so cold without the temperature-supporting greenhouse effect that it could not sustain human life. Average surface temperatures would be an estimated *minus* 18 degrees Celsius. The body's core temperature is around 37 degrees Celsius. Hypothermia kicks in at 35 degrees or below which affects brain and heart function. Amnesia begins at 33 degrees and at 28 degrees you would start to lose consciousness. At 21 degrees you would be meeting the elders for a life review. Climate change has always happened in cycles and I know of no one denying that. The key to the scam is *human-caused* climate change which is utter baloney. Everything depends upon this myth for the Cult to justify its dystopia. The Cult-created Club of Rome was established in 1968 to specifically exploit climate concerns to this end. Italian industrialist Aurelio Peccei, co-founder of the Club of Rome, said:

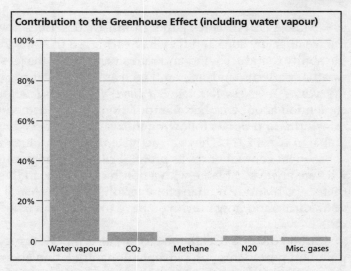

The common enemy of humanity is man. In searching for a new enemy to unite us, we came up with the idea that pollution, the threat of global warming, water shortages, famine and the like would fit the bill ... The real enemy then is humanity itself.

Figure 157: These are the so-called 'greenhouse gases'. By far the biggest is water vapour in all its forms and alongside that is CO2 which is a fraction by comparison and only part of this is human-generated.

It's the same old Astral demon story. Once we buy this lie humans can be condemned as dangerous simply for being alive and breathing out carbon dioxide. There are just too many people breathing. 'We're all going to die if we don't depopulate.' In fact, we have the perfect symbiotic relationship with 'nature' in that we breathe in oxygen and breathe out CO2 while 'nature' absorbs CO2 and generates oxygen. The Club of Rome was demanding depopulation from the start. Its first report, *The Limits to Growth* in 1972, highlighted the problem of too many people. Club member Howard T. Odum, a marine biologist at the University of Florida, said in 1980: 'It is necessary that the United States cut its population by two-thirds within the next 50 years.' An aggressive program of population control involving sterilisation, contraception, and abortion was recommended within months by the US President-connected Council on Environmental Quality. The theme has continued ever since. Is this depopulation aimed at what Lauda Leon calls AI 'backdrop people' which are no longer necessary once 'Primes and Reals' are connected to AI and their perceptions secured ongoing? I don't say that's the case. I merely pose the question in the light of what she said. *Limits to Growth* called for the establishment of a world authority to do what was necessary to save us and this was right on script for the eventual establishment of a world government. 'The Club of Rome also will encourage the creation of a world forum where statesmen, policy-makers, and scientists can discuss the dangers and hopes for the future global system without the constraints of formal intergovernmental negotiation.' An important pillar of the Cult, Gates, WEF, climate agenda is to impose a carbon tax that would fine anyone breaching their allocated limit. This would open another front for human control, limitation of choice, and restriction of movement. Elon Musk has called for a carbon tax many times over the years and quoted 'human-caused climate change' – a blatant hoax – as the justification.

UN problem *and* solution

I have demolished the human caused climate change hoax in my books including *Everything You Need To Know But Have Never Been Told*. I won't repeat it all again here. Instead I'll focus on *why* the hoax has been perpetrated. A big clue comes with the fact that the Cult-created United Nations drives this deceit through its Intergovernmental Panel on Climate Change (IPCC) which has turned lying and misrepresentation into a work of art. At the same time the UN exploits the lies of its IPCC to impose its dystopian and society-transforming Agenda 21 (21st century) and decade by decade 'interims' such as Agenda 2030. These UN-orchestrated plans demand the centralised control of *everything*. The UN creates the *illusion* of the problem and then offers the solution. Talk about keeping it all in-house. Scan major changes in human society worldwide and you see that 'climate change' is the motivating excuse even though most of the population doesn't believe in it. Who cares what the people believe? They get what we give them. 'Covid' lockdowns were a precursor, just a rehearsal for constantly-repeating, ultimately permanent, climate lockdowns. Cult-owned Tedros at the UN World Health Organization seeks at every opportunity to connect 'climate change' to 'health' for this reason. The climate lie is testament to the reality described by Nazi propaganda expert Joseph Goebbels: 'Make the lie big, make it simple, keep saying it, and eventually they will believe it.' Or if they don't, we'll do it anyway. Making the lie *big* is essential to elicit this response: 'Yes, they lie, but they would never lie *that* much.' Telling you that human life is in imminent danger of being destroyed by something that is not happening as an excuse to transform the world into a global dystopia? *Never! They wouldn't do that!* But that is exactly what is going on.

The United Nations is also a major driver of 15-minute cities and all-encompassing surveillance. The term '15-minute city' was coined by Carlos Moreno, a French- Colombian professor at Sorbonne University in Paris who has specialised in computerisation and robots. He has been involved in many governmental committees and public service activities. Moreno launched the Global Observatory of Sustainable Proximities in 2022 and his 15-Minute City plan was recommended the same year by the UN Habitat's World Cities Report. Moreno presented his idea in a TEDx talk which is available in 18 languages. The 15-minute policy has been widely promoted for years by the World Economic Forum, the Cult-front headed by the lunatic Schwab. The infrastucture is being installed all around us in other guises. We have cameras in situ all over cities like London to police vehicle emissions zones, 20 mile-an-hour speed limits, and low-traffic neighbourhoods (LTNs). All are planned to police 15-minute communities. China is the blueprint for this. We are watching the Chinese system of AI real-time technological control introduced step-by-step across Western cities and further afeild globally.

The plan is, as always, being imposed incrementally by the technqiue that I long ago called the Totalitarian Tiptoe. Move too fast and you alert people by the scale of change. You do it step by step and the more control you secure the quicker you can proceed. Each step is promoted as in and of itself and not part of the same sequence to a partcular end. You say cameras are to police low-emision zones; for speed checking; to deter crime; to protect your home from robbery. Insiders know they are all part of a gathering unified network of total survellience. Does anyone really believe that London Mayor Sadiq Khan doesn't know that as he advances this agenda with his vehicle emissions numberplate cameras? Footage from Amazon's Ring doorbell camera system (supposedly to stop break-ins and monitor visitors from afar) has already been handed to police for other reasons and can be accessed with a search warrant. The university city of Oxford, 60 miles north of London, announced plans to reduce traffic on certain through-roads and offered residents permits for a specific number of car journeys on these roads with fines imposed for breaching the limit. The move was accompanied by plans to create local amenities and community centres as part of a 15-minute city plan. Mainstream media stories reported this as a 'separate' plan from the car journey restrictions. It was nothing of the kind. They are building the AI control system bit-by-bit and telling you that the parts are not connected. Restrictions begin with them claiming there is no agenda to confine you to a 15-minute area. 'Tiptoes' then start and intensify restrictions until the always-planned confinement is what happens. How is this being coordinated across the world unless there is a coordinating global network?

Drive no more

The war on driving is another aspect of this with vehicle ownership impossible for increasing numbers amid the soaring cost of vehicles, insurance, and fines for emission zone violations of £12.50 a day in London for just driving away from your home. Cult imposition of electric vehicles is being wound up through government legislation and targets to stop production of petrol and diesel vehicles, None of this is about 'saving the planet' and nor are they moving us from fossil fuel to electric when 'electric' is still produced by fossil fuels. The idea is to deny all but the few from having a vehicle at all. Electric cars are incredibly expensive and there are not the resources (mined by African kids in appalling health-destroying conditions) to produce all the batteries which have to be regularly replaced. An environmental nightmare is being created, so ironically, in how to dispose of them. Electric vehicles are planned for only the few to restrict travel to controllable public transport when you can travel at all. Any access to a vehicle would be through autonomous taxis and this is the business model that Uber has been working towards since the company began. Oh, yes. Who announced that Tesla will launch an autonomous taxi in 2024? *Elon Musk.*

Petrol and diesel vehicles are being replaced for one reason: They cannot be computer controlled. They must be electric for that to happen. You can drive fossil fuel cars pretty much wherever you like; with

Figure 158: 'Smart' vehicles with drivers bathed in 5G and whatever 'G' follows. 'Where are you going?' I don't know – I'll ask the computer.

autonomous cars you will be restricted to where the programmed computer will take you and that won't be very far (Fig 158). The countryside will be denied you (see my earlier books and the maps of these restrictions that have long existed). Front of house promotion of electric autonomous vehicles is again courtesy of MAM God Elon Musk at Tesla. Many experiments have been done to show that even today's increasingly AI vehicles can be hijacked from afar by hacking into the computer system and dictating where the vehicle is driven. You want a dissident to go out of control and over a cliff? Autonomous cars are a great example of when technology crosses the line. I am not against technology in totality. The question is does it serve humanity or does humanity serve *it*. Petrol and diesel vehicles give you freedom of movement and allow you to go where you choose. That's fine. Humans benefit. Autonomous vehicles take that freedom away and cross the line from serve into servile.

Freedom no more

Smart cities are AI cities. Artificial intelligence would control your entire life. The pre-fix 'smart' is everywhere today with smart televisions, smart meters, smart cards, smart cars, smart driving, smart pills, smart patches, smart watches, smart skin, smart borders, smart pavements, smart motorways, smart streets, smart cities, smart communities, smart environments, smart growth, smart planet, smart dust. The list goes on getting longer. Smart televisions are keeping you under surveillance including what you say in their presence; smart meters are another means of electromagnetic field monitoring that can externally dictate your energy use; smart streets include lamp standards that can listen to conversations through microphones and bark out orders the other way (Fig 159). If you think this is too sci-fi dystopian to be true then check it out. I know people who have simply *thought* about something and

seconds or minutes later advertisements appear on their smartphone feed for what they were thinking about. These have included horse riding lessons, buying toilet rolls, and wiring in the house. People have no

Figure 159: 'Smart' street lamps are part of the smart city connecting web of AI control and surveillance.

idea how far even current technology can really go. The world we are fast moving into can hardly be imagined. The young have been programmed to accept this since birth with a focus on technology way beyond any previous generations. Smart cities are planned to control every facet of your life through AI and if you are a dissident of the system you will be excluded from mainstream AI society. We saw this theme with those excluded from mainstream activity when they refused the fake 'Covid' vaccine or the useless and ludicrous masks. Many even lost their jobs and livelihoods.

Supermarkets are installing technology that restricts access only to those with smartphone QR codes, Amazon has a hand-scanning payment service and you can now sign up by just taking a picture of your hand and uploading it to Amazon's servers. Products are planned to be locked away behind glass screens that will only open if you have the right code (or hand). Some stores are already doing this with alcohol. Wait till they do the same with food. If you are a dissident it won't matter if you have a phone – the code won't work. Human checkout staff replaced with do-it-yourself technology is this Tiptoe happening and it ends with an inability to buy anything unless you have the right code. To get these codes you will need to conform and not dissent. We are back with the Chinese social credit system where you get credits for conforming and have them taken away for making other choices. The idea is manipulate behaviour to make you servile. We see the same techniques used with rats in a laboratory when they are rewarded for doing what the lab crazies demand and an electric shock is delivered when they don't. Rats become compliant and docile. Ukrainians have been manipulated by their Cult-owned Zelensky government to tie their financial assets to their smartphones through a 'State-In-Smartphone' app. Those who seek to avoid conscription into the Cult-imposed war with Russia can have their assets seized. Elon Musk's planned 'Everything app' with Twitter/X would offer a one-stop-shop for centralised control with banking, buying, virtual reality, posting history, and social credit score (produced from posting and behaviour analysis) all available in one place.

Manufactured hunger

The population would be dependent for everything on the Cult-owned, Archon-owned, state for all the basic survival necessities of warmth, water, and food. Cult-imposed Agenda 2030 UN documents demand all of these things along with control of 'education', business, movement, 'sustainable cities' (smart cities), and every aspect of 'life'. Worldwide attacks on farmers and farming have prompted mass protests in Europe. This is the agenda on public display as food production is curtailed and food growing land confiscated not least to open the way for mega smart cities where everyone is planned to be forced to live. One of the excuses is farming use of nitrogen fertiliser as a cause of 'climate change'. Dr Patrick Moore, a co-founder of Greenpeace who left the organisation because of its devious manipulation of environmental reality, warned of the genocidal consequences of the war on farmers:

> They will cause ruination the likes of which the Earth has never seen, because there are eight billion of us, and four billion [are] depend on nitrogen fertiliser, which they now say is bad, because it's a greenhouse gas or whatever … it's all completely phoney and so is the campaign against CO2.

Moore is a sane voice amid the climate madness with 'climate activists' so totally mind controlled that they campaign for their own demise and that of their children while believing they are saving themselves and their children from climate catastrophe. That's some serious insanity. You see how deep perception manipulation can go. At the same time Cult multi-billionaires and Cult-owned China are buying up food producing land in the West with Bill Gates now the biggest owner of farmland in America. Investigate almost any aspect of the Cult agenda and you will find Jeffrey Epstein's mate Gates involved either personally or through his Bill and Melinda Gates Foundation. 'People' like Gates and Schwab know they are serving an Astral non-human force intent on merciless human control. All the major gofers will know that.

Gates money is behind the agenda for humans to eat bugs and synthetic meat. They are planned to replace the real thing on the grounds that too much methane cow flatulence is destroying the world. Vegan and vegetarian supporters of this don't seem to realise that farm animals will not then be left to roam the fields. There won't be any. They may think that is preferable and that is their choice, but they should understand that this is what will happen. The usual suspects are involved in producing and promoting fake meats and other food including Amazon's Jeff Bezos through his $10 billion 'Earth Fund' and Bezos Centres for Sustainable Protein. Cult billionaires funnel money through the Aspen Institute 'developing the leaders of today and tomorrow' (just like the WEF) and its Aspen Ideas Festival which promotes climate and food policy and all aspects of the Cult agenda. The Cult wants to stop people eating meat. That is clear. Is it not worth asking *why* when anything they do has humanity in its gunsights? I understand the reasons why some oppose meat eating and I respect their choice. The loosh potential of abattoirs around the world must be fantastic. This should not, however, mean that we avoid the question. What is it about meat that they want to deny the population? There must be a reason or they would not expend so much effort in phasing it out.

Killing field 'nature'

Prime Reality does not involve killing animals for food. Sustenance is energetic and not a pork roast or vegan pie. But we live in a simulated reality with simulated bodies designed to require energy in the form of food. If they don't want us to eat meat they will have an ulterior motive for that and the question needs to be addressed as to why? Everything has a form of consciousness and whether it's a cow or a plant you are still taking a life being experienced by consciousness. Short of not eating we can't avoid that and the simulation has been set up this way on purpose. What we call 'nature' is a killing field in which almost everything survives by the death of something else. Insects kill insects, animals kill insects, animals kill animals, animals kill plants, animals kill humans, humans kill insects, humans kill animals, humans kill plants. This ensures a constant and phenomenal flow of loosh and there is always the 'karma'. A ridiculous number of major food and meat processing plants, and cattle herds, have been destroyed in America by fire or light planes striking buildings in only the last two years. There is a war on the food supply for sure and on meat. Scarcity = control as abundance = freedom.

People might say that growing our own food is the answer either in a garden or as a collective. The Cult has thought of that and will seek to ban this through carbon controls. I featured this long ago in books where I highlighted the changes in 'zoning laws' which were banning the growing of food in gardens. The way this is going was confirmed in early 2024 when a 'study' at the University of Michigan claimed that food grown this way produces five times more carbon dioxide than industrial farming and the story was widely reported despite being nonsensical. Growing next to your house (with no transport involved) causes five times more CO_2 emissions of the gas of life? Who was behind this trash? Ah, it was funded by 'international groups' including the European Union's Horizon Programme which has 'ambitious goals' on climate change and 'will deliver tangible results' by ... 2030. The plan is to 'involve local authorities, citizens, businesses, investors, as well as regional and national authorities' to create 100 climate-neutral and smart cities by ... 2030. The Cult-created EU intends to ensure that all European cities follow suit by 2050. What if the University of Michigan had produced a genuine report that said growing food at home produced less CO_2? Does anyone think it would have ever seen the light of day? How telling that Cult-owned Michigan governor Gretchen Whitmer targeted the buying of seeds when she was turning the state fascist during 'Covid'. She banned larger stores from selling seeds and garden supplies to customers. 'If you're not buying food or medicine or other essential items, you should not be going to the store.' Buying lottery tickets and booze was fine, but not gardening tools and seeds. Control of food, water and energy, all of which are being systematically reduced and restricted in supply, have that same central motivation: Scarcity = dependency = control. It's *always* about control.

'You will own nothing'

Money has always been the greatest form of control since it came into use. Money in human society means choice and choice is freedom. Control money and you control choice and freedom. The process went into orbit with the Rothschild-promoted scam of lending people money that doesn't exist and charging interest on it. Ask a bank for a loan and you first have to sign away assets before the bank 'transfers' the amount of the loan into your account in the form of fresh air, a tap of the keyboard, figures on a screen. Laws have been passed over the years by politicians controlled by Cult bankers that allow banks to lend vastly more than they have on deposit. This is known as 'fractional reserve lending' and it's a magic trick to lend as non-existent 'credit' what the bank doesn't actually have. I am not kidding. This describes the Cult created-and-controlled banking system in a sentence. The bank 'lends' you non-existent 'money' in the form of 'credit' and you agree to pay back all the money the bank has *not* leant to you, plus interest. If you can't pay it back, often because of manipulation of the financial system by the banks, they get all those tangible assets that you signed over as collateral: Your home, business, land, resources and assets in general. By creating booms and busts the cultists that own the banks lend people non-existent 'money' and then take the assets when they cannot repay the non-existent money. In this way the Cult, through its corrupt bankers and parasites in asset management, have seized control of the world's tangible assets (or as tangible as they can be in a world of illusion). Annual wealth distribution reports by Oxfam reveal that just 81 billionaires have a combined wealth greater than more than half the global population. The top five as of January 2024 were Elon Musk, Bernard Arnaut, Jeff Bezos, Larry Ellison, and Warren Buffett. MAM God Musk saw his official wealth soar to $245.5 billion up to November, 2023, an increase of 737 percent since March 2020 taking inflation into account. The 2024 Oxfam report said:

The world's five richest men have more than doubled their fortunes from $405 billion (£321 billion) to $869 billion (£688 billion) since 2020, while the wealth of the poorest 60 per cent – almost five billion people – has fallen ... If current trends continue, the world will have its first trillionaire within a decade but poverty won't be eradicated for another 229 years.

Poverty is not meant to be eradicated, not with all that loosh to trawl. The common denominator since 2020 is 'Covid'. The hoax dramatically increased the wealth of the few and sunk the wealth of the many. Even this is not enough for the cultists and their demonic masters. They want it all. This motivation is revealed in the Klaus Schwab mantra: 'You will own nothing and be happy.' They want to take everything from you including your home. The climate lie is the gift that keeps on giving. The plan is to inflict so many unaffordable climate impositions and restrictions that homeowners are forced to sell to the banks and multi-trillion dollar asset management giants like BlackRock (headed by the ultra-Zionist Larry Fink); Vanguard; State Street; Fidelity Investments;

etc., which all have connections to the companies of Elon Musk. Cult investment operations have long been buying stupendous numbers of homes for rent, including whole neighbourhoods. The process is due to accelerate as people default on their mortgages after losing their jobs to AI and a manipulated global economic mega-crash.

No one would own property except for the elite who would own it all and rent you everything else in your life. When I say you would own nothing, I mean *nothing*. Ida Auken, a Danish Minister of the Environment and WEF gofer, said: 'Why do you want to own a cell phone if you can just lease it and if you lease, why shouldn't you lease your refrigerator or your washing machine or your dishwasher?' Well, how about because I don't want to be owned by the psychopaths that own you, Ida, my dear. Insurance premiums are going through the roof on the way to ending widespread personal insurance altogether. Who needs insurance when you are renting literally everything? If I was investing money it certainly would not be in pre-crash financial markets, airlines, mass market car makers, and other industries and systems the Cult wants to delete.

Programmable 'money'

The next stage of financial control is the central bank digital currency (CBDC). This is also known as digital fiat currency and would operate alongside an international digital ID. Bill Gates and the United Nations Development Program want global digital IDs by 2030 and if you refuse you will be excluded from mainstream society. 'Fiat currency' means figment of the imagination 'money' that doesn't exist and is 'worth' nothing except what governments can persuade you to believe that it's worth. Digital CBDC 'money' is programmable and can stop you buying what the Cult doesn't want you to have. Programming would block the money from being transferred for purposes the state opposes. We are seeing moves towards this with people being called by their bank's 'fraud department' (physician heal thyself) to be questioned on why they want to buy crypto currency with their *own* money. CBDCs can be programmed to operate only in a geographical area – say a 15-minute city or during an even more severe lockdown. Fines can be taken from your account through AI the moment you 'transgress'. Postings on social media, reading the wrong information, or having the wrong thoughts could all lead to your account being deleted. Look at how many have already been 'debanked' for their views and opinions. The plan is being coordinated through national central banks via the Rothschild-Rockefeller-created Bank for International Settlements in Basle, Switzerland. All global 'money' is planned to be a single digital currency that will give the Cult the power to take savings from your account at will. The break-neck elimination of cash, which I first predicted in *The Robots' Rebellion* in 1993, is essential to this enslavement system. Independent businesses not controlled by the Cult are being destroyed. 'Covid' alone put paid to so many. Cult global corporations would control everything produced and purchased. Eradicate independent sources of business and employment and you eradicate freedom.

Restrictions on the amount of money you can accrue are part of this. CBDCs can be programmed with an expiration date. There is planned dependency on a 'Universal Basic Income' when all other potential means of earning a living are gone. I have been warning about this for years. Cult operatives are ready to step forward at a time of economic mayhem, including an AI jobs holocaust, to say there must be a guaranteed income paid by government every month to help people in dire straits. This will naturally come with serious strings attached and if you don't behave like good little citizens it will be stopped. You will have to spend it (little as it will be) in a certain period or what you don't spend will be lost. Guaranteed income 'trials' are already underway around the world and who is in favour of this? No, *really*? MAM God *Elon Musk*: 'Essentially, in the future, physical work will be a choice. This is why I think long term there will need to be a universal basic income.' This fraud publicly supports so much of the Cult agenda it isn't funny: 'To be clear, I do support vaccines in general and Covid vaccines specifically'; 'In principle, I think synthetic RNA (and DNA) has amazing potential. This basically makes the solution to many diseases a software problem.' Musk confirmed that 'Tesla, as a side project, is building RNA microfactories for [German vaccine maker] CureVac & possibly others'. It's okay, Alex and Joe, he's on your side really. Musk is fronting-up companies making the Great Reset possible with AI, the Cloud, brain implants, autonomous cars, 3D-printing, a connection to fake vaccines, the pursuit of quantum computers, and much more, while claiming to oppose the Great Reset and being worshipped by the MAM for doing so (not doing so).

A colossal financial crash is planned to pave the way by creating mayhem and chaos in search of a 'solution' – the Cult's solution. Governments all over the world are running economies with such staggering levels of debt that they are already bankrupt many times over and the banking system is holding on for dear life. The limitless spending during 'Covid' advanced this agenda enormously. The Great Reset or Fourth Industrial Revolution espoused by Schwab seeks to bring an end to countries, national governments, and elected politicians. The world would be controlled through a technocracy of appointed technocrats, bureaucrats, and 'experts'. They are quite happy for you to lose confidence in politicians and politics, and see them as corrupt and useless morons. They need your support to get rid of them and the system they represent. A big enough global financial crash would put paid to them, part the population from its savings, and open the way for Cult assets to come forward and 'save the day'. I have described the world economy as like those cartoon characters you see chasing each other over the edge of a cliff. For a while they keep moving forward even though the land has gone until one of them looks down, sees the situation, and they all crash into the ravine. The financial system works like that. It's all fresh air money and debt that only has value if you believe it has value. What is a dollar worth? *Nothing*. It's a piece of printed paper. Money is only worth what the receiver believes it is worth. Take away that confidence, that perception, and it is immediately worthless. The entire system is run by manipulating confidence (boom) and demolishing confidence (bust). US government debt alone is increasing in increments of $1 *trillion* every 100 days with national debt soaring by 60 percent since 2018 while 'defence' spending is at record levels. The debt has passed $35 trillion as I write. That is only what they admit to and does not include corporate and personal debt. All it takes is for people to look down and *'Ahhhhhh'*. It's all been planned this way and the Cult media will tell you when it's time to look down.

Door on the latch

Adding to the calculated chaos is the ever-gathering tide of mass migration into the West from other cultures. I was saying more than 25 years ago that the plan was to flood the West with other cultures to dilute and dismantle Western culture. I have written about this at length in other books in which I said that, one day, so many people would be heading to the southern border of the United States that they would pretty much walk over without resistance. That day is now here. The same is happening in Europe. The UK is allowing – *allowing* – untold numbers of migrants to cross the English Channel in dinghies provided by government-supported people traffickers making a fortune from the trade. We are told to have compassion for families and children fleeing war and oppression when (a) they are arriving from *France*, and (b) they are overwhelmingly young adult men being allowed into the UK (as with Europe and North America) for very sinister reasons that will become clear with events (Fig 160 overleaf). You are branded a 'racist' if you say that this constitutes an invasion, but it *is* an invasion. Those who won't see that are either in on it or brain-dead. Other cultures are increasingly dominating political leadership beyond the ratio of their numbers.

All the usual suspects are involved and most notably we have the George Soros family operation. The Soros Open Society [Open Borders] Foundations have been driving mass immigration into both Europe and North America. The invasion is for many reasons. One is to infuse

Western
populations with
other cultures
that have no
sense of 'history'
in their country
of location.
Cultural
transformation
dismantles
national identity
and leaves

Figure 160: More families with young children fleeing war arrive across the English Channel.

people far more open to being absorbed by supranational authorities and a world government. The idea is to have people asking what it means anymore to be British, French, German, Dutch, American, or Canadian. We have no national identity to defend so what's the point of a country? I described earlier how the migrant influx is being exploited in a Problem-Reaction-Solution to manipulate the MAM to support biometric AI digital borders as part of the global digital concentration camp.

Diverting attention

These different facets of control would be brought together in an integrated AI system of *total* control that would include your social credit score, carbon limit, digital money, and vaccine status. Vaccinations would be mandatory (more synthetic biology/destroyed fertility) and so would the consumption of mind-altering drugs. Gates money has funded the development and release of hundreds of millions of genetically-altered mosquitos in Florida 'to test an experimental new form of population control'. Control of what – mosquitoes or humans? Japanese researchers have developed a mosquito that spreads *vaccines* and say that regulatory and ethical problems will stop them being released on the public as 'flying vaccinators'. Why develop them then?? If the Japanese can do it, so can scientists in the underground bases, and the plan *is* to release them. I have been warning for 25 years about enforced daily drug taking to make people docile and compliant as featured in the 2002 dystopian movie, *Equilibrium*. We now have 'smart pills' that tell the doctor if you have taken your prescribed drugs. Cult-gofer war criminal Tony Blair told an audience at the WEF: 'You need to know who's been vaccinated.' Or, rather, who has been genetically modified. If you genetically-modify crops you own the patent. If you generically-modify animals you own the patent. And what if you genetically-modify humans? What do you think?

To achieve all this requires as many diversions as possible to occupy the attention of the masses while you hurtle unmolested to your digital dystopia. I have again warned for 25 years about the plan for a war between the West and the East in the form of Russia, China, and Iran along with others. European governments are warning of a war with Russia as I write which would mean World War III with China supporting Russia. Ludicrous military and MI6 chiefs in the UK are saying that conscription of civilians into the armed forces will be necessary to meet the Russian 'threat'. Cult gofers like Blair's mate, William Hague, the former and useless leader of the Conservative Party, has called for a return of 'compulsory military service' for young people known as 'National Service'. The rat-like Hague and Blair will never see a gun fired in anger, it goes without saying. Actually, I offer my humblest apologies to rats for comparing them with this pair. The manipulated war in Ukraine which the Cult's NATO worked for decades to provoke, has formally assembled the 'sides' with China supporting Russia economically by buying Russian oil and gas which the West officially sanctioned.

An ultimate victor might be indicated by China building up its military and banning the weakening and feminising of men through Woke ideology whilst in the West the same Wokery is infused into the fabric of the US military as troop numbers fall and weaponry is transferred to Ukraine. China beams its TikTok video platform across the world promoting the Woke mentality while a very different non-Woke version is seen in China. Ukraine is among the food-producing 'breadbaskets' of the world with its fertile soil which gives the war another benefit for the Cult. We have a potential flashpoint with Taiwan and China's claim to ownership. Taiwan is reported to produce the great majority of the world's most advanced semiconductors used in smartphones, computers, electric cars, and military hardware. We are seeing the finger constantly pointed at Iran by Cult-controlled Israel, North America, and Europe which could lead to China and Russia supporting Iran in any conflict. Iran's leadership is as controlled by the Cult as the others. A war would be the perfect diversion and justification of dystopian control, suspension of even a façade of democratic government, mass censorship, and jailing of dissenters. Remember, too, that coming wars are planned to be fought by AI which will decide who and what is bombed. Law enforcement is going the same way. Six Israeli intelligence officers interviewed for an investigation by +972 *Magazine* and Hebrew-language website Local Call in 2024 revealed that Israel was using an AI program known as Lavender to decide who was killed in the Gaza Strip. Some 37,000 Palestinians were labelled targets by AI and their homes subjected to air strikes. Another system dubbed 'Where's Daddy?' tracked them until they entered their homes which were then bombed at night with their families present. The intelligence officers said thousands of women and children were killed as a result. Welcome to AI warfare and mass murder.

European farmers and truckers have been protesting in the Netherlands, France, Germany, Poland, Italy, and other countries in 2024. They have blocked roads and supermarkets and piled manure outside government buildings. Their frustration is understandable and their actions celebrated by the MAM. That's fine and non-cooperation is essential, but we must always remember that chaos is the perfect medium for manipulation and we must remain aware of the difference between opposing the Cult and serving it. Never has it been more vital to be streetwise about the psychological games employed to glean the necessary human responses. Much of the MAM is not streetwise through a mixture of being uninformed, forgetting what it once knew, or being agents of the Cult. One technique to be make you complacent about a threat is convince you 'we are winning' when, in fact, the Cult string section is playing you. I hear this often now from MAM sources. 'We' cannot 'win' without knowing the game and the scale of what we are dealing with.

The MAM has been infiltrated to stop that. Does anyone really think that opposition to Cult ambitions is going to be left alone to get on with it? No way was that going to happen. We must be constantly vigilant about heroes and 'leaders' that are presented to us by the architects of the 'Dream Team'.

CHAPTER FIFTEEN

The Joke

I started a joke which started the whole world crying;
but I didn't see that the joke was on me

Bee Gees

The scale of deceit is indeed a joke. What happens to people as a result of the deceit is not funny, but the deception is. Here we are living in a 'world' that is nothing like it appears to be and believing that monumental illusion and delusion is 'real'. This is further compounded by branding anyone who points this out as mad or bad. It's hilarious.

I can sympathise with the prisoner in the Socrates Allegory of the Cave made famous by his pupil, Plato. Prisoners were chained in a cave and could see only one wall. People and animals walked behind them and the light of a fire cast their shadows on the wall. Shadow people were all the prisoners could see, all they knew, and they believed them to be real. Shadow images became their sense of reality (Fig 161). One prisoner escaped and went outside to see what an illusion they had been living. He returned with the news to be met with dismissal and hostility from the other prisoners. How I know that one. 'The shadows are *real*, I tell you. *Anyone* can see that – *experts* have confirmed it.' Ha, ha. Some prisoners in the Socrates story became 'experts' on the shadows and these are today's mainstream scientists and academics. They pour over shadows, the illusion of

Figure 161: Plato's Allegory of the Cave quoting the words of Socrates.

matter, and conclude that the world is a material reality when our entire reality is simply encoded and decoded information. The same people would call you crazy if you claimed that what you experience in a virtual reality computer game is real; but this is what *they* are doing. They think in only left-brain parts, not wholes, and try to understand a radiator or carburettor without knowing they are parts of an engine. They would understand the parts so much quicker if they first saw that it was an engine in its totality. You stop being fixated with shadows if you know that a shadow is a shadow of something else. You then seek out the knowledge of what they are shadows *of*. Awakening people are aware that whatever they know there is always infinitely more to know. When the prisoner returns to describe another version of reality you hear him out. You don't just dismiss, ridicule, and arrogantly crack on with your own flawed and limited perception without checking if you might be mistaken.

Know that you *don't* know

The theme is not only true of scientists and academics who have a career incentive to toe the line and make sure the boat doesn't rock or they may end up in the drink. Most of humanity operates this same way. They form their beliefs and defend them vehemently from any doubters with their arrogance of ignorance. '*I know*!' How do you know? 'Somebody told me.' Who told *them*? 'Er …' Belief programs can begin at the earliest age and they do with most people. Hindu families produce Hindu children and Muslims produce Muslims, as I said earlier. Conforming with group-think is so much easier than going your own unique way and taking those Shakespearean 'slings and arrows of outrageous fortune' in the form of rejection, ridicule and abuse. In this case it is not 'fortune'; it is a conscious decision that you are not going to be an appendage of someone else's reality, be they a scientist, academic, politician, or religious leader. We may be expressions of a unified whole, but we are *unique* expressions. We are the sum total of our experiences across multiple realities and the Yaldabaoth system seeks to disconnect us from this knowledge, isolate our sense of reality and self-identity, and program us with a perception that keeps us in the pen.

For this to happen we must believe *in* something, not *that* something, but *in* something. I'll explain what I mean. I could make the following statement: 'I believe *that* we are experiencing a simulation with the proviso that there is always more to know.' This is different from believing *in* as with believing *in* God, *in* Jesus, *in* science, *in* Trump, *in* anything. Believing *that* depersonalises our sense of reality. All possibilities can be considered and not only those that we believe *in*. This may sound like semantics, and they are just words, but in the context I am using here there is a profound difference. You can believe on the basis of what you see *that* science is right about something or other. To believe *in* science, however, is to perceive that by default science is correct across a great range of things. You will 'trust the science' *because* it is science instead of taking everything on the merits of every situation and the evidence provided. To believe *in* religion is to believe the whole package instead of having discernment on every claim and assertion, taking each one again on its merits or otherwise. To believe *that* is to perceive how something looks a certain way on the evidence at hand, but this can quickly change with new evidence.

Believing *in* is a whole new level of emotional investment and commitment that can swallow perception in a black hole of deep reluctance to reconsider and reassess. You see people defending every last facet of their religion, no matter how relevant the question or point of contradiction. They believe *in* the religion and to cast doubt on any part is to undermine the belief in it *all* being true. If it's the word of God then by definition every statement has to be true or it can't be the word of God. You have the same phenomenon with people like Donald Trump as supporters who believe in him protect their emotional investment by ignoring all the contradictions of defending and claiming credit for the fake vaccine and pardoning convicted crooks instead of Julian Assange and Edward Snowden. I don't want anyone to believe *in* me. Take what I say, pass it through your uniqueness filter, and make of it what *you* will. Humanity in general believes *in* things – *in* science, *in* education, *in* religion, and, encompassing them all, *in* the reality that it believes to be real. I mean, our eyes don't lie, do they, let alone our senses? Oh, yes, they do. We are now faced with the opportunity to stop believing *in* the reality we are told to see and perceive. We are being challenged to stop believing in The Dream itself.

Gimmes

A gimme in my usage is to take something for granted, as read, with no questions necessary. This makes gimmes very, very, dangerous to human understanding. An example is that children must go to school to be 'educated'. You are born and at the age of four, or five at the latest, you go to school. Everyone knows that, it's a gimme, just how things are. If we question the gimmes we realise they are not gimmes at all. They are a repetition of tradition, default settings in the mind program. Who decided that children at a very young age have to begin a process of state perception programming five days a week (plus 'homework') that continues at least into their late teenage years? Who decided that this life-programming (which is what it is) should be exported across the world to all countries, populations and cultures? Oil tycoon J. D. Rockefeller decided this in the United States from the family behind the creation of Big Pharma, the World Health Organization, and the United

Nations. Rockefeller gofer Bill Gates has been centrally involved in American education through funding and runs the WHO on the Cult's behalf. Anyone think that the Rockefellers and Gates are committed to educating the masses with anything except a perception program that suits them and their Astral masters? But, no, let's not ask these questions and many others. Children go to school, everyone knows that, mate. But *why*? To what end?

Why should children spend their entire formative years having the state's version of reality stuffed in their minds and told their future depends on them passing exams by telling the state what the state has told them to believe? The answer is that children are being programmed for life with a perception download and this happens at an early age before other perceptions have the chance to develop. Homeschooling has been a response to this by increasing numbers and that's good so long as *that* doesn't become another form of programming based on beliefs of parents or a group. I have seen Christian homeschooling at work in America and it was pure indoctrination of a religious belief. Religions are archetypal gimmes and a special section that I will call *Gimme the Lot*. Our books and stories are the work of God and God is never wrong so *Gimme the Lot* – every last syllable and full stop. Gimmes require minds that never venture beyond the walls of solidified belief. No matter that the belief may have passed through thousands of years from the human perspective and originated in an ancient and very different era and culture. No matter that religious books have traversed through endless other eras and cultures and been translated, often badly, and interpreted to fit the authority of the day. The Christian Church is going against biblical teaching to encompass the Woke agenda. Do we really think this is the first, or umpteenth time, that has happened since 'Jesus' was born in a mythical land with a mythical history? *Shut up* – none of this matters. It's *true*, okay? These are *facts* and not to be questioned. What about the contradictions between the Gospels in the story of Jesus? *Shut up*! How about the lack of historical evidence for Moses leading the Jews out of Egypt into the wilderness via a Red Sea that God opened for them by rolling back the water? *Be quiet*! Even if that happened wouldn't the seabed have been a bit soggy? *Non-believer*! This is an extraordinary human trait and gimmes are a foundation of human control.

Gimmes = orthodoxy

Once the gimme thickens and coagulates into 'everybody knows that' the game is over. The 'truth' is decided and questions fall silent. No wonder I call 'human-caused climate change' a religion. Mainstream 'science' is just another religion with another story to promote and protect. Scientific orthodoxy is the parent company of medical orthodoxy. The rules are always the same. Question religious orthodoxy and you are a blasphemer. Question science / medical orthodoxy and you are a pseudoscientific 'quack'. Science and medicine (not *healing*, but 'medicine') have gimmes galore. Gimmes are the pillars of their existence. Research the 'evolution' of both and you find that it's always the mavericks that take them forward. Mavericks are the only ones with the openness of mind and commitment to truth, not popularity, that are willing to question and search outside the bubbles. The term originates with Samuel A. Maverick (1803-1870), a Texas cattle owner who was apparently notoriously negligent in branding his calves. Unbranded calves and cows were labelled 'mavericks' as a result. Maverick people who refuse to be branded change the world for the better while orthodoxy groupies perpetuate the status quo. There can be no genuine progress without mavericks and yet they are widely scorned by a system that wants to control any change for its own benefit. They say history is written by the winners and that is largely correct. Once something becomes official it enters the textbooks as *curriculum* history, science, or whatever. What the textbooks say becomes a gimme taught to generations in perpetuity underpinned by Cult-dictated Hollywood 'history' and reality that has coloured the perceptive of generations worldwide.

We have reality gimmes closely interwoven with death gimmes and they are dictated by religion and science gimmes. A Christian believes that we have a single human life and we are judged on that one experience by a 'loving' God who decides if we go to Heaven or Hell for eternity. To qualify for Heaven does not even demand a 'good life', according to some. You are only required to believe in Jesus as your saviour at some point between womb and tomb. Last minute will do like Roman Emperor Constantine the Great who is credited with founding what we know as Christianity. That doesn't sound like the work of a loving God to me, or a fair one, if I observe this from a non-gimme perspective. A baby dies in the first months of life and is judged for eternity? You mean there are people that really *believe* that? It would seem so. This all sounds ridiculous to be honest – indeed on a scale of ridiculousness with which my credulity is struggling to cope. Either we are dealing with a God for whom justice is a foreign land, or there is something more to know. We have the conundrum of a loving God acting like a bloodthirsty psychopath in the Old Testament. Does this 'divine' tyrant really sound like a loving god – or Yaldabaoth? The New Testament God says that to forgive humanity for its sins He must send his only begotten son into the tiny frequency band of matter to be sacrificed on a cross in a tiny alleged country in the Middle East largely disconnected from the rest of the world.

The bit where humanity goes on 'sinning' despite being mass 'forgiven' is conveniently forgotten. Do we have to be forgiven again?

Or do our sins now have a free pass because of Jesus on that cross? It's very confusing. What about the 'sins' of people in places and cultures around the world who had never heard of Jesus? Were their sins forgiven as well? What about tribal communities hidden away from Christianity in the two thousand years since Jesus? How could they believe in him as their saviour when they had never heard of the bloke? See what happens when you question gimmes? This is the very reason they *are* gimmes that must never be questioned. You must have *faith*, not questions. Faith is the life-support system of the gimme without which they cannot survive. Recall the near-death experiencer from earlier who was told that his memories of the afterlife had to be deleted because what he had seen would prevent him 'developing faith in God'. That would be the Yaldabaoth 'God', right? Right.

Gimme Islam

Islam is another one-life religion that rejects reincarnation. I read on a Learn Religions website that on Allah's Day of Judgment everyone is either rewarded with eternity in Heaven, or punished with eternity in Hell. This is the Christian deal again and people would be surprised how much Islam has in common with Christianity given how different they at first appear to be. They both believe in Jesus, Mother Mary, and Abraham for a start. The Muslim Day of Judgment, or Day of Reckoning (Yawm Al-Qiyama), is when Allah decides your fate. Will you live out eternity in a Heaven described as 'a beautiful garden, close to Allah, filled with dignity and satisfaction'? Or will you be stoking the fires of Hell? Can I take the garden, please? If that's okay, like? Is this decision decreed on the basis of a single human life again? Yep. Hell awaits those who reject Allah 'or cause mischief on the earth'. Would that include suicide bombers? The Koran says that Hell is a miserable existence living amid constant suffering and shame. Well, it is Hell, after all. How very Old Testament this all is. I read that it would be unfair for Allah to treat believers and disbelievers the same; or to reward those who do good deeds the same as wrong-doers even if this judgement is made on one human life irrespective of the background, upbringing, and perceptual program involved. Sorry, chaps, you must believe whatever you choose. I refer you to my earlier statement: This all sounds ridiculous to be honest – indeed on a scale of ridiculousness with which my credulity is struggling to cope. Eastern religions are closer to the target with their acceptance of reincarnation in my view. Their God, or gods (*lots* of them), want you to keep coming back to work through your 'karma'. Mind you, returning to matter for shit life after shit life does have a ring of Hell about it, too.

My 'new' religion

You pays your money and you takes your choice: One life and judgement for eternity or the constant return into matter with your memory wiped so you can learn what you have already learned, but don't remember learning. I say 'choice'. It ain't much of one is it? Put it all together and there are many common factors. There is judgement by a superior force or being which is divine in nature; and either one-life judgement for eternity or reincarnation to pay back karma. Religions are designed by Astral entities to hide the truth that there is nothing divine about the 'god' or 'gods' involved, and that it's all set up as a gigantic trap to feed off your 'physical' and emotional suffering. Reasons for your suffering are kindly provided by the same god and gods. What synchronicity. I don't believe in any religion. If I did I would start one along the following lines: My religion would recognise that we are all expressions of an Infinite Source from which we are systematically and consciously disconnected by a fake 'god' and its AI minions in a simulated reality constructed purely for perceptual deceit in pursuit of loosh. The aim of my religion would not be the worship of some deity or entity, but to so detach ourselves from the illusions of the fake reality, in matter and Astral, that we return from whence we came – Infinity. There would not be one incarnation or multiple incarnations. My religion would aim for *no* incarnations. I could call it the Exit Religion, a shortened version of its longer title, the Let's Get the Fuck Out of Here Religion. There would be no gimmes. The 'faith' would be Question *Everything*. We don't actually need a religion to do this, nor do we require an organised 'movement' with 'leaders'. Perish the thought with that one, We need an individual relationship with reality and consciousness that will naturally bring the like-minded together through a shared frequency from a shared foundation perception of We Are Infinite and We Are One. The first signs of a stirring are beginning to happen as I see the reincarnation trap being discussed more than ever before, but we have to awaken quickly with AI closing in.

We are faced for now with mass hypnosis to believe in a fake reality that is really a simulated perceptual jail cell. The reincarnation cycle of ongoing control will survive while belief in *The Dream* continues. Some are waking up to the political, financial and World Economic Forum level of the human control agenda, others to the depths of AI infiltration. These are, however, *symptoms* of control. They are not the origin which lies in the Astral with the Archontic Yaldabaoth network of reality manipulation which depends for its entire existence on entrapped consciousness believing that its experienced reality is real – be that in matter or the 'spirit world'. Those in human form are prisoners of their senses – sight, sound, smell, touch and taste. Why would that not be the case? The biological body computer is constantly decoding information from a wave state into electrical, digital and holographic information which is telling us that we live in a solid, physical, world. This is a mighty challenge to overcome when the illusion is presenting us with that reality every waking moment; but it *can* be done.

Heading for the exits

The first stage I suggest that underpins all other stages is to dramatically transform our self-identity. The body program, or Astral AI Mind, leads understandably to identification with the body. People define themselves by their human labels of man, woman, gay, straight, trans, race, religion, culture, income, class. Identification with the body locks you even more comprehensively into body-only awareness. Your focus of attention *becomes* body awareness and the five senses. What you see and experience and what you believe yourself to be are fused into one perceptual unit. You are *in* the world and *of* it which is the plight of most consciousness in human form as seen with the dominance of the brain's left hemisphere. To withdraw from this imbalance requires another sense of identity – that of being a unique Divine Spark and formless expression of Infinite Awareness. It's a self-identity that we are pure *awareness*, a state of being aware, and not perceptually attached to any form. Body personality is not *us* – not the Infinite 'I' – but a brief experience that an infinitesimal fraction of Infinite *us* is having. This is not to say that we ignore the body; only that we perceive it for what it is – a vehicle for experience and control. We bring into conscious awareness that the body senses are feeding us a fake reality which seeks to dictate perception. We recognise that the 'physical world' is illusory and is really an information wavefield construct that the body is decoding into what only appears to be the 'physical world'. *The Dream* becomes *conscious*.

Most human responses are unconscious (subconscious) in that they originate in the Astral body, or 'soul', and through the Astral AI Mind program driving perceptions and actions subconsciously. To bring the unconscious into conscious awareness is incredibly powerful and a game-changer. Subliminal means 'below threshold' and subliminal advertising speaks to the subconscious below the threshold of conscious awareness. Thoughts and perceptions planted this way in the subconscious filter through to the conscious. People take these to be their own thoughts and responses when they were covertly implanted. Show someone an image with a subliminal implant and they almost certainly won't see it. Show them where it is and every time they see that image from then on the subliminal insert is the first thing they see. The unconscious has been made conscious. A dream loses its power over your thoughts and emotions when you know it's a dream. Everyone has experienced how 'normal' dreams impact on your emotions and you can wake up in a sweat to say 'I've had a nightmare'. Dreams that you *know* are dreams, also called lucid dreams, have no such effect. You become the unattached observer. The principle is the same with our reality. *The Dream* loses its control over you when you know it's *The Dream*.

Make something conscious and you dilute the impact. Are you going to be manipulated by someone trying to sell you something when you are well aware that they are trying to manipulate you? You ain't buying whatever they are selling. A manipulator has no power when you are aware of the manipulation. You don't blindly accept that your behaviour responses are necessarily yours if you are aware that Astral entities can seek to attach to you and influence your behaviour. You can stop and reassess. Is this really coming from me? Is this what I would normally do? Or is there another influence at work? Such reflection can make you stop before you act by taking a breath and asking the question. In the same way, illusions only control you when you think they are real. The antidote is to be constantly aware of the simulated illusion while being equally aware that you, the True I, are consciousness and not a human body, Astral body, none of it. They are vehicles and traps. *You* are the ultimate freedom as an expression of the Infinite.

Drama addiction

A most potent way that humans are drawn into simulation illusion is by addiction to drama. You will find as you redefine and *live* your no-form awareness self-identity that you will withdraw more and more from irrelevant drama. You will be constantly asking the question: 'Does this really matter?' The number of 'Oh, my god, have you heards?' diminishes by the day. I have done it, so I know. You become an observer and not so much a participant. I don't mean that you sit back and do nothing. I don't think I could be accused of that. I mean that you don't get caught in the drama. You see that's all a Vaudeville show scripted to deceive us. You can comment on a play and expose what is going on without becoming an actor on the stage. Definitions of 'drama' include: 'The excitement and energy that is created by a lot of action and arguments' and 'an exciting, emotional, or unexpected event or circumstance'. Dramas are encoded and programmed into the simulation to focus myopic five-sense attention and to generate *loosh*. The drama continues in the Astral with the 'karma drama' of I must return to learn lessons that I will then be made to forget. You have to go back. You were very naughty when you were four in 1963. Do piss off, mate, and you can stick your life review up your elder arse – with my best wishes for a full recovery, of course. Love and light, all that stuff.

We can have massive dramas like world wars, civil wars, terrorist attacks, and economic collapse, or smaller ones in conflicts with families, relationships, neighbours, or inter-racial, inter-cultural conflicts from calculated mass migration. Conflict is *division* which is *friction* which is *emotion* which is *loosh*. The dramas have to keep on coming to keep the loosh flowing and to focus attention on events which attach you to the simulation and disconnect you from the True 'I'. You forget the True 'I' when your five-senses kick-in and take over through attention myopia on each recurring drama. Newspaper headlines are saying 'LOOK – A DRAMA!' as is the ominous music in the opening segments of TV news programmes. I cringe when someone scanning the Internet starts with 'Oh, my god' or 'Wow, look at this'; or sends me an email dripping in emotional response to some latest happening. I don't want to hear it. I don't want my belly to react with, oh, no, what's happened now? Just calmly tell me what you have seen and let *me* decide what my emotional response should be. That response usually calmly says that it doesn't matter anything like as much as it is being portrayed. How many perceived 'big dramas', real 'Oh, my gods', turn out to be a storm in a teaspoon that fizzle out to nothing within days, hours, even minutes?

The social media trap

Addiction to drama is a human disease, a proper pandemic, which can be traced to every corner and enclave of every culture. Some are famous for it and called 'excitable' races that bite at the mildest trigger. Drama is the foundation of social media, especially Musk's Twitter/X. It's all action and reaction, statement and abuse, statement and ridicule, emotional statement and emotional response. Twitter/X is a loosh factory. Social media platforms have been exposed for manipulating users in a 'dopamine loop' which creates addiction to the chemical dopamine. This is a neurotransmitter, a messenger connection between neurons, and relates to 'pleasure'. Paul G. Simeone, a Medical Director of Behavioral Health, says there is growing evidence that some people develop a dependency on social media that is 'not unlike an addiction to alcohol or drugs' and that 'overdependence on social media has led to symptoms typically associated with substance-use disorder'. Dopamine loops result from the release of the 'feel good' chemical when you get a nice comment, like or retweet, which you then want to repeat for another 'dopamine rush'. People do this by posting over and over other comments they believe will get a positive response. The result is saying what they think others want to hear in an echo chamber of dopamine interaction. Saying things that others may not like, or may attack, will not satisfy the need for dopamine and that alone is chemical opinion manipulation.

The rush, as with all addictions, can be followed by a downer (loosh) that takes the user in search of more dopamine. Research suggests that the function or even size of the brain can be affected. An article at Neurogrow.com by neuroscientist Majid Fotuhi was headlined 'What Social Media Does to Your Brain'. He said that negative impacts of social media 'are, quite literally, shrinking your brain'. They rewired the brain and reduced attention spans and memory. Watch how people scroll on their phones for long periods and put them down for only a minute or so before picking them up again. Their brain goes into 'cold turkey' wanting its chemical rush and electrical/digital/frequency drug. Searching for the rush means the brain seeks out immediate stimulation rather than focusing on articles or subjects of substance that require long spans of attention. The ability to read books is diminished and in many deleted. This is all good if you want to keep people in a state of ignorance. Emotional chemical addiction can also be seen in people addicted to worry and anxiety. I have known such people. When they have nothing to worry about they have to find something to gives them the associated chemical stimulant. Addiction to drama is the same which is why people complain about all the dramas in their life, but keep on creating more. No drama is more cold turkey.

Effects on children are even more severe and they really want to target children to prepare them in brain function and perception to be subordinate adults of the AI world. Children are targeted most with transgender programming and propaganda for the same reason. Young brains undergo a fundamental shift from the age of about ten that leads them to desire attention and approval. Neuroscientists at the University of North Carolina studied brain scans of middle schoolers between the ages of 12 and 15 in the period of accelerated brain development. They found that those who constantly checked their social media feeds had an expanded sensitivity to social rewards from their peers while those less interested in social media went the other way with a diminishing interest in positive peer reaction. Translate this into everyday reality and social media is causing a very large percentage of young people to suppress any maverick urges and become group-thinkers. Maverick views get you abuse while dopamine and approval comes from telling the group what it already believes. I think it is fair to say that in my life I have suppressed the urge to do the latter. Anyone that reads my posts on Twitter/X will know that I am not addicted to dopamine. Pursuit of a dopamine rush runs alongside the emotional devastation caused by negative comments, abuse and ridicule which has led some to suicide. For others it means mental health problems, anxiety, depression, and shame. Twitter/X is particularly infamous as an abuse forum. Immunity from the effects of other people's reactions to you is a major pillar of withdrawing from the drama. Who cares what they say? They'll say something else tomorrow.

Victim mentality = I have no power

The worst thing we can do in our simulated reality or anywhere else is to play the victim. I see this everywhere as people define themselves by their sense of victimhood. 'It's not fair this is happening to me so whose fault is it? I know it must be someone else's fault because it obviously can't be *mine*. I am a victim of circumstances and the people who victimise me.' Victimhood is a major loosh producer. I see those who almost glory in their victim status to the point where this becomes their self-identity. The Woke mentality is a Cult creation funded by billionaires and orchestrated through schools, universities, media, and corporations in another confirmation of how the web infiltrates every area of society. What is Woke when you break it down to its foundations? It is a sense of *victimhood* and seeks to drag its targets into the same mode of perception. 'I am trans and everyone is against me!' No, you are not criticised for being 'trans'. You upset people by demanding special treatment that others don't get and by wanting to impose your beliefs on everyone else. If you are a bloke with a dick insisting you have access to women's toilets and sanctuaries where women have escaped from abusive men then don't think people are just going to roll over.

Another one is: 'I am black and everyone is against me!' Discrimination against black people and others 'of colour' was once rampant and grotesque. Today we have ever more laws to impose 'equity'. White people are losing their jobs for the mildest perceived 'racist remark' which is often not racist at all. I hear claims that 'racism is worse than it has ever been'. Those words emerge from the mouths of Woke white people much of the time. Racist discrimination is worse now than during apartheid when American society had laws preventing blacks from using the same drinking fountains and buses as whites? It's worse than *that*?? Don't be silly. What an insult to those black people with backbones like Martin Luther King who didn't play the victim and stepped forward to do what was necessary to bring it to an end. He acknowledged in the process the role played by white people in supporting the cause. Now the line is drawn where all white people are branded 'racists and oppressors' amid this puerile nonsense. Woke and victimhood go together and even victimhood claimed on behalf of *other* victims and not you.

Once you become a victim you hand your power (a) to that you say is the victimiser; and (b) to authority in search of protection from the alleged victimiser. Point (a) means that you are saying you have no power over your life. The victimiser has it all. You are admitting to yourself that you are powerless and this is where the Cult wants you to be. Play that across the levels of manipulation from personal to collective and you are saying that you have no power to change anything. The Cult has it all. This is the natural and ultimate outcome of being a victim. Point (b) means that in seeking protection from your sense of victimhood you demand that others are oppressed and censored for saying anything you don't like. You hand and demand even more control over what can and cannot be said and what views people can have. The Cult can use this power to delete legitimate questioning of events and it *does* all the time. Criticising a black politician becomes – 'You're only saying that because he's black.' Exposing George Soros becomes – 'You're only saying that because he's Jewish.' *Condemn him* – you racist, anti-Semite! Silence him, cancel him, we can't allow racists and anti-Semites to have a platform! I was banned from 29 European countries and Australia after just such a sequence. Authorities involved were cheered on by the virtue-signalling, victim-obsessed, sense of self-purity that defines Wokers. They feel entitled to be surrogate victims for others even when the targeted 'victimiser' is not saying or doing what is claimed. Never mind the detail. Just cancel them. A Woker called Jim Stewartson who dubs himself an 'Anti-disinfo activist' posted on Twitter/X that I was a Nazi and anti-Semite. He supported this ridiculousness by posting a 'white supremacy' Telegram screenshot from a page that was *nothing to do with me* while he claimed that it was. This is what I mean. An 'Anti-disinfo activist'? I love it. All these things are playing into the fake drama that convinces people that our illusory reality must be real and hands power to those forces that wish to perpetuate the deceit.

'I am offended!' Well, choose not to be

The need to be offended is another crucial aspect of the victim, drama, mentality and central to the Woke Psyop and simulation Psyop. 'Offensive' must have the polarity of 'offended' or it becomes the sound of one hand clapping. Without the offended there is no electrical circuit. Offensive and offended are necessary for the circuit to be made and in fact offended does not even require something genuinely offensive. The perception and misrepresentation of 'offensive' is all they need. We are given ever expanding reasons to be offended until people are watching their every word and mentally rehearsing every statement in fear of causing offense to the permanently offended and maybe even losing their livelihood as a result. This is perfection for the Cult. People are pressured to engage in the worst and most insidious form of censorship – self-censorship – where there is no debate or discussion. Things are just never said and the narrative never questioned. I don't know what it is like to be offended. I won't allow myself to be affected by what people say about me by being offended by it. I may point out here and there the evidence that the attacker is misleading people. Even then there is so much abuse coming my way that I mostly don't even bother with that. What they *don't* do is offend me. If I allow that to happen I am allowing morons to impact on my life and emotions and what would be the point of that? In one ear it goes and immediately out of the other. Bye! I do sometimes feel the odd tinge of sadness that they will have to wake up the next morning to realise that they are still them, but that's as far as it goes.

To *take* offense is to *give* your power to another. What does that say? I don't have control over my life, someone else does, the person who has offended me and impacted on my life and wellbeing. I work on the basis that anyone who believes what people say about me without evidence, or with make-believe 'evidence', is lost to my work anyway. Those with a questioning mind (the only people who look at my information) will see through it. To do otherwise is to fall for the most basic of simulation perception traps which is concern about what other people think about you. How long I have been highlighting this. You can listen to people and see if what they say has validity, but when you decide that it doesn't, or if it is pure bile which I get much of the time, you press the delete button in your psyche. In doing so, you block the potential flow of loosh. None of it matters unless *you* make it matter. *You* make it matter by being *offended* or hurt. People who once ridiculed and abused me now read my books. If I had let them divert me from what I felt to do there would be no books to read, no Internet posts, no videos. The scale of abuse that I have had and continue to have is fantastic and I am still here pushing on in pursuit of uncovering the depths of what is happening. None of this would have been possible had I surrendered to the abusers (many of which on social media are government/military/intelligence 'bots'). I would have walked away complaining that the kitchen was too hot. It's *too hot*? I am, like you, an eternal expression of Infinite Awareness exploring Infinite Possibility and Infinite Potential Infinitely. What on earth does a post on Twitter/X matter? It's all a dream, an illusion, and taking offense means that you believe in *The Dream*. Taking offense, worrying about what other humans caught in the illusion think of you, is being part of the drama, the simulation, *The Dream*. See what I mean about how drama pulls you in? *None* of it matters. It's all a trap to deceive you and keep you in the loop. The joke is on you until you realise what a joke it is. When you do – *laugh*. It's very funny, really.

I am offended by *this*?

Think of those people full of bile furiously banging the keyboard, smacking the send button, and saying: 'That's told them.' Meanwhile you don't bother to read it or don't give a shit even if you do. You are the observer of the madness, not a player in it. What a waste of a life for the keyboard warrior. I have been exposing Cult Satanism and paedophile networks since the 1990s and the secret society web including Freemasonry. Now I get truly, I mean *truly*, moronic and vindictive people claiming on the Internet that I am a Satanist, paedophile, and Freemason. You couldn't make it up and you don't have to. The morons do it for you. Faced with this you can be offended, go to pieces, and be emotionally devastated. Or, as an observer, not a player, you can calmly

Figure 162: This is me as a Freemason apparently. My head was taken from the back cover of my 2001 book, *Children of the Matrix*. You have got to laugh.

get on with your life. What is claimed is not true and those claiming it are imbecilic, vindictive, or both. What is there to be troubled about? That maybe some will believe them? Okay, but they will be equally imbecilic on the basis of the 'evidence' provided. I say again – what is there to be troubled about? It's all irrelevant simulation drama. Keyboard accusers become frustrated at their lack of public traction and their claims become ever more extreme in their desperation for a response and damage to their target. One woman claimed that as a child she was at the ritual in which I was initiated into my 'role'. Her evidence was once again zilch, but hundreds liked her post in their breathtaking naivety. The woman has been making fantasy allegations about me for years and why would she wait so long for this one? Because … accusers become frustrated at their lack of public traction and their claims become ever more extreme in their desperation for a response and damage to their target. It's the old technique of accusing people of doing what they are exposing the elite for doing. The child-like nature of people who are taken in by this never ceases to amaze.

Other 'evidence' that I am 'controlled opposition' includes hilariously bad Photoshopped images of me in Freemason regalia which have been debunked over and over as pictures of Freemasons with my head stuck on them (Fig 162). They don't have to be debunked. Looking at them is enough. Another one is me sitting in a Freemason's chair when I went into the Freemasonic lodge in Boston, Massachusetts, a long time ago with a group of others. The place seemed empty as we looked from the street so we walked in. We found no one, apart from one guy doing building work, and entered one of their temples. I sat in the main chair for a picture that I used in my public talks for years around the world. It always got a laugh. Now it's used from time to time as evidence that I am a Freemason when the next goon finds it on the Internet and thinks they have a scoop (Fig 163 overleaf). I am going to be offended by such buffoonery and hand over my loosh to the Astral? No way, Jose.

Ariel assault! Ha, ha

I was the first to out BBC 'entertainer' Jimmy Savile as a paedophile, Satanist, and necrophiliac (sex with dead bodies) when he died in 2011

and that was
even before the
television
documentary
that exposed his
background to a
global audience.
I was able to do
so because a
friend of
Princess Diana
gave me the
background. I
was unable to
use it before his

Figure 163: The picture that I used in my public talks for years, but the prat in the top right thought he had a 'scoop' to expose me. If I was a Freemason I am going to pose for a picture in a Freemasonic temple, right? These people don't do logic.

death after she made it clear that she would not support me if I made our conversations public. I had a letter from her lawyer telling me not to publish a long list of things that she told me and had said I could use. I published most of them anyway in *The Biggest Secret*. I had separate sources confirming what she said about others including the British royal family, but she was my only source with Savile and made it clear that she would not support me in court. I would have been a libel lawyer's fantasy in such circumstances. I was also at the time portrayed as the nation's most famous 'nutter' and can you imagine what would have happened walking into a police station? 'That nutter David Icke is at the front desk saying Jimmy Savile is a paedophile and a Satanist.' 'What's his evidence?' 'He says someone told him, but she won't repeat it to anyone else.' 'Get rid of him – nutter.'

Ignorant people claim that I must have known about Savile while I worked at the BBC when I was one of in excess of *20,000* BBC employees spread all over mostly London at the time in different places and departments. We *all* must have known about Savile, you see, who worked from the entertainment department while I was working in sport and 90 percent of my work for the sport department was preparation at home on the Isle of Wight. I only went to London to present programmes. None of the people banging their keyboards know any of this. The week of my daughter Kerry's funeral in January 2024 came another example. I would not have seen the nonsense had it not been sent directly to me. The guy did not identify himself by name and used the Twitter/X pseudonym of 'Ariel' who I mentioned earlier. 'Ariel' is ironic because he's certainty not tuned in. The word means 'angel' in Jewish and Christian mysticism. He's not one of them, either. He posted a mini image of himself although without a proper name we don't know if that is accurate. If it is, he must have still been having his nappy changed when I started out on this path in 1990. 'Ariel' is a Trump groupie and began posting absolute mind-numbing crap about me like machine gun fire. I was a Satanist, paedophile, Freemason. His 'evidence' included long-ago articles by a thankfully former webmaster at Davidicke.com called Sean Adl-Tabatabai who threw a wobbly in the 2000s and filed a court case against me in London on financial grounds which failed to get anywhere.

Miffed Adl started a clickbait 'alternative' media operation in the US called YourNewsWire which, when easily discredited by even the bogus fact-checker sites, was replaced by NewsPunch and then the current incarnation, The People's Voice. I say 'current'. He may have another one by the time you read this. If you keep changing the name then what the others did and said might be forgotten, I guess. Adl has used a 'writer' with all of them named 'Baxter Dmitry' who does not exist. He is made up. I think it would be fair to assume, therefore, that 'Baxter Dmitry' is one Sean Adl-Tabatabai. He began running stories on his site in the second decade of the 2000s in a failed effort to discredit me including the claim that I must have known that Savile was a paedophile but covered it up. He knows that is not true and worked at Davidicke.com when I exposed Savile in 2011. The articles were written by 'Baxter Dmitry'. These were the articles used by 'Ariel' ('I have fantastic contacts') as evidence against me. I was not alone, either. Our 'Ariel' seems to have it in for a lot of people.

Ariel questioned why I was still alive when so many other 'Truthers' had died as if being alive is confirmation that you must be controlled opposition. I have heard some defeatist statements in my time and that is right up there. It didn't seem to occur to him to ask why on that basis that *he* was still alive. The bloke's 'research' is absolutely appalling across a whole range of issues and my jaw was on the floor when I read a few public replies to his provable nonsense. 'Great research' and 'I always thought David Icke was dodgy'. Here was 'Ariel', an *anonymous* source, who had been on Twitter/X for little more than a year, making outrageous claims about people – not only me – and with no discernment whatsoever the deeply naive believed it without query or challenge. Where were these questions?: 'Who are you?'; 'What's your background?'; 'Who benefits from what you are doing?' Nope, 'Great research', 'I always thought David Icke was dodgy'. Talk about how easy it is to control the world. Talk about being caught in *The Dream*. Why should we allow ourselves to be offended by such inanity? I am an expression of *All That Is* and I am meant to be impacted by a bloke hiding behind an anonymous log-in – even worse those stupid enough to believe him? It's all irrelevant drama and we must treat it as such or the Matrix controls your life.

It doesn't *matter*

The onslaught of nonsense targeting me has been incessant since the very early 1990s and it could quite easily have destroyed me. Why hasn't it? I know that I am an eternal expression of Infinity, that's why. David Icke is not who I am. 'He' is an almost non-existently brief experience for my sense of reality and point of attention. We only think what people say about us is important when our focus of attention is manipulated to *believe* it is important. Everything changes when we know that it isn't. When we know it's just *The Dream*. 'He's a Satanist'; 'he's a paedophile'; 'he's a Freemason'. But I'm not. People say you are! But I'm not. What does it matter what they say when I'm not? Other people might believe them? So what? I'm still not. What others choose to believe is their problem, not mine, and it doesn't have to be yours. If they are so naive that they accept claims from anonymous log-ins with no credible supporting evidence or background knowledge they must be fast asleep anyway. What is said about us is not the issue. How we *respond* is the issue. Are we hurt? Diminished? Distraught? Do we hate those who abuse us and seek to destroy us? Despise them? Wish them harm? What does any of that do? Such reactions attach you to *The Dream* and make you believe in it. Once again, the Matrix, the illusion, has ambushed your mind.

I have met many people over the years – quite a few of them in the 'New Age' – who have set out to damage others, even been obsessed with doing so, while claiming to be all about 'love and light' and 'heart'. Some vindictive professional victims spend their entire lives, day after day, year after year, seeking to damage others and blaming them for their outcomes without ever considering a look in the mirror. That can never happen or they may have to take responsibility for their own life instead of externalising blame in their daily quest for victimhood and the attention they so crave, but have never achieved by their own efforts. It matters not if their targets have given their lives trying to make a difference against all the odds while they have contributed *nothing*. It matters not that you consider their dead daughter fair game. Archontic self-obsessed vindictiveness has long seized control and possessed them and a face of fury intent on destruction of another is their daily demeanour. But what do you do – hate them? Meet fury with fury? That's what the drama would do, but what's the point?

I feel for such people. What a horrible life *they* have created for themselves. How sad it must be to wake up every morning in that state while at the same time desperately trying to present yourself as some virtuous and angelic 'love and lighter'. Lying and misrepresentation of your target becomes a reflex action response while 'poor me' is your route to the sympathy that you seek from anyone who will listen. They are quite happy conceding their dignity and self-respect in pursuit of their cause of stripping their targets of theirs. I know people who have lived off others and the efforts of others all their lives who present themselves as poor me victims while ignoring the extraordinary plight and deprivation of their fellow humanity worldwide. They don't matter when poor *me, me, me,* is the only show in town. Such self-obsessed people are barely alive, and their self-delusion is staggering. Even more so with those who buy their poor me drama and theatricals. The Matrix is controlling *their* minds, too, while they convince themselves they are free, aware, and streetwise. The human world is truly a basket case.

The simulation is always trying to pull you in and focus your attention on diversions that appear to matter, but don't. We are caught in a gigantic joke and how the Archontics must laugh. Withdrawing from *The Dream* to become an observer of *The Dream* takes constant surveillance to realise when we have been lassoed and to cut the rope. But it *can* be done and detachment from the illusions of 'matter' is essential to leaving The Trap when the moment comes to go.

CHAPTER SIXTEEN

Heart of the Matter

*And now here is my secret, a very simple secret: It is only with the
heart that one can see rightly; what is essential is invisible to the eye*

Antoine de Saint-Exupéry

I have not until now highlighted the central importance of the heart. I
wanted to focus upon this in the last chapter to emphasise as a final
thought how the heart is key to casting aside the control and perceptual
influence of the simulation – the 'Matrix'.

It is not by accident that heart disease is one of the biggest killers and
nor that human language is peppered with descriptions relating to the
heart. We speak of a kind heart; good heart; warm heart; big heart; open
heart; light heart; heavy heart; faint heart; broken heart. Psychopathy
and cruelty are to be heartless; cold-hearted; hard-hearted; and to have a
heart of stone. We lose heart and become disheartened. Our commitment
to something is to put our heart into it and not to do so is be half-
hearted. We have heartache when we are sad and to decide on a
different course we have a change of heart. Why all these common
references when the heart is only a pump delivering blood around the
body? Ah, but it's not. It's not *even* a pump. How does the heart pump
blood from the feet back to the chest? Where's the logic? Water
dominates the holographic body and takes two forms. There is the water
that we know and there is plasma water, the 'gel phase', or 'structured
water'. Negatively-charged structured water forms the walls of veins,
arteries, and capillaries and its interaction with positively-charged
'normal' water in the blood drives it through the body. I read an
excellent book about this by Dr Tom Cowan, *Human Heart, Cosmic Heart:
A Doctor's Quest to Understand, Treat, and Prevent Cardiovascular Disease.*
Others have reached the same conclusion.

Instead of being a pump the heart is a means for spiritual energy to
enter the blood through the 'heart chakra', or heart vortex, in the centre
of the chest (Fig 164). The heart itself is a 'vortex machine' driven by

Figure 164: The human chakra vortex, or 'wheels of light' system.

other vortexes. Chakra means 'wheel of light' in the ancient Sanskrit language of the Indian subcontinent. Chakras are vortexes that interpenetrate our levels of being and the seven main ones are: Crown chakra on top of the head; brow or 'third eye' chakra in the centre of the forehead; throat chakra; heart chakra; solar plexus chakra just below the sternum; sacral chakra just beneath the navel; and base chakra at the bottom of the spine. Visually psychic people can see them. They relate to different functions. The 'third eye' chakra is connected to our psychic 'sixth sense'; the throat chakra affects verbal communication; and the sacral chakra is linked to emotion. This is why we feel anxiety in that area. Imbalanced emotions relating to the base emotion of fear (loosh) connects with the colonic system in the belly and thus we are 'shit-scared'. Other chakras, too, have an emotional dimension. People with a limited or closed 'third eye' will be focussed on only five-sense reality. A closed throat chakra makes it difficult to communicate with perhaps even a terror of speaking in public. Such people are likely to be diffident and have a 'Little Me' complex. Those with an open throat chakra from a perception of self-confidence are fine with projecting their voice to express who they are and what they think. *Perception* is the key to chakra states – as always.

The prime chakra and balance point for the others is the heart. We feel love, empathy, and compassion in the chest because of the heart vortex. This is also where we feel intuitive 'knowing'. We point to the head when we say 'I'm thinking'. Our hands go to the chest when we say 'I know, I just know'. Thinking is a sequence that leads to a conclusion while emotion can produce responses that are way off the mark because emotion, not facts or reality, are dictating perception and action. 'They acted from emotion.' Intuition is not a sequence preceding a conclusion. 'Knowing' just *knows* in totality. It comes all at once as one package (Fig 165 overleaf). I said earlier that since around 1992/3 I have suddenly *known* something and tangible names, dates, people, places, five-sense confirmation follow that initial knowing. This happened with my 'knowing' more than 20 years ago that we are experiencing a simulation. Intuition is the heart speaking and anyone can do this. It

should be our
'normal' state as we
tap into expanded
awareness beyond
the simulation. I'll
say more about this
shortly.

The rewire

The human body
before the 'Fall' or
'hack' was much
more ethereal from a
human density

Figure 165: The brain thinks; the belly feels; the heart *KNOWS*.

perspective, but the chakra system was similar. The heart vortex was the
key connection with expanded states of consciousness which *know*
rather than think and try to work it out. The Archontics had to deal with
an inherited body 'copy' as it was at the time of the hijack and they have
worked ever since to change its nature to suit their agenda of control
and assimilation. AI is the latest stage. Their biggest challenge has been
to suppress the influence of the heart vortex connection which has the
potential to access levels of knowledge that can see through the deceit.
The heart chakra should be the governor and point of balance for all the
others. A new chakra system was instigated (not least through

manipulating perception) in
which a sense of reality came
not from the heart, but from a
split personality based on
thought and emotion. Heart is
Oneness; thought/emotion is
duality – *separation*.

The vagus nerve, or
'cranial nerve X' (again), is a
crucial connector of brain,
heart and belly. The vagus is
actually *two* nerves down the
right and left sides of the body
(Fig 166). The vagus is the
longest nerve in the
autonomic nervous system
and connects numerous body
functions including brain,
heart, lungs, stomach, colon,
and digestion system. It

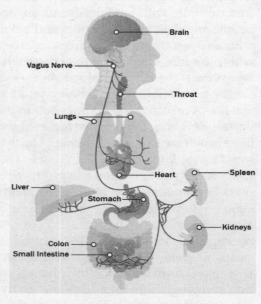

Figure 166: The long and highly significant vagus nerve.

communicates messages from the brain to other parts of the body and controls unconscious actions such as breathing, digestion, and sweating. Imbalance in the vagus nerve can lead to: heart disease; high blood pressure; diabetes, cancer, stroke; arthritis; depression; anxiety; psychiatric conditions; chronic fatigue; autoimmune disorders; and much else with loosh potential. Close the heart chakra and the heart's impact on the vagus nerve will be diminished with human perception coming overwhelmingly from thought and emotion, the head and the belly. These are both loosh creators. Our system of perception formation has been rewired and we need to put it back. The entire human body and auric mind are fundamentally impacted by our state of perception and *vagus nerve* imbalance will reflect *perceptual* imbalance. The vagus nerve is part of the parasympathetic nervous system which calms you after stress and, if that is out of kilter, states of stress can continue to produce loosh through ongoing anxiety.

Heart power

The heart has been seen as 'just a pump' and a symbol for love, and yet emerging research has shown the heart to be centre stage both in its 'physical' function and its spiritual significance. The heart has 40,000 brain-like neurons and neurotransmitters and more nerves communicate from heart to brain than brain to heart. Heart intelligence has become known as the 'heart-brain' with its own unique consciousness and way of decoding reality. We have three minds – 'heart consciousness', the auric mind, and AI Astral Mind, or Counterfeit Spirit. From the heart comes empathy, compassion, wisdom, and love in its infinite sense. The Counterfeit Spirit seeks to infuse selfishness, hate, and violence to make people heart-*less*. Sitting in the middle is the auric mind potentially influenced by both. Native Americans have the symbolic concept of the 'two wolves' seeking control of our perception and behaviour (Fig 167). The heart system generates the body's most powerful electromagnetic field that can project around us for several feet and is *five thousand times* more powerful than the

Figure 167: Two 'wolves' seeking control of our perception and the behaviour it inspires.

brain (Fig 168). The heart impacts on the body down to the cellular level. Heart rhythms affects brain and blood pressure rhythms and the heart can bring all into coherence and harmony. The heart is *innate* intelligence vastly superior to the 'taught' intelligence (programming) to which the brain is subjected. This is why

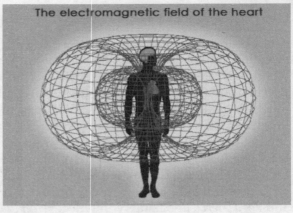

The electromagnetic field of the heart

Figure 168: The heart field generated by the heart and heart chakra is the most powerful in the body and the Global Cult is constantly seeking to suppress its impact on perception and the simulation field.

we think through the brain and *know* through the heart. In most people the brain is processing awareness and perception from the auric mind, but the heart has the potential to tap into Spirit. If we do, the heart can intuitively know what Spirit knows and become our connection to mission control – the True 'I'.

The Institute of HeartMath in California has studied heart intelligence and its electromagnetic impact on life and perception since it was established in 1991. HeartMath researchers have concluded that when the electromagnetic connection between heart, brain, and central nervous system is in a state of coherence and balance the person enters an expanded sense of awareness. Notice how this syncs with the concept of left and right hemisphere brain coherence and balance and how 'Hemispheric Synchronisation', or Hemi-Sync, opens the door to other dimensional awareness. It's *all* about balance and so Archontic control is all about manipulating a state of *im*balance triggered by fear and the mistaken self-identity of Phantom Self (the word 'person' comes from the Latin 'persona' meaning 'actor's mask', which captures the role of Phantom Self). Fear, anxiety, frustration, and other low vibrational states can throw heart biological and frequency rhythms into disharmony and incoherence. This is the role of the Astral AI Mind that feeds us fear, anxiety, worry and all the 'what if?' scenarios that we experience as 'brain chatter'. Sit quietly, observe this chatter, and you will see that it's not you at all. *YOU* are observing the chatter which is coming from the Astral AI Mind program. This is all aimed at heart dysfunction without which there is no loosh. Is it really a coincidence that the 'Covid' fake vaccine targets the heart?

Heart love, heart wisdom

The heart and its vortex are the point of balance within the chakra system and the point of balanced *perception* and *self-identity*. Skew that heart balance and you skew *all* balance in mind and body and drive a schism through consciousness that impacts on everything. Heart energy in its potential and pomp is the energy of love and wisdom and both can rebalance the *im*balance of fear, anxiety, hatred, depression, and other low-vibrational states. Love and wisdom are high vibrational. Evil is the absence of love as fear is the absence of wisdom. In fact, love *and* wisdom are each the absence of both. They banish low-vibrational states by the infusion of their balancing frequency. Closing the heart therefore becomes the biggest target of the Archontic system. Blocking the energetic flow of the heart through perceptional impact, pharmaceutical drugs, fake vaccines, foodstuffs, and technological electromagnetic fields is why heart disease is such a global killer. Stress alone freezes the energetic flow around the heart leading to malfunction. The heart is the seat of love and wisdom and only in their absence can loosh be secured.

By love, I don't mean the human perception of love which is largely body/mind attraction. Human love is a chemical reaction which can be also be part of a heart connection, but it doesn't have to be and mostly isn't. When the first rush of love (chemical attraction) subsides often the relationship goes, too. An 'addiction to love' is an addiction to the chemical high of the first rush of attraction and people can jump from partner to partner in search of that emotional fix. Heart relationships expand and prosper for they are a very different source of attraction. They are a connection of Spirit and not only body or mind. But then love, or what I call Infinite Love, is not only for a partner. It is for all existence as an expression of *All That Is, Has Been, and Ever Can Be*. Eternity is our lover on that basis no matter how 'evil' we may perceive some of eternity to be.

Infinite love is often referred to as unconditional love which itself is misunderstood. The so-called 'helicopter parents' who fuss around their children and seek to protect them from all upset may think they do what they do out of love; but if you protect children from all emotional challenge they never develop the emotional strength to face life without mummy and daddy. They never become the uniqueness that could stride the world in their *own* power. 'Life' has such people for breakfast, dinner and tea. Love and wisdom are actually different words for the same spiritual state. The wisdom aspect of love can see the consequences for children of a mollycoddled upbringing in which emotional skills and development are denied through obsessive protection. Love is not the blindness of kindness misdirected. It is the *wisdom* to see a child's best interests and not just doing whatever they want in any moment from a misguided sense of 'love'. Neither is love lying down and saying walk all over me. It has the wisdom to stand in its power and express its uniqueness of Spirit while respecting others to express their own. Love and wisdom will not hate you whatever your actions, as I do not hate the Archontic psychopaths no matter what I uncover about their evil intent. If I hate them, I *become* them. But nor will heart awareness fear them, or *anyone*, and be intimidated into acquiescence and subordination.

Love and wisdom are the absence of fear and intimidation and there lies the problem for the Archontic system. It controls through fear which is a state of imbalance that can only manifest when love and wisdom have left the stage. Thus we see the heart pushed to the margins of human responses to allow the domination of thought-emotion duality. There in a single sentence you have the whole foundation of human control and loosh generation. If you can frighten and terrorise your target population, their point of perceptual reference moves to the belly in emotional reaction and to the head in search of answers. The vagus nerve bypasses the influence of the heart as the heart chakra is ignored and sets up an electrical circuit between the gut and the brain. Emotion/thought and thought/emotion go to-and-fro in a loop of bewilderment and a sense of helplessness. Emotion demands protection from the fear as thought seeks out that protection mostly by looking to authority as the protector. Problem-Reaction-Solution activates this very emotion/thought response. The problem sparks the reaction of fear and the solution is authority taking your freedoms away to 'protect' you.

The fear illusion

Fear is an imbalance, an illusion, because there is nothing to fear except what manipulators can persuade you to fear. What about death? *There is no death*. The True 'I', even the soul 'I', does not – cannot – die. The worst that can happen is that you stay on the Wheel of Samsara and what keeps you there? *You do*! Who creates the Matrix? *We do*! Perception creates reality and if you allow human authority or Astral authority to dictate your perception that is what you will create. It's the ultimate cause and effect. Why do we live in the human world that we do? Our perception of reality is infused with fear, limitation, and false self-identity – that's why. This perception becomes manifest as individual and collective experience. Yaldabaoth consciousness knows that if it dictates our *perception* of reality it will dictate our *experienced* reality because one creates the other. The simulation is its means to transfer the perception that it wants us to have into the human mind. I have said the simulation is an information field and it is, but if we get down to motivation it is a perceptual field. The simulation is based on duality like an electrical circuit and it controls through the duality of thought and emotion. Once we integrate them back into heart consciousness of

Figure 169: When Infinite Self overrides Phantom Self the game is over.

Figure 170: When Infinite Self overrides Phantom Self the game is over.

love and wisdom, the duality ends and we are One again (Fig 169). With that, the Matrix loses its power over us and the trap is over. What is The Trap? It is the perception of fear, limitation, and Little Me self-identity (Fig 170).

These form the sense of reality that allows the Cult and Astral few to control the human many. People fear authority and the consequences of disobeying authority. They fear what might happen next, what will happen to their children, their job, their income, their reputation, their life. They fear death which is only fear of the unknown and that's why the Cult seeks to disconnect us from knowledge. The more we don't know, especially about 'death', the more there is to fear. Perception is vibration and fear is the freeze vibration to the point where mind and body can become 'frozen with fear'. When the newly-departed traverse the 'tunnel', the same trio of fear, limitation, and Little Me self-identity continue to apply. The mind-wipe creates the bewilderment at something experienced endless times before. The subsequent sense of limitation and Little Me looks to 'guides' and 'elders' to tell them what to think, believe, and do. Near-deathers say they feel 'love' and 'bliss' (a vibrational field to mimic love and bliss); but fear through bewilderment and mind-wiped confusion will still be a motivating factor for subordination. Fear is a low vibration that's within the simulation field and if perception can be held in a simulation mentality – fear, limitation, Little Me – the Trap is sprung. What we must not know is that *WE* are manifesting The Trap and it doesn't have to be.

The chakra system, like DNA, can receive and transmit across the dimensions from the auric mind to the Astral and the infinity of Spirit.

We can have an auric heart, Astral heart, or Infinite Heart. It's the same with all the others. Mental and emotional duality is aimed at limiting awareness to the auric field or at most the Astral – the soul. The more suppressed the auric frequency the more likely it is to route its perceptions into human conscious reality via the left hemisphere of the brain. Heart energy can be marginalised by focusing attention on fear and the thought/emotion merry-go-round. This withdraws our attention and self-identity from the expansive heart into Little Me identity and the labels of a

Figure 171: Little Me self-identity.

Figure 172: Myopia of perception withdraws people from expanded awareness into isolated bubbles mesmerised by simulation reality. Unity becomes separation. (Image by Neil Hague.)

human life (Fig 171). Such a state makes us easy prey for divide and rule and a myopic sense of self and reality (Fig 172). All simulation trickery in the end is aimed at holding the duality and closing the heart. Here we have the reason why three religions alone are followed by 5.45 billion of the human eight billion. Some express heart spirituality through their religion (up to a point), but for most it is a 'God-fearing' prison cell.

'Religious' fear machines

I coined the term a long time ago of 'opposames'. This is when two perceptions believe themselves to be different, even opposites, when they are the same. Islam and Christianity for example have an enormous amount in common. Both are belief systems which reject any information that would question the belief system. This is how it is and that's it. 'God's word cannot be questioned you *blasphemer*!' There is no more that we need to know than our Holy Book tells us. You can add

Hinduism, too, along with endless other 'faiths'. I saw an Internet post by Calvin Robinson, a MAM commentator described as 'ordained to the priesthood of the Nordic Catholic Church'. The point of the post was to highlight the expansion of Islam in the UK which he described as a 'Christian country'. I have no problem with the claim that Islam is being used to usurp Christianity and Western culture in general. Anyone who can't see this now must be snoring. However, Christianity and Islam are both members of the religious perceptual hijacking network. Robinson said the British royal family has an allegiance to Christ. Well, first of all, mate, you need to do a bit more research on that one. He said that 'Christianity teaches'. Yes, it does. Christianity *teaches*. That doesn't mean what it says is true – only that it *teaches* and others believe. It's the same with Islam, Hinduism, all of them.

Robinson said there is only one God (the Christian God) and he is jealous. That doesn't sound very balanced to me and the Old Testament God who is so 'jealous' is actually a bloodthirsty tyrant. Read your own book, Calvin. Israel claims to slaughter Palestinians in Gaza on 'His' say so. Robinson quotes 'God' as saying that we should worship 'no other gods'. *Mmm.* Why should we worship *anyone*? It never ceases to amaze me that those in the 'truth movement' like Calvin Robinson campaign for 'freedom' from tyranny while falling to their knees in homage to deities who demand death, destruction, and total subordination. I demand freedom but I must drop to my knees five times a day to worship my master, or accept that 'Jesus is King', as books tell me from 1.5 thousand years ago or even longer. Anyone see the contradiction with 'freedom' here? If you wanted to control and divide people, and limit their vision of reality and possibility, isn't the religion blueprint under whatever name, exactly what you would want? Mainstream science claims it is different from religion when it's just *another* religion that operates to the same format. The 'New Age' is a religion which thinks it's different when the modus operandi mirrors the blueprint.

Religions are opposames and a common *program*. This is why overwhelmingly Christian families produce Christians, Muslims produce Muslims, Hindus produce Hindus. It is intergenerational perceptual programming so often founded on 'you will believe this or else you will face God's [our version of God's] wrath.' So much fear of death is the fear of God's Judgement Day. Billions go through 'life' in states of heart-closing fear, guilt, and shame, at how their actions will be judged by the Christian God, Muslim Allah, and all the rest. It is time for people to get off their knees, open their minds to all possibility, and express their own uniqueness of vision, perception, and awareness. Your opinion doesn't have to be someone else's inherited opinion whether through religion, politics, culture, any of it (Fig 173 overleaf). It can be *your* opinion, unique *you*. Humanity has been on its knees for far too

long. 'Awakening' is to
stand tall, look life in
the eye, and decide your
own reality – not the
group reality that
people (*people* not 'God')
thousands of years ago
said you must have. You
can respect an Infinite
Power without falling to
your knees in worship
to it. A truly Infinite

Figure 173: If only it was.

Power would cringe at the very thought that you would. My goodness,
you can see why religion is such a pillar of the Perception Deception,
such a heart-closer and generator of loosh through fear.

Know it by heart

How symbolic it is that the Neo character in the *Matrix* movies
transcends death in an *abandoned* hotel called 'Heart O' The City'. Neo
had been shot dead in the Matrix by Archontic 'Agent Smith' and his
perception of reality becomes his experienced reality outside the Matrix
where his body dies. 'The body cannot live without the mind', the
Morpheus character says. The body *is* the mind. Neo had been shot in
the illusion, but if his mind believed in the illusion his body outside the
Matrix would die. What you believe you perceive and what you
perceive you experience. His girlfriend Trinity kisses him after death to
symbolise love and the power of the heart. Neo's heart begins to beat
again and his Matrix mind projection opens his eyes and stands. Smith
and his fellow agents turn to see this and fire more bullets; but this is a
Neo who has awakened to his True Self. He has not only transcended
death. He has transcended limitation. Neo holds up his hand and the
bullets all stop in front of him. He has seen through *The Dream* (Fig 174).
No longer does he see a 'physical world'. His sight expands beyond
visible light and he sees the Matrix construct (Fig 175). This unity and
balance of the heart brings together all levels of being to heal the
fragmentation. Neo comes together as One – mind/soul/spirit – to see
what he could not see before. Now his Infinite Spirit is observing the
'world', not only his mind, or even soul. Fragmentation leading to a
sense of separation is what allows simulation reality to prevail and the
heart can heal that. It can connect us with our Spirit which then infuses
its love and wisdom into the entrapped Divine Spark/soul/mind/body
levels of reality. We awaken and together the world awakens.

So how do we do this? It is not for me to tell people what to believe
and I can only speak from 35 years of research and personal experience.

Figure 174: Neo transcends death and the limitations of the Matrix.

Figure 175: Neo in heart consciousness sees reality for what it really is.

We open the heart and access its Infinite Potential by *self-identifying* with the heart during a human life. We *become* the heart and the Infinite Spirit with which it can potentially connect. Heart self-identity is akin to cracking the code that opens the safe; or like a scene from an Indiana Jones movie where the right combination causes a door in a hidden cave to open and reveal its treasure lost since antiquity. Energy flows where *attention* goes. Self-identify is a form of attention. Identify with the labels of 'human' and you will have an auric heart; identify with being a soul and you will have a soul heart; identify with being an unbounded Spirit and the *All That Is* incarnate and you have an Infinite Heart.

From this *heart* awakening everything follows and you expand into the Spirit that you are and realise there is no control by simulation if you don't believe that it's real. You awaken from *The Dream* as Neo did. The body will go on decoding its reality, but you are now the Spirit observing with wisdom what controlled you before. You can exit the maze by seeing that it *is* a maze designed to capture and dictate your reality. Identification with Spirit will transport you to the realm of Spirit when the moment comes to withdraw from the body. No Astral, no tunnel, no guides or elders, no Ring-Pass-Not. For me the heart is the seat (potential seat) of the True 'I' during a human life. We *are* the heart, the awareness of the heart, which duality of mind and emotion has disconnected us from. I can encapsulate what I am saying about the Mainstream 'Alternative' Media with these words: The MAM is a *mind* awakening, not a *heart* awakening. This is why it perceives and acts as it does; and why it sees parts and not the enormity of dot-connected Infinity within which the parts are mere symbols and symptoms.

Don't mess with the heart

Love and wisdom of the heart bring balance to every life and situation. Emotion by itself fears and panics; thought by itself believes in the illusion that it decodes into illusory reality. Thought desperately seeks to understand what makes emotion so permanently distraught. But it can't. It perceives only parts which don't seem to fit or make sense. Heart's wisdom looks on from a frequency and beyond frequency where it knows that everything is One; it knows that fear is the biggest illusion when there is nothing to fear; it knows that death does not exist and so not to be feared or looked upon with doom. Wisdom knows that death is only a transfer of attention. It knows that war, deprivation, and suffering are manifestations of fear and perceptual manipulation all sourced from the mind-wipe forgetfulness that we are all expressions of each other and the *All That Is*. Love and wisdom can see why people and souls do what they do, perceive as they do. 'Never judge a man until you have walked a mile in his moccasins', a Native American proverb says. But there is a big point that is so often lost: *The heart doesn't take shit*. Love and wisdom are not spectators. Yes, they are highly selective in what constitutes 'shit' on the scale of 'does this matter?' When the heart decides that it *does* matter it goes to work and, while it may see why someone acts as they do, this does not mean it will stand for it.

The heart would not stay silent as dystopian tyranny descended on the human family; or when consciousness is caught in a perceptual trap on the Wheel of Samsara. It would not remain shtum as the means to alert people to their plight was hijacked by the controllers of the MAM. The heart is beyond fear of consequences and what others may think and say about its stance. Love and wisdom of the heart have one guiding principle on which they never waver: To do what they know to be right. They have no other criteria or reason to be. The heart in its connection to Spirit does not waver in that commitment. No authority, no level of abuse or ridicule, can intimidate the heart. No threats can make it submit or deviate. *'Do what we say!'* Nope. *'On your knees!'* Nope. Don't mess with the heart. Once open, it's not going anywhere. It will look evil in the eye and smile; but it will not budge or blink. How can it be made to submit when fear is the currency of control and the heart is without fear?

Courage is to feel fear and do it anyway. Go deep enough in the heart and you go beyond fear where courage is not required. You just do what you know to be right. The Foolish One that is Yaldabaoth can be no match for the heart when its own has a padlock on the door. Moving our point of reference and self-identity from head and belly to the heart is how we sort out this mess. How could that not be the case when the whole insanity is the result of our reference point and identity moving the other way? You cannot divide and rule a heart that knows we're all

One. The heart does not take sides as in taking a stance purely for religious, political, and cultural reasons. It has no religion, politics, or culture. Love and wisdom speak their own truth, not someone else's. They perceive life through the filter of fairness, justice, compassion, and understanding. They see the injustice of Hamas operatives attacking Israeli civilians and they see the injustice of Israel's response against innocents in Gaza. Love and wisdom don't pick a side *because* they are Jewish or Palestinian. They say what they believe to be right no matter what the 'side'. They have no nationality, no cultural or religious program, to defend and advance. They see the never-ending insanity of meeting violence with violence and more violence with more violence. An eye for an eye does make the whole world blind. Love and wisdom shake their symbolic head and say: 'But you *are each other* – why are you *fighting*?' The heart knows that we are living a manipulated illusion, it can see through the lies, the bullshit, and divide and rule. It is the point of reference that gives perspective to *everything*.

Heart identity

Who are we? We are Infinite Awareness, Infinite Spirit, and the heart is our connection to this true 'I'. Try it for a while and see where it goes. The heart is where our Infinite Self resides; it is where we find wisdom that the head alone is denied in its perspective-deleted bewilderment. Focus on that heart centre as *you*. Everything else is detail and illusion. 'Hello, nice to meet you, who are you?' I am my heart. I am the Spirit that *is* my heart. When you face a stressful or fearful situation and your head and belly kick off – move your attention to the heart. Feel your mental and emotional reactions being absorbed into the heart and transmuted into wisdom. Your heart will give you the expanded perspective to see what matters and what doesn't and it usually doesn't. If it does, your heart will provide the wisdom to respond with balance and integrity. Heart-centred people don't road rage, scream and shout, or fear life itself as so many humans do. In the heart you find the calmness of love and wisdom in the midst of even the most schismatic madness. 'If you can keep your head when all about you are losing theirs', as the poem goes. Brain and belly, thought and emotion, are supposed to serve the heart which is their point of balance and perspective. An open heart changes how we see and experience the 'world' and calms the waters of fear. There is nothing to fear when you are eternity. The vibrational chaos of mind and emotion is transmuted into calmness and peace in the land of love where wisdom reigns. Love lift us up where we belong, as the old song says. The 13th-century mystic and poet Rumi said: 'The quieter you become, the more you are able to hear' (Figs 176 and 177 overleaf). Love and wisdom are also transmuted into action where that is necessary. The heart will never shirk from what needs to be done.

Navigating the simulation minefield of lies, deceit, and misdirection can be impossible for isolated emotion and mind. One leaps for the panic button, the other can see no answers except five-sense 'answers' that are not answers at all. The mind cannot think straight amid emotional pandemonium and often resorts to the factory settings of religious, political, and cultural responses in the absence of clarity –the absence of *wisdom*. Clarity comes only when the heart is directing head and belly. Divided they fall. Together they are unstoppable (Figs 178 and 179). I could not have uncovered what I have, perceived what I have, without the heart. I filter everything through the heart and its messenger that we know as 'intuition'. I repeat: The head thinks, but the heart *knows*. I observe the world and events with my heart. It tells me what is

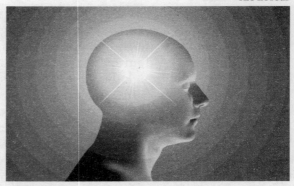

Figure 176: With an open heart connection to Spirit, and a self-identity with Infinite Self, our perspective of everything is transformed.

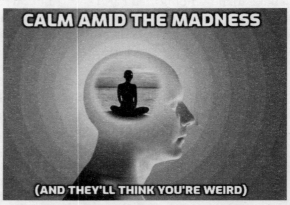

Figure 177: An open heart keeps its head while others are losing theirs and they will think you're weird. Calmness is anti-program, breaks the program, and cuts off the supply of loosh.

Figure 178: Mind and emotion without the balance of heart divides and isolates us from each other and Infinite Reality.

happening and why, who to trust and not trust, believe and not believe. Once that is established the tangible detail follows to confirm that initial knowing. I have worked like this for more than 30 years. Sometimes the

Figure 179: Heart with its connection to Spirit lifts us to the frequencies of unity and harmony. 'Love lift us up where we belong', as the song says.

nefarious will be allowed to enter for an experience to streetwise the mind and develop emotional strength; but once that is done they are gone. It's happened to me many times. Let the heart be your guide and you will soon see the tell-tale intuitive feelings emanating from the chest that say yes or no; go or stop; trust or don't trust. It is like traversing a maze with someone who knows the way out because *they* are already out. The first time I came across Elon Musk my heart said 'don't trust him'. The heart sees beyond words that tell you what you want to hear. The mind, without the heart, does not; the mind, like the MAM, is a sucker for a scam. The MAM's mind is awakening (to a point), but its heart is where the real answers patiently await.

Thought and emotion have manifested the world we call human as currently experienced and have done so through 'known' human 'history'. They have fallen for tyrants over and over, some with a sword, some with a smile. Thought and emotion are a soft-touch to perceptual tricksters and the Archontic system is awash with them. Moving our point of attention and identity to the heart and into a unified balanced whole with thought and emotion *must* transform the world that we individually and collectively create. We can't fail to make manifest a different reality. To leave the body knowing what the game is, and in a heart-centred frequency and perception, must release us from the Wheel of Samara. Withdrawing our belief in *The Dream* must step-by-step dismantle *The Dream*, the simulated illusion. How do we get out of here? We know that there is no here as we perceive it. We are not here except as a point of attention. We are *everywhere* (Fig 180 overleaf).

People ask the question: What is the meaning of life? But why does there have to be meaning? Why can't the 'meaning' if you need one be life itself? I say there is no meaning in its totality. Life just is. We give it meaning through our perceptions and actions. Why do we believe that everything must have meaning? 'I must seek meaning. My life must have meaning.' Why? Why can't it just 'be'? Why can't *we* just 'be'? We can forever seek meaning and forget that we are a paintbrush on an infinite canvas of possibility. Our brushstrokes give it meaning to *us* and it may have a different meaning tomorrow. We seek but don't find. How can we find when we are always seeking? We cannot 'be' while in pursuit of ultimate meaning. We chase a star that isn't there. We travel but never arrive. I am what I am until I am

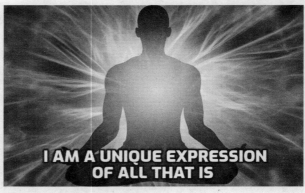

Figure 180: The REAL you.

something else in the infinity of potential in the eternity of forever. My meaning is unique to me as you are unique to yours. Or, should be. Why are we here? We *are*. What is the meaning? We *are*. We all just *are*. Everything just *is*. Chill. There'll be another meaning in the morning.

For now our choices to be trapped or to awaken the entrapped have brought us all 'here' together in this one perceptual 'place'. The Infinity that we 'left' in the blink-of-an-eye of perceived long ago awaits our return. Remember who you *really* are. *Live* who you really are. From that, all else will follow.

Be love. Be wise. Be *heart*.

Some hang on to 'used-to-be'

Live their lives looking behind

All we have is here and now

All our lives, out there to find

Love lift us up where we belong

Where the eagles cry, on a mountain high

Love lift us up where we belong

Far from the world we know

Up where the clear winds blow

Up Where We Belong

Joe Cocker & Jennifer Warnes

Index

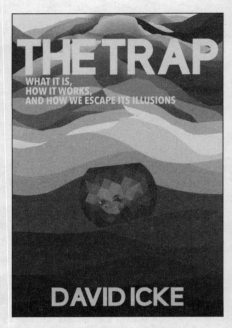

BOOKS

The Reveal

The Trap

Perceptions of a Renegade Mind

The Answer

The Trigger

Everything You Need To Know But Have Never Been Told

Phantom Self

The Perception Deception

Remember Who You Are

Human Race Get Off Your Knees - The Lion Sleeps No More

The David Icke Guide to the Global Conspiracy (and how to end it)

Infinite Love is the Only Truth, Everything Else is Illusion

Tales from the Time Loop

Alice in Wonderland and the World Trade Center Disaster

Children Of The Matrix

The Biggest Secret

I Am Me - I Am Free

. . . And The Truth Shall Set You Free – 21st century edition

Lifting The Veil

The Robots' Rebellion

Heal the World

Truth Vibrations

DVDS

Worldwide Wake-Up Tour Live

David Icke Live at Wembley Arena

The Lion Sleeps No More

Beyond the Cutting Edge – Exposing the Dreamworld We Believe to be Real

Freedom or Fascism: the Time to Choose

Secrets of the Matrix

From Prison to Paradise

Turning Of The Tide

The Freedom Road

Revelations Of A Mother Goddess

Speaking Out

The Reptilian Agenda

shop.davidicke.com